R. Todd Godwin received his PhD from the School of African and Oriental Studies (SOAS), University of London, and now lectures at the Institute for Orthodox Christian Studies, Cambridge, UK and in the United States at the University of Tennessee at Chattanooga. He has published in peer-reviewed journals on the early medieval Church of the East.

D1560156

'Ever since its discovery in the seventeenth century, the Xi'an (Nestorian) Monument, the oldest Christian monument in stone to be found in China, has been a source of controversy and fascination. Earlier Catholic scholars had hoped to see in it evidence of Catholic mission to Tang China, but modern scholars now regard it as an important document on the diffusion of the Church of the East along the Silk Road and in pre-Modern China. The present volume – by a scholar who does not shirk the enormous linguistic demands of mastering the bilingual text of the Monument and of the relevant historical sources – is a landmark publication which will benefit both the series study of Eastern Christianity and the general reading public with an interest in an extraordinary but too often neglected testimony to early East–West contact.'

Samuel N.C. Lieu, Emeritus Professor, Macquarie University, Sydney and President, Union Académique Internationale (UAI)

'Godwin's book is a magnificent exploration of one of the most important themes in the new global medieval history: Persian Christians in the empire of Tang China. Not unlike the Silk Road itself, this study brings East and West together in one overarching Eurasian world view. Erudite and subtle, Godwin weaves together all the languages and literatures of Mesopotamia, Iran, Central Asia, and China to create a vivid textile of religion, culture, and political dominion. Godwin places his own bold argument within a history of debate over the incredible Xi'an monument that extends back to the time of Voltaire. Students and scholars interested in the Asian history of Christianity – obscured by unfamiliar languages and historical sources – will find in this book the hidden pearl of a remarkable story. Godwin has uncovered this story with a sincerity of research that is reminiscent of golden age scholarship and the work of Paul Pelliot himself. This is history on a grand scale, invoking the rise and fall of empires, intrepid missions across thousands of inhospitable miles, and the durability of monastic institutions that are still with us.'

Scott Fitzgerald Johnson, Associate Professor of Classics and Letters, University of Oklahoma

'This is a groundbreaking study that is soundly based on both Chinese and Syriac primary sources. It demonstrates compellingly that the Church of the East in Tang China and in Sasanian Persia saw itself as an active participant in maintaining the Empire and ensuring its very survival through the blessing of Christ dispensed through its ascetic leaders.'

Steve Eskildsen, Professor of Philosophy and Religion, International Christian University

PERSIAN CHRISTIANS AT THE CHINESE COURT

The Xi'an Stele and the Early Medieval
Church of the East

R. TODD GODWIN

I.B. TAURIS

LONDON · NEW YORK · OXFORD · NEW DELHI · SYDNEY

I.B. TAURIS
Bloomsbury Publishing Plc
50 Bedford Square, London, WC1B 3DP, UK
1385 Broadway, New York, NY 10018, USA

BLOOMSBURY, I.B. TAURIS and the I.B. Tauris logo
are trademarks of Bloomsbury Publishing Plc

First published 2018
Paperback edition published 2019

ISBN: HB: 978-1-7845-3880-4
PB: 978-1-8386-0013-6
ePDF: 978-1-7867-3316-0
ebook: 978-1-7867-2316-1

Series: Library of Medieval Studies 4

To find out more about our authors and books visit
www.bloomsbury.com and sign up for our newsletters.

*Special thanks to my mom and dad, my academic advisor at
SOAS, Erica Hunter, and The University of Salzburg's* International
Conference on Syriac Christianity in Medieval Central Asia and China.

CONTENTS

A NOTE ON SOURCES AND THEIR USAGES

In terms of Chinese sources, though this study centres on the Xi'an stele, it relies upon the standard Tang sources – familiar to Sinologist but not the Eastern Christianity and early Islamic historians to whom the study is partly directed. These are the *Jiu Tangshu* 舊唐書 (the 'Old Tang Record', compiled in 945), the *Xin Tangshu* 新唐書 (the 'New Tang Record', compiled in 1060), the *Cefu Yuangui* 册府元 龜 (the 'Great Tortoise of National Archives', compiled between 1005–13), the *Tang Huiyao* 唐會要 ('Tang Collection of Notabilia', compiled in 961), the *Tongdian* 通 典 ('Complete Institutes', compiled between 766–801) and the *Zizhi Tongjian* 資治通鑑 ('Comprehensive Mirror Aid in Governance'), compiled in 1084 (regarded as one of the world's first rigorously analytical and 'scientific' studies of history). The *Siku quanshu* 四庫全書 (SKQS) electronic data base, is a computerised and searchable version of the vast and virtually complete library of Chinese historical materials compiled in eighteenth-century China under the directions of the Qianlong Emperor (1711–99), and is a great boon to scholarship.[1] It is not an overstatement to say that SKQS and the availability of the Tang sources online has revolutionised the study of Tang culture and many other aspects of Chinese history. Standard Buddhist sources in Chinese have been consulted.[2] In terms of the other Christian documents from Dunhuang first made available in English translation by Saeki, while they do make an occasional appearance here as well, they are not as central as some might wish. A basic conviction here is that by putting the Persian and Central Asian background of the Church of the East on a better footing, and beginning with their connections to a key epigraphical source such as the Xi'an stele first, a road to further progress, in terms of understanding the royal and ascetic footing the Church of the East stood upon between Persia, the first Arab empires, Central Asia, and China, in the early medieval period is opened which others can help explore and help nuance.

Numerous sources in Syriac, Arabic and Greek have been consulted for information about the western side of the early medieval Church of the East, Syriac and Arabic of course being a language in which the church itself wrote. Key among these are Paul Bedjan and Oskar Braun's collections of so-called Persian martyr acts in Syriac, Thomas of Marga's ninth-century Syriac *Book of Governors*, and the tenth-century Arabic *Chronicle of Se'ert* appear in the notes throughout the study. The Syriac letters and law book of East Syrian Patriarch Timothy I (727–823) constitute the basis of Chapter 3.[3] An occasional reference to a Middle Iranian, a Turkic or Tibetan source will appear as well.

A NOTE ON THE ROMANISATION OF CHINESE CHARACTERS

The Pinyin system of romanisation of Chinese characters has been employed throughout the study. Chinese studies protocols are still in flux and without widely agreed upon standards, so rather than present the reader with an array of approaches, I have tried to err on the side of consistency and the most common approaches. I have avoided the more scholarly convention of putting a hyphen between Pinyin syllables used shows linkages between words (*yan-jiu* 'research', for example), and followed the system of many Mandarin dictionaries which simply joins the two words (*yanjiu*) – a terrain readers of Chinese will navigate easily. When confusion over meaning could arise (xi'an vs. xian for example, the standard Mandarin pinyin apostrophe has been used (Xi'an). In terms of capitalisation, another headache generator for Sinologists, for titles of books and articles written in both modern as well as pre-modern Chinese, an attempt has been made to capitalise the first word only, but places 'book' or 'sutra', Jing, or Shu, also in capitals – thus one will find *Wei Shu* [*Book of Wei*] and *Hua hu Jing* [*Sutra for Converting Barbarians*].

Cast of Principal Characters

Adam [Syr. ܐܕܡ, Chn. Jingjing 景淨]: the son of Jazbōzēdh, who had likely grown up in China, was a native speaker of Chinese, and who composed the text of the Xi'an stele.

Aluoben [Chn, 阿羅本, Syr. *Rabban*, ܪܒܢ, 'teacher'): a major figure in the narrative the Xi'an stele; presented as having established relations between the Sasanian court in exile and the rising Tang Chinese empire, following the Arab conquest of Persia, and making the Church of the East important within these relations.

Isho'yahb III: Patriarch of the Assyrian Apostolic Church of the East from the year 649 to the year 659, a period in which the church was under definite but seemingly non-coercive rule by its new Arab governors. Through Isho'yahb III the monastic foundation of the church's long-range connections through the Silk Routes from Persia into China are shown to have been firmly in place, confirming the picture given by the Xi'an stele.

Jazbōzēdh [Syr. ܝܙܕܒܘܙܝܕ, Middle Persian *yaz-dan buxt*; meaning 'One Saved by God']: a priest [*chorepiscopus*], and major actor within the narrative presented in the Xi'an of the Church of the East's utility to the Chinese court. He had most likely come to the Tang Empire as part of a fighting unit after being invited there by the court in order to help quell the disastrous An Lushan rebellion (755–62).

Khosrow II: Sasanian Persian monarch from the year 570 to the year 628, under whom the Persian Empire reached its greatest expansion ever and reached far into Roman territory, and whose connections to Christianity were at times instrumental in this imperial expansion.

Mar Aba: Patriarch of the Assyrian Apostolic Church of the East from the year 540 to the year 552. It was partly through Mar Aba's charisma that Sasanian Persia re-established itself along the Silk Road and reconnected the world economy from China to Rome, cut off by the Hepthalite Empire.

Tang Dezong [唐德宗]: Emperor of China from the year 780 to the year 805, and during the period in which the Xi'an stele was composed and set in place. Having ascended the throne only shortly before the stele was made, and at the relatively late age of 38, Dezong came to the throne and was able to draw upon experience accumulated over a long period and a succession of Tang courts. One main feature of these earlier reigns was an inability to deal with the long-term effects of the disastrous An Lushan rebellion (755–62), the string of rebellions and connected border incursions that followed. Emperor Dezong's wisdom and experience lend credence to the idea that what is said in the Xi'an stele about the Church of the East's continuing utility to the court and empire is not merely flattery and opportunistic rhetoric.

Timothy I: Patriarch of the Assyrian Apostolic Church of the East from the year 780 to the year 823, and during the church's move to Baghdad and its becoming part of the Abbasid Caliphate's intellectual and cultural enterprise. Timothy I's interest in projecting the church's mission into Central Asia, visible in his letters and extant texts, developed as the church was becoming part of both the Abbasid court and Tang court in ways which parallel one another.

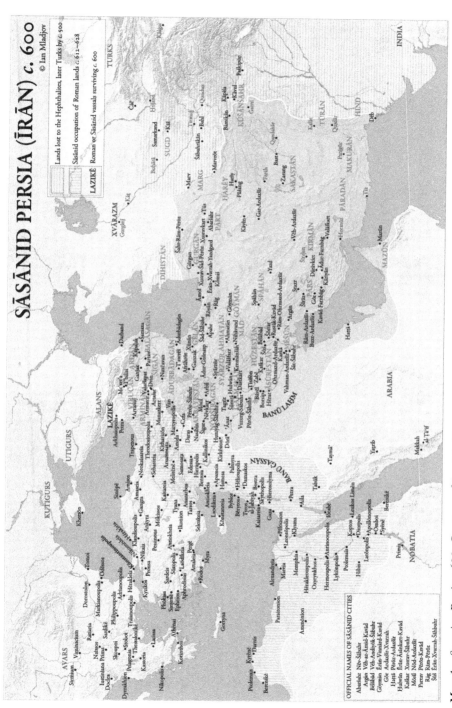

Map 1   Sasanian Persia c.600. Courtesy of Ian Mladjov

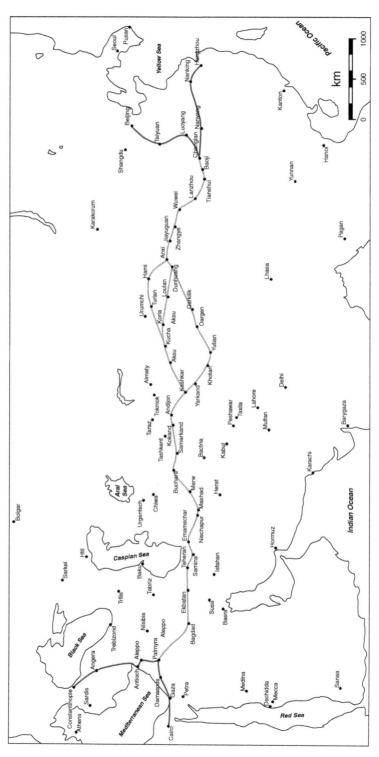

Map 2 The Silk Road during the Sasanian and Tang Empires

INTRODUCTION

'The king that never dies' here has been replaced by the king that
always dies, and suffers death more cruelly than other mortals.

Ernst Kantorowcz[1]

The still sizeable Christian populations of the Middle East and their
plight are not part of Western discourse about western Asia in the
way that many of us would like. A moment's reflection on the types of
photographic images appearing in Western media in recent years
portraying Eastern Christianity indicates, at least partly, how the
process of erasure works in actual practice. As relations between
Russia and countries to its west have degenerated over recent years,
Western media have begun to turn to certain photographic images.
This is being done in an attempt to explain the source of these
political tensions and offers readers a visual language of interpreting
this political tension. For example, in one set of images an Eastern
Orthodox priest, with his gold vestments, surrounded by a throng of
clergymen similarly clad, sends water from a ritual vessel high into
the air before it lands on both soldiers and armaments.[2] A line of
tanks as well as an array of guns and ammunition spread on a nearby
table all receive a thorough dousing as throngs of faithful look on.
In another set of images the Russian president and Russian police are
shown walking side by side with Eastern Orthodox Church leaders,
again festooned in their golden vestments and carrying sacred objects
(icons, crosses, censors, jewelled bibles), as part of a procession
through the streets of Russia's capital city. 'This is what Russian

Christianity is', we are told along with these images. 'Russia is not like us, for it is a country in which the rituals of state and a culturally embodied form of religion align with traditional values and power.'[3]

But there is intellectual amnesia about Christianity's long-held connections to political power present here too, along with a representation of whatever might be happening in Russia currently. Relationships between European royal families and elites and the legitimation of their alliances for public consumption took place through a sacramental and culturally embodied form of Christianity well into the twentieth century.[4] This did not begin with Charlemagne's well-known coronation by Pope Leo III on Christmas Day in the year 800. It can be traced back beyond Constantine to the Bible, and the tensions created by a Messiah standing in the Davidic line of kings, yet whose 'kingdom is not of this world' (John 18:36).

Shortcomings within the study of Christianity in early medieval China and across the Middle East may be traced here as well. The Tang Chinese Empire (617–907) was one of the most cosmopolitan and expansive periods within all of Chinese history, and its diplomatic and cultural connections across early medieval Central Asia and Persia led to Syriac Christians, known as the Church of the East, being granted an official place at the Tang court from 638 to 845.[5] A high degree of closeness between the Tang emperors and the church came about as a result, to which the Middle Chinese textual record related to the Church bears ample witness. This closeness was once referred to by Y.P. Saeki (1871–1965), an early pioneer in the study of the Middle Chinese materials related to the Church of the East, as 'emperor worship'.[6] For Saeki this 'emperor worship' ultimately caused the Church to disappear in China.

Rather than seeing a church on its last legs because of its close relations with political power, this book argues for the existence of agency and mutuality within the East Syrians' relationship not only with the Tang court but other early medieval courts. The book does this on the one hand by examining the relationships between culture and power obtained between the Tang court and the Church of the East's elites through a lens not shaped by modernist political discourses. It does this also by highlighting the Church of the East's elites' ability to reflect and reconstitute the culture of the Chinese court through its relationships with other courts and what the study refers to as the church's *longue durée* across Persia and Central Asia.[7] The East Syrians' vaunted roles as interregional arbiters and power holders within the late Sasanian Persian church are held up in this regard, and set next to the church's known survival in Central Asia after the fall of the Sasanians and with likely close proximity to Sasanian royals eking out an existence in the same region. Sasanian royals' survival in Central Asia and with Chinese support, the subject of increasingly focused research, has shown that Tocharistan, Kawulistan, and Zawulistan, each Hindukush principalities, were bases for royal Sasanians in exile along with Tang China before leaving the Hindukush for China in the second half of the eighth century.[8] This work deserves to be built upon.

Although there is a tradition of Western academic research arguing that the Church of the East in the Sasanian Persian Empire (225–651) was an integral part of the Persian state, the Xi'an stele, set in place in 781, allows the church's connections to the Persian state even after its fall to be seen in bold relief, quite literally.[9] The stele provides a means of studying the cultural basis and long durational continuity of the church's Persian formation and makes visible how this was augmented and mediated within the church's relationship with the Tang Chinese state and court through the seventh and eighth centuries, the church's connection to the Persian state having been established in 410 and at the Synod of Isaac. The study is directed both towards generalists and specialists in Eastern Christian studies, the study of early Islam, and the study of the early medieval Silk Road, for whom the *longue durée* of the Persian formation and trajectory of the East Syrians ought to be better known. The Xi'an stele's phrases *gong zhen xuanwang* ['together [we have] repaired the Imperial Net'], and the donor section of the stele where the Syriac word *mdabranoutha* [ܡܕܒܪܢܘܬܐ, Divine Leadership/ Economy] is found, along with the multiple references to the East Syrians in China as 'Persian Monks' [*Bosi seng*], are argued to be keys to this trajectory as these elements reflect both the East Syriac church in Tang China's leaders' Christian ascetic tradition as well as their ongoing reflections on the church's Sasanian Persian and courtly-centred past. Looking at the combined heritage of these elements and by reading across the Syriac and Chinese primary sources, something heretofore unattempted within the scholarship, makes possible a history of the church's elites' manipulation and reflection of the courtly spaces and courtly culture open to them between the fifth and ninth centuries, something that will be of service to scholars and students of Middle Eastern Christianity for whom the Chinese sources are inaccessible yet for whom such themes are relevant. As such the book opens avenues for others to further explore ways in which the East Syrian church's Middle Eastern and Christian identity held together with its identity as an elite religious body not just in Tang China and vis-à-vis its courts and emperors, but across a series of empires and as part of a church able to stand apart from, yet also integrate itself with, a range of cultures in the period. One of the key services the study provides is a methodology, empirically grounded, for studying the multicultural nature of the Church of the East in this period, which also seeks to come to terms with its fundamentally imperial nature. One result of these investigations is an understanding of the seemingly audacious statement made in the Xi'an stele that, through its asceticism and rituals, the church and its elites could save the Tang Empire from annihilation. Another result, more far reaching, is a presentation of Eastern Christianity during the first two centuries of Arab rule over the Middle East, which is neither characterised by passivity and a lack of agency, a presentation at odds with aspects of contemporary historiography, nor a presentation of Eastern Christianity that is deracinated and homogenised for modern Western consumption.

Between Dhimmitude and Emperor Worship:
East Syrian Agency and Its Historiography

In order to better understand why such a reassessment is needed it is important to look more deeply into the work of one of the early pioneers in the study of East Syrians in the Tang dynasty, Peter Yoshiro Saeki (1871–1965).[10] Christian and Manichaean documents in Chinese were discovered during his lifetime in Dunhuang, a city set within a corridor along the last leg of the Silk Roads leading into China. Dunhuang held a series of caves that had been used for centuries by China's multicultural elites for various purposes: as ancestral veneration grottoes, as sites of Buddhist pilgrimage and art, etc.[11] The Dunhuang cave containing the Christian and Manichaean documents is thought to have been a text graveyard of sorts, sealed off in the ninth century possibly to protect its contents from the growth of intolerance towards Central Asia's and China's multi-religious early medieval past.[12]

Saeki's translations into English from their Middle Chinese made these texts widely accessible for the first time; and his efforts in contextualising these documents in relation to one another, to the standard Tang historical sources, and to early medieval Syriac Christianity as then understood, were simply remarkable for their time.[13] The most important Middle Chinese Christian document, the Xi'an stele, set in place in 781 (which was rediscovered in 1625 having probably been covered and concealed in the late Tang period), had its interpretation shaped by Saeki and among this corpus of documents and historical setting as well.[14] Although the view emerging within the scholarship on Eastern Christianity during the first two centuries of Arab rule over the Middle East is steadily maturing, it still often characterises it as passive and lacking agency.[15] A different view emerges, however, when we investigate and hold together the Tang Chinese, Sasanian, and early Post-Sasanian period and context of Syriac Christianity, and attempt to develop a binocular vision for these interrelated contexts, and do so around certain key themes. The Xi'an stele as a key document, but other Chinese primary sources as well, bear traces of the East Syrians' Persian past and its continuation in the period of early Arab rule, and contain an as-yet-untold story. One useful interpretive point of entry is found by returning to Saeki. There is a non-sacramental and anti-royalist component surfacing in his interpretations that leads to unfounded conclusions. This component obscures the Persian and courtly nature of the Church of the East's presence in Tang China, and the degree of agency the East Syrians held in relation not just to the Tang court, but in relation to a range of non-Christian courtly and imperial contexts. It obfuscates as well what will be called in this study the Late Antique and early medieval East Syrian church's Persian *longue durée*.[16]

Saeki on occasion referred to the existence of 'emperor worship' in the corpus of Tang Christian documents, and held the understanding that this was unwise and hasty on the part of the East Syrians in Tang China. It not only made them vulnerable but caused them to disappear in China altogether. Though he placed the term 'emperor worship' within quotation marks, suggesting he knew the term was imprecise and only a working concept, this was for him part of the church's Greco-Roman Christian heritage – brought to China, not discovered there (in Saeki's view).[17] Not only was the 'emperor worship' thesis part of Saeki's general characterisation of the political nature Church of the East in China, it was also part of his (erroneous) understanding that the church disappeared in China *because* of its being killed by 'too much imperial favour'.[18] For Saeki, the East Syrians in Tang China not only lacked sufficient connections to other regional courts (also erroneous), which made their situation precarious, but gave away their political will. Saeki's perception that the Church of the East in the Tang Empire was ultimately bureaucratic, top-heavy, and unconnected to the populace outside the court and to the courts of the surrounding region, thus leading to its disappearance in China, persists within the scholarship today, and needs re-examination if the study of the political nature of the East Syrians in and across early medieval China, Central Asia, and the Middle East is to be seen holistically.[19]

As Saeki wrote in 1916:

That the Nestorians who were driven from Edessa to Persia, and thence to Central Asia, and finally to the Middle Kingdom – sometimes sheltered by Arabs and sometimes by Hindoos [sic] – should have performed this great work of leavening Chinese thought with Theistic conceptions, reminds us of that 'Stone which the builders rejected but which became the chief Corner-stone! But what lessons can we learn from the history of the Syriac Church in China? This depends on how we study this Inscription. If we mention the failures of the Nestorian[20] mission in China, we should say first of all, that they did not raise up native workers. The foreign missionaries relied on themselves too much. We see hardly any native Chinese priests amongst the seventy-five names inscribed on the sides of the Nestorian Stone.[21] Again, it appears to us [also] that the missionaries relied too much upon Imperial Favour. They died or were smothered under too much favour from principalities and powers as a State Religion so often is. 'Too much kindness', in this case', killed the cat!' A State Church is a national confession of God, and the nation which disowns or ignores God is doomed; but the state protection of religion is apt to lead to state corruption of religion too.[22]

In Saeki's *The Nestorian Documents and Relics in China*, published in 1951, and as part of his discussion of the *Jesus Messiah Sūtra*, a text in which the Chinese sovereign is clearly attributed with sacred and numinous qualities, Saeki puts forth the view that the church's elites made the unwise move towards emperor worship in an attempt to win favour with the Chinese court:

> 'Emperor Worship', as well as the worship of other distinguished persons, was an old institution both in the East and in the West ... It is therefore no wonder that our Nestorian author should declare here {in the *Jesus Messiah Sutra*} 'all the sacred superiors {i.e. rulers} are no other than the gods born into this world'.[23]

Saeki's consistently placing quotations around the words 'Emperor Worship' suggests of course that he can be forgiven, and even thanked, for bringing an important scholarly problem before us. Though his assumptions stem from his lack of knowledge of the Chinese East Syrians' connections to Central Asia and Persia, there is a shortcoming within his interpretations as well. For Saeki the elites of the East Syrian church could not, and did not, share in and reflect the charisma of the Tang China court without violating itself and its God.[24] There is no sense of an 'open courtly charisma' within Saeki's interpretations, or any sense of the long-range political constitution of the church – how it, the church's elites, and their culture might have reflected political relations with neighbouring courts and carried what will be termed here as its own divine agency with it.[25]

Saeki's interpretations have a parallel in the scholarship on Syriac Christianity in late Sasanian Persia and early Arab rule; and it is here one begins truly to understand why an empirically-based reassessment of Saeki's emperor worship and imperial favour thesis is needed, and what can result from a robust re-assessment of the source and constitution of East Syrian agency in and across its multiple early medieval imperial contexts. The concept of 'dhimmitude', or legal subjugation under Islamic law, for example can be found within areas of the scholarship and popular writing on Christians under early Arab rule.[26] One important early twentieth-century scholar of Syriac Christianity in the Persian Empire, Jerome Labourt, quipped famously that 'it does not matter to the slave what particular master it serves'.[27] Stephen Gero, more recently, has argued for greater freedom in the church than Labourt saw, but dismissed the notion that the church was part of the Sasanian state by the time of its demise, writing that in its connections to the state 'the way was being prepared for the imposition and supine acceptance of inferior, marginal *dhimmi* status in the Abbasid period'.[28] Michael Morony, in his important work *Iraq after the Muslim Conquest*, suggested that the way in which the Church of the East fell into this state of servility was through the disunited nature of its monastic faction and scientific factions (a suggestion that is questioned later in this study), and the church's resultant inability to sustain a culture which could stand independently from the legal shadow cast upon it by the non-Christian courts who ruled over it through the later part of Sasanian Empire (225–651) and the early period of Arab rule.[29] Even more recently Samuel Moffett has written:

> a better metaphor than the 'sword', as far as Muslim-Christian relationships were concerned, would be a net, for after the conquest Christians found themselves caught in a the web of Islam but not usually under its sword; the net, if not always comfortable, was at least safer than the sword.[30]

One reason these and other scholars have failed to develop a more nuanced understanding of East Syrian Christianity's ability to reflect imperial power and stand flexibly in relation to it, both before and after the Arab conquests, is that these scholars are not reading the Sasanian Persian, Tang Chinese, and early Arab rule period historical materials together and through an integrating hermeneutic of the courtly space. The early Arab imperial setting is a period of world history with enduring contemporary relevance, and an important source for probing and reconceptualising relationships between religion and power in general, but particularly those that stem directly from and exist in connection with the region currently. Given the difficulty of developing expertise in each of its sub-domains, it is perfectly natural that this documentary record is not read holistically and with an eye to the Chinese context more often. The same limitation occurs on the Chinese side of the scholarship. Lin Wushu, for example, has directed attention to Saeki's assertions about why Christianity disappeared in China and countered them by showing that it was the 845 rescript from Emperor Tang Wuzong [唐武宗] (r.840–46) that ended the Christians' first phase of official status in China, not its culturally embodied character or its closeness to the Chinese emperor or court.[31] But Lin's treatment of the issue is far too localised, and leaves the impression that the political character and long durational identity of the Syriac church in China was simply an artefact of its being granted position by the Chinese court.

Samuel Moffett has offered the field a helpful metaphor in his characterisation of Christian–Muslim relations as a 'net' in his important volume on the history of Christianity in Asia. Arguably an articulation of political realities present within both sets of sources as well, this metaphor can serve as one among several combined beginning points for reorienting the discussion towards the necessary binocular vision. The Dunhuang document commonly called the *Sūtra of the Hearing of the Messiah* [*Xuting mishisuo jing*, 序聽迷詩所經], for example, contains language in which the Tang emperors, church elites, and the Christian God are shown to be part of a common familial fabric and a shared imperial charisma, one suggesting that the culture of the church was a conduit for the power of the empire, could be an extension of the Tang court, and could be unproblematic as such:[32]

> One who serves the Heavenly Lord[33] wrote this book in order to explain the doctrine [of the church] ... All beings have fear[34] of the Heavenly Lord who controls the life and death of all beings, and guides and controls the stupid gods. If all human beings fear the Heavenly Lord, then they should also fear the emperor. The fortune of the predecessors of the emperor was immense. The Heavenly Lord helped them take office.

This understanding, one in which the culture of the East Syrians, meaning the ascetic practices of their leaders, their standing before the Tang emperors having been granted office both by God and the emperor at once, and the way in which the church, its families, the empire, the emperor and the church's elites all constituted a family, borrowing an imperial Confucian trope, went unnoticed in Saeki's interpretations.[35] They are present, however, in the most important document concerning Christianity in the Tang Empire, and the document that can best serve to reorient scholarship on Eastern Christianity under early Arab rule by the inclusion of Chinese sources. This document is the Xi'an stele.[36]

The Xi'an Stele's Sasanian Persian *Longue Durée*

The Xi'an stele was set in place in 781 by the Church of the East and the Tang court in what was then China's capital city of Chang'an.[37] Uncovered in 1625 by workmen digging just outside the ancient capital, modern Xi'an, the Xi'an stele, as it is known, dazzles the eye today as it surely did in the short seven-year period that it stood in place during the reign of emperor Tang Dezong [唐德宗] (r.780–805).[38] The text of the stele was written by Adam/Jingjing, the son of a priest, a *chorepiscopus*, of the Church of the East who had most likely come to the Tang Empire as part of a fighting unit after being invited there by the court in order to help quell the An Lushan rebellion (755–62).[39] Adam's father, Yisi [伊斯] (Middle Persian, Jazbōzēdh), is presented as a key historical actor within the historical narrative presented in the stele, whose service to the Tang Empire during the rebellion and after (the stele can be understood to say) is shown representative of the church and its elites' long history of good relations with the Tang court and emperors.[40] Written in or before the year it was set in place, 781, in 1,900 Chinese characters and 50 words of Syriac, the stele is presented as a commemoration of the establishment and official recognition of the Chinese diocese of the Church of the East by the Tang court beginning in 638 and continuing to 780. The stele is commonly thought of as containing a beginning (doxological) section, a middle section, and a final, donor section, wherein the names of those responsible for the stele are mentioned.[41]

The reception history of the Xi'an stele being now four centuries long, it is impossible to summarise succinctly. Paul Pelliot's study notes on the stele, published posthumously by Antonino Forte, present a précis for key studies arranged chronologically until the early twentieth century and as such remains highly valuable.[42] The stele's seventeenth-century reception history dealt with the Tang Christians' relationship to the Chinese court and emperor only in so far is it could celebrate them and make them part of Roman Catholic evangelisation efforts in China.[43] If Christianity had been welcomed by previous Chinese courts and emperors, Jesuit missionaries could now say Christianity was not a colonial European imposition on China. Though the seventeenth and eighteenth centuries were the beginnings of both Syriac studies and Syriac printing in Europe, as well as Rome's rediscovery of Oriental Christianity in both India and the Middle East, the Syrian and Persian background of the Tang period Christians, and certainly the community's basis in Syriac monasticism, all went unnoticed.

As modern scholarship on the Xi'an stele could not and did not begin until the early twentieth century, with the discovery of the Dunhuang Christian and Manichaean documents, nineteenth-century studies of the stele are crucial documents in development of European Sinology, but are not crucial for understanding what the stele can tell about Syriac Christianity under early Islam or the Persian and courtly formation of East Syrian Christianity. It is only in the last two decades that the study of Christianity in Late Antiquity has come to include Iran.[44] Though much important work has been done on Syriac Christianity in medieval Central Asia, the Peter Brown school of Late Antique historiography and its sophisticated analyses of asceticism and the social functions of monasticism and its ability to transmit imperial power has not yet arrived in Central Asia along with it.

In directing attention to the all-important issue of what prompted the writing and setting in place of the stele in 781 in the first place, Max Deeg has drawn attention to changes having just taken place in the Tang Empire's tax structure initiated by Emperor Dezong, known as the *Liangshui fa* [两税法] or 'Double Tax System'.[45] Having ascended the throne only shortly before this, at the relatively late age of 38, Dezong came to the throne able to draw upon experience accumulated over a long period and a succession of Tang courts. One main feature of these earlier reigns was an inability to deal with the long term effects of the disastrous An Lushan rebellion (755–62), the string of rebellions and connected border incursions that followed, and the general chaos the Chinese empire was in during the period, without which no understanding of what a foreign religious body with an Iranian and ascetic formation was doing and could do can be ascertained.[46]

That the Xi'an stele community thought of itself as a monastic unit whose spiritual support and prayers (and, as explored below, fighting power) had aided the Tang emperor and court in the past and should be relied upon again is abundantly clear from the text of the stele.[47] The spiritual bond they thought to exist between emperor, court and the church's monastic élites is expressed in concrete terms in the text of the stele. The stele speaks for example of the church as having at one point *gong zhen xuanwang* [共振玄網], i.e. 'together repairing the Imperial Net', and *juwei jueniu* [俱維絕紐, reconnecting the threads which have been broken], asserting both that the group was indispensable and that the emperor had himself worked with the group to ensure the Tang empire and court's survival. The phrase *zhen xuanwang* [振玄網] has received differing translations. Daoist Wu Yun [吳筠] (d.778) composed a text called the *Xuangang lun* [玄綱論] at the beginning of the An Lushan rebellion, which he submitted to the court and emperor, a title translated by Jan De Meyer in his excellent study as 'maintaining the mystic mainstay'.[48] James Legge, in his classic study of the stele, translates the stele's expanded sense of the phrase as they 'joined together restoring the mysterious net'.[49] Pelliot translates this 'ensemble ils soulevèrent la corde mystérieuse' as 'together they elevated the mysterious chord'.[50] Deeg translates it as 'richteten gemeinsam das geheimnisvolle Band', 'together they directed the mysterious band'.[51]

There are imperial Chinese, Central Asian, and Persian trajectories within the phrase that Pelliot and Deeg, authors of the two most important commentaries on the stele, overlook, as they focus on the phrase's connections to the Dhūta Inscription [the *Toutuo sibei Wen'*, 頭陀寺碑文], a sixth-century Buddhist temple inscription in which the phrase is used in connection with the important Mahāyāna figure Nāgārjuna (c.150–250) and his having 'repaired the net of the Dharma'.[52] The Xi'an stele's author, Adam, was drawing upon pre-Buddhist classical Chinese sources outlining the metaphysics of

Chinese imperial ideology, though not excluding contemporary Buddhist dimensions as well.[53] One motivator for this translation is that non-Han individuals residing in the Tang Empire had constantly to negotiate their relationships with the court, as the primary sources for the Church of the East clearly show, their connections to Central Asian and Iranian commercial, military and cultural resources sometimes being a boon and sometimes not.[54] Moffett's insightful characterisation of early Muslim–Christian relations as a 'net' and the timely need to re-evaluate the place of Christians living under early Islamic rule on the basis of material provided in Chinese sources is another motivating factor.

The choice to translate *gong zhen xuangang* as 'together we have repaired the Imperial Net' also focuses attention directly on Saeki's anxiety over 'emperor worship' in the Tang East Syrians' Middle Chinese materials and provides direction as to how to probe and resolve it. This effort is aided by turning to the sophisticated analyses of early Christian asceticism appearing in recent decades and the way in which this has been brought into the study of Christianity in the Sasanian Empire more recently.[55] The donor section of the Xi'an stele, written in Syriac, and its reference to the term *mdabranoutha* [ܡܕܒܪܢܘܬܐ], often translated as Divine Economy, is crucial in this regard. This section reads:

> In the year 1092 of the Greeks [780/81 CE], Mar Jazbōzēdh [i.e. Yisi] the priest and chor-bishop of Kumdan, the royal city, son of the late [lit. resting soul] Milis the priest, who was from Balkh, a city of Tocharistan, set up this tablet of stone on which is written the [divine] leadership [*mdabranoutha* ܡܕܒܪܢܘܬܐ] of our Saviour and the preaching [pl.] of the fathers to the kings of the Chinese.[56]

Visible here is an imputation of the power of Christ to the leaders of the Church of the East and an understanding that this transmission of power gave them agency in relation to the Tang court and the 'kings of the Chinese'. The writing and setting in place of the stele itself appears as an evangelical proclamation. The Persian Christian monastic tradition and the ascetic nature of leadership in the East Syrian church is referred to in the stele's use of the term *mdabranoutha*. The term has the root d-b-r, denoting leading/directing.[57] The term is a translation of the New Testament Greek term *oikonomía*, translated often as 'divine dispensation', or 'divine economy', and stands syntagmatically in relation to the Greek term for 'house/household', οἶκος.[58] In the Greek-speaking church of the later Roman period the term *oikonomía* came to be related to monastic discipline too, to monastic leadership and monastic administration, through semantic links to the verb οικονομέω, 'to maintain a household'.[59] As the monk in charge of monastic discipline came to be known as an οικονόμος (administrator), and through the largely shared Greek-Syriac speaking monastic culture of Late Antiquity, the groundwork was laid for notions of leadership within the Syriac churches to be articulated through the term *mdabranoutha*. Erica Hunter has asserted that the term *mdabranutha* be translated 'monastic way', a helpful suggestion given that the Church of the East in the late Sasanian Empire, and during early Arab rule, as well as in the Tang Empire, was led by ascetic elites.[60]

The monastics of the Xi'an stele are also identified as 'Persian monks' here and in other Tang sources.[61] Pride in the Sasanian Persian past and its connection to Sasanian emperors can be found in the Syriac primary sources from this period of the church's history. Astronomer families working within the Tang court alongside the Church of the East's elites clearly identify themselves with Sasanian Persian royal lineages two centuries after the Sasanians' demise.[62] Tang historical sources show Persian monks accompanying Persian kings to the Tang court well into the eighth century and working as intercourtly liaisons.[63] The Xi'an stele, for example, tells readers that it was 'Persian monastics' [*Bosi seng*, 波斯僧] who came to the Tang Empire in the period of emperor Tang Xuanzong [唐玄宗] (r.712–56) and 'repaired the Imperial Net'.[64] An individual named Aluoben [阿羅本] (Syr. *Rabban*, ܪܒܢ, 'teacher') is a major figure in the narrative of the Xi'an stele and can be characterised as a Late Antique 'holy man' in the manner of historian Peter Brown and the school of research into Christian asceticism following him.[65]

Recent scholarship on Tang Christianity has drawn a great deal of attention to the official names given by the Tang government to Christianity and the change that occurred in this in 745, and as such it is a way of relating these two areas of inquiry.[66] The name change of

745 has been studied extensively, but the original name for Christianity given by the Tang court has not. Chinese sources indicate this name to have been 'The Persian Religion', *Bosi jiao* [波斯教] (lit. Persia[n] Teaching/Religion).[67] Antonino Forte (1940–2006), the most important scholar working on the Tang Christian materials in the later twentieth century, cautiously asserted that the reason for this name was not simply because 'Christianity comes from Persia', as the extant Tang sources containing and reproducing the edict state, but rather because Christianity was both an important institution in Sasanian Iran and within its court, and one that continued among Iranians residing in the early Tang Empire well after 651.[68] Though Forte showed less surprise at this in other parts of his work, he has written, with seeming surprise, that 'it is curious that the term "Persian" is applied to Christianity, which originated outside Persia, and not to Mazdaism (Zoroastrianism) or Manichaeism; it's as if when Christianity was introduced in China, it was *the* 'Persian' religion *par excellence*'.[69] Characterising Aluoben as a Late Antique holy man supports Forte's views on the title 'Persian teaching' for Christianity in the early Tang sources and in the Xi'an stele as having derived from Christianity's importance within the Sasanian court and its continuance in the Tang context. It also supports the translation of *gong zhen xuangang* as 'together we [i.e. the church's elites and the Chinese emperor] repaired the Imperial Net' because it highlights the leverage and mutuality the church's elites understood themselves to have had and their ability to transmit what theoretical work in the history of courts leads one to refer to as 'the imperial charisma' of the Tang Empire.[70] This undercuts Saeki's 'emperor worship' thesis and certain Syriac scholars' assertions of dhimmitude within the church in this period, along with Moffet's understanding that the mesh in which the Church of the East was drawn, not just to the Tang court but a series of imperial courts in this period, was one in which the church's elite agency and leverage was negated.

In the late eighth-century Tang context, the terms *xuangang* would have had great rhetorical impact within Dezong's court and within a Tang Empire reeling from two decades of instability stemming from the An Lushan rebellion and the continued border incursions, which were intrinsically connected.[71] Wu Yun, in the first year of the An Lushan Rebellion, had used the term in the title of his manual for support for the empire's spiritual elites, should the case arise.[72] Wu Yun expressed the understanding, arguably in line with Adam's thinking, that imperial monastics, through their asceticism and spiritual support for the Tang Empire, could participate in the personal charisma of the emperor himself, and even share in the emperor's bodily health and be an extension of his wardrobe.[73]

Wu Yun's and Adam's suggestion that the Tang Empire's ascetics could act as extensions of the emperor's person and sustain the court's charismatic constitution may also be deemed mere rhetoric.[74] But comparisons with ways in which religious elites participated in imperial political structures in other parts of the ancient and medieval world and the language used to represent them suggest otherwise. In ancient Rome, imperial priests distributed approved imperial portraits and statues, inaugurated public works, games, and calendars, and were said to act as extensions of the *genii* of Roman emperors.[75] The Hebraic conception of divine anointing, signified through the verbal root מָשַׁח [*mašaḥ*, to anoint] and its permutation מָשִׁיחַ [*mašiaḥ*, 'anointed one'], resulted in configurations in which divine power and charisma were shown to rest on individuals in a concrete and material fashion, and political and sacerdotal power were mutually implicative. This material embodiment of divine power could also rest upon individuals who were not Jewish, as long as God was thought to have acted through them.[76] This tradition of representing the interaction of earthly and divine power through material transference and contagion, signified by oil, was one in which kingship and those who shared in the charismatic constitution of the king's court stood in symbiosis. When the psalmist writes that 'the Lord is King; He is robed in Majesty', this symbiosis and sharing are seen in connection to clothing, and were indicative of perduring ways of thought among ancient and medieval peoples about the way in which political power and sacerdotal power rested on individuals, their clothing, and objects of courtly patronage. This is a way of thinking that may be akin to that pre-Early Modern European world described by Ernst Kantorowcz, in which a mystical continuity existed between kingship, the person who happened to hold the office, and the Christian clerical establishment, termed by him the 'king's two bodies'.[77] Saeki and other interpreters' failure to understand this and early medieval Syriac Christianity's long durational nature accounts for Saeki's consternation over 'emperor worship' in the Tang East Syrian materials.

In the Christian Roman Empire of the fourth century and after, the charisma of emperors is also shown to have been open to participation by the scholarly and ideological elite; Eusebius is an exemplar of this in both his panegyric to Constantine and his biography of the emperor.[78] By the fifth century, Christian ascetics had come to be part of this tradition and through it had come to stand on equal footing with emperors. A conception of open imperial charisma appears in the Syriac hagiographical tradition of the sixth century, as represented by the Syriac *Life of Joshua the Stylite*, where ascetics stood on equal footing with emperors when not perched on columns and performing acts of extreme asceticism and commandeering large groups of lay followers as a result.[79] The *Life of John of Tella*, like the *Life of John*, written by John of Ephesus, shows an early sixth-century Christian culture having emerged in the borderlands of Rome and Persia.[80] As N.J. Andrade writes, imperial charisma was held and transmitted by ascetics within this culture and 'as part of a clerical hierarchy and a network of priests and monks that cut across the frontier of the Roman and Persian empires'.[81] This culture's vision of an open imperial charisma, shared by emperors, courts, ascetics, and holy objects alike, was the ground from which sprang John of Ephesus' styling of John of Tella as a figure of resistance against both the imperial mandates of the Eastern Roman and Sasanian Persian empires. The term *politeia*, a Greek loan word in Syriac, is at the centre of the articulation of the political vision of the openness and transferability of imperial charisma found in the texts of this culture. When Persian Emperor Xosrō II (r.590–628) acquiesced to the Eastern Roman demand to involve Church of the East leaders in negotiating the end of a long period of war between the two powers and returned the pieces of the True Cross taken from the Church of the Holy Sepulchre in Jerusalem as a sign of renewed peace, the field of operation of this imperial charisma and as part of a trans-imperially placed Christian culture commandeered by ascetic elites was being made visible.[82]

The imperial charisma-wielding ascetics of the Eastern Church can be found in the Sasanian Persian Empire and shaped its trans-regional courtly culture just as they did in the eastern Roman Empire. The East Syrian church moved with the fallen Sasanian royal house into Central Asia and China after the Arab conquests and carried the Sasanian royal house and its legitimacy with it.[83] The courtly asceticism of the Tang East Syrians is more properly understood, however, by looking to the development of East Syriac Christianity in the sixth and seventh centuries in the heart of the Sasanian Persian Empire (225–651). Such a move builds upon some of the theoretical foundations of the study of Christian asceticism and power within the Late Antiquity paradigm, and its notion of the 'rise of the Holy Man', in the context of the official Christianity of the later Roman Empire.[84] This work can be built upon too by turning to the best theoretical tools available from the field of Cultural History, to which the Late Antiquity paradigm owes much.[85]

This study will translate the Syriac term *mdabranoutha* as 'Divine Economy and Divine Leadership' and use them interchangeably in order to highlight both the vaunting of individual leadership and ascetic prowess within the church denoted by the term, as well as the collective and shared agency within the church and its forward movement within history, as seen in the sources. The Xi'an stele's monastic and ascetically-led community stands, for example, in a tradition stemming from the Syriac *Acts of Thomas*, the Syriac letters of Patriarch Mar Aba I, the travel narrative surviving from Cosmas the India Traveller,[86] the letters of Patriarch Isho'yahb III and ascetic literature of his period,[87] Isho'dad of Merv and his *Book of Chastity*, the letters of Patriarch Timothy I, and Thomas of Marga's *Book of Governors*,[88] among other works, in which the long-range, social cohesion and adaptability, and historical mandate (to use the language of Persian, Turkic and Chinese courts) of the church is shown to have had intrinsic connections to its asceticism and its ascetic leaders. This understanding of the church as a house traversing and encompassing large swaths of space and time, led by ascetic athletes, comes from literary images found in the East Syrian ascetic tradition, having emerged from the church's commercial roots in the Silk Roads and sea trade spanning the globe from the Mediterranean to the Indian Ocean and to China.[89] Elizabeth Fowden, Scott

McDonough, Richard Payne, Cynthia Villagomez, and Joel Walker, among others, have opened new avenues for analysis of the ways in which the culture of Christian ascetic power transcended borders and was tied to Christianisation during the final phase of the Sasanian Empire and the two centuries following.[90] Sebastian Brock, Matteo Comparetti, Touraj Daryaee, Antonino Forte, Janós Harmatta, Anonino Painano, and Richard Payne have done important work on the closeness of relations between the Church of the East and the Sasanian court, providing building blocks for understanding how the two became part of Tang hegemony in Central Asia after the fall of the Sasanians, and building on the previous generation of work done by Arthur Christensen and William Young.[91] Sam Lieu has explored the re-opening of the Silk Roads in the late sixth century and the twilight years of the Sasanians.[92] This historiography can be set next to work on the spread of Christianity into Sogdiana at the same time, and more generally on Sasanian–Tang relations.[93] The result suggests the 'repairing [together] of the Imperial Net' that would occur in the period of the Xi'an stele, and where the long-range social positioning and interimperial culture of the Syro-Persian church was seen by the church as binding China and Central Asia together (captured in the phrase and explaining its origins), was one of only several acts of binding which would take place between the church and imperial courts between 410 and 780 and as centred in the church's ascetic and long durational culture.[94]

The term Divine Leadership/Economy (Syr. *mdabranoutha*, Grk *economia*) of the Xi'an stele also offers an empirical foundation for understanding the East Syrians of the Tang, their encounter with the Chinese empire and court, the political character of the church as seen in the late Sasanian empire and afterwards, and for understanding their view that their asceticism could sustain the Tang court and emperor. The demise of the Sasanian Empire and the simultaneous rise of the Tang, which created an opportunity for the Church of the East to use its ascetic resources in the Tang courts (honed in the late Sasanian Persian setting) constitutes a fruitful area of research not yet fully appreciated. Glen Thompson suggests that there was a Christian presence already in the western area of China and between the two Tang capitals, Xi'an/Chang'an and Luoyang, before Aluoben's arrival facilitated developments.[95] Local Tang Christians, consisting of Sogdian, Persian, and Turkic migrants and immigrants, likely asked the Catholicos (head of the Church of the East) in Persia to send a bishop for them as he did for the Christian Hephthalites, who were also missionised by Sasanian Church of the East members.[96] This builds upon the hard evidence that exists for the eastward spread of Christianity towards and into China before the seventh century. The granting of official status to the Church of the East in 635, which likely came under imperial and intercourtly auspices, is better understood in relation to this evidence. The *Synodicon Orientale*, a collection of East Syrian synods and their canons between 410 and 790, records that by 424, four of the cities of Khurasan, i.e. Viz, Nisapur, Merv and Herat, were represented by bishops.[97] By the time of the Synod of Mar Aba in 544, Merv had become a metropolitanate, ranking seventh in seniority after Beth Lapat, Nisibis, Basra, Arbil, Kirkuk, and Rev Ardashir. The city's fortifications, its proximity to the Merv river, its links to Turkic tribes, and its placement on the trade route to Herat and Balkh in one direction, and to the great Khurasan trunk road eastward to Seleucia-Ctesiphon in the other, were likely responsible for its elevation to metropolitan status.[98] Its bishops appear to have been placed in the city in order to negotiate within the city's and region's intercultural and political relations.

Though studies are now emerging that place emphasis on the church's monastic and ascetic culture as its sustainer in multiple settings following the fall of the Sasanian Empire, termed here the church's Persian *longue durée* – this is an area of research that can be expanded.[99] Michael Morony points to an increase in mission activity and the establishment of monasteries and schools among both Syrian Orthodox and the Church of the East in the final years of the Persian Empire.[100] It can be argued that the development of missions and educational institutions gave the Church of the East capacity to operate outside imperial constraints, occurring both in the late Sasanian setting and in the period of early Arab rule, but less emphasised in the Chinese setting. Scholarly work has long recognised that it was the church's cultivation of Hellenistic learning and other long-range cultural and intercultural competencies that aided its survival in the Abbasid context.[101] This needs to be further understood in connection to the monastic-ascetic bases of the Church of the East and be seen as part of what connected its Sasanian Persian and Tang Chinese settings.

Commentators have used the term 'cultural mediator' to refer to the Church of the East within these settings and as it performed this function in terms of its monastic and scholarly activities. Dimitri Gutas makes a distinction between the church and the court (i.e. the Abbasid court and the late eighth and early ninth-century church), and asks whether the church or the court led the movement. Gutas overemphasises the Abbasid court's influence, paints the Church of the East as a passive player and without agency, and excludes the expressions of ascetic agency and elitism found in the letters of Patriarch Timothy I.[102]

Adam Becker has recently shown how the monastic culture of the Persian church allowed it to traverse the transition between Sasanian and early Arab rule.[103] This, in turn, allowed the church to become part of the Chinese imperial setting and was part of its mobile, Persian, and agency-holding identity in the church's second major imperial and courtly setting.[104] For example, the School of Nisibis was a major component in the Persian church's self-conception in its use of the 'the divine garment of names', a conception first seen in Ephrem the Syrian and a notion that had spread widely in Syriac Christianity. The 'divine garment' was thought present in scripture and nature, and was a metaphysical and hermeneutical stance toward the world which gave the Syriac churches a trans-regional mobility, since it stressed reading and placed texts and the creation of textual universes at the centre of its mobile identity.[105] Jacob of Serug would refer to God as a 'divine scribe'.[106] The Persian martyr books show new converts to Christianity not being called Christians, but rather, 'students', building on a conception seen in Greco-Roman Christianity in which conversion to the right way of life came through choosing the right philosophical school.[107]

The Aristotelianism of the school of Nisibis, something that made the school well known even in the West, was an important part of this concept and something that enabled the Persian church to manoeuvre adroitly within the Sasanian Persian court, a practice it arguably carried into imperial China.[108] The medical faculty that was part of the School of Nisibis aided in these connections as well, by making the church mobile and adept within courts. That logic and science were cultivated at Nisibis contributed to the church's ability to debate in imperial courts.[109] These components surfaced within the Persian church's monasticism and in its courtly relations. While Isho'yahb III clashed with the Persian church's monks because of the division between coenobitic and anchoritic factions, he himself being more closely tied to the former and their interest in Greek learning and connections to the Persian aristocracy, these two branches of the Persian church's monks should not be seen as separated. Ishodoneh's *Book of Chastity* shows Evagrius's views on learning and prayer, though his Origenist and semi-Gnostic tendencies were condemned in the West, had flourished in the Persian church and became part of its trans-imperial and trans-regional culture.[110] The *Book of Chastity*, like Thomas of Marga's *Book of Governors*, stemming from the same period and context, is replete with a Sasanian Persian memory, one in which Christian ascetic elites hold agency in relation to imperial power through their thaumaturgical abilities and their Persian lineages.[111] Babai the Great (*c*.551–628) would join together the ascetic and scholarly sides of the Persian Church of the East's monasticism and make it a trans-imperial, and specifically Persian, form of monasticism. This is found again in the Church of the East's Xi'an stele and its language of imperial nets and extendable imperial bodies, their repair and sustaining, and the binding of the church to the court and the emperor's charisma.

The understanding of the Persian *longue durée* of the Tang East Syrians developed here holds these threads together and builds upon them. It is offered as a response to Saeki's hypothesis of 'emperor worship' and meant to reorient the discussion of the nature of Syriac political agency held under early Arab rule by starting with a key document within the Middle Chinese East Syrian corpus: the Xi'an stele. While Saeki indeed did not understand the extent to which the elites of the Church of the East did not merely represent Persian imperial power during and after the Persian Empire's fall, but also 're-presented' it, the significance of the way in which this study can reorient the study of Eastern Christianity under early Arab rule is of significance far beyond Saeki and what might result from expanding the scholarship on Syriac Christianity in the Persian empire and early Arab rule period. If we begin to take seriously the seemingly absurd notion, presented in the Xi'an stele, that the East Syrian church's ascetic elites could 'repair courtly/Imperial Nets', and could represent and sustain the emperor's own flesh and family, his imperial court, charisma, and imperial mandate, an edifice of Western humanitarian thinking that fails to understand that there is or ever was a Christian presence in the Middle East and across Asia, and continues to think of Christianity as an essentially Western phenomenon, is also issued a needed challenge. As much as Western secularist thought in its postcolonial moment longs to dissociate itself from its colonialist past, its assertion that non-Western peoples can have their religions and traditional culture, but it itself cannot and has outgrown the need for such things (unbeknownst to Russia), simply reifies the same teleology of progress found in Hegel, Spengler, and other architects of colonialism's intellectual edifice.

The culturally denuded and antiseptically cleansed subjectivity of postcolonial historiography can also be said to contain a shadow in so far as it is extremely interested in the complexities of interactions between coloniser and colonised, subject and sovereign, and the notion that culture and power not only interpenetrate one another but allow the subaltern to collaborate both with and against its own interests and that of the power holder. The window upon Eastern Christianity this book opens also involves a call for a more robust engagement with this shadow element within postcolonial historiography. The approach to the Persian and courtly *longue durée* of the Tang East Syrians developed here has been informed by the work of, for example, French sociologist Pierre Bourdieu (1934–2006), and Bourdieu's conceptions of *habitus*, field, and dispositions.[112] Christopher Beckwith's empirical but theoretical work centring on what he and others have called the *comitatus* is an essential synthetic component. A German historiography of courts stemming back to Max Weber and his notion of charisma, along with Weber's conception of 'worldly asceticism' [*Innerweltliche Askese*], despite seeming to share roots with the matrix of Western historiography the study attempts to critique, has also been employed as an interpretive tool.[113] As the book is first and foremost an empirical study of documents, these theoretical excursions have been relegated to an appendix.

It is indeed important to keep in mind that an investigation of the Persian royal dispositions and Persian *longue durée* of the East Syrians

is ultimately an empirical venture. Joseph Wieshöfer indicates that
during the late Sasanian period a tension arose during the period of
Khosrow I's reforms between social grandeur and courtly pomp and
social lineage.[114] In times of crisis, as occurred through the sixth and
into the seventh century, the higher nobility could force a ruler to put
lineage before courtly ritual and regalia usage. This changed with
Khosrow I:

> The rank of a Parthian or Persian nobleman remained more or less
> independent of royal favour until the end of the fifth century. Until
> that time, the unruly heads of great noble houses [Suren, Karin,
> lords of Andegan, etc.] admitted only nominal allegiance to the
> central power. In their hereditary territorial domains they were
> virtually independent of the king. This changed in late Sasanian
> times. Symptomatic is the way in which the wearing of belts,
> rings, clasps, and other sartorial distinctions now required royal
> approval.[115]

These sartorial distinctions, signifying numinous and imperial
courtly power at once, and becoming connected to the Church of the
East's Persian *longue durée* and Divine Leadership tradition, were
carried not just beyond the temporal and geographical confines of the
Sasanian Empire (ending in 651), but were carried into Tang period
China, the elucidation of which has far reaching implications and is
relevant to a range of readerships.

The East Syrian's presence in Tang dynasty China has long been
subject to the projections of under-informed interpreters, thus
revealing as much about the tenor of the times of the interpreter as
about the lived identity of those who produced the middle Chinese
corpus of texts stemming from the Luminous Religion and their
history across a range of early medieval world empires. While the
Sasanians' connections to the Tang Chinese empire in Central Asia
have been treated in a small number of articles, the East Syrian
church's connections to this history have been left untouched. As the
field of Late Antiquity extends itself eastward and the spread and
deep-rootedness of Syriac Christianity in central Asia becomes better
understood, a more extensive and integrative treatment is in order –
and especially one that draws upon Peter Brown's and his followers'

discovery of the social function of early Christian monasticism and asceticism. Saeki's unfounded intuition that the East Syrian church's elites interacted with the Tang court and emperor on an asymmetrical footing, such that it caused the church eventually to disappear, is an intuition that many modern people do share and might share. The recovery of connections the East Syrian church might have had to the indigenous cultures on the edge of China's vast empire, and which helps better understand the way in which their Middle Eastern identity related to their Chinese enculturation during the Tang period, has vast implications that extend well beyond academia. The same can be said for a deeper investigation of the question of whether the church's vaunted place within the Sasanian Empire continued and had a place in the early Tang Empire, as it supported Sasanian royals up to the mid eighth century and referred to Christianity as 'The Persian Religion'. Let us be clear, however, that the history of the Persian agency argued visibly in the Xi'an stele and to be delineated in the following pages is part of a scholarly endeavour, and that being careless about what is in historical sources will ensure that these possibly wider effects never materialise. In that regard the book targets three specific elements in the Xi'an stele, then moving out from then in both time and space. These are the *mdabranoutha* / 'divine economist' and 'Persian monk' designations, and the claim made by church's ascetic elites to have 'repaired' the 'imperial net'. The study moves out in time and space from these elements and makes visible the agency they bequeathed to the church's leaders and within its monasticism within four phases or chapters, and which are focused on in the following ways as part of the book's larger thesis.

Chapter Summaries

The book is divided into two parts. Part I is entitled 'What's in a Name?'. The first chapter, 'The Late Sasanian Court and Divine Economy', treats the East Syrians' agency within the Sasanian setting and court through the cultural strength of the church's asceticism and monasticism, showing that this allowed the Sasanian court to be carried, quite literally in one instance, into the early Tang imperial setting.[116] To make this argument, the chapter looks to Tabari's description of the burial of Yazdegird III by Christians, to the travelogue of Cosmas the India Traveller, and to developments in the late Sasanian period in which Sasanian courts and emperors played roles in the affairs of the church. It also looks to Church of the East elites taking on roles in Sasanian interimperial diplomacy, and Persian Christian queens and their patronage objects. By examining the way in which these elements appeared and were sustained within the interimperial and ascetic culture of the East Syrians on the eve of the Arab conquests and surface in the Divine Economy tradition of Patriarch Isho'yahb III, an understanding can be gleaned of why the early Tang court named Christianity 'the Persian religion', an important background ultimately for understanding the rhetorical assertions of the Xi'an stele under focus in the entire study, and allowing the degree to which East Syrians were autonomous during early Arab rule to come better into focus.

The second chapter, '"Repairing the Imperial Net" before the An Lushan Rebellion', examines further the early Tang imperial setting in which the Church of the East was given the official title by the Tang court of 'the Persian religion'. It has long been known that Sasanian royals fled to Central Asia following the fall of the Persian Empire, entered Tang imperial social space, and were aided by the Chinese. What has not been examined within the secondary scholarship is the Church of the East's place within this. This chapter and the next one argue that that the East Syrians and Sasanian royals in exile conferred agency and leverage upon one another and in relation to the Tang court. The church's diplomatic and cultural contacts with Central Asia and the Eastern Roman Empire, examined in Chapter 1, surface within the Chinese primary sources and can be shown to have continued after the fall of the Sasanian Empire, showing that East Syrians very likely played a role in strengthening Sasanian restoration hopes and were known to have remained alive up to at least the 740s. Though the scene changed after the An Lushan Rebellion (755–62) and Battle of Talas 751, we are able to know much more about the content of the Chinese designation 'the Persian religion' and about Persian royal continuity even within the name 'Daqin religion' (as the church came to be called in 745) than we had previously, which has important implications for both Syriacists interested in Sasanian Persia and Persian historians interested in the role of Syriac in early medieval Iranian history. It allows us to reassess

Saeki's emperor worship thesis and the Xi'an stele's notion that Syriac Christians were a 'sacred net' around the Tang court in connection to their asceticism as well.

Part II, 'The Lord is King: He is Robed in Majesty' begins with the third chapter, 'The *Habitus* of Patriarch Timothy I', which examines the early Abbasid setting of the church and how its social leveraging capabilities changed, were 'repaired', from the early Tang (pre-An Lushan and pre-Abbasid) setting of the previous chapter, and in relation to the imperialised articulation of ascetic leadership found within the extant writings of Patriarch Timothy I (r.780–823). The chapter centres upon another challenge to Saeki's views, his dictum that the study of Christianity in the Tang period begins and ends with the Xi'an monument, arguing that an understanding of the Abbasid setting and the social leverage the church's elites gained within the early Abbasid court and a sequence of courts across Central Asia simultaneously is crucial for understanding the rhetorical assertions the Church of the East's elites were making in the late Tang setting, and the degree of agency they possessed there.

The fourth and final chapter is entitled 'The Court of Emperor Tang Dezong as Imperial Net, and the Church of the East's Persian *Longue Durée*'. This chapter examines the consolidation of relations between the East Syrian church and the court of Tang Dezong (r.780–805), which took place after the An Lushan Rebellion. After the earliest part of Dezong's reign, one in which the church's connections to the Tang court were jeopardised and curtailed, the imperial charisma of the Tang court can be argued to have been extended once again to the Church of the East and its long range, Persian, ascetical constitution – its *longue durée* thus being once again fully operational and 'repaired' (in the language of the stele). The chapter examines the church's connections to the eunuchs of the late Tang court in this regard, as well as to esoteric-imperial Buddhism. It was this set of connections that led to the Church of the East Metropolitan Jingjing/Adam and the Esoteric school master Prajña working together on the translation of a Buddhist sūtra for Emperor Dezong in the year 787, something that shows with specificity how agency and imperial charisma transmission occurred between the church's elites and the Tang court. The effects upon the church of the rise of Chancellor Li Mi (722–89) and the success of his programmes for integrating the foreign fighters in the Tang who had come 30 years earlier to help put down the An Lushan rebels, as well as Li Mi's changes in border policy, are also examined in this regard. Both were a boon to the Church of the East. By looking ten years beyond the Xi'an stele and into the late 780s, when Li Mi and the connections noted above occurred, the Church of the East's understanding of itself as a group whose asceticism could foster and sustain the Tang court is shown to be prescient, and Saeki's understanding of a church in which agency and imperial involvement with the Tang court were antithetical, is again shown to have been unwarranted.

PART I

'WHAT'S IN A NAME?'

CHAPTER 1

THE LATE SASANIAN COURT
AND DIVINE ECONOMY

Introduction

The scholarship of Antonino Forte (1940–2006) stands as a leading edge of the research on Iranians in Tang China. The designation 'Persian Religion' [*Bosi jiao*, 波斯教] given by the Tang court to the Church of the East prompted puzzlement and scepticism on the part of this leading scholar, however. Forte wrote that 'it is curious that the term "Persian" is applied to Christianity, which originated outside Persia, and not to Mazdaism (Zoroastrianism) or Manichaeism; it's as if when Christianity was introduced in China, it was the "Persian" religion *par excellence*'.[1] Forte's scepticism that the Church of the East's religion could have been the main representative of Persians in Tang China is shared by other high-profile scholars.[2]

Forte is less sceptical on this point further on in his discussion of the topic.[3] He asserts that: (1) the Tang court would never have allowed the propagation of a religion based only on the visit of a sole monk, Aluoben, and the welcome Aluoben was given by high-ranking official Fang Xuanling would not have been offered to anyone without connections to the Sasanian court; (2) when Peroz III (Yazdegird III's son) in 677 requested a temple be built in Chang'an, he was likely following the precedent set by his father and his court at the time of Aluoben's work as a diplomatic liaison for the royal house, suggesting this temple was probably Christian and not Zoroastrian; (3) in Sasanian Persia, Christianity had received state protection such that, as Forte writes 'there is nothing strange in this being carried over into China';[4] and (4) Church of the East leader Jilie (Syr. Gabriel?) is shown as being sent from a political body referred to as Persia in Chinese sources and as accompanying its envoy to the Tang court in 732. It is the third point that will be singled out in this chapter and the next as a foundation that allows the research question raised in the Introduction to be addressed, i.e. what gave rise to the Church of the East's rhetorical assertions in the Xi'an stele and its notion that its ascetic leaders could represent the Tang court and its imperial charisma, and in what sense was the Church of the East's identity within the Tang Empire courtly and Persian. Marshalling data and arguments such as this of course speaks to Saeki's assertions of 'emperor worship' and his inability to understand the Church of the East's Persian *long durée* in the Tang.

Tabari's Account of the Death of Yazdegird III and East Syrian Involvement

The description of Yazdegird III's death in 651 as recounted in Tabari's *History* provides a good beginning for these directives.[5] There, following his murder in 651, the final Sasanian monarch, Yazdegird III, is shown as having been given a funeral conducted not by the Persian Zoroastrians *mobeds*, but by a Church of the East cleric in the region of Tocharistan and Bactria.[6] Found in the narrative are consistent views on kingship, the Church of the East's sharing in the Sasanian *comitatus*, and an understanding that religion and kingship are inseparable – statements regarding these being attributed just to Yazdegird III himself by Tabari and by the Church of the East's leaders.[7] In the final vignette in these Yazdegird III passages, Tabari includes an imagined recounting of a Church of the East Bishop also stating his own views on the burial and why his Christian community should wish to be involved:

a man from Ahwāz named Iliyā', who was the Archbishop of Marw, learned of the murder. He assembled the Christians who were under his authority and said to them 'the king of the Persians has been murdered, the son of Shahriyār son of Kisrā. Now Shahriyār is the child of Shīrīn the believer, whose just conduct and beneficence toward her coreligionists you must know. The king [that is, Yazdegird], had a Christian lineage, [and we should note as well] the honour that Christians obtained during the reign of his grandfather Kisrā, and the good previously received by them during the regime of certain kings among his ancestors. He even built some churches for them and settled [the debts] of some of their coreligionists. It is therefore fitting for us to bewail the murder of this king because of his generosity, [which was] commensurate with the beneficence of his ancestors and his grandmother Shīrīn towards the Christians. Now I think it right that I build a tomb [nawus] for him and his body and bear his body in honour in order to inter it there. Thus the archbishop ordered a tomb to be built within the garden of the archbishops in Marw/Merv.[8]

The Church of the East had been granted an official place at the Tang court and named 'The Persian Religion' only 13 years earlier.[9] Though Sasanian–Chinese relations were growing closer in the waning years of the Sasanian Empire, and this occurred as the Church of the East's connections to the Sasanian court appear to weaken, the ascetic, Persian, and long durational character of Syriac Christianity as practiced east of the Tigris was such that the Church of the East was able to 'carry' the Sasanian house into Central Asia and into the early Tang Empire's hegemony there. Exploring this adds empirical weight to Forte's inclinations about the nature of the name of Christianity in the early Tang and the larger theses of the study.[10]

The Church of the East's elites carrying Yazdegird III's body to his tomb into the garden of the archbishops in Merv and celebrating the monarch's burial as it would a fellow member of the body of the church stand as visceral representations of the Divine Economy doctrine seen in the Xi'an stele and its connections to the church's ability to represent imperial power. Seen within the Tabari passage is an understanding of imperial charisma, xwarrah, and its powers of contagion with respect to objects of material value and holders of military power and high social office.[11] This is illustrated by the mention of family bonds transpiring over generations between the Church of the East's leadership and Sasanian royals and in connection to the beneficence of the imperial family. Each of Tabari's accounts of the incident indicate the final Sasanian monarch moved along with an escort and with an array of courtly paraphernalia, a *comitatus*, ultimately to the city of Merv, and where wealth holders were re-established as members of the Sasanian inner circle.[12] In each account Yazdegird III is shown seeking the help of a local Marzban in Merv.[13] Turks, holders of wealth generated from water irrigation and agriculture, and local military officials under Turkic authority also feature in each of the accounts, indicating connections to the Church of the East's capacity as mediators and transmitters of Greco-Roman culture to Turkic peoples of Central Asia, as explored later. The imperial charisma transmission seen there was part of the Divine Economy tradition and the church's worldly asceticism seen in the Xi'an stele and the name 'Persian Religion' given to the church.[14]

Cosmas the India Traveller and Divine Economy

The travel narrative of Cosmas the India Traveller provides a way of moving further into these connections.[15] At the centre of the book is a bridge-building exercise between the Syro-Persian and Greek Christian worlds that is to be extended outwards to the entire world. In the book's opening sections this centres on two individuals: the first is Pamphilus, Cosmas' monastic elder in Jerusalem, with whom he has maintained a long-running written correspondence.[16] Pamphilus is the monastic elder responsible for Cosmas' choice to leave his life as a merchant and become a monastic writer and purveyor of prophetic visions and Christian merchant literature. The second is an ascetic figure who loomed much larger in the interregional, Greco-Syriac, Christianity of the period: East Syrian Patriarch Mar Aba (r.540–52). As he speaks to Pamphilus in the text's opening section and readers overhear their correspondence, Cosmas' allegiance to both a line of ascetic leaders and an attempt at integration of a secular and religious learning urged by the text can be seen. Readers encounter constant attention to detail, in the manner both of a scrutinising scientist (note the scientific naming of Cosmas' eye disease), voyager and accountant, or a Biblical scholar standing in the tradition of Theodore of Mopsuestia. Readers also encounter a social body self-confident enough to support fallen royal houses within the expansions of the Chinese Empire beginning to take place outside the text. As Cosmas writes:

How long I put off the composition of my work regarding the figure of the world, even though other admirable men as well as thyself frequently urged me to undertake it, you know best of all. O dearest, God-loving and Christ-loving Pamphilus, a man worthy of that name, since all holy men love thee – a sojourner in the earthly Jerusalem, but enrolled among the first-born and the prophets, with whom when of yore I knew thee only by report I was knit in the bonds of warmest friendship ... You ceased not pressing us to compose a treatise about the Tabernacle prepared by Moses in the wilderness, which was a type and copy of the whole world, as I explained to thee personally by the living voice in a cursory way, not as communicating opinions and conjectures of my own framing, but what I had learned from the divine scriptures, and from the living voice of that most divine man and great teacher Patricius [Mar Aba], who when fulfilling the vows of the Abrahamic rule, set out from Chaldea with his disciple Thomas of Edessa, a holy man who followed him wherever he went, but by the will of God was removed from this life at Byzantium. Patricius [Mar Aba] propagated the doctrines of holy religion and true science, and has now by the grace of God been elevated to the lofty episcopal throne of all Persia, having been appointed to the office of Bishop Catholicate of that country.[17]

His attempt to combat the learning of 'the Greeks' (non-Christians), and present an integrated account of the Christian world view, one in which the cosmos, the structure of Christian trade networks, and the biblical account of the world and the church's basis in ascetic leadership co-inhere, is also present. As Cosmas, speaking of his monastic elder, writes:

But you again pressed me to proceed with it [Cosmas' travelogue], loading me with condemnation upon condemnation if I refused, and assuring me that the work would be useful for the guidance of life and for the study and understanding of the divine doctrines, as well as for a refutation of the Greek [i.e. pagan, non-Christian] preconceptions; while showing that the whole scope of divine scripture has respect to the future state, as is most pointedly affirmed by the Apostle when he says: For we know that if the earthly house of this our tabernacle were dissolved we have a building of God – *a house not made with hands, eternal in the heavens*. When in these and such like terms you appealed to me, and it was beyond my power to gainsay the injunctions laid upon me by your piety, I consented, trusting to receive the benefit of your prayers; while making supplication ourselves that the divine grace without which we can do nothing aright might be vouchsafed to us in the opening of the mouth, so that we might be able without polished and artistic modes of expression, but in the simple words of ordinary speech (while grace manifests her own peculiar powers), both to teach her foster-children the divine knowledge of the doctrines, *the lives of pious men, and the figure of the world and its origin*, without ambiguity; as well as to describe with all readiness, and to communicate ungrudgingly, what we ourselves have freely received from God.[18]

Cosmas' interest in the church as a mobile, cohesive, leverage-holding social body led by ascetics and their followers must be seen against the realities of Sasanian Persian economic relations of the early seventh century when the text was composed, as well as the late eighth century when the Xi'an stele was composed. For Cosmas, Persian Christianity and its traders are in touch with all the known world. In the following passage one notes the reference to the 'full ecclesiastical ritual', the notion that China lies at the end of the known world, and that Persia's Christian traders have a divine right to trade there. As he writes:

The island [Taprobane] has also a church of Persian Christians who have settled there, and a Presbyter who is appointed from Persia, and a Deacon and a complete ecclesiastical ritual. But the natives and their kings are heathens ... The island being, as it is, in a central position, is much frequented by ships from all parts of India and from Persia and Ethiopia, and it likewise sends out many of its own. And from the remotest countries, I mean Tzinista [China] and other trading places, it receives silk, aloes, cloves, sandalwood and other products, and these again are passed on to marts on this side ... farther away is the clove country, then Tzinista which produces the silk. Beyond this there is no other country, for the ocean surrounds it on the east. This same Sielediba then, placed as one may say, in the centre of the Indies and possessing the Hyacinth receives imports from all the seats of commerce and in turn exports to them, and is thus itself a great seat of commerce.[19]

Cosmas' exquisite attention to detail and the way in which he narrates his convictions about the worldwide spread of Christianity and its agency stemming from its leadership under ascetics and knowledge-holders give readers a sense that they themselves are participating in the divine plan unfolding in connection to each of these nodes. The shared Sasanian Persian and imperial Greek nature of this divine plan and its existence within Persian Christian trade networks is repeatedly emphasised.

Though Cosmas had great respect for Persian Christianity and its merchant and inter-courtly connections, because the Greek-speaking Roman imperial church was an official supporter of Christianity, for him this made it the superior political and economic empire and ultimately the winner of the economic contest taking place between the trading empires. This is reflected in a story Cosmas tells about his fellow Greek-speaking Christian merchants trading on the Island of Taprobane and winning the island's king over to support for Greek merchants, Greek coinage, rather than Persian coinage.[20] Whether this really happened as Cosmas states, or he witnessed it himself, is not an issue, for Cosmas' impression that these events took place reflects consciousness of the economic changes taking place within the merchant circles in which Cosmas did in fact move.[21] Menander the Roman guardsman provides a contemporaneous account of Sogdian merchants visiting the Persian court seeking to trade silk from China on behalf of the Turkic suzerains under whom the Sogdians then lived and traded.[22] This occurred after the Hephthalite Empire, which had for a century exacted tribute from the Sasanians, fell to Turkic power and a political and trade alliance between the Sasanians and the Turks. Cosmas' vision of the world is better understood by placing it next to Tabari's description of Yazdegird III's burial, thus supporting Forte's assertions about the name 'Persian Religion', and making each part of the Persian agency seen in the Xi'an stele of the late eighth century.[23]

Zachariah of Mitylene, the Sasanian *Comitatus*, and *Mdabranoutha*

The Roman Empire, a partner in this alliance too, would soon find itself, its Christian traders, and their Persian Christian trader colleagues benefiting from the fall of the Hephthalites and the opening of the overland silk route into China.[24] Though this was a contest in which non-Christian Sasanians would lose much, it was not the case for Sasanian Christians. Zachariah of Mitylene (*c*.465–536) offers insight into the inter-courtly connections of Christians, both Chalcedonian and non-Chalcedonian, and the way in which the economic losses experienced by the Sasanian Persian Empire vis-à-vis these changes in Central Asian and Roman trading relations were accompanied by new articulations of Christian leadership in which asceticism predominated. Seen also in the previous excerpt, the following passage further indicates ways in which Christian merchants and Christian knowledge holders worked in tandem with Christian missionaries and ascetic holy men among the Hephthalites. As Zachariah writes:

> Now in the land of the Huns about twenty years and more ago some men translated some books into the native tongue; and the origin of it, which the Lord brought about, I will relate as I heard it from certain truthful men, John of Rhesaina, who was in the monastery founded by Ishokuni close to Amida, and Thomas the tanner, who were carried into captivity when Kawad carried away captives fifty years and more ago. And, when they reached the land of the Persians, they were again sold to the Huns and went beyond the gates and were in their country more than thirty years; and they took wives and begot children there. But after about this space of time they returned and told us the story with their own mouths as follows: After the coming of the captives from the land of the Romans, whom the Huns had taken away with them, and after they had been in their country for thirty-four years, then an angel appeared to a man named Kardutsat, Bishop of the country of Arran, as the Bishop related, and said to him, 'Take three pious priests and go out into the plain and receive from me a message sent to thee by the Lord of spirits, because I am guardian of the

captives who have gone from the land of the Romans to the land of the nations and have offered up their prayer to God. And he told me what to say to thee.' And, when this same Kardutsat, which, when translated into Greek, is Theokletos, had gone zealously out into the plain and had called upon God with the three presbyters, then the angel said to them, 'Come, go into the land of the nations and warn the children of the dead, and ordain priests for them, and give them the mysteries, and strengthen them; and behold! I am with you and will deal graciously with you there, and signs shall ye do there among the nations, and all that is needed for your service ye shall find.' And four others went with them; and in a country in which no peace is to be found these seven priests from evening to evening found a lodging and seven loaves of bread and a jar of water. And they did not enter by way of the Gates, but were guided over the mountains. And, when they reached the place, they told these things to the captives, and many were baptised, and they made converts among the Huns also. They were there for a week of years, and there they translated books into the Hunnic tongue.[25]

The chronicle goes on to describe both the Roman and Persian emperors' involvement in Christian missionising and trading work among the Hephthalites. Its indication that supplies were sent only when the Roman emperor found out what was taking place, sending both 'commodities and sacramental vessels', is important in this regard. The introduction of horticulture and building techniques by the missionaries is described in conjunction with mass baptisms. The Persian emperor too is described as being involved in the commercial aspects of this exchange and involved in a Christianisation process and in the weakening of his Zoroastrian dietary observances.[26] As Zachariah writes:

For one week of the year the king of Persia also, as those who know relate, has separated himself from the eating of things strangled and its blood, and from the flesh of unclean beasts and birds, from the time when Tribonian the Archiatros came down to him, who was taken captive at that time, and from our serene king came Birowi, a perfect man, and after him Kashowi, and now Gabriel, a Christian of

Nisibis. From that time he has understood his food is not polluted according to the former practice, but rather it is blessed, and so he then eats it. And Joseph also, the Catholicos of the Christians, is high in his confidence, and is closely attached to him, because he is a physician, and he sits before him on the first seat after the chief of the Magians, and whatever he asks of him he receives. Out of kindness towards the captives and the holy men he has now by the advice of the Christian physicians attached to him made a hospital, a thing not previously known, and has given 100 mules and 50 camels laden with goods from the royal stores, and 12 physicians, and whatever is required is given; and he is in the king's retinue.[27]

Christians on both sides of the Roman-Persian border in the final years of the Sasanian Empire devised grandiose metaphors to describe the expansive and trans-regional positioning available to those who worked across the cultural and trade networks of the two empires – metaphors such as 'standing on the two shoulders of the world', or 'seeing through the two eyes of the earth'.[28] As seen through the eyes of Cosmas and Zachariah, the Church of the East's contemporaneous regional position and place in history suggest that this vision was grounded in economic and cultural realities.

This is a vision of this world that is at odds with earlier scholarly views of the late Sasanian court, its demise, its place in the movement of history, and the place of the Church of the East in relation to these developments, and where the late Sasanian Empire was seen as a centralised and powerful monarchic state.[29] A confederation of Parthian and Sasanian families sharing power is now being pointed to, and a Sasanian faction that, up to its final days, had to work to secure loyalty from its clients, Parthian families and elites.[30] The Church of the East's facility as a knowledge holder, able to navigate the historical conditions of the time through the cultivation of this knowledge holding and its wealth, can and should be seen as part of its Divine Economy tradition and its Sasanian Persian *longue durée*.

Inter-courtly Physicians, Rhetors and Rome

This can be further understood by looking to the beginnings of official Christianity in the Sasanian Empire and its connections to official Christianity in the Roman Empire. There were negative consequences for Persian Christians stemming from the granting of official status to Christianity in the Eastern Roman Empire in 315. Elements within Persian ruling circles began to be suspicious of Christians' allegiance to the Persian state. In some cases such suspicions were justified; cross-border spying involving Christian clerics on both sides of the border began in the fourth and continued well into the seventh century and expressed the betwixt and between nature of Christian life between the Persian and Roman empires.[31] One specific development in the Roman Empire's trajectory towards official Christianity which did not help Persian Christians was its beginning to see itself as the protector of all Christians, including those beyond the borders of its own empire, as seen in Eusebius' *Life of Constantine*, which reproduces a purported letter from Constantine to Shapur I in which Constantine presents himself as the protector of Christians both within and outside Roman political boundaries.[32]

Persian Christians' adherence to a faith shared by a bordering empire that differed from the official religions of their own empire and its inevitable tensions were resolved temporarily in 399 when an edict of toleration was granted by Sasanian Persian emperor Yazdegird I (r.399–420) to the Persian church following a period of peace with the Roman Empire.[33] Aspects of the tension created by the Persian church's ties to Rome were offset by developing closer ties to the Persian court. The late fourth and early fifth century was a period in which, as occurred in the synod of Isaac in 410, the church would embrace aspects of Persian authority within the church itself. Persian monarch Yazdegird I for example was given a place and named within the very liturgy of the church. The synod was convoked by the Persian king himself, as indicated by the *Synodicon Orientale*. The synod adopted a recommendation as well that moved the Persian church away from Rome structurally and politically.[34] Persian cities were to have only one bishop, elected by bishops having authority conferred upon them from the Metropolitan and the Bishop of Seleucia-Ctesiphon.[35] Zoroastrians were also given freedom to worship inside Roman territory, another example of the confluence of imperial and religious tensions occurring.[36] The Persian church moved closer to Rome in certain ways too, as it adopted canons for liturgical feasts to be celebrated concurrently with the West, along with the adoption of the Western creeds stemming from the Councils of Nicea in the year 325 and Constantinople in 381.[37]

A backbone within the cross-border medical and knowledge holder tradition that gave Syriac Christians in Persia roles as cultural mediators between their empire and that of Rome was the School of Nisibis. Adam Becker says of this series of centres of learning that they

> could range from gatherings in local churches for the elementary study of scripture to informal study circles which met in specific locations within monasteries to independent institutions with a multi-tiered hierarchy of offices, where students engaged in a detailed study of biblical exegesis and acquired an acquaintance with Aristotelian logic; the foremost and most influential of the East Syrian 'schools' was the school of Nisibis.[38]

The roots of the school of Nisibis are in the school of Edessa, a city 200 km to the west of Nisibis. Edessa, nestled within the Roman Empire, that had held on to links established with regions to the east and beyond the empire's borders forged when the school's disciples, connected to Ephraim the Syrian, had lived within the Persian Empire and migrated westward when the Persian Empire's borders expanded in the mid fourth century. The population of the city of Edessa had given the school the name 'school of the Persians' or the 'Christian *Didascalion* for the Persian'.[39]

Following the decisions made in 431 at Ephesus against the Antiochean and diphysite theology to which the East Syrians adhered, pressures began to mount against the school at Edessa, forcing it eventually to move back into Persian territory and to the city of Nisibis, something that happened in stages throughout the fifth century.[40] At the school in Edessa, as in other schools within the Syrian tradition, pupils began textual training learning to read the Psalter and went from there to reading in Old and New Testaments.[41] The theological tradition of scriptural interpretation based in the writings of Theodore of Mopsuestia then followed.[42] 'Because Edessa had an advantage in view of its geographical location, being located between the Hellenistic culture and that of the Syrian orient, it utilised this advantage by employing Greek philosophy in its curriculum', writes Arthur Vööbus.[43] Work translating secular and sacred learning from the Greek into the Syriac languages contributed to the intercultural and interimperial nature of this environment. Aristotle's logical works, tied to the culture of rhetoric, argumentation, and intercultural encounter at the centre of this environment, were emphasised.[44] Within this setting emerged a tradition of Christian doctors serving in diplomatic roles between the Persian and Roman empires.[45]

By the fifth century doctors were involved at the very highest ambassadorial levels.[46] Marutha of Mapherqat († c.420) is one of the better-documented doctors who served in interimperial negotiations in the fifth century.[47] Hailing from Mesopotamia, an intercultural and educational centre for Persia long at the centre of Roman and Persian interimperial relations, he became the Roman ambassador to Persia near the time of the Synod of Isaac and represented Constantinople on as many as three missions to Persia, in 399, 406, and 410 (the year of the church's first synod). Marutha, who was received as an 'apostle and messenger of peace whom God in his mercy sent to the east, mediator of peace and concord between east and west', played a large role at the Synod of Isaac and interacted with the Persian king.[48] The letter of accord he brought with him to the council from the Greek fathers was translated into Pahlavi and read to those assembled, including the king, a process indicating the monarch's interest in the events.[49]

The Roman church historian Socrates records Marutha's successful treatments of the Persian king's headaches, something said of Tang Christian doctors and their emperor on one occasion also.[50] Marutha's influence was also felt in other areas of diplomacy between Persia and Rome. He was once able to persuade the Persian king to repeal a death sentence for a Christian prisoner.[51] Socrates' own words are worth examining in this regard:

At this time Christianity spread in Persia for the following reasons. Between the Romans and Persians embassies constantly take place; varied, however, are the reasons why they constantly send embassies back and forth. This necessity then also at the time entailed that Marutha, the Bishop of Mesopotamia, whom

I mentioned briefly earlier, was sent to the Persian king by the Roman emperor. The Persian king found the man very pious and treated him with honor, just as it befitted a man loved by God. This irritated the Magians who had much power over the Persian king; for they feared that he might persuade the king to become Christian, for with his prayers Marutha cured his chronic headaches, which the Magians had been unable to treat successfully. Then he promised Marutha that he could build churches where he wanted. This is why Christianity spread among the Persians at this time. At this time Marutha left Persia and went back to Constantinople. But soon after he was sent back in the context of an embassy, but the Magians tried to trick him again. This is why many of them were punished. The king however held Marutha in high esteem. He loved the Romans and welcomed their friendship too. And he nearly converted to Christianity after Marutha passed a further test, together with Ablass, the Bishop of Persia. For by spending their time fasting and praying, these two drove out a demon that was torturing the king's son. But Yazdegird died before he fully converted to the Christian faith; the throne then passed to his son Bahram during whose reign the peace between Rome and Persians was broken.[52]

While Socrates' words must be treated with caution, a dynamic is observable through them in which Greco-Roman medicine conferred cultural capital and leadership status, was part of inter-courtly settings and Roman and Persian interimperial relations, which the East Syrian church cultivated in relation to its asceticism and which shows a connected trajectory running from the fifth century, with the official recognition of the church, to Cosmas and Zachariah, and ultimately to the Xi'an stele, its Divine Economy rhetoric, and its ties to the scientific and ascetic acumen featuring in its presentations of Yisi and Aluoben. The way in which doctors with training in Greek medicine and philosophy gained access within Roman and Persian courts, not only because of their training but also because of the social mobility they gained in the court of the neighbouring empire, help us to better understand the world view of the Xi'an monument and the extent to which Adam took seriously its suggestion that East Syrian ascetic elites could sustain the personal charisma of the Tang emperor.

Medicine, like philosophy and rhetoric, was seen in the Roman Empire as both an empirical discipline, offering training to individuals for scientific work, but also giving useful knowledge for work in government service. Sophists, or philosophers, like medics, also followed a career path that could lead into work for the court and empire. It is through these means that individuals with this training became part of the church hierarchy, as seen in the case of Zacharias of Sura who was an archdeacon in the Roman church.[53] There are grounds for arguing that the Romans were likely aware of the popularity of Greek medicine at the Persian court and that they wanted doctors to serve as diplomats so as they could, in addition to their use of persuasive speech, use their powers of empirical observation to gain and transmit knowledge of Persia back to the Roman court. As will become apparent, this can probably be said for the Persian side also.

One doctor who worked within this interimperial matrix was an individual named Stephanus, involved in negotiations with Khosrow I when the Persian army besieged the city of Edessa in 544. Stephanus was dispatched in an attempt to persuade the Persian king to leave the city.[54] In addition to his ability to think extemporaneously in consonance with his training in medicine and philosophy, Stephanus was chosen because he had cured Khosrow I's father of an ailment.[55] Zacharias of Sura was sent following the death of the Roman emperor Justin II (r.565–78), by the then reigning Roman empress Theodora, as envoy to Persia 'with full power to treat'.[56] Zacharias was dispatched as the Roman court's highest-level envoy.[57] He was successful in negotiating a truce. Zacharias was sent to negotiate again later within the Persian court for the Roman court.[58]

One of the ways in which the inter-courtly and trans-imperial abilities of the church would make their way beyond the Persian Empire after its fall would be the inculcation and maintenance of this identity through the continuance of the church's monastic institutions in following centuries. It is no accident that the first ascetic figure whose life is recounted by Thomas of Marga in his book of church leaders is Abraham, a Patriarch clearly identified

with the figure of the Hebrew bible and father of all monotheistic
Semitic people. His 'virginity and holiness went out to all nations',
readers are told.[59] Babai the Great comes to the fore during the
reign of Khosrow II; standing in the lineage of Mar Abraham and
Mar Aba, he led monastic reform and expelled from monasteries
monks who had taken wives.[60] The next Patriarch came from Hira
and was trained at Nisibis, also railing against monks with wives,
part of which led to these leaders' understanding and modelling of
the faith being 'spread all over the country'.[61] Thomas of Marga has
the following to say about the role of ascetic leaders, their
interimperial mobility and roles in shaping the East Syrians'
standing in Sasanian patronage matrix through the embodiment of
its leaders' charisma in objects of culture:

> When king Khosrow wished to build a convent to Shīrīn his wife,
> in the country of Beleshphar, he sent to the city of Edessa, to the
> good man of worthy memory, Shamta, the son of Blessed
> Yazdin, telling him to bring from there copies of the Holy
> Scriptures, Prayer Books and Lectionaries which were to belong to
> the convent. And after he had gone there, and finished his
> business, he brought with him for Rabban a large Service Book,
> and he asked for Rabban's prayers and set out for his country. And
> all the books which Rabban wrote with his own hands, were
> copied from the service book which the honorable Shamta brought
> to him, and in the greater number of them may be found
> 'Mar Shamta, the son of Yazdin, the prince of believers, gave this
> service book'.[62]

As powerful ascetic holy men began to play interimperial roles and
shape the relations between Persia and Rome – 'the two shoulders
of the world' – and the buffer polities that existed between them,
the Church of the East's ability to secure and maintain patronage in
the late Sasanian court increased.[63] Although waxing, waning, and
being lost by the church for an extended period in the early
seventh century, the connection between pedagogy and courtly
patronage within the Church of the East's monasteries and schools
began to be shaped in such a way that the church was increasingly
able to stand apart from its imperial court. In the text *Cause of the*

Foundation of the Schools, a work coming from the late sixth century, the history of the school of Nisibis is narrated as a history of Patriarchs.[64] Leaders are seen as embodying not only the learning community but also the Church of the East itself. John of Beth Rabban is described, for example, as 'disputer' and is spoken of in a positive manner as being involved both in Khosrow I's court and the imperial expansions that occurred in his time. John is said to be one who 'begat spiritual sons without limit, and took up a beautiful name in the kingdoms of the Romans and the Persians'.[65] As men wielding ascetic power began to play interimperial roles and thus shape the culture of patronage in the late Sasanian Empire, these men and the culture to which they were connected both pulled East Syrians towards their court while giving them an ability to stand independently apart from it. It was this 'royal dialectic' that would become a conduit for the survival of Sasanian royal culture in Tang China.

Mar Aba I, the Fall of Hephthalites and the Re-Opening of the Silk Road

One of the central figures in this set of developments is the twenty-seventh Patriarch of the Church of the East, Mar Aba I (r.540–52), appearing as a central figure also in the travel narrative of Cosmas the India Traveller. Mar Aba led the Church of the East during the fall of the Hephthalite Empire and the related re-opening of the Silk Road. He also led the church during the period of unprecedented imperial and commercial expansion within the Persian Empire that started with Emperor Khosrow I (r.531–79) and the reforms of Khosrow I.[66] Mar Aba's prominence in the history of the Church of the East coincides also with the extensive restructuring of church structures and practices that occurred under him, resulting in the Canons of Mar Aba and as recorded in the *Synodicon Orientale*.[67] His ability both to secure and maintain courtly patronage for the church yet also steer an independent course for it occurred through the vehicle of East Syrian monasticism and asceticism; as such it contributed to its social cohesion and adaptability of the church and the culture within the church that would give rise to the literary image of Aluoben in the Xi'an stele and its rhetorical assertions.

There are two lengthy accounts of the Patriarch's life, and both aid in understanding and contouring the details of these developments. One appears in the *Life of Mar Aba*, in the collection of Paul Bedjan.[68] The other appears in one of the most valuable sources for the Late Antique and early medieval Church of The East, the *Chronicle of Se'ert*.[69] The latter text has been dated to the ninth century.[70] Both accounts present Mar Aba as an inter-courtly, trans-imperial, and ascetic and wonder-working figure.

Mar Aba is shown in each narrative as having spent his formative years travelling in the Roman Empire.[71] This gave him facility in Greek, which he employed alongside Syriac, the prestigious missionary language of the Late Antique Levant, and Middle Persian, the language of the court of the empire to which he belonged. His learning is shown in the accounts of his life to be part and parcel of his repertoire of cross-cultural communication and courtly debating abilities. These were skills that allowed him not only to win converts to the Christian faith but also to secure patronage and good standing with emperors and holders of power in regions on the edges of the Persian and Roman empires.

The *Chronicle of Se'ert* presents Mar Aba converting to Christianity and leaving the Zoroastrian faith of his ancestors precisely because of the reasonable nature of Christianity and its being amenable to rational argument. Upon being persuaded of the reasonable nature of the Christian faith, the zealous new convert is shown immediately proceeding to found a convent in the important regional trading and cultural hub of the city of Hira.[72] This he achieved through cultivating relations and political ties with the son of the Arab king Na'man, the son of another powerful Arab ruler, Al-Moundir.[73]

The narrative in the *Chronicle of Se'ert* shows him then going to the city of Nisibis, where he further excelled in rhetoric and learning. Following this, a journey to Roman territory and to Constantinople is presented. It was here that his scientific knowledge was put on display.[74] The emperor was so impressed by the entourage that he refused to slight the East Syrian Church and its diophysite theology as his advisors and bishops wished him to do. This was 'a sign of respect'.

It is Mar Aba's relationships with the mid sixth-century Persian court and Persian emperor Khosrow I, however, that are of greater importance. Both texts tell of a 'cat and mouse' game taking place in which the Zoroastrian leaders attempt to win the emperor to their side, deal severely with Mar Aba, yet fail and themselves fall victims to their own schemes. The *Chronicle of Se'ert*'s account, for example, notes that Mar Aba incurred the ire of the Mobeds specifically because 'he had prevented the Christians from marrying more than one woman and had cancelled the decisions of the judges' (with regards to marriage).[75] Though this 'royal dialectic' ends in imprisonment and long exile in both texts, Mar Aba is triumphant in the end, and it is through his ascetic powers and merchant connections, and the sacramental and material bases binding each together within the church, that this occurs.[76]

In both texts this period of imprisonment ends with the Zoroastrian Mobeds experiencing a comeuppance and Mar Aba and the East Syrian community and culture as a whole becoming vindicated. The *Chronicle of Se'ert*'s account shows the conflict being resolved by a debate in court and with the aid of objects of material culture associated with the church, in this case a cross, in conjunction with the use of reason and science as embodied in the church's leaders standing as Persian elites and Christian elites at once. The text reads:

> There was, made by his own hands, a cross of plaster, which the schoolchildren used with advantage as a key to open the door of their minds and have their minds penetrated by instruction when one of them found it difficult. God opens their spirit when one of them took a small piece of this cross. When the cross was placed at a house filled with mice, cats and lizards and which were demons who lived in the house of Piraeus [a Mobed], and when Mar Aba took possession [of the cross] and had exorcised the demons, they went away forever, not daring to approach it again. *God replaced them [the demons] with people of science, letters and propriety* and [because of this] the institution of fire-worshipers were singing their guttural cries ... All this took place following the controversy and questions which were debated *in the presence of the king* between the Catholicos and a man [a Zoroastrian debater], *one of the nobles of his nation*.[77]

The *Chronicle of Se'ert* indicates Mar Aba won this debate in court both by means of the material objects of sacramental Christianity and by impressing the emperor with his use of 'ingenious arguments'.[78] The argument used had a basis in the scientific and metaphysical arguments actually being debated in the Persian court at the time, as shown in the migration of Greek philosophers to Khosrow I's court and written about by Agathias. It has connections to the re-opening of the Silk Road in the period of Mar Aba's life and the trans-regionally placed Christian trading community Mar Aba regarded as his flock, and his and their participation in the 'soft power' of the Persian Empire.

In this regard it is necessary to note the way that both texts present Mar Aba as continuously bound to the Persian emperor's place of residence both before and after the Hephthalite Empire had come seeking their own Christian Bishop to be consecrated by Mar Aba. This suggests the Church of the East's sharing in the Sasanian *comitatus*. As the text edited by Bedjan reads:

> Afterwards [after the Hepthalites came seeking a Bishop] the King of Kings said in a calm and friendly manner, go and compose letters to the Christians of that province, that if the king does not want to feel good will [towards them], then with sword, bow and arrow they will be accused; fighting will take place against them and anyone who remains will be dead, whether he be a Magian, Jew or a Christian. After conveying the message ... God told the King of Kings to tell him [Mar Aba]; and he commanded that the blessed one have his chains loosened, and to be moved into the place where the king of kings had his winter quarters.

The Life of Mar Aba in the Bedjan collection offers further narrative but again emphasises that Mar Aba was required to remain living within the Persian monarch's residence – though given the freedom to move wherever he wished, he was still positioned within the narrative as an extension of the emperor's charisma and authority. The text reads:

> After some time, the Prince of Hephthalites, sent a priest to the King of Kings, and many Christian Hephthalites wrote to

the blessed [Mar Aba] asking them to give a Bishop to the whole of the Hephthalite kingdom. After the priest came to the king and had made known the matter of his mission, he [the emperor] was surprised at what he heard and marveled at the great power of Christ....afterwards the King of Kings sent him [Mar Aba] to province of Bet Huze [near the capital, Seleucia-Ctesiphon] and by God's work and his concern, many priests were saved from death, and the church's blood was not shed. He comforted her [the church] and filled her heart with the words of sacred doctrine. Then he [Mar Aba] returned to the court of the King of Kings, where he was allowed where he wanted.[79]

An exploration of the context in which Mar Aba mediated courtly relations with the Hephthalite kingdom and the court of Khosrow I reveals a set of tensions stemming from the Christian merchant culture the Church of the East shared with the Roman Empire and the Church of the East's ability to work extra imperially and perform tasks non-Christian Persians could not.[80] On the other hand, these tensions stem from the expansions of the empire taking place concurrently and during the 20-year period in which Mar Aba was a bishop and then Catholicos, and because of Khosrow I's interest in using the Church of the East as a means to this end.[81] This would have allowed Khosrow I to build upon relations between the Church of the East Hephthalites and Turks occurring under the reigns of Kavad I (488–97, 501–31) as the empire's administrators and tax collectors.[82] This set of tensions, when unpacked, explains the emphasis on material culture and proximity to the emperor's person seen in both narratives of Mar Aba's life. The narrative ends not just with Mar Aba sharing the Sasanian emperor's dwelling and with the emperor not allowing Mar Aba's body to be buried until the emperor decreed it a fitting time to do so, but also with Mar Aba's body being devoured by the Christian community and consumed like a sacrament, followed by a statement indicating that as this occurred 'the holy priests consecrated a Bishop for the Hephthalites, and the people of the Lord, and the joy has grown through the Divine Economy'.[83]

Procopius records silk traders coming from Sogdiana wishing to trade with the Sasanians, and the Sasanian court dramatically refusing by buying and then burning the Sogdians' silk in front of them.[84]

Menander the Guardsman shows that as a result of this, the Sogdians and their Turkic overlords simply brought the silk trade around and north of the Sasanian Empire and established a trading partnership with Constantinople.[85] Procopius shows that 'certain monks coming from India' [τινὲς μοναχῶν εξ Ἰνδῶν], likely Sogdians, approached Justinian, willing to convey to him the technology to grow and cultivate silk, and the emperor accepted their terms.[86]

The Sasanian court denied Turko-Sogdians access to their silk markets because they wished to remain in control of the silk market and the high price they were able to exact for it up until this time. That the East Syrians of the Persian Empire would have had some leverage in and around these tensions can be gleaned through the passages from Cosmas and Zachariah. The *Chronicle of Se'ert* also notes that:

> The cause [of this persecution] was this: the great Marzbans had plundered a boat, which came from India and which was filled with objects and things precious – a huge value belonging to a Greek trader. This went to the Emperor of the Greeks, which he obtained a letter for King of Persia in order to claim these items. They [the Mobeds] denied it, but were forced to make it clear. That's when, in revenge for the Greek trader incident, they stirred the king by their intrigues against the Catholicos and against all Christians.[87]

The text's reference to India indicates it speaks of the same Christian trade network into the Roman Empire referred to by Procopius. It relates to information also found in Procopius that Justinian entered the Turko-Sogdian trade network north of Sasanian territory not simply to reduce economic expenses, but through the desire to avoid trading with an enemy. It suggests as well that while Christian traders and church elites, either Diophysite, Miaphysite or Chalcedonian, could have gained proximity to the Sasanian court and could as easily lose it, they had perduring value to the Sasanian court through such tensions.

The asceticism cultivated by the Christians of the period should be seen in relation to both their cross-border economic activity and Christian traders' ability and willingness to sacrifice material comfort in order to extend markets and faith domains. Mar Aba and the East Syrian culture led by him was one that built upon earlier foundations, such as the men described in John of Ephesus's *Lives of the Eastern Saints*. Though monasticism came to Persia in the fourth century and was brought to Mesopotamia by practitioners fleeing Roman persecution instigated by the Emperor Valens (r. 364–78), persecutions by Chalcedonian Orthodox emperors and Magians in the sixth century had the effect of scattering East Syrian schools of learning all over Iraq/ Persia.[88] As a result, schools were built in the regions of Mada'in, Hira, Kashgar, Maysan, and in the villages of Adiabene and Bet Garme. Through Mar Aba's reforms, the trade wars of the late sixth and early seventh century, and the ability of Christian merchants and ascetics to work in tandem to spread faith markets and markets for material goods, this culture laid the groundwork for the church to carry the Persian court into China and to become part of early Tang China's colonial holdings in the mid seventh century. The way in which the Church of the East was able to operate as a robust, socially cohesive and long-range adaptable social body, able to mediate courtly relations through the operation of its elites and transmit Sasanian imperial power, seen here in connection to Mar Aba, can be seen once again in the following passage from the *Chronicle of Se'ert*:

> It is reported that Mar Aba brought from the barbarians a man of tall stature, and of course clothing. He [Mar Aba] showed himself very gracious in his dealings with him, he even cut his hair, and cleaned his clothes of rough wool, and ordained him for the Persians. Then he led him before the king [Khosrow I] and instructed him how to comport himself in front of the king. When the king saw [this] he was amazed at the wonder that the Catholicos had carried out and because he had cleaned up [the man so] and groomed him, because before this the king had first witnessed [the holy man's appearance] and discerned his [highly uncourtly] condition.[89]

Patriarch Ishho'yahb III, Divine Economy, and the Sasanian *Comitatus*

As the Sasanian house was falling and the incidents described by Tabari took place, the Church of the East was led by Isho'yahb III (580–660), its thirty-fifth Patriarch.[90] Over 100 of his letters are extant. These were published by Rubens Duval in 1905, when he published the Syriac along with a Latin translation. Isho'yahb III lived and wrote his letters during the crucial period in which Arab armies were just beginning to take control of Persia and alliances with power-holding families in Persia and Mesopotamia were being forged.[91] It is still an open question in the scholarship to what extent permanent Arab governing institutions were in place at this time, and the position of Christians defined clearly in relation to the new empire that ruled over them.[92] Though this would be different under Umayyad rule, starting in 651, the world of patronage by Arab rulers is only glimpsed in the letters from Isho'yahb III, but within the letters from his final years especially, one gains a glimpse into the thought world of the church as it entered Tang patronage along with Sasanian royals.[93] It is important to recall that the Divine Economy (*mdabranoutha*) tradition of the Xi'an stele is one asserted in reference to the 'fathers' of the church, and thus the agency with which the church's elites stood in relation to the Tang court, and the setting of this in relation to the Sasanian court's *longue durée* can be probed in relation to the church's Patriarchs. One such exploration will be offered here, with Isho'yahb III, and another with Timothy I, in the third chapter.

Before the establishment of stable rule by the Umayyads in Damascus, and during the period in which the power struggles that characterised Arab and Muslim politics before Caliph Mu'āwiyah and his military victory over Caliph Ali, there was no 'scorched earth policy' and both property and political independence existed for the Christian communities in Mesopotamia, Iran, and former Roman territories newly under Arab control.[94] This is borne out in the archaeological record even more than in the historical sources.[95] There was in fact a vigorous attempt by the Arab conquerors only to chase, subdue, and execute Sasanian leaders, a zeal that did not extend beyond the Sasanian ruling class remnant. The *Chronicle of Se'ert*, for example, says that after a period of five years of turmoil, stability returned and things were much better and they were treated with benevolence.[96]

Isho'yahb III's links to Christian institutions that have their origins in the Sasanian Empire can become apparent by looking at the namesake figure of Isho'yahb II (638–45), with whom the thirty-fifth Catholicos shares many connections.[97] He was also Patriarch of the Church of the East during the Arab conquest of Mesopotamia. The *Chronicle of Se'ert* relates information concerning Isho'yahb II's involvement in negotiations with the new Arab rulers.[98] He is recorded as having approached Arab leaders to win guarantees for the treatment of Christians in the Sasanian Empire.[99] Two approaches to the Arab conquerors were made, one by Isho'yahb II's emissaries to Abu Bakr (r.632–4), Muhammad's successor and a second by Isho'yahb II himself to the caliph Omar ibn al-Khattab (634–44).[100] The second of these, at least according to this recounting, resulted in Caliph Omar granting the Church of the East a charter of protection.[101]

The accuracy and even the veracity of these portrayals may be doubted and should be accepted in only a tentative manner.[102] However, Isho'yahb II was Patriarch of the Church of the East at a time when the Persian church was involved in much interimperial diplomacy and trans-regional commercial activity. A self-understanding and *habitus* was present among Church of the East leaders, of which Isho'yahb II was an extension and which may well have been passed on by him and other leaders to such figures as Isho'yahb III, as the primary source materials which will be reviewed will shortly reveal.[103] The first recorded Christian excursion to China arrived in the Chinese capital Xi'an in 635, during Isho'yahb II's reign; diplomatic relations with the Roman Empire being engineered by Isho'yahb II, referred to in one primary source from the period, suggest that Isho'yahb II may well have been active within diplomatic ties between the Church of the East and its first Arab rulers.[104]

The *Chronicle of Se'ert* indicates that during the year-long reign of Sasanian empress Boran (Pr. Poran), Isho'yahb II was sent on an ambassadorial mission to negotiate with Roman emperor Heraclius.[105] Because the involvement of the Persian church's leaders in Persian diplomacy by the early seventh century was a long-standing tradition, it may be proposed that such traditions extended into the Church of the East's tenure under early Arab rule, albeit in different form, and that may have been a mechanism that was passed on to other Church of the East leaders who were part of the transition in the period of early Arab rule. The ascetic figure from the Persian

Gulf, Mar Yonan, shown at the beginning of his hagiography written
during the period to have connections with Greek Christian
Emperors such as Constantine, provides support to such
suggestions.[106]

Isho'yahb III and the trans-regional elite culture within the
Church of the East of which he was a part had links to shared
theological negotiations with the Roman Empire. The *Chronicle of
Se'ert* suggests that in response to theological questions raised by
Emperor Heraclius to Isho'yahb II, the Catholicos

> answered his request, only under the condition that the deacon
> who read out loud the diptychs and which bore the names of
> certain Patriarchs and fathers, suppressed the name of Cyril,
> because of the schism and master of the impious doctrine.[107]

The author of the *Chronicle of Se'ert* concludes this incident by
indicating the Roman emperor accepted all that Isho'yahb II
wished and with agreement between the two Churches represented
over the issue of Mary, the mother of Jesus, who is curiously called
'the Theotokos', and, following this incident, indicating that
help was offered from the Roman Church to the Persian Empire
and to Empress Boran.[108] The negative positioning of the Syrian
Orthodox Church seen in this passage is most salient and striking.
The rivalry posed to the Church of the East by the Syrian Orthodox
church continued through the Sasanian–Arab rule transition
and was deeply part of the social chaos the church had to deal with,
as the discussion of the letters of Isho'yahb III below will show.
It was not only as troublesome for the church as was early Arab
rule itself, as the primary source data introduced below will
illustrate, but was tied to, and part and parcel of, the ways in which
the church came to terms with and responded to Arab rule, an
assertion that will become clearer as this chapter proceeds.
Secondly, the link with the Roman imperial church and the Church
of the East, seen being forged here in this passage from the
Chronicle of Se'ert, was something seen earlier in the Sasanian period
and in the ascetic figure of Mar Aba. Because this too constituted
one of several points of continuity between the Sasanian and
Arab rule periods for the church, this suggests that the church's

trans-imperial nature was partly what allowed it to bridge the Sasanian and early Arab periods.

Isho'yahb III was himself part of this diplomatic enterprise, continuing a long-held tradition, for the church had long been involved in trans-imperial diplomacy and this trans-imperial element had long been part of the way it cultivated its leaders. His personal qualities as well as family background – he came from a background of wealth and status – undoubtedly assisted in this role. Educated at the schools of Nisibis, he was consecrated Bishop of Mosul and the Metropolitan of Arbil and Mosul before becoming Catholicos. The location of his bishopric in Mosul was geographically close to the arena of Greek and Persian fighting and may have been part of what pulled him into this orbit of power holders.[109]

Thomas of Marga, while writing in the ninth century and some two centuries after the events, records Isho'yahb II's diplomatic mission to the Roman Empire highlighting the culture in which the Church of the East's leaders were reared, and was transmitted by them to the élite layer of the church in the period of early Arab rule. He writes of

> Bishops, who were wise, *instructed and understanding men*, and with them were also our holy Isho'yahb of Nineveh … who through Christ our Lord, the Lord of the worlds and the Governor and Guardian of *the two countries and of the whole world* gave these shepherds mercy in the sight of the Greeks, and they received their assembly and their petition as if they had been the angels of God.[110]

This passage in Thomas of Marga's *Book of Governors* connects Isho'yahb III to the ascetic Rabban Jacob, a charismatic figure linked to Bet Abhe monastery, an institution that was involved in sustaining and passing on Persian Christian cultural power and wealth well into the late eighth century, when the Xi'an stele was set in place. This monastery, and the ascetic figures connected to it, were also connected to Isho'yahb III's father, his cultural and symbolic capital, thus showing how it was gleaned and transmitted both within his family and within the culture of the monastery through the Sasanian-Arab rule period. It is revealed in the passage for example that Isho'yahb III was the son of a Persian nobleman, a man whose name, Bastomagh, means 'man of large estates'.[111] Isho'yahb III studied later at the school of Nisibis, an institution known to have long-held links to the trajectories of power and prestige within the church. Cultural connections to Isho'yahb III's family were not as extensive within Isho'yahb III's network of relations as would later be the case, as Isho'yahb III's father did not have much to do with the running of the monastery itself and likely only patronised it. But it is clear this changed with Isho'yahb III, and that he became a locus of more intense cultural patronage and in connection to his cultivation of himself as an ascetic figure within the church as an island of cultural power, an enthnarchy transmitting its Sasanian royal heritage into its ascetic leaders.[112]

Monasticism was part of both the Church of the East's identity and its power, not solely at the end of the Sasanian period, a period in which the church was experiencing much chaos and political ostracism. It was also a support upon which the church stood and moved into and through the period of early Arab rule. Thomas of Marga provides ample data on this and on the monastic revival that occurred in the late sixth and early seventh century.[113] He also comments on the role of Isho'yahb III in monastic revival and his patronage of monastic institutions. Writing about Rabban Ananisho, who is called 'the doctor, the monk and the compiler of the *Book of Paradise*, Thomas of Marga states:

> let us place his noble acts among [those of] his companions, for happiness at the right hand of our Lord Christ is [also] laid up for him with them. Now this blessed man Ananisho and Isho'yahb his brother came from the country of Adiabene; they were both trained in doctrine in the city of Nisibis, being children of the school and love and household of the blessed Mar Isho'yahb [Isho'yahb III]. They became disciples in the Great Monastery of Izla, as the books which belong to them in the library of this monastery testify, *for they show that they were written by their hands there.* Now Abba Ananisho having lived the life of an ascetic with all excellence, and having his mind constantly fixed upon the works of the ascetic fathers, determined to go and worship in Jerusalem. And from there he went to the desert of Scete, where he

learned concerning all the manner of the lives of the ascetic fathers, whose histories and questions are written in books, and concerning their dwellings, and the places in which they lived.[114]

The text emphasises Isho'yahb III's place as a patron of learning within the church, as well as the interregional nature of the monastic *habitus*. The links between the institutions of Izla and Nisibis, a shared cultural space in which Mar Isho'yahb III and Ananisho came into contact, were part of this *habitus*. The text continues to show how the nature and extent of the scholastic reform that was taking place at the time involved the incorporation of ascetic holy men and their charismatic authority.[115]

The culture that is exposed in this text is one that was not only trans-imperial and interregional, having links with the Sasanian past and moving diachronically across time, but one that also moves synchronically, i.e. traversing then contemporaneous imperial boundaries within time. The Church of the East's constitution as an inter-courtly, mobile, house-like, social body, one having cohesion as a social unit during and following the Sasanian Empire, connects to the Divine Economy tradition of the church's Xi'an stele and its rhetoric of imperial charisma participation is apparent as well.

Isho'yahb III and the '*Rulers of this World*'

The earliest direct reference to the church's new Arab rulers appears in a letter written as Isho'yahb III was about to become a Metropolitan within the church.[116] According to the dating scheme devised by Duval and what is known about the temporal course of the Arab conquest of Iran, the letter can be dated to between 635 and 640.[117] Though the reference to the new Arab rulers comes only at the end, the entire final section of the letter will be quoted in full as this portion of the letter shows the range of concerns through which Isho'yahb III thought about and talked about Arab rule, the nature of the church as a social body in his thought and rhetoric, and the range of rhetorical devices he turned to in order to express his concerns and assert his leadership within the church. The letter begins with a discussion of an East Syrian Bishop who had stood strong against the incursions of the Syrian Orthodox in the East Syrians' domains and had recently removed Syrian Orthodox clergy sympathetic to East Syrian theology and politics. It reads:

> Blessed Qamiso the Bishop, who removed the one who worships the idols [showing him to be] a fool to the common concerns of his work, and [spoiling] the inheritance of the good of the body of his children, in the instruction he gave for the orthodox faith, and for its sons. So, it is too, as fathers of the faithful, of every one of you who is of good report, [standing as] insignias of pure belief in the life of the body, your heritage and wealth, of the faith, you honour and what is left to your jurisdiction and governance. Perhaps when the armour of the prayer is upon you, the hope of being with the Lord will strengthen you. So the almighty help of God in faith and prayer be with you, keeping all of your fathers, and wealth and the government of honour of your country at this time, in such a way that there was not one of them the cause of the slander. You can [easily] find an excuse to inaction and carelessness. But, when seizing the opportunity, you will have judgement upon you at the time of the judgment of God, so confess to any justice of God, whose judgments are most correct.

> I know, oh weak men, because of the defiance against you, you think that reading this letter, perhaps you will be tired by another letter before you read it. Perhaps you would be. I am weary of this for my own sake and of writing to you concerning this matter, though it is necessary.

> I think at this time the business of your prayers, too, rather than a letter instances is necessary. However, before the God of his grace, mercy you will, I am a sinner and should see and know how you are, and how you can keep your good hope of the faith of our fathers guarded. If guarded, and if you are aware of these things and how they can happen or not, in other words, it is whether these things happen which do away with your perfection of your Christian faith, which is most important. I wanted to prove this to you, although it may seem otherwise to other people. Until you carry the zeal of the faith of our lord to your hearts, minds, tongues and hands, there is being created in you an impure seal, which is thrown by Satan and his minions upon the door or your church.

You are showing appropriate concern to the church; to build it, to enrich it, its sanctity and holiness, and this is fitting to the church of God. But going into one of the churches of any [other] and to enter into the mysteries in any place and to be partakers of the divine mysteries, this may not be permitted you, by the word of our Lord. If that would happen, you will cause false rumours. You are [also] saying along with the heretics that it is by the order of the Arabs that this trouble has come. It is in no way true. It is not done by the Arabs. For they do not help those who say that God, the lord of all, suffered and died. If it so happens that they give assistance to them, yet, you can tell the Arabs about this and persuade them of this matter, if this is a thing about which you are concerned rightly. Come, therefore, oh men, my brethren, inspect all things wisely. Render to Caesar what is Caesar's and what is God's to God. May you with God the most high God, who is able to make all grace abound to worshipers, keep you in every good work, bring it to completion, so that you do the will of him, at any time, through all the days of your life, do so, Amen.[118]

While it is difficult to know what effect this letter had on its recipients, what is noticeable in the letter is the in-group/out-group dynamic of the letter's rhetoric and this rhetoric's basis in biological and familial metaphors, thus connecting it to the Divine Economy tradition.[119] The text urges its readers to think of the church as an institution as both a physical and familial body, one under imminent threat. The letter refers repeatedly to 'the faith of your fathers', the risk of making an 'impure seal', and the threat of 'rejecting the perfection of the Christian faith', etc. The letter invokes and exhorts readers with injunctions – only 'the true believers' can ensure that the 'fathers of the faith' are not lost. Heresy, a set of 'tares in the field' (from another part of the letter) when removed, can insure the purity of the church's 'sons and daughters'.[120]

Isho'yahb III's mention of Arab rulers comes at the end of the letter. Shoring up East Syrian identity in opposition to the long-standing Syrian Orthodox threat appears more important to Isho'yahb III than do the church's new Arab rulers. The urging of fear at biological and familial impurity within the church social body is seen more in conjunction with the Syriac Orthodox threat than any threat perceived from Arab rule. However, both sets of concerns are bound together.[121]

The reference to 'those who say God suffers' refers to the Theopaschite controversy and suggests Isho'yahb III had been accustomed to this issue arising in dealings with Arab rulers. The reference to rumours and the fear that they may spread, as seen in the text, also show that Isho'yahb III is concerned that the church's Arab rulers distinguish sharply between East Syrians and Syriac Orthodox, and is backed up by the threat of excommunication:

> going into one of the churches of any [other] and to enter into the mysteries in any place and to be partakers of the divine mysteries, this may not be permitted you, by the word of our Lord. If that would happen, you will cause false rumours.[122]

This moral universe, and the institution it was attached to and created in, was also trans-imperial and inter-courtly, spanning temporally the boundary between the periods of Sasanian and early Arab rule over the church, extending beyond the geographical borders of the new Arab empire. It also extended metaphysically beyond the temporal boundaries of the present world, as seen in the text's references to 'inheritances', the 'will of God' working underneath the church's present situation, and the final 'judgement of God'. In this way, contemporary empirical support is given to the trans-imperial self-understanding of the church seen in Thomas of Marga's presentation of it, the latter stemming from the ninth century, and in which Isho'yahb III is portrayed as the creator and sustainer of an inter-courtly church, and a church with a Sasanian *longue durée* and subsequently part of the *mdabranoutha* tradition.

The next reference to the new Arab rulers found in the corpus of Isho'yahb III's letters appears in a letter to a monastic audience.[123] The connections to the ascetic foundations of the *mdabranoutha*/divine economist tradition can thus be seen in the letter. The letter is written to the monks of the monastery of Mar Qardagh. One key issue discussed in the letter is the payment of tribute, or *jizya*, to the church's new Arab rulers: 'those who rule the world in these times, as is fitting' [ܐܝܟ ܕܙܕܩ ܠܗ ܕܠܘܬܗ ܡܨܛܘܒ].[124] The notion of what is 'fitting' (*zdaq*) appears prominently in the letter, and is ultimately tied to the notion of paying taxes to the church's new Arab rulers. In this regard Isho'yahb III first makes an effort to remind his readers that they are part of a social body, one with a divine lineage, and standing upon the shoulders of the great ascetics of the past. He reminds the group that they are passing on this tradition as a collective social body, and that paying taxes and respecting monastic hierarchies as they do so are constituent parts of the social body and its traditions. The letter reads:

> For lo and behold, God and Qardagh are with you, to whom is good and right for you to head towards as a headmaster. Sprout forth together, holding fast to them. In being disobedient in holding fast to them, it is us also [the Bishops] that you refuse. However, if you hold yourself apart from them, it is clear that a great judgment shall be suffered, as you know. Because it may be through lack of knowledge [of such things], I write to you here about your [monastery's] founder, and because this is not clear to you entirely, this conversion of the mind on this matter to which I refer, as some testimony to our heritage.[125]

The letter goes on to say that the monks should remember their great heritage through Mar Qardagh connects ultimately to East Syrian monasticism's founder, Abraham of Kashgar. The spirituality of this tradition, the wealth of its monasteries, and the ecclesiastical hierarchy, all of which are connected to and were in need of tighter regulation and cohesion in the early years of the Arab rule over the church, are interconnected elements in Isho'yahb III's thinking. The letter comes back to the interconnected themes of wealth regulation and the streamlining of authority as part of the shared ascetic practice of the group as it refers to the church's new Arab rulers.[126]

The Church of the East's Divine Oἶκος in the Early Arab-Ruled Persian Gulf

The final set of references to the Church of the East's new Arab rulers appearing in Isho'yahb III's letters comes from the last phase of his life. Eight letters from the 650s survive, written in response to the unravelling of the Church of the East's authority and its structure, which occurred in its dioceses in Qatar, Bahrain, Oman, and India.[127] While this set of letters finds Isho'yahb III trying to rein in recalcitrant provinces and leaders, and anxious about the state of the Church and his authority, the divine economist tradition and its salience is also found in the letters. Isho'yahb III can be seen in these letters repeatedly returning to the notion that he, the Church, and its leadership should be seen as a mediator and medium for temporal power, and that the church constitutes an inter-courtly and metaphysical social body on a sojourn towards both an earthly and heavenly paradise. As such, and as this section of the chapter will argue, monastic culture and asceticism are shown articulating a sense of identity that draws upon the church's place in the merchant communities of the early Islamic period Persian Gulf.

This connection between monastic and merchant culture is increasingly being demonstrated by archaeological research on the East Syrian churches of this region and in this period.[128] Carter has found and documented a burst of monastic activity in the seventh to ninth centuries, arguing that data from Sir bani Yas, al-Qusur and Kharg suggests the Island's sites should be dated later than has been previously thought.[129] He notes that the monastic building activity referred to in the letters of Isho'yahb III adds support to the findings from archaeology. Monks who had left previous lives as merchants appearing in the textual record, similar to Cosmas the India Traveller, lead Carter to suggest that the early Arab period rulers may have left alone lucrative Christian trading centres in strategically positioned island settings where the pearl trade flourished.[130] Payne suggests that the appearance of mobile, house-like thaumaturgical adventures, the kind that appear in the hagiography of Mar Yonan, 'addressed the challenges posed to ascetic ideology by the expansion of Cenobotic institutions', and that in such episodes 'consumption is rendered part of the ascetic ideology and community identity through the holy man's act'.[131]

There are two passages from this section of Isho'yahb III's letter in which the church's new Arab rulers – 'those who rule over the world at this time', and to whom 'God has given rule over the world at this time', in familiar phraseology – appear. As the earliest one reads:

As for the Arabs, to whom God has at this time given rule [*shultana*] over the world, you know well how they act towards us. Not only do they not oppose Christianity, but they praise our faith, honour the priests and saints of our Lord, and give aid to the churches and monasteries. Why then do your *Mrwnaye* {Bahrainis} reject their faith on a pretext of theirs? And this when the *Mrwnaye* themselves admit that the Arabs have not compelled them to abandon their faith, but only asked them to give up half of their possessions in order to keep their faith. Yet they forsook their faith, which is forever, and retained the half of their wealth, which is for a short time.[132]

As the first of the two letter texts reads:

You stupidly wrote {to the Arab authorities} and sealed your revolt against God. And you took the statement of your rebellion to the tribunal of the secular princes, and you did all this, in order to cut yourselves off completely from the hope of church life.[133]

And the reference latest in date reads:

Since your so-called Bishops would not have been satisfied by your hostile impiety to the Church of God, they have aimed to show off their rebellion to the earthly rulers and even to the Great Prince {Caliph Uthman}, the chief of the princes of this time. To do this is to behave contrary to the government of the Church of God, and they have in reality been despised by the princes, just as their rebellion ought to have been.[134]

Despite the fact that the first and the last two texts are written to different audiences, noticeable in the texts taken together is the idea of the church as a divine social body. It is a 'house', in both the familial and economic senses. It is also a house of God in the theological sense and with a close identification with monasticism in Isho'yahb III's thinking. The church is also a body and house which carries its members across historical time and geographical space, wherein its members' earthly and heavenly sojourning is mutually implicated. A look at the background of the Church of the East's dioceses in the Persian Gulf and their history is instructive in terms of what happened in the period of early Arab rule and the specifics of what is taking place in each of these texts with regards to Isho'yahb III's articulation of church authority vis-à-vis changes brought on by Arab rule.

Fars was an independent church before the fifth century, but in 415 it recognised the leadership position of Seleucia.[135] At the same time, the Bishop of Fars was made a Metropolitan Bishop; and his headquarters was made in the seaport town of Revardashir, at the northeast corner of the Persian Gulf.[136] This Metropolitanate stretched far wider than normal, as church regulations stipulated that a Metropolitan was only to have six to 12 bishops under him, and if the number became more a new Metropolitan was to be granted.[137] There were many bishops under the Metropolitan of Fars, the precise number only vaguely apparent in a string of diocesan sees stretching from Kerman and possibly Baluchistan, with at least eight in Qatar and Bahrain and the nearby islands, and another two in Oman. There were missions in Sokotra, off the coat of east Africa, each connected to the seat of Fars, worth mentioning as well, along with Bishops in India also standing in relation to the see of Fars. In the sixth century the Metropolitan appointed a bishop in Kalyan, a seaport near Bombay.[138]

These structures began to change, however, in the early years of Arab rule. Bar Hebraeus, the twelfth-century Syriac Orthodox polymath, indicates that the Pars/Persian and Indian diocese began at this time to claim they were separate from the Patriarchal seat in Seleucia, and to extol their links to Syrian missionary Mar Thomas.[139] Ibn Tayyib refers to a development 'during the time of Isho'yahb', not specifying whether it was Isho'yahb II or III, that 'Metropolitanates of Halwan, Herat, Samarqand, India and China were established'.[140] William Young, arguing against Alphonse Mingana that this must be Isho'yahb III and not Isho'yahb II, asserted that Isho'yahb III's letters only make sense on this issue given the assumption that when they were written Simeon's province of Fars still included India, and that it was Isho'yahb III who created a separate Metropolitanate for India.[141] One way of interpreting the letters in which Arab rule is referred to is that Isho'yahb III was attempting to bring Bishop Simeon to submission, as is indicated in the letters themselves in numerous places, and was dividing this vast unwieldy province into three parts, and creating two new provinces with separate Metropolitan Bishops: Qatar and India.[142] Isho'yahb III was apparently therefore simultaneously streamlining and diversifying the large and expansive structure of the Church of the East at this time, something the Arab conquest of Iran necessitated.

John Healey has added to the work undertaken by William Young showing further that the text referring to the Bahrainis and their apostasy, as quoted above, can be seen within the context of the controversy that developed between Isho'yahb III and Simeon the Bishop of Fars about the Metropolitanate of Revardashir.[143] Healey has pointed out that the Arab expansion caused a separation to occur between Fars and Seleucia.[144] Because of this, new bishops in the church could not very easily go to Seleucia for approval and confirmation. This eventually drove a wedge between Beth Qatar and Revardashir and the Patriarch. Because of Arab rule, the precise details of which are faintly discernible in the historical record, in this region, as Young states 'Simeon [Bishop of Fars] was treating as his own empire'.[145]

The broad outlines of what transpired in order to cause Isho'yahb to write the letter to Simeon are that after Isho'yahb III became Catholicos in 649 he demanded the submission of the Fars Bishops and Simeon, but not only did the Revardashir Bishops assemble their own synod and decided to reject this, they also, apparently, notified Arab authorities. In response to this Isho'yahb III called a synod to condemn the bishops.[146] Later sources show that Isho'yahb made a personal visit to Revardashir and the diocese was reconciled with Seleucia but that a degree of autonomy was granted to the Metropolitan of Fars from that point forward.[147]

The main thrust of the letter, besides assuring its readers that Arabs were friendly toward the Christian religion, its holy men and monasteries, was firstly that the bishop of the region needed to come and talk with the Patriarch in person. For the moment, however, and in lieu of this meeting, Isho'yahb III wanted to press upon the bishop his second main point: that this apostasy had taken place because apostolic succession had not been understood in the correct way.[148] Isho'yahb III's understanding of apostolic succession is contrasted with Simeon's apparent view that laying on of hands was something that could be bought and sold, was, in the rhetoric of the letter 'nothing more than a money making business'.[149]

In the Qatar letters especially, what is discernible is that Isho'yahb was exerting his authority in ways similar to how he was doing this in relation to the situation in other places in the Metropolitanate of Revardashir.[150] The issue that constantly surfaces in these letters is that of invalid ordinations, termed in the letters 'cutting the body off from the head', and the reliance upon the Arab rulers for support against the Patriarch: 'You stupidly wrote [to the Arab authorities] and sealed your revolt against God ... going to the secular princes in order to cut your selves off completely from the hope of church life.'[151]

It is stated in this letter that Simeon and his followers attempted, apparently in vain, to get the support of the Arab authorities for their schism. A set of oppositions therefore exists in the text not only between the worldly rulers and the heavenly church – 'going to the princes who now rule this word' for help with your nefarious interests, he seems to say, is 'contrary to the government of the church of God'. Isho'yahb chides those who have done this: 'for they have in reality been despised by the princes, just as their rebellion [against the Church] should have been'. Isho'yahb III therefore seems to think the Church's new Arab rulers are on his side rather than on the side of the schismatics. This suggests that in his mind at least, Isho'yahb III was representing and connected to sources of power, perhaps not as closely tied to the new ruling court as was the case in the fifth- and sixth-century Sasanian context, but imperial and trans-imperial sources of authority nonetheless.

CHAPTER 2

'REPAIRING THE IMPERIAL NET' BEFORE THE AN LUSHAN REBELLION

Introduction

The Xi'an stele's phrases, '[we] repaired/sustained the Imperial Net' [as interpreted, not translated here] and 'binding the broken threads', were chosen ostensibly with reference to events affecting the Church and its leaders late in the reign of Empress Wu Zetian [武則天] (r.690–705) and early in the reign of Emperor Xuanzong [玄宗] (r.712–756). They have a context in the late eighth century and following the An Lushan Rebellion too of course. The goal of this chapter is to illustrate the early part of this continuity.

The Empire Strikes Back: Persian Agency in the Early Tang Period Church of the East

To better understand the dynamics that held between the Church of the East's elites and the Tang court and emperor, standing also behind the Wu Zetian and Xuanzong sections of the Xi'an stele and part of a symbiotic arrangement incorrectly interpreted by Saeki, it is helpful to investigate the designation of the early Tang court for the church and its elites as both 'Persian' and 'monastic' in the early Tang Empire. The name change of 745 from 'the Persian Religion' to 'the Religion of Daqin', has been ably studied within the secondary scholarship.[1]

The mid and late eighth-century setting of the Tang court's nomenclature for the Church of the East and why the name change of 745 occurred has been probed by helpful studies.[2] However, this cannot be said of the context of the initial naming decision, which was made in 635.

The restored edict reads as follows:

> The texts and teaching of Persia, originating in *Daqin*, came [to China] after being transmitted and practiced [in Persia], and have long since been practiced in China. Thus it was that when the monasteries were first built [in China], they were named accordingly [i.e. Monasteries of Persia]. Wishing to show people that it is necessary to learn their origin, the Persian Monasteries/Temples in the two capitals are to be changed into Monasteries/Temples of *Daqin*. As for those established in the Prefectures, and Commanderies of the Empire, they too should conform to this.[3]

Here it is seen that the Church of the East's presence in the early Tang Empire was tied to its monasteries. It also indicates that in the third decade of the Tang era and in the reign of Emperor Daizong [太宗] (r.629–49) the Persian nature and the monastic nature of the Church became tied together by official decree.[4] The edict appears to indicate as well that the Church of the East was not only thought of as a foreign entity, but was to be reminded of this.

Though the Church and its elites may appear to have been without agency and leverage in this regard, the ties to its monasteries and the church's connections to the foreign trader communities in Chang'an and Luoyang and the Silk Roads leading into Central Asia, seen in the passage, standing alongside the church's remaining connections to its Persian past, would have afforded the Church of the East's elites a means of circumventing this lack of agency. For example, the edict indicates that the Church of the East and its 'Persian Monasteries' were given official position not only in the empire's two capitals, Chang'an and Luoyang, but in the 'all the regions of the realm' [*tianxia zhufu junzhi zhe*, 天下諸府郡置者]. As these connections existed simultaneously with the church's ties to the Tang court, it stands to reason that the worldly asceticism and the elite, Persian and inter-courtly agency seen within the church in previous chapters would have carried over into the early Tang setting.

Arguments for why the phrase 共振玄網 [*gong zhen xuangang*] has been interpreted and translated as 'together we repaired the Imperial Net' having been offered in the introduction in connection to the period of Emperor Dezong, it is appropriate at this juncture to study the phrase within the reign of Emperor Xuanzong (r.712–56).[5] Previous research has explored the background of Sasanian royals' becoming part of the Tang state apparatus.[6] Knowing that this occurred simultaneously with the granting of place within the Tang court to Persian monk Aluoben, an attempt must be made to access the courtly *habitus* and leverage the church and Sasanian royals might have had within the orbit of the early Tang court, and before and leading up to the period of Empress Wu. Looking to the presentation of Aluoben, Jilie, and the other early Tang Church of the East elites (those 'nobles' [貴], from the 'Metal Region' [金方貴緒]) in the stele in this way gives further specificity to the argument that the inter-imperial nature of the Church of the East in the Tang Empire and the leverage held within the court by its elites generated the phrase 'sustaining/repairing the Imperial Net'.

Emerging as a leader within the church at precisely the time the Tang court gave the name 'the Persian Religion' to Christianity, it is important to recall that Aluoben was squarely identified and connected both with Persia and with monasticism in the official language of the designation for the church. The *Tang Hui Yao*'s version of the Promulgation Edict indicates this and in language that closely resembles that of the stele, characterising him also as a 'Persian Monk'.[7] Aluoben and Jilie (along with late eighth-century figures to be discussed in Chapter 4) can also be argued to be representatives of the church's worldly asceticism: elite, Persian, nation-representing monks, in whom political power rested and was invested.

The church's monastics are shown to sustain not just the Tang court, but the cosmos itself, with their asceticism and within the stele.[8] The emphasis on asceticism for the good of the Tang Empire's living and dead seen in this portion of the stele – i.e. asceticism done 大庇存亡', for the increase of those living and not', and acts of 'benevolence and humanity', 仁惠, 'going out with the sound of the strike of a wooden gong', 擊木..之音 – should be seen against the fact that the Church of the East elites are identified not just as monastics in the Xi'an stele, but as *Dade sheng*, 'Grande Seigneur de la Loi, gardien du royaume', in Pelliot's rendering.[9] Aluoben is also referred to as a *Shangde* [上德] '[un home d'] une vertu supéreure', in Pelliot's rendering, and is presented as a realm-guarding, or nation-representing monk, recalling the *Guo-shi* [国師] or 'national teacher' designation given to some Buddhist teachers.[10] Aluoben is also shown as a monk with extraordinary physical, intellectual, and political powers, a 'holy man', arguably, in the parlance of the study of Greco-Roman Late Antiquity. He is shown learned in astrology, physically robust, and able to serve as a diplomatic elite and inter-courtly liaison at once.[11] Aluoben had the power to bind communities together with his own charisma and his sharing in that of the Tang emperor. Patronage gifts presented to the emperor signify this, as does the emperor's having taken to the texts of the Church of the East into his own private quarters for perusal. As the text reads:

> In the time of the accomplished Emperor Daizong, the illustrious and magnificent founder of the dynasty, among the enlightened and holy men who arrived was the most-virtuous Alouben, from the Middle East[12] (Daqin). Observing the azure clouds, he bore the true sacred books; beholding the direction of the winds, he braved difficulties and dangers. In the year of our Lord 635 he arrived at Chang-an; the Emperor sent his Prime Minister, Duke Fang Xuanling; who, carrying the official staff to the west border, conducted his guest into the interior; the sacred books were translated in the imperial library, the sovereign investigated the subject in his private apartments; when becoming deeply impressed with the rectitude and truth of the religion, he gave special orders for its dissemination.
>
> In the seventh month of the year 638 CE the following imperial proclamation was issued: 'Right principles have no invariable name, holy men have no invariable station; instruction is established in accordance with the locality, with the object of benefiting the people at large. The greatly virtuous Aluoben, the kingdom of the Middle East (Daqin), has brought his sacred books and images from that distant part, and has presented them at our

chief capital. Having examined the principles of this religion, we find them to be purely excellent and natural; investigating its originating source, we find it has taken its rise from the establishment of important truths; its ritual is free from perplexing expressions, its principles will survive when the framework is forgot; it is beneficial to all creatures; it is advantageous to mankind. Let it be published throughout the Empire, and let the proper authority build a Middle Eastern (Daqin) church in the capital in the Yi'ning ward, which shall be governed by twenty-one priests. When the virtue of the Zhou Dynasty declined, the rider on the azure ox ascended to the west; the principles of the great Tang becoming resplendent, the Illustrious Breezes have come to fan the East.

Orders were then issued to the authorities to have a true portrait of the Emperor taken; when it was transferred to the wall of the church, the dazzling splendor of the celestial visage irradiated the Illustrious Portals. The sacred traces emitted a felicitous influence, and shed a perpetual splendor over the holy precincts. According to the Illustrated Memoir of the Western Regions, and the historical books of the Han and Wei dynasties, the kingdom of the Middle East (Daqin) reaches south to the Coral Sea; on the north it joins the Gem Mountains; on the west it extends toward the borders of the immortals and the flowery forests; on the east it lies open to the violent winds and tideless waters. The country produces fire-proof cloth, life-restoring incense, bright moon-pearls, and night-luster gems. Brigands and robbers are unknown, but the people enjoy happiness and peace. None but Illustrious laws prevail; none but the virtuous are raised to sovereign power. The land is broad and ample, and its literary productions are perspicuous and clear.[13]

Aluoben's presentation as a holy man is conveyed in several ways in this text, and part of a more general joining together of the Daqin region's political and spiritual power (imperial charisma) with that of the Tang Empire, which includes the very person of the Tang Emperor. The stele indicates that Aluoben, in the context of the early reign of Daizong, was part of a setting in which the imperial radiance of the Tang Empire and the religions of Central Asia and its holy men coalesced, where it became true that: 道無常名; 聖無常體 [*dao wu changming, sheng wu changti*, the Dao is without an invariable name, and but the Sage is without an invariable place].[14]

This presentation of Aluoben and the other Church of the East elites in the stele and the 'sustaining the sacred chord' phrase to which they are connected are better understood when seen as having emerged within a context in which Sasanian royalty occupied shared ground within the early Tang Empire and court with them, and as building upon the articulation of leadership within the Church of the East seen in the previous chapters. Leaders such as Isho'yahb III were able to hold and transmit imperial charisma and Sasanian royal traditions and transferring the inter-imperial capabilities of the church's elites of the Sasanian context to a later setting. Aluoben, his church, its elites and Sasanian royals used and built upon these foundations by finding places together within the Tang court and military and within Tang colonial expansion programmes that the Tang used to regulate the economy and products of early medieval Central Asia, and did so both as Persians residing within early Tang hegemony, but also as inter-imperial monastics.

Prince Aluohan of Persia: 'Nation Founding Duke' and 'Prominent Clansman'

One way of looking back through the binding together of the Church's elites and the Tang court seen in the Wu Zetian section of the Xi'an stele, and exploring the way in which the Persian and monastic character of the Church offset the apparent lack of agency seen there, is by turning attention to 'The Stone Tablet Set up in Memory of Prince Aluohan of Persia' (616–711), discovered in 1903 in Luoyang.[15] This inscription, in the present author's rendering, reads:

> 1. [this] Memorial [has been] erected for the Great Tang ['s] Persian Chieftain, General of the Right Wings of the Imperial Army, Upper Pillar of State (2) Metal Region/Town['s] National Founding Duke, [and] Persian Military Lord (3) A Lord [with] the common name Aluohan, the hope of [his] people, a Persian. In the Xianqing era (656–661) (4) Gaozong, the heavenly emperor and

great lord, in order to give special designation to those with talent and ability in the Western Regions, invited (5) [Aluohan to court]. Being received as General of the Western Gate, he served effectively (6) And serving as an ambassador [and] inviting and making peaceful the barbarian federation of Fulin, at Fulin's Western border (7) a stone monument was erected, which is still towering [like a mountain], [and] still propagating the way of the heavenly empire, [and] actualizing the beckoning of the barbarians' hearts (8) Numerous countries were purged and cleansed, and even now have peace and stability. How can it not be that with such a good leader (9) great success will not come? And for Empress Wu Zetian he called upon numerous barbarian kings, and constructed the Sky Pillar, many generals have met success, and this is not the only thing! This is indicated at the Lin pavilion, [as] the result of this is well known; [and] [by the fact that] there [is] there images at the Cloud Table, without which there would be no record (12) On April 1st of the year 711 [his time] came cruelly to an end; for at the age of 95 (13) he died in his own private residence in the eastern capital (Luoyang). The winds of sorrow, and the sun of remorse, and their clouds, made their way across the sky [on that day] (14) The wailing of sorrow accumulated, and the tears of remorse moved on (15) to the longest road. Oh what cries (16) from his son Juluode, [who] bemoaning to the highest heaven's ill-fated net, and with beating of the head on the ground, caused thunder around the grave; [his] tears gnawing [away such that they they] engraved [this] stone (17)

The now century-long tradition of scholarship on this inscription has yielded a set of building blocks that can serve as a basis to be added to by scholars more familiar with the Mesopotamian corpus and setting the Church of the East, its rootedness in the Sasanian Empire, and the political nature of the church's monasticism holding sway through the Tang period.[16] Each of these threads, held up in comparative light with the inscription, allows further counter arguments to Saeki's assertions that the Church of the East had no agency in the Tang imperial setting to be made. This is particularly relevant in terms of what the inscription says of Sasanian royals having prominent position in the orbit of the early Tang court, signalled by the inscription's reference to Aluohan as the 族望 *zu wang*, [of prominent clan].[17] This can be set aside the elements within the inscription showing the extent to which Persians played roles within Tang hegemony during the reign of Empress Wu, who wrought extensive innovations within Tang imperial Buddhism, adding therefore to the Church of the East's elites' ability to function within the Tang court and empire as national monks and as an extension of the emperor's charisma (the 'Imperial Net').

Though Forte has rendered several services to the scholarship on the Aluohan epitaph as part of a general urging of restraint within interpretations seeking to find connections with the Church of the East, he was also unaware of, or uninterested in, the leverage and agency sharing that existed between Sasanian royals, the church's elites, and the Tang court, which become apparent with analysis of the inscription. Forte showed that Aluohan cannot be the Luohan of the Xi'an stele, as the latter lived into the 740s, and that interpreting Aluohan's name as Abraham is unfounded.[18] He has emphasised as well that Aluohan's religion is not discernible from the epitaph, in spite of earlier theories that 宣傳聖教, 實稱蕃心, [propagating the way of the heavenly empire, [and] actualising the beckoning of the barbarians' hearts], in this author's rendering, indicated that 聖教 *shengjiao* connected Aluohan with Christianity.[19] And though Forte has added considerably to our knowledge of what this was, he has not carried this into a discussion of the Church of the East's elite position within the Tang Empire. Given that *shengjiao* refers to Tang imperial ideology, and that Persians had a vaunted place within this ideology, this opens an avenue to the exploration of the leverage and agency to the Church of the East's elites held in relation to this, which is apparent in the inscription, as will be shown.

Forte has suggested as well that the place to which Aluohan was an ambassador to 拂菻 [Fulin], mentioned in the inscription, has more than one designation in Middle Chinese sources; and though it was long thought to refer mainly to the eastern Roman Empire, Forte suggests it may also have been the country of Khulum near Balkh, which had been under Western Turkish rule but newly subjugated by the Tang when the Church of the East entered official patronage within the court.[20] Ma Xiaohe [馬小鶴], however, has taken this much further and provided an important breakthrough in the study of the relationship between the Aluohan inscription and Fulin, and thus the Church of the East's elites. It was in Fulin where Aluohan

> served as a leader of, and made peaceful, the barbarian federation, and where a stone monument was erected, which is still towering [like a mountain], [and] still propagating the way of the heavenly empire, [and] actualising the beckoning of the barbarians' hearts.

Ma argues that the reason some contemporaneous Chinese and Iranian documents imply that Tocharistan and Fulin were the same is because they were: the latter was a shortened form of Fulin-Kapisha [拂菻罽婆].[21] Ma surmises that when Tocharistan became a Persian protectorate under early Tang hegemony, it was either renamed or returned to the name Fulin-Kapisha, pointing out that the protectorate included an area that had previously contained Hephthalite territory, taken over later by the Sasanians, as discussed previously. Drawing the Persian connection out further, Ma seeks to build upon Pelliot's argument that the phonetics of Fulin in Middle Chinese correspond to an Iranian pronunciation, and come originally from Rum Caesar, a pronunciation that Ma believes dates to the Hephthalite and Kushanian periods, when, as is known, Kushanian kings could also be called Caesar.[22] Coinage from the seventh century indicates that there was a fiercely independent and anti-Arab mood in the air in the region, which may have been derived from a confluence of Sasanian restoration designs and support of this within Tang imperial expansion hopes.[23]

The Church of the East's ability to carry Persian royal habitus beyond the temporal and geographic borders of that empire may well have been put to use in this political setting, an assertion that can be supported by a number of strategies for engaging the textual record, as the exploration of Empress Wu Zetian's *Mingtang* and *Axis of the Sky*, mentioned in the inscription, and its connections to imperialised Tang Buddhism, looked at in more detail below, will show. However, it is fitting at this stage to delve further into the connections to the Sasanian Persian royal house hinted at in the Aluohan inscription and the agency this would have given the Church of the East's elites. Tabari and other Arabic sources record that Yazdegird III wrote to the early Tang court for assistance in his final years, suggesting that the Church of the East's ability to win support with a range of imperial courts and carry Sasanian power and influence beyond its borders may have been seen as attractive.[24] Tang sources describe Peroz III (Yazdegird III's son) being granted the position of military general in the Tang army by the Tang court, and the same being given to his son Narseh, suggesting the Church of the East would have had reason to carry their Sasanian connections eastward.[25] Upon the death of Yazdegird III, Peroz III would have taken the title Šanšah, 'king of kings', and would have been referred to as such in Tocharistan, whose outpost there is described in the Tang annals.[26] One indication of how deep the royal ties between the Tang and the fallen Sasanian ruling house were is that at Qianling, near Xi'an, there stand today two statues of Sasanian Persian royals among the statues of foreigners standing at the entrance of the funerary Mausoleum of Emperor Gaozong (r.650–83) and his consort, Empress Wu Zetian.[27] Though they are both headless, one of them bears the inscription 'Nanmei' [Great Head of Persia]; the other 'Peroz, king of Persia, Grand Central of the Right Courageous Guard and Commander in Chief of Persia'.[28] The notion, as Forte suggests, that Sasanian patterns within the royal habitus of the Church of the East's elites would not have been nurtured within this atmosphere, seems unlikely.

Tang sources allow the three-way connection between the Church of the East's elites, the Tang court and empire and Sasanian royals holding place within Tang hegemony to be explored in detail. *The Old Tang Records* recounts:

> In the late Sui period the Western Turkic Tong Yabghu Qaghan (d. 628) invaded and attached the country [of Persia]. [As] the Persian King Khosrow [II] was killed by the Western Turks, his son Shiroe was installed; he oversaw the county, and Persia was a vassal state to the Qaghan. When the Qaghan died, command passed because of this to Persia, and did not return to the western Turks. Shiroe passed away a year later. The wife of Khosrow II was made ruler, but the Turks killed her. Shiroe's son, Kavad [II] was made king. He fled into Fulin, and the people [of] the county [of Fulin] welcomed him. [But] they made him, Yazdegird III, the ruler, as he [Kavad] passed away in two years.

In the 21st year of the Zhenguan era (627–49) Yazdegird [III]'s envoy offered to the court a beast, named the lively rat snake, shaped like a rat and with bright blue color, 89 inches long, and able to enter to holes of rats. Yazdegird becoming weak, he was made a chieftain and entered Tocharistan. Even before arriving, he was killed by the Arabs. His son was Peroz [II]. And being offered protection by the Qaghan, he entered Tocharistan. At the beginning of the Longshuo era (661–3) Peroz told the [Tang] court that he was being invaded by Arabs and asked for armies and to be rescued. The emperor promulgated that, in the southern prefecture of the Longzhou area, commanding Wang Mingyuan to set up the Western Regions, making its prefectures and provinces, and through this series (chain of polities) Sistan was made the Persian Area Command. And Peroz was made its commander. And after this Peroz sent envoys to court. In the Xianheng era (670–674) he himself came to court, and Gaozong took pity on him making him a general.

In the third year of the Yifeng era (676–679) it was commanded that the Vice Minister of Appointments, Pei Xingliang command the armies of the crown and return Peroz as king of Persia. Taking him on the long road, [Commander] Xingling, in Sui'ye prefecture of Anxi province, turned back. Peroz alone resisted, but could not enter his country, and was killed by the Arabs. His ministers lasted for more than 20 years. And his tribe was more than a thousand. After being scattered and having difficulties, in the second year of the Jinglong era (707–10), he came to court and was made the Right Wing Army Commander. No matter what [though], with his sickness and death, his country went into decline. But his people carried on. From the tenth year of the Kaiyuan era (713–41) to the sixth year of the Tianbao era (742–56), a full ten envoys came to court, bringing local products: Agate beds, and did the Fiery Haired Rope Festival dance, and unbored pearls. In the beginning of the Qianyuan era (758–60), the Arabs and Persians attacked Guangzhou together. They destroyed storage buildings, burned them, and escaped by sea. They returned to court in the Dali 766–79 era.[29]

The New Tang Record allows more of this context to be seen, though differently, and states:[30]

> Says in the 12 year of the Zhenguan period, [not 21st] Yazdegird {III} not being a lord, was made a Chieftain, and fled to Tocharistan. While on the way there the Arabs killed him. His son Peroz {II} entered Tocharistan to flee. Envoys speaking of difficultly [to the Tang court], Gaozong not being able to command[31] from afar, invited an envoy. In order to deal with Arabs, he sent an army to Tocharistan. In 661 they were invaded by the Arabs. Then the emperor placed emissaries in the Western Regions Protectorate, making Sistan the Persian area command, and making Peroz its head. But it was suddenly destroyed by the Arabs. Though he could not found a country, in the In the Yifeng era (676–679) he entered court and was made the Right Wing of the Army. When he died this was the start of his son Narses being made a Son of the Court.[32]

At the beginnning of the Tiaolu era (679–80) the court invited Pei Xingjian to command the Persians and return them [to their throne], making Narseh king of his country. Extending the Persian road far, he made it go to Sui'ye prefecture of Anxi province. And there Xingjian came back. Because Narseh was a privileged foreign guest for twenty years in Tocharistan, his clan remained scattered and in difficulty for 20 years. In the beginning of the Jinglong era (707–10) he returned to court and was made a Left Wing of the Army. Though sick and in decline, the Western Regions continued. In the Kaiyuan period the Persians and Arabs attacked Guangzhou together.

The references to 'carrying on of his people' and to 'extending the Persian road far' by General Pei Xingjian in the above passages are among the most interesting, as this indicates the presence and shape of the agency of Sasanian Persian leaders with connects to Tang hegemony. This is the case even though Narseh was a *zhizi* [質子, hostage, son of the court], does not show precisely that Fulin and Tocharistan were the same political entity as suggested by Ma, though it does show them being spatially close and both being part of the base of operations for Sasanian royals being made part of early

Tang hegemony. The extent and reality of the church's elites' *habitus*, i.e. the embodied nature of their subjectivity and worldview, having connections to courts through the region (to that of Turks, to Romans through a shared religion, to Arab and Chinese court, explored in greater detail below), comes further into view through these details as well.

It is in an Iranian apocalyptic text called the Bundahišin, composed at an unknown date after the fall of Iran to its Arab conquerors, where these issues come into clearer focus.[33] The text indicates that the notion was alive in the period that Iranian royal theology was passed to the Hephthalites in Central Asia, suggesting the validity of Ma's theories and bearing connections to the Church of the East's relations to Hephthalites. It preserves a fiercely anti-Islamic sentiment and the notion that Iranian religion is held within the Sasanian royal line and those able to transmit the imperial charisma of its family line:

> During the reign of Peroz son of Yazdegird I, there was no rain for six years, and severe distress and hardship befell the people. Again, Khushnavaz, the ruler of the Hephthalites came, and killed Peroz. Kavad and his sister handed a fire altar to the Hephthalites as security ... when the sovereignty came to Yazdegird III, he ruled for twenty years; then the Tajiks (Arabs) moved into Iranshahr in large numbers. Yazdegird could not stand in the battle with them. He went to Khorasan and Turkestan, and asked horses and men for help, and they killed him thither. Yazdegird's son went to Hindustan, and brought a valiant army. He passed away before coming to Khorasan. That valiant army was disintegrated, and Iranshahr remained with the Tajiks (Arabs). They promulgated their own code of irreligion [*ak-den* (i.e. Islam)], and eradicated many usages of faith of the ancients, enfeebled the Revelation of Mazda-worship ... And from the beginning of creation to this day, no calamity greater than this has befallen; for owing to their misdeeds, on account of supplication, desolation, distressing deeds, vile law, and bad creed, pestilence, want, and other evils have made their abode in Iran. One says in the Scripture, 'Their wicked rule will be at an end. A community will come with red ensigns and red banners, and will seize Pars and the districts

of Iranshahr up to Babylon, and they will weaken the Tajiks (Arabs)'.[34]

Interestingly the text also refers to Fulin and the presence of restorers of Sasanian glory (*xwarrah*) in Central Asia and the 'Romans' ('Arumans'):[35]

> After that, the Turkish army will move into Iranshahr in large number and with many banners will desolate this prosperous and sweet-smelling Iranshahr, will disintegrate many thriving families, will perpetrate much harm and distress to the men of Iranshahr ... And when the Arumans will arrive and conduct the government for a year, at that time, one will come from the frontiers of Kabulistan, with whom there will be glory, also of the royal family, whom they will name Kay Vaharam; and all men will return with him, and he will rule even over Hindustan, Arum, and Turkestan, over all the frontiers. He will remove all impious beliefs, and having restored the Revelation of Zarathustra, no person will dare to come in the public with any other belief. 'And in the same period, Peshotan son of Vishtasp will come from the direction of Kangdez, with a hundred and fifty holy men. He will eradicate the idol temple which was their secret place, will establish the Warharan fire in its cradle, and will properly proclaim and restore the Revelation' ... the sun will stand at the zenith of the sky. Of earthly beings, they will first raise the dead body of Karsasp son of Sam, who will smite Bevarasp with the mace, and kill and withhold him from the creatures. The millennium of Soshyant will commence; as the millennium of him, the body builder [i.e. reanimator, resurrector] is for fifty-seven years. As regards these three sons of Zarathustra, such as Ushedar, Ushedarmah, and Soshyant, one says, 'Before Zarathustra wedded, they had consigned the glory [*xwarrah*] of Zarathustra for preservation, in the sea Kayansah to the glory of the waters, that is to the Yazad Anahit'. They say, 'Even now they are seeing three lamps glowing at night in the bottom of the sea. And each one of them will arrive when it is their own cycle'. It will so happen that a virgin will go to the water of Kayansah in order to wash her head; the glory [*xwarrah*] will mingle within her body, and she

will be pregnant. They will one-by-one be born thus in their own cycle.[36]

The ascetic and bodily nature of Sasanian courtly restoration ideology and restoration hopes, though to what degree the Christians would have thought in these terms, is intriguing and merits further scrutiny.[37]

By 745 the Christians had come to think of themselves as Tajiks/ Daqins, one indication that perhaps the thinking seen here was either not part of the church's elite agency or had been usurped by it.[38] That the name Daqin arguably represents the Iranian ethnonym Tajik, and was chosen by the Church of the East as Muslim domination of Central Asia spread and Iranians, though not necessarily adopting the Muslim faith, began to be integrated into the cultural and forces that came to make up the Abbasid Empire and Revolution.[39] The Persian dimensions seen in the Xi'an stele and the Li Su gravestone make it perfectly natural that East Syrians would want a name having continuity with their Persian past. Manicheans began to refer to themselves as Tajiks in this period too.[40]

But this chapter is focused on the pre-An Lushan/Battle of Talas era. By 648, and under the capable leadership of Emperor Daizong (r.626–49), both the Eastern and Western Turks were subjugated and the Tang Empire took control of all the major trading cities which rimmed the Tarim Basin – Yarkand, Khotan, Kucha, Kashgar, Karashahr, and Turfan.[41] Daizong adopted the title of Heavenly Qaghan, made ample use of his Turkic ancestry and understanding of Turkic military culture, and gave the local lords he conquered places within local governance using a form of rule called the Jimi system [羈縻制 *Jimi zhi* or 羈縻府州 *Jimi fuzhou*, *jimi* meaning 'to restrain and lure', i.e. 'carrot and stick'].[42] He thus created a unified imperial ideology that insured easy governance of regions still under Turkic and other domination locally, but within Tang imperial hegemony. The command units from which these envoys came were part of the self-rule administrative and political organisation for subdued Tang border regions, and first introduced by Commander Li Daliang [李大亮] (586–644) in 630.[43] By the 650s it had come into wide usage, and began to decline by the 740s.[44] The system, intended for foreign rulers or tribal chiefs that were either militarily subdued, had surrendered or assimilated naturally into the Tang's vassal states, and encouraged local hereditary rule. Zhou Weiyan writes of this vassalage system that:

> the rulers of these regions received their duty from the central authority while keeping their original status, and passing on their duty to heirs. They were to provide annual tribute, following the foreign policy and were superintended by the central authority. In terms of foreign policy, they would collaborate with the officials sent by the central authority in administration, participate in military affairs of the central authority's interest, and obey the assignation made by the central authority.[45]

'Mysterious Items of Foreign Cunning': Imperial Buddhism, Worldly-Asceticism and Persian Agency During the Period of Wu Zetian and Xuanzong

In terms of our ability to look back through the Wu Zetian-Xuanzong/'we have repaired the Imperial Net' section of the Xi'an stele, and through this gain access to and learn something of the leverage and agency provided the Church of the East's elites by its combined Persian and monastic character represented there, several additional passages can be held up for comparative analysis. These passages extend as well what can be said of the Aluohan gravestone and epitaph and the light it sheds on the Persian aspects of the elite nature of the Church of the East's leadership, i.e. that which gave then an ability to choose and be chosen and the tensions that held sway therein. Both passages counter Saeki's characterisation of the church in the Tang period and address Forte's suspicion that there may have been more to the Persian designation given to the Church of the East by the Tang court than met his eye. One passage appears in the *Tong Dian* [通典].[46] As the text states:

> The first year of the Longshuo era [661], there was established, in Tocharistan, prefectures and counties. Wang Ming Yuan, Commissioner responsible for establishing districts and sub-districts in Tocharistan presented [to the throne] a book entitled

Memorials of the Western Regions. At the same time he offered up the suggestion that west of Yutian (Khotan) and east of Persia, sixteen kingdoms should be established as separate governments and with 80 districts, 180 sub-prefectures and 126 military prefectures; [he also suggested] that there should be put a pillar in the kingdom of Tocharistan to commemorate the Imperial Virtue. The emperor consented.[47]

This next passage comes from the *Cefu Yuangui Record* [冊府元龜].[48] Here an important reference appears reflecting events not only contemporaneous with, and connected to, the 'we repaired the Imperial Net' episode referred to in the Xi'an stele, but where the figure of Jilie (Gabriel), responsible for 'our repairing the Imperial Net', and referred to within the same section of the Xi'an stele, also appears. In this portion of the text, Gabriel, a 'Persian monk and others [i.e. other monks]' are described as bringing *qiqi yiqiao* [奇器異巧, wondrous/mysterious items of (i.e. made by) foreign skill], to court and, through their own influence and that of a newly appointed official, bringing these items before the emperor and disturbing his passions and sense of equanimity. This took place when Emperor Xuanzong (r.712–56) had just ascended the throne, he ruled *in absentia*, and the confluence of power around the court was not yet settled.[49] As such the passage sheds more light on the Xi'an stele writers' understanding of what 'the imperial net' was and how it was 'repaired'. These two passages, taken together, also provide insight for contemporary interpreters of what the conditions for this were, along within insight into the *habitus*, or lived social context and agency of the church's elites, and the role of what has been termed 'worldly asceticism', i.e. the church's elites' shared connection to the Tang Empire and emperor's charisma and body, and how the church's elites maintained a sense of independence despite the closeness indicated by such language of solidarity with the court. The passages also indicate what the habitus of the church's elites was between the periods of Empress Wu and Xuanzong and the role of imperial Buddhism within this. As the passage reads:[50]

Liuze, in the second year of Kaiyuan period [714], was appointed as Inspector for the Department of the Domestic Service of the

Emperor and as Censor for the General Affairs for the Court for Lingnan. Together with Zhou Qingli, who was the Director of the Board of Foreign Trade and the Lieutenant-Colonel of the Magisterial Guard of the Right, he selected and supervised the presentation to the Emperor of devices, on a large scale, which were strange and of foreign skill, which they had made by Jilie [Gabriel], and a number of Persian monks. Liu presented his official address to the Emperor stating: your official has heard that one ought not look at things which one may covet, so that the heart does not riot from this, knowing that if one sees what he covets his heart cannot but riot. Sire, surreptitiously seeing that Qingli and others had some devious things engraved-smelted, engraved and assembled for distribution, [I noticed also they] used the admiration of this skill for luxurious items and the admiration for foreign treasures, as trickery. Such being the case that [for the sake of] the Principle of the Empire, let this be denounced by the Sacred Emperor as a great parasite, and under pain of severe punishment, as this degrades[51] and wearies the Sacred and Imperial Design. [In] the Ancient Code in former days, the correct way was, if a structure beyond expenses was to be built for your Majesty, or if an unbearable pair of chopsticks were [given] by an overly loyal courtier, this was [seen] beyond the imperial opulence. Moreover, it would be stated in no uncertain terms that in the Imperial Regulations: anyone who makes unduly ornate devices, through suspicion of the masses, shall be put to death in accordance with the Monthly Laws, which state: there is no making of crafty and licentious things which agitate the Imperial Sovereign's heart, crafts being that which is said to be of bizarre techniques/artistry, and mysterious ability. Agitations is what is said to be causing the loosing of the passions. [Zhou] Qingli and his cohorts desire to charm the emperor's will, shaking and disturbing his heart. If Your Majesty believe it so, thus it is best to undertake to command the whole empire [to be involved in such a disturbing of the heart and its passions]. If Qingli and his cohorts dissemble [in such a way], are they not opponents of the Imperial Code? Your majesty has ascended the throne recently, but the regions [of the empire] have absolute confidence[52] that [you] ought to clearly state that [the virtues of] thrift and humility are codes of conduct for frugality [and when existing] on a wide scale [then] the myriad common people of the empire will be most happy and prosperous.

The *Cefu Yuangui Record* passage above indicates that items of merchandise and clothing, along with the artisans who made them and the officials who allowed these items to be brought to court, constituted the Tang court and acted as an extension of the emperor's person and charisma, shaping even his bodily health. That the emperor's and court's charisma was thought to radiate into both the empire's colonial land holdings and its imperial sea ports is evident in the passage. As Emperor Xuanzong had just come to the throne and the constitution of his court was undergoing reshuffling, the mechanics of the court had become open to view, along with the patronage field, or *habitus*, within which the Church of the East stood in relation to the early Tang court and emperor. A concrete illustration is thus found of Norbert Elias's understanding of courts as reflecting the social order, and within a context far removed from his focus of early modern Europe.[53] In so far as the early Tang court and emperor's charisma is seen to have radiated far beyond Chang'an and Luoyang and into the Tang's colonial land holdings, and where items made in greater Persia and Persian linked Central Asia and the Sea Silk Routes were all part of the social cosmology of the Tang court, what constituted the 玄綱/天綱 ['the Imperial Net'], is also exposed, along with church's elites' courtly status (i.e. standing) as individuals with a group identity holding the ability to be 'chosen', i.e. *élitus*, as well as with the ability to choose, *élire*, within the 'long arm' of the Tang imperial court.

In order to understand these interconnections and the Imperial Net more fully it is helpful to look at the development of imperial Buddhism in the reign of Empress Wu, and its roots in the Gaozong and Daizong periods. This gave agency to those of non-Han ethnicity residing in the early Tang Empire, to Persians in particular, and appears, as will be shown below, to open doors for the church's elites as monastics and as knowledge holders. It is also in this connection that the *Tong Dian* and *Cefu Yuangui* passages can be brought together and made to speak to one another. The *Tong Dian* passages indicate that Tocharistan stood at the top of the string of Western polities made part of Tang hegemony, where the 'imperial virtue' was commemorated, something seen also in the Aluohan epitaph. The text mentioned in the *Tong Dian* passage, the *Xiyu Tuji* [西域圖記, *Memorials of the Western Regions*], was presented originally to Emperor Gaozong by 玄奘 [Xuanzang] (*c*.602–64).[54] Xuanzang can be referred to not simply as a Buddhist monk, but as a Tang imperial Buddhist monk, for his geography and travelogue was presented to the court following a tour of Chinese Buddhist-linked Central Asia and northern India in the manner of Rudyard Kipling's imperial tour, before submitting his geography to the throne.[55] The text then allowed the participation of the Tang emperor within his and the empire's lands held in Central Asia and their Persian leadership in Tocharistan, where the shrines established for commemorating the 'imperial virtue' there, meant that the asceticism practiced by the emperor, as exemplary religious leader, and shared by elites across religions, made Tocharistan a nexus point in this transmission. These are trends that continued under Empress Wu Zetian and that surface in the *Tong Dian* passage, the *Cefu Yuangui Record* passage, as well as in the Aluohan gravestone and epitaph.

One way that the agency and *habitus* of the church's elites can be better understood in relation to this is through focus upon the Tang governmental position called the *sabao* [薩寶, caravan leader] and its connection to the Church of the East.[56] The *sabao* institution, though it has been studied ably in recent decades resulting in a rich research literature, can be understood as a mediating point between Tang ideology and its Central Asian subjects and as a more important institution than has been heretofore realised.[57] Wei dynasty sources indicate that *xian* temples served as law courts in which disputes between foreigners residing in China were settled.[58] The term 祆 [*xian*], used in Tang sources to refer to the god of any Central Asian religion and generalised to refer to the god of any Persian or central Asian religion or to the religion itself, is crucial in expanding how we think about the *sabao* institution.[59] Though the term was privileged in the direction of the Persian state cult, Zoroastrianism or Mazdaism, because Chinese contacts with Persia took place on a vastly wider scale and from an earlier pre-Tang period than they did with Christianity or Manichaeism, faiths that only seem to have acquired fully-fledged state connections during the Tang, though built on earlier precedents and cultural footing such as Christians' and Manicheans' roles in trade, and

Christians' roles in inter-courtly diplomacy.[60] There are references to both the practice of Zoroastrianism and the existence of Persians in China from the Northern Wei dynasty (386–535) and its annals, the *Beiwei Shu* [北魏書] indicating the term's earlier uses.[61] However the earliest reference to a *xian* [Western or Persian] temple being built in China is in a description of the *Liangjing xinji* [两京新記, *The Records of the Two Capitals*] compiled by the major official historian of Xuanzong's reign Wei Shu [韋述] (fl.713–57), and from 621 indicates the term being used near the time when the Church of the East's first monasteries were built there as well.[62] This reference, found under the heading 'Buzheng ward', shows the institution of the *sabao* being linked to the notion, reads:

> In the Buzheng ward [of Chang'an] in the south west corner, in 621, there was set up a western region divinity temple. The western regions divinity is known in Buddhist texts as Maheśvara. In the temple there is an official of the *sabao* 薩寶 [caravan leader] department who presides over the sacrifices over the divinity, or alternatively a foreigner carries out the job. Mr Bi says that as for the foreign divinity issue and for the whole story of it, consult the Northern Wei annals where it is shown that this temple was set up under Dowager empress Lingtai.[63]

This reference resembles the Xi'an stele's reference to the establishment in 638 of a 波斯寺 [Persian Temple] in the Yi'ning [義寧] ward of Chang'an for the foreign [*hu*, 胡] monk from Daqin named Aluosi (likely correctable to Aluoben) and at close proximity in time, where it can be assumed that this language reflects the mindset of the officials involved with regulating the temple/monastery and thus the cultural resources available to the Christian enclave to negotiate its place within its new milieu along with Sasanian royals.[64] The concentration of Buddhist temples in the Buzheng ward where this earlier temple was put, as evidenced by the surrounding passages in the *Liang jing xin ji*, as well as the high number of Buddhist temples in the Yi-ning ward, as is suggested by reading in the other entries on the ward's temples in the same section of the *Liang jing xin ji*, suggest that the Tang court associated the Church of the East enclave and network with other Persian religions, Buddhists, and adherents of

Turkic religions, all thought of as part of the *xian* religion by the Chinese; in addition, the Chinese saw each as part of its shadow empire, and made the *sabao* an at-once-merchant-and monastic figure, a vanguard force in early Tang China's colonial project.[65]

The *Wei Shu* records information in its section on Sogdiana, suggesting the involvement of Sogdians in running these temple courts and monastic market places at an earlier stage.[66] Lin Wushu, based on archaeological and epigraphical work at Sogdian grave sites, puts forth the assertions that all *sabao* were Sogdian, four generations of Sogdian *sabao* could be identified among the graves he investigated, and that Zoroastrian courts and Sogdian *sabao* were at the centre of Chinese immigration policy.[67] Various etymologies for the term *sabao* have been put forth, from the Syriac *saba*, 'Patriarch', to Sogdian *sarthavak*, and Uighur *sartpau*.[68] Albert Dien shows that there are Buddhist usages of the term in its Sanskrit *sarathavaha* form that likely passed through Middle Parthian *s'rtw'*, Khotanese *satavaya*, and into similar terms in Tocharian and Uighur, arriving at the Sogdian term *s'arath*, meaning 'caravan'.[69] Its caravan leader and 'shepherding' connotations made the term a frequent metaphor for a Bodhisattva.[70] The Chinese term *daoshi* [導師, master, guide] and *shizun* [世尊, world honored one], appears as translations of *sabao*.[71] The fact that the latter term, *shizun*, appears as a name for Jesus Christ in one of the Church of the East's early documents written in Middle Chinese, the *Discourse on Monotheism*, suggest the *sabao* institution was becoming part of the elite culture of the Church of the East and as they worked between the Tang court and the Tang's markets. Assimilation into Chinese culture had occurred for Iranians through the monasteries and temples and associated with *sabao* as both merchant and monastic leaders for generations, and it is thus natural that the *sabao*'s dual role expresses itself in Church of the East's theology.[72]

If the *sabao* were a link between monastic and merchant cultures and the realm of culture that gave the church's elites agency — made them elites in fact, and thus part of the Tang's Imperial Net — it is helpful to look at the practice of scientific patronage among the Tang's colonial subjects more widely. One starting point in this venture may be a passage in the Church of the East's *Discourse on Monotheism*, not suggesting this text comes necessarily from the early

Tang period, and what appears to be the presence of Aristotle's unmoved mover concept within this text.[73] As that text reads:[74]

> There is neither pillar nor prop to support heaven. Unless the one God does so, how can heaven remain so without falling from above? This is due to no other than the mysterious and wonderful power of the one God. Were this not for the action of the one God, who could have supported [it] and have prevented it perpetually from falling?[75]

And slightly later in the text, and completing the notion presented to its interlocutors:[76]

> But the power of God exists, and by which all things without exception were made according to his will. For instance, it is like a man shooting an arrow. We see only the arrow fall, but we do not see the archer himself. Although we do not see the archer, we know that this arrow cannot come of itself, and there must be someone who shot it. For that reason we know that by virtue of the divine power of the one God heaven and earth are made neither to crumble nor to fall, and that because of this divine power, they will remain steadfast for ever and ever. Although we do not see the upholder [of the world], we do know that a divine mysterious upholder [of the world] must exist. For instance, as soon as the impetus given to an arrow by the archer is exhausted, the arrow must fall to the ground. Likewise, if the divine power were not working, heaven and earth must needs fall to pieces. But, but virtue of this divine power, we know that heaven and earth do not decay.[77]

The Church of the East's connections to the spread of civilisation among Turkic peoples were reviewed in a previous chapter. Their ability to hold status within early Arab rule period courts came partly from their scientific *habitus*, something that built on foundations the Church of the East had established with the Sasanian court. It is known that during the seventh and eighth century, Greco-Roman scientific texts and thought were spreading into Tibet and Central Asia, and in a milieu in which Iranians and Iranian Christians were doing missionary work. It is reasonable to assume, therefore, that the appearance of Aristotelian metaphysical notions within the apologetics of the Church of the East in the Tang setting stems from these larger developments.[78] One would expect such currents to surface within Tang courtly patronage of the church's elites as well, and within those elites' ability to share in, and articulate, the Tang court's and emperor's charisma and heavenly mandate.

A passage appears in the *New Tang Record* in this regard. During the reign of Emperor Gaozong (r.650–83) a physician named Qin Minghe [秦鳴鶴] is recorded as having cured the emperor of a headache through use of a technique involving bloodletting.[79] While the family name of Qin may indicate the doctor came from Daqin (western regions), controversy remains surrounding the physician's origins.[80] Upon investigation of the trepanning or bloodletting techniques Qin used, as it is described in Tang sources, Huang Lanlan [黃蘭蘭] maintains that they are similar to those of fifth-century Greek physicians such as Cassiodorus (c.485–c.585) and Dioscorides (first century) and suggestive of Roman and Syriac Christian links, however immediate or remote, seems more likely. The skill of this medical officer and his being rewarded at court for curing the emperor appears in more than one official Tang source.[81] The *New Tang Record*, however, states:

In the third year of the Yifeng era [678] all the officials and a barbarian chieftain were called into the imperial presence, meeting at the Guangshun Gate. The emperor's head hurt and he could not see. Medical officers Zhang Wenzhong and Qin Minghe said: if the circulatory system is off balance, pierce the head and it will improve. The empress from within the court[82] had been favored by the emperor to a dangerous extent and able to monopolise him herself; she said angrily: '[doing] this deserves execution. The emperor's body, how can you settle this by stabbing it for blood?' The doctors bowed their heads and begged for their lives. The Emperor said: 'for a physician to discuss an illness, how can he be blamed? I can't stand this dizziness. Let him do it'. The doctors once or twice lanced him. The Emperor said: my eyes are clear now! Before he'd finished speaking, the Empress from within the screen bowed twice and said 'heaven has bestowed upon us some teachers', and in person carried silks and jewelry and placed them upon them.[83]

This passage is most interesting, however, because of the appearance of Empress Wu within it, and the way in which Emperor Gaozong appears as a *Rex Absconditus* within it and Empress Wu, as well as the physicians, appear as extensions of the charisma of the emperor and the Tang court. Huang Lanlan maintains that an early Song dynasty compilation may be turned to for support for the assertion that Qin (Tajik/Daqin) Minghe was a Western doctor. That text states: '大秦 善醫眼及痢、或未病而先見、或開腦出蟲' [Western (Tajik/ Daqin) doctors are good for eye and dysentery treatments, or for disease prevention and observation, or opening up the brain and releasing its ailments], and Huang's assertion is given further support by what the passage says about foreign advisors in Empress Wu's court.[84] For example, while Huang asserts that the courtly assembly and parade of officials at the Guangshun Gate took place because of the foreign doctors' and chieftains' arrival, something not ultimately provable, what must be noted is the fact that in the passage the foreign chieftain arrived in close temporal proximity to the healing of the emperor, and during a time in which Wu Zetian was beginning to use foreign technicians, especially with Buddhist monastic connections, and Wu Zetian is shown placing courtly patronage items (silk and jewellery) on the doctors and extolling the graciousness of heaven in bestowing upon the empire and court a teacher, a *guoshi* [國 師], again recalling the 'national teachers' that had become such an integral part of the Tang court's connections to Central Asia, wherein the Church of the East places a role, in the late Tang period.[85] Wu Zetian is thus seen expanding both her and the empire's power with the aid of foreign elites and as part of a major trajectory within the Tang cosmopolitanism. This gives further support for Huang's thesis that Qin Minghe was a Western doctor, which, given the connections between Greco-Roman medicine and leverage among Turkic peoples seen in previous chapters, suggests the presence of the cultural orbit (the *habitus*) of the Church of the East and its elites.

It is the above passage's reference to what 'heaven has bestowed', however, and the connection to astronomy, astrology, and cosmology in the Tang, that is of most relevance to the argument that, in order to understand the elite and courtly nature of the Church of the East in the Tang, it is crucial to look both at its 'Persian' and monastic (i.e. Buddhist) connections, and the way in which the church bound itself, then broke away, then rebound itself to the court during the periods of Empress Wu and in the early Xuanzong period (as shown in the Xi'an stele). The issue of foreign elites sharing and supporting the mandate of heaven and the imperial charisma of the Tang during the period of Empress Wu is a topic that can in fact be centred on the issue of cosmology and Buddhist monasticism. Nowhere is the link between Western foreigners' technical skills and the leverage they held in relation to her court derived from their roles in the field and politics of cosmology (à la Bourdieu) more in evidence than in the fields of astronomy and cosmology. One should note as well that in the passage above, Empress Wu Zetian is shown demurely to peer from behind screens and to be (at least ostensibly) concerned with placing the emperor's person (his charisma) before her own. This is a type of asceticism, and can be thought of in terms of the courtly asceticism seen in the 'mysterious items of foreign cunning' passage on the one hand, and the 'commemoration of the imperial virtue' reference seen in the *Tong Dian* passage on the other, as well as to the many references in Tang sources to the emperor's practice of virtue affecting the empire as a whole, which are especially abundant in reference to the Ming-tang construction project pursued by Empress Wu Zetian.

While the Chinese emperor was involved in approving calendars at least from the Jin dynasty [晋朝] (265–420) onward, astronomy and the need for foreign technical experts having astronomical skills begins to play a much greater role in the Tang than in previous dynasties.[86] The Tang calendar was revised eight times over the Tang's three centuries, whereas in previous dynasties the custom was to have one renewed and revised calendar per dynasty.[87] Foreigners, Indians and Persians in particular, began to hold positions in the imperial astronomy department as they had long held in the translation department before the Tang. Some of these positions were held within clans and families running several generations. A grave was discovered in 1977 outside of Chang'an showing that an Indian astronomer clan held positions within the Tang astronomy bureau for over 100 years.[88]

The Aluohan gravestone and epitaph indicates that Persians participated in Empress Wu Zetian's Mingtang and Axis of the Sky projects, both of which were rich in astrological and cosmological symbolism. As for the Axis of the Sky, Forte suggests that foreigners, most likely Persians and Indians together, would have set it up for Empress Wu and probably paid for it as well.[89] Made in celebration of the beginning of one of the most pompous and audacious of her reign periods, the Axis of the Sky was full of propagandistic and cosmological symbolism. The name in Chinese – The Great Zhou Period (690–705) Axis of the Sky of the Myriad Countries Exalting the [Imperial] Merits [大周 萬 国 頌 德 天樞] – is revealing in terms of its ideological functions and its allowance of non-Han to participate in Tang imperial charisma sharing. Forte suggests that a deal of sorts might have been struck between the Tang court and the Persian community, making them give their support for a Buddhist monument in return for the help they received against Arab attacks in Tocharistan and Tang support for their designs to rebuild a Persian state there (he rules out any massive conversion to Buddhism on the part of Persians during this period). The reference in the Aluohan epitaph to the commemoration of imperial virtue and the spreading of the teaching of the empire calls for other similar developments, and in connection to Tang imperial Buddhism and Tang astronomy taking place under Empress Wu Zetian, should be looked at more closely.[90]

It is instructive as well to look at the connections between cosmology and Manichaean technical elites having relations with the Tang court during the period of Empress Wu. Forte surmises that Aluohan might have been involved in the introduction of the first Manicheans to the Tang court, a meeting that took place in 694.[91] Whether or not Aluohan was Manichean is difficult to ascertain, but Forte suggests that as the highest ranking Persian in China at the time and with deep connections to the army and court, and as one involved in the propagation of the cosmological symbolism tied to court ideology at the time, it seems likely that Aluohan would have known of the Manichaeans in Central Asia who practised astronomy as part of their religion. Knowing the date of Mani's death was part of the Manichean liturgical year and had to be carefully calculated and accurately recorded and observed using an almanac called *The Seven Luminaries*.[92] Given the close connection between the Tang's own imperial legitimacy and its calendar and the Tang encouragement for neighbouring states to accept its calendar as part of its ideological pacification campaigns, it is likely that Aluohan would have crossed paths with Manicheans in the Tang patronage matrix. Sam Lieu writes that:

> While not attending to the spiritual needs of merchants, [Manichaean] priests may have served as consultant astrologers to the local courts [in Central Asia]. We find in a Saka document of the seventh century many calendar details which are clearly Manichean liturgical terms. This suggests that in the small Saka kingdom of Maralbashi there existed a community of Manicheans in that period with close contacts with the aristocracy through their skills as astrologers and diviners.[93]

If the late seventh and early eighth century was a time when Persians and Indians were viewed favourably within the Tang court because of their usefulness in colonial politics against external threats such as the Arabs, it is natural that new developments in astronomy, very likely having roots beyond the world of Manichaeism, came to be a driving force that only added to this mixture and the way in which the Tang royal house articulated its relations with its colonial subjects through imperial astrology. At the end of the second decade of the eighth century, designers of 'strange and wonderful devices' were invited to the Tang court and caused a stir internally while escaping criticism themselves. This occurred within the same Persian milieu in which Persians, and by implication Persian and Persian community-related Christians, found a place in Tang colonial designs.[94]

The periods between and including the reigns of Emperor Gaozong (r.650–83), Empress Wu Zetian (r.690–705), and into the early reign of emperor Xuanzong (r.712–56), were periods in which cosmology, foreign relations and colonial assimilation ideology converged.[95] Church of the East and Manichean elites based in Tocharistan and Balkh, shown in the sources achieve agency within the Tang Court through their skills in astronomical calculation and instrument making, may shed light on the type of

items brought to court in the 'wondrous items of foreign skill' seen
in the *Cefu Yuangui Record* passage above. However, the Xi'an stele's
Wu Zetian and early Xuanzong section, i.e. the 'breaking and
repairing' of 'our Imperial Net' passage, states that late in the reign
of Empress Wu the church's elites were attacked by Buddhists
(in 698–700) in the Eastern Capital, and that the vulgar/criminal
gentry attacked the church in 712–13. It is necessary therefore to
address what may have been taking place and given rise to these
events and their mention in the stele, remembered three generations
later. It is possible to say generally that the system of ideological
control and imperial regulation set in place by Empress Wu was
unravelling in the late 690s.[96] Jilie/Gabriel and Aluoben are after
all *bhandantas*, and are referred to as such repeatedly in the Xi'an
stele; it was the *bhandantas* who played such a large role in bringing
Wu Zetian to power and orchestrated the *Dayun Sutra* commentary
and the ideological drive that accompanied it.[97] Individuals
rising to power during Wu Zetian's reign also did so by becoming a
Kaiguo gong [開國公], a position also mentioned in the Aluohan
gravestone and epitaph.[98] Wu Zetian's court began to turn
against the Empress's costly and interventionist foreign policy
late in the 690s, as Turkic and Tibetan power were on the rise,
and the Zhou court had to begin offering royal brides to Qaghans'
requests.[99]

The Tang restoration set in place by the weak rulers Zhongzong
and Ruizong (705–12) saw the ideological and hegemonic
system developed by the long reign of Empress Wu continue
unabated yet staggering. This cannot be said overall of the reign of
Xuanzong, whose measures against the bloated monastic system
of Wu Zetian had taken effect by the 720s, though implementation
of them was underway by the beginning of the Kaiyuan period, i.e.
Xuanzong's reign.[100] Though it took many years to take hold, this
breaking of the monks' connection to the officials did eventually
take hold.

Cefu Yuangui records Iranian astronomers coming to the
Tang court and attracting the close involvement of the
emperor only five years after the date of the event described in
that passage.

The *Cefu Yuangui* states:[101]

in the sixth month of the seventh year of the Kaiyuan era [720] a
memorial was sent to court about the ruler of Tocharistan named
Zhihanna[102] presenting an astronomer-magus[103] to the court.
The learning and intelligence of this person was subtle and
deep. When questioning him there was nothing he did not know;
[he said]: I[104] humbly beg for your imperial favour that you
should call up this person and closely question him on the purpose
of our activities, your servants, and the various methods of our
teaching. When you realise that this person has skills and abilities
like this, I hope and request that you order him into imperial
service[105] and that in addition that you set up a dharma hall[106]
and that he should minister to us and nourish the empire
according to the basic teaching.[107]

This passage shows not only that the Church of the East's elites were
mediators within Tang imperial affairs, as holders and representatives
of a post-Sasanian Persian royal and courtly identity; it shows as well
that they were linked to the military and cultural exchanges taking
place between the Tang and its western regions. Buddhist, military,
and scientific/cosmological cultures were also part of this shared
patronage field, and were economic exchanges supported and
solidified cultural exchanges. The way in which the heavenly
mandate and the imperial charisma of the Tang court, shown as
articulated through and in relation to the Church of the East's elites'
participation, both in their Middle Chinese corpus and the official
Tang sources, is thus set in a wider context and offers explanatory
support.

One notices also that Jilie/Gabriel appears in the passage above, as
well as in the 'mysterious items of foreign cunning' passage, *and* in
the Xi'an monument's 'our repairing the Imperial Net' section.
Gabriel was not only an elite, a *gui*, a *bhandanta*, the likes of which
played such a large role in bringing Wu Zetian to power, but also an
'elite', from the 'Metal Region'. It is highly likely that the numerous
references to the metal city appearing in the old Tang Record during
the Zhongzong and Ruizong periods, and in connection to Tibet, are
referred to here.

For the Zhenguan era (626–49) and in its 14th year (640) the *Old
Tang Record* indicates: 'Tibet sent an envoy presenting [to the Tang

court) a thousand metal items of gold for a bride [in exchange for a royal bride].'[108] Then, in the Jinglong era (707–10) and its third year (710), the *New Tang Record* reports that:[109]

> Tibet's king dispatched the envoy Xi Dongre to the court bestowing gifts from the area {Tibet}. In the spring, a teacher at the capital went to Shandong on account of a pestilence, {as there were} many dying. In Hebei, and Henan there was a great drought, and he did rites of protection for the Princess of the Metal City, who then fled to Tibetan king {named} Sanpu. In the spring and in the fourth month, 14th day, by the Successor to the Prince of Yong, {named} {Li} Shunli, she was made the princess of the metal city, and went to the Tibetan king.

Also in the same year, and in the same text, it is recorded that:[110]

> In celebration of the new residence in the metal region, Princess An le [684–710] gave a banquet for vassals and scholars. In the first phase of the eleventh month, the imperial ancestral rites celebrated in the southern suburb of the capital city, when the Empress ascended the ritual platform for the second libation, the Left Vice President of the Affairs of State, {formally known as} the Duke of She, Wei Juyuan [631–710], completing the libations. And amnesty was then declared for the empire. It was seen that a line of prisoners and the unforgiveable were all being done away with, and various criminals moving out {of prison} and returning {to normal life}. So in the capital the literati and military, and with the input of the upper nobility, and together with the fourth rank down to the first rank, the officials at the capital also dealt with the shepherds/grazers, by reducing them from third to fifth ranks., their seniors then receiving this plan. A proclamation was made on the third day of the month. On the first phase of the {next} month, rites at the son of heaven's ancestral tomb were observed. In the second phase of the month, First Degree, Second Class Military Commander, Doulu Qingwang [624–710], Duke of Rui, passed away. The Tibetan King[111] sent his Prime Minister Xiang Sandu in exchange for her {Princess An Le}.

There are many intriguing connections in the above texts between the Church of the East's courtly and monastic elites and Tibet, the Metal City Princess, Tibet, the social upheavals within imperial Chinese society that accompanied Empress Wu Zetian's loss of power, and the slow and chaotic transition to the reign of Xuanzong.[112] While it must be acknowledged that the Xi'an stele refers to *Jinfang gui* [金方貴, aristocrats of the Metal Regions], in Legge's rendering, and not *Jincheng gongzhu* [金城公主, the Princess of the Metal City], or *Jincheng gui* [金城貴, Metal City elites/aristocrats], it must also be pointed out that the only reference in either of the Tang records to *jin-fang* is to an 'ambassador for the economic streamlining of the *Jin-fang* road' [金方道經略大使] and within a discussion of Turkic relations and the Tang military positions and units, and the economic exchanges set up to deal with Turkic relations in year five of the Kaiyuan era (718), i.e. at precisely the time with which the texts seen above deal.[113] It appears reasonable, therefore, to associate the language used of Jilie in the Xi'an stele with the Tang sources' numerous references to *Jincheng gongzhu* [金城公主]. It is telling, as well, that the Metal City Princess is presented by the Song era compilers of the Tang records as having irresponsibly opened the Chinese Empire's prison system's doors, which likely coincides with their disdain for the overly close relations with Tibet and Turks of her era and the Wu Zetian era in general. This, as well as the fact that the princess is shown setting up residence and banqueting scholars on the edge of Tibet, and just on the eve of her 30 years as a patronage bridge within a royal marriage linking the Tang and Tibetan empires, sheds light on the Church of the East's elites and their inter-imperial character, and the previously seen connections held with Sasanian royals, both as transmitters of Sasanian royal and imperial charisma, but also as liaisons to Turkic and Central Asia semi-nomadic polities as bearers of medical, scientific, and religious knowledge. Such connections, concentrated not only in the Church of the East's leaders, but precisely within leaders remembered within the church three generations later as shown within the Xi'an stele, appear within a passage within the *Cefu Yuangui* and from slightly further into the reign of Xuanzong:

In the twelfth year of the Kaiyuan period {725} and on the 5th of the eighth month, the king of Persia[114] sent the head {military} leader Pannami accompanied by Bishop[115] Jilie/Gabriel to the imperial court. They bestowed upon the leader the rank of Guoyi,[116] while the monk was presented with a set of purple coloured robes[117] and fifty bolts of silk.[118] And they were sent back to their country.[119]

PART II

'THE LORD IS KING: HE IS ROBED IN MAJESTY'

CHAPTER 3

THE *HABITUS* OF PATRIARCH TIMOTHY I

Introduction

The Tang Empire's colonial *Jimi zhou* system began to decline in the 740s.[1] The decision by the Tang court to change the name of the Church of the East and its religion from the 'Persian teaching', to the 'Da Qin teaching', came in 745.[2] These two changes also came only a decade before three of the most momentous events in all of early medieval history worldwide – the Battle of Talas in 751, the An Lushan Rebellion (755–63), and the Abbasid Revolution (750–62).[3] It is probable that the Tang court's decision to change the name of the Church of the East was made because it saw that the church could no longer be considered part of its colonial project in Central Asia through use of Sasanian royals, and sought a new name accordingly. Though Barrett's proposition that the rise of imperial Taoism might have been behind the name change is not incompatible with the general outlines of this book, it is appropriate to ask how the Persian, royal, and ascetic nature of the church, seen in the previous two chapters, was reconfigured in this new setting and might stand behind the elements in the Xi'an focused upon within this study as a whole. For the Tang court to associate the Church of the East with its Persian past too overtly would have created problems for the church as it began to negotiate its way through the Abbasid Revolution and the move of the Caliphate to Baghdad in 762, a move that the East Syrian Patriarchate would soon make with the new Abbasid

Caliphate and from which other Christian groups would be excluded.[4] Any study of the way in which the Church of the East renegotiated its position within and between the imperial courts of the period, and 'repaired its Imperial Net' following the An Lushan Rebellion and Abbasid Revolution, must begin with these basic facts.

Yoshiro Saeki once boldly asserted that 'the study of Christianity in the Tang period begins and ends with the Xi'an stele'.[5] While such a statement still stands today, the church's move to Baghdad, along with the Abbasid Caliphate and the rise of a Patriarch like Timothy I (r.780–823), whose interest in projecting the church's mission into Central Asia is visible in his letters and extant texts, and in which integration of the church into the Abbasid court and its extensive empire in the region can be seen, all developments concurrent with the Xi'an monument's appearance, suggest the statement must be reconsidered.[6] For as has been argued, the Church of the East of the Tang dynasty was an inter-courtly, elite, worldly ascetic, social body, one that drew creatively upon its Sasanian Persian past and did so continually as it renegotiated its place within and between imperial courts. The construction of a view of Sasanian Persian culture within early Abbasid ideology and within the Church of the East of the period concurrently, and changes within the nature of kingship across the region, provide other ways in which Saeki's statements discussed in the introduction can be reassessed.

The picture emerging within the literature points to interconnections between the shape the church took in in its post-An Lushan Rebellion phase within the Tang empire, trends within the church under the leadership of Patriarch Timothy I, and the inter-courtly, and the worldly ascetic culture that existed in Bactria, a former home base for some of the key leaders within the late eighth-century Chang'an branch of the church. This chapter will therefore analyse the corpus of Syriac writings from and related to Patriarch Timothy I against the historical background of the early Abbasid Empire, and the church's dual relationship to Central Asia and the Abbasid court in Baghdad. In doing this the chapter will argue that the Middle Persian-speaking branch of the Church of the East at Chang'an was connected to an inter-courtly, trans-imperial, and worldly ascetic culture that held sway across the entire region. This would have given Church of the East agency and leverage in their interactions with the Tang court, and is reflected in the Xi'an stele's rhetorical assertions.

In such endeavours historians are beset methodologically with, on the one hand, a vast and ever widening documentary record and secondary literature. On the other there is a sparse and fragmentary, literary and epigraphic record spread over vast territories and existing in multiple languages.[7] However, clear trends are visible in the secondary literature and in the primary sources with regards to the inter-courtly nature of the cultures of the region and the way in which the Church of the East stood within them and drew upon their resources.[8] In the late eighth century connections between world religions, courtly patronage, and itinerant knowledge holders and preachers were coalescing across the region, giving rise to a worldly asceticism of which the Church of the East would become master. This was taking place in areas where the Church of the East and the Abbasid Empire had shared influence, and where Tang China's influence in Central Asia was waning in the face of the rising Tibetan and Uighur empires. Many of the major imperial polities between the Abbasid and Tang empires had not only chosen and were choosing a world religion, but were also developing knowledge production in an inter-courtly diplomatic apparatus that worked in tandem, a climate that can be linked to the Xi'an stele's long durational Persian nature. In so doing, the societies making up the cultural corridor between Abbasid ruled Baghdad and the Tang Empire were restructured in such a way that royal dispositions, inter-courtly relations and world religions became a feature within the region's geopolitical shape and order. There are grounds for referring to this as an 'emergent phenomenon'.[9]

This emergent phenomenon can be explored *mise en scène* by probing the extent to which the Middle Persian-speaking group within the Chang'an branch of the Church of the East was able to draw creatively upon its Sasanian past in order to achieve agency within the Tang court by means of developments taking place within the Church in Mesopotamia following the Abbasid Revolution and by means of its ascetic constitution. One way of doing this is by attempting to set the existing corpus of Syriac documents stemming from and relating to Patriarch Timothy in relation to the sparse documentary record relating to Medieval Bactria and Central Asia and the earliest phases of the Abbasid court.[10] In these documents, the period and context can be read through the study's main theoretical constructs of *habitus*, *comitatus*, transmission of imperial charisma, and worldly asceticism, to good effect, i.e. resulting in a new picture of the trans-regional standing of the church at Chang'an and the agency it held in relation to the Tang court, an analysis that will be extended in the following chapter by looking more specifically at the church's late Tang context.[11]

The worldly asceticism appearing in Timothy's Syriac corpus can be studied in relation to the Xi'an stele's reference to clergy within the church who wore white robes, or in Saeki's rendering: 'the white-robed scholars of the luminous religion'.[12] Similar references appear in the letters of Timothy I, the *Historia Monastica/Book of Governors* of Thomas of Marga (r.837–50), the works of Ibn al-Ṭayyib (d.1043) and Bar 'Ebroyo (1226–86), indicating the extent to which not only Timothy but the greater church was concerned with such an issue following the changes that took place within the church stemming from the Abbasid Revolution.[13] These multiple references, spanning several centuries, indicate that Timothy and the greater church were concerned with this issue. These references can be analysed and contextualised in relation to changes taking place within the structure of the church and within its understanding of leadership and authority, something occurring within the church from Baghdad to Chang'an, and in relation to changes taking place within the Abbasid Empire itself, and within the structure and shape of kingship, royal patronage and its religious underpinnings, across the entire region. As the imperial and courtly centre of the Abbasid Empire in Baghdad was becoming more firmly integrated with the empire's periphery in the first half of the eighth century, processes related to and reflective of this surfaced within the Church of the East.[14] An analysis of the available primary source data, centring on the issue of clothing and the cultural regalia of the church studied through the book's theoretical apparatus, provide a tentative basis for asserting this.

The Church of the East's *Noblesse de Robe* and Emergent Central Asian Kingship

The Xi'an stele refers to Yisi as being a member of the white robed-wearing clergy. The text indicates that the level of virtue exhibited by Yisi is a new achievement among the Tang's monastic orders: 'Among the purest and most self-denying Buddhists, such excellence was never heard of; but now the white-stoled members of the Illustrious Religion see it in this man; such excellence from whom has heretofore not been seen.'[15] It is important to note these are the very last words of the stele before its list of monks, where Christoph Baumer suggests that the white robes indicate possible Manichaean or Islamic influence, or both, citing evidence that Abbasids were called 'the white robed' in Chinese.[16] While it is difficult to rule out such a suggestion entirely, given that the Church was on such cordial terms with the Abbasid court, it is difficult to imagine a coterie of Umayyad dynasty supporters existing within the Tang branch of the church. While the Manicheans were known to distinguish clergy ranks by colour among their clothing, given the antipathy towards the Manicheans among the Abbasids and the closeness between the Church of the East and the early Abbasid court, it is difficult to imagine this conflation either. Paul Pelliot, saying nothing about the Abbasid or Umayyad connection, and not discounting a possible Manichaean connection, points out that a distinction between black and white robed clergy was and is found among the Chalcedonian Orthodox, which he assumed also existed within the Church of the East of the period.[17] Pelliot was correct in his intuition that because a distinction between secular, white robe-wearing, lay clergy, and celibate, black or darker robe-wearing clergy, had long been part of the Chalcedonian Orthodox church, it was likely part of the Church of the East as well.[18]

That a non-celibate order of the clergy was an issue undergoing lively discussion during the Patriarchate of Timothy I and within the Church of the East from Baghdad to India and to China is given support within the letters of Timothy I, in the later Syriac writer Bar 'Ebroyo, and in ibn al-Tayyib, who wrote in Arabic. Bar 'Ebroyo, discussing the Patriarchate of Timothy I, writes:

It was commanded then, at that time, by Timothy, of the Bishops of the Persian region, to wear white clothes, in the manner of seculars [lit. elder sons of the world], to eat meat, and to take wives. It was not allowed however of the Catholicos of Seleucia. They [the clergy of the Persian region in response] said: 'We are disciples of the Apostle Thomas, and we have nothing in common with Mar Maris.' [and in response to this] Timothy then joined them together and gave them a Metropolitan, named Simeon, who he enjoined not to eat flesh, nor marry, [and of the householders he urged] not to wear white garments and garments other than of wool. And when he allowed him to ordain Bishops, they were complete [without needing the confirmation of any other authority]. They were not obliged, like other Bishops from other provinces, to go visit the Catholicos. This custom of the *hyparchie*, even to this day, remains in force.[19]

The eleventh-century Church of the East writer Ibn al-Ṭayyib has the following information to add.

As far as far off lands like China and India are concerned, there was, up to the days of Mar Timothy, difficulty along the roads. So Bishops used to assemble together to name their own Metropolitans. And because of the difficulty arising and the trouble which came up against these episcopal seats [al-kasra] in the days of Mar Timothy ... [the sentence is completed by a marginal note from Ibn al-Tayyib, stating]: Timothy prohibited Bishops ordaining Metropolitans and forbade even the sending of letters, which had been the custom of the Catholicoi, which were used by the Catholicoi in the ordaining of a Metropolitan. The hand-written materials [al-khatta] included letters and permission for the ordination; the Bishops placed this upon the back of the ordinand as if it [the letter itself] was the deputy for the hand of the Catholicos. Timothy forbade this and the letters too. It was the case [instead] that the Catholicos would send a staff, and cloaks and he would send some of the bishops or Metropolitans. They, this hyparchie, would assemble and name the Metropolitan, by putting on his back the gospel with the letters of the Catholicos.[20]

Readers are told more about these new arrangements, the role of the *hyparchie*, and the new structures of the far-flung Church in the following section of the same text from Ibn al-Ṭayyib:

> From the letters of Timothy to the believers [*ahl*] of India [it was stated that] they not first go to the king, in times of the election of a Metropolitan but rather to the Patriarch, who will attend to the ordination. The matter can only then, in the end, go to the king, if he is wise, God-fearing and well versed in the records [*al-kitib*]. In his letter to the leader, the head of the believers in India, [i.e. Timothy] [he said that] he would stop the Metropolitan ordaining priests without him [Timothy] and without any bishops; and [Timothy] said that it was necessary that priests name bishops, and for the deacons to ordain priests, and that the higher yield to the lower be subject to them. This is in contrast to the canons of the church which commanded that the lower completely obey the higher back to the final one at the end, who is in Rome and the deputy of Simon Peter.[21]

The situation being described in these texts indicates that Timothy I was urging streamlining and consolidation within the Church's clerical structure. It is important to note that this is a structure that was simultaneously 'top-down' yet also 'bottom-up', giving power and autonomy to local leaders, while also insuring that the church's Patriarch in Baghdad would remain the sacral helm of the church. What is most important, however, about the struggles over church structure and authority seen taking place between Chang'an and Baghdad is the attempt being made to incorporate both celibate and non-celibate/householder modes of religiosity within the church as a social body. As will be argued, this had, quite literally, far-reaching implications.

Later in the chapter a close reading of the corpus of Timothy's letters will be presented in order to attempt to access what was happening within the church's organisational structure and the extent to which that environment alone yielded these statements and convictions. However, the debates and political tension at work within the late eighth-century Church of the East from Baghdad to Chang'an need to, and can, be contextualised in relation to texts from both within and outside the church. This allows the long-range social cohesion and trans-imperially Persian and ascetic character of the church to be understood. The tension between celibate and non-celibate modes of church leadership constituted a *habitus*, i.e. a contextualised, bodily, dispositional repertoire making the church a socially cohesive set of agents responding to changes within its inter-imperial setting and through the worldly asceticism part of its imperial structure since the Sasanian period. The *comitatus*, part of the church's social constitution in earlier historical contexts, played a role here as well as it allowed for the transmission of imperial charisma.[22]

The term *habitus*, coming appropriately from church Latin, and referring to a monastic and clerical garment, allows Bourdieu's understanding of the social body to be easily imported.[23] Timothy I had a conviction that he could send objects conveying his sacred power, i.e. stoles, staffs, and letters, along with a willingness to allow this and the ascetic power that also adhered to these objects, to be delegated locally. The local Chang'an church had a similar understanding and can be tied to specific changes taking place within and in relation to the rise of the Abbasids and to trans-regional developments taking place there with respect to kingship and the carrying of royal dispositions within the elite's ranks.[24] This way of understanding the context settles several long-standing puzzles within the historical milieu. It is well known for example that during Timothy I's early years as Catholicos he attempted, successfully, to subdue leaders within the Persian branch of the church to come under his control.[25] The often-noted historical conundrum around the fact that the date of erection of the Xi'an stele, in 781, was after Timothy had come to power, becomes interpretable within this framework.[26] The fact that the name of the previous Catholicos, Henanisho, appears in the text of the Xi'an stele, indicates that the community either did not know the previous Catholicos had passed away or was opposed to Timothy's position as the new Catholicos. Because of the known strength and speed of the postal system (*al-barīd*), which had been developed and put in place within the Abbasid Empire, and linked together its capital, Baghdad, the new Patriarchal seat of the Church of the East, not only with the Xi'an stele community's former home base in Bactria, but linked all three of these areas together, it is highly unlikely that the group did not know of Henanisho's passing.[27] If this conflict can be tied to what is known about Timothy I's attempts to subdue the Persian branch of the church, a set of developments reviewed below, this understanding can be combined with what is seen in the texts above about Timothy's simultaneous restructuring and divulging of authority within the church through clothing and material objects.[28] More to the point, however, is that such analyses can provide support for an argument that this conflict was over what was Persian within the church, was tied to ways in which agency and trans-imperial leverage was being both negotiated and restructured within the church, and was part of the evolution of imperial power and the routinization of imperial charisma in the interconnected Abbasid Caliphate, its deepening Central Asian colouring, and the shape of imperial patrimony in Chang'an.

These observations also make it possible to extend what was said in earlier chapters about the Persian nature of the *comitatus*. Beckwith lays stress upon the role of merchants and economics and says the *comitatus*, while ultimately a military guard unit set up around sovereign leaders, as part of the 'deep structures' of the political cultures of Eurasia, functioned within the transformations taking place between China, the Iranian world, Central Asia in the eighth century, responsible for similarities in architectural patterns, modes of literacy, the shapes of imperial courts and families.[29] The phenomenon of soldiers and fighters willing to join such units and defend them unto death, something that formed a cultural paradigm appearing not only in the Sasanian context but that played a role well into the Islamic period and in the Arab-Turko-Iranian polities active between China and Baghdad in the eighth century, cannot therefore be thought of simply as a mode of kingship. It is rather a type of extended familial social organisation. Beckwith writes of how the attack strategies of the Arabised Central Asians/Central Asianised Arabs (he suggests that in the end it makes little difference which appellation is chosen) who led the Abbasid revolution and overthrew the Umayyad Caliphate in Damascus were mirrored in the Turko-Persian/Iranian assaults that took place against the Tang dynasty in the same period.[30] 'No one knows precisely how the An Lushan and the Abbasid revolution are connected', he writes; however, 'both were planned long in advance by merchants', to which can be added, and by military-merchant families/dynasts.[31]

The similar cultural patterns in architecture, literacy and institutions that can be seen emerging across the region and during the late eighth century involved Tibet as well, and can there too be tied ultimately to a change in what constituted the structure of the family and the structures attendant upon it.[32]

Though the often-found attempt to link the architectural styles of the early Abbasid period to its ideological campaigns and to north India has been astutely criticised by Lassner, a building style did in fact emerge in the region, as seen in Tibet, in which the imperial court was placed at the centre of both an imperial geography and cosmology and began to symbolise, as Beckwith writes, 'the emperor's position as a righteous Buddhist ruler and the establishment of Buddhism as the state religion of the Tibetan Empire'.[33] The patronage of Buddhist literacy and learning that was brought by monks from all parts of the Buddhist world that Tibet incorporated into its new empire by the end of the eighth century took place at its new imperial monastic-court complexes, and appears to have paralleled developments in the early Abbasid Caliphate, the late Tang empire, and the Uighur, Qarlug and Khazar empires.[34] Each of these polities made the emperor into a father figure and his retinue into an immediate family, extended after this into the rest of the body politic as an extended family, each linked to the other and to higher rungs of power through an arrangement of imperial charisma through material objects and positions around the local courts which conferred and instituted this power.

Similar ideas about kingship appear among the Eurasian cultures between and bordering China, extending through Central Asia and into northern territories ruled by the Rus, Caucasian federations, Avars, and Khazar Turks.[35] Sasanian motifs emerge mixed within Christian and Turkic articulations of courtly ideals among the trading communities of the Eurasian belt and bordering the Abbasid Empire. Ibn Fadlan (active 920s) described the Jewish Khazar court and the Turkic-Abrahamic culture that had arisen within it after the polity's conversion to Judaism in the late eighth century.[36] At centre of the polity was its king, serving as a cosmological-sustainer. He stood withdrawn from the empire's social life, yet acting as a sacral element with it. This paralleled changes that had taken place in Arab kingship. The last Arab Caliph to lead the Hajj pilgrimage to

Mecca, ceasing after this to run the empire and becoming a sacral element within it, was in the period of Timothy I.[37] That the memory of the Sasanian Persian Empire and its imperial glory could become a powerful Christian symbol in this setting is confirmed by a vignette depicting Khazar culture written by an Abbasid geographer named Istakhri. Ibn Fadlan sought to include Istakhri's account of an Avar Turkic polity living to the north of the Khazars. This Christian culture called itself the *sarīr* (سرير), using the Arabic word for throne.[38] Istakhri notes:

> The people of Sarīr are Christians. It is said that their throne, which is gold, once belonged to a king of Persia, and when his rule came to an end it was brought to Sarīr by one of the Persian kings. I have heard that it was one of the sons of Bahram Chubin. Kingship has remained among them down to our day. It is also said that this throne was made for one of the Khosrows many years ago.[39]

Patriarch Timothy I appropriated imagery associated with thrones within his articulation of his authority and the authority of the church within the Abbasid Empire. While he held a notion of Roman primacy and city of Rome as the seat of St Peter, Timothy understood his church's authority and its Patriarch as sharing in St Peter's primacy. The shared ecclesial imperial charisma stemming from each radiated out through the Abbasid Empire through Timothy's rule over the eastern world as part of the Abbasid Empire. He writes:

> Christ appeared in our flesh, as is shown. If Christ appeared in the flesh out of David, but David was a son of Abraham, and Abraham is from us, out of the East, then it is well known that Christ in the flesh is from the East. Therefore, the source of life and the source of the Christians, appeared from the east, and it was then divided into four heads of a whole garden of the Catholic Church, and from there we drink divine spiritual moisture from the kingdom of heaven. And just as the origin and source of water is attributed to a well, that which comes out of Eden to water the garden [of the earth], and is derived from the fact of the heads of the four [the world's four oceans through to proceed from Eden], though one of whom, in bodily form [Christ], he drinks for the whole

world. Even so with our throne, the East, and from the time of the redemption of the fountain of life at the beginning [Christ as second Adam], it ascends upwards from here, and the order of this first principle is observed. If Rome for the sake of the Apostle Peter had primacy and this principle is still preserved, then how much more is Seleucia-Ctesiphon standing in the line of St Peter.[40]

Similarities are evident between the worlds of Cosmas the India Traveller and Timothy appearing in the above passage, where the church is a great throne and tabernacle extending through time and space. Also similar with Cosmas is the role of Sasanian Persia as a cultural hub and *axis mundi*, through which the church's culture made its way through imperial social space and time.[41] This occurred for those associated with the church through the reading of the church's literature in the Syriac language, and by becoming familiar with the royal Sasanian Persian lineage of the church, its saints, relics, and texts. As Timothy I writes:

By reading our books you can be on the side of the martyrs, that is to say through acts of the martyrs who had completed their martyrdom in the east, which have *existed as a body* starting from Marutha Mapharqat the bishop, who had been sent by the king of the Romans in the days of the Persians with a message to king Yazdegird I, at the Patriarchate in Seleucia-Ctesiphon. The acts of martyrdom killing Holy Marutha occurred there, as a fountain for use by our writers, but as the place at which he composed his chariot [his body]. The very many bones of the martyrs, which he removed to the city of the Blessed, the 'country of the Martyrs' as it is called up to the present day, is there. With the generosity from the palace, he had been honored with the gifts of the king's possessions, and so all those things [bones of the Martyrs] were of even higher value, as it was only Yazdegird I, the king, who was asked to transport the Blessed one and his martyrs' chariot when he reposed.[42]

A clearer indication of the connection between Persian royalty, the East Syrian ascetic tradition, their shared *longue durée*, and an illustration of the social function of the Divine Economy tradition, could not be asked for.

Persian Knowledge-Holders in the Long
Orbit of the Abbasid Court

Wrangling over the issue of celibate and householder asceticism between Timothy I and the Chang'an church, rather than being a contest over how to define the long-range nature of the church, were two different ways of asserting that the church had such a nature. An analysis of the role played by speakers of Persian languages in the Abbasid Revolution and the development of Abbasid ideology in connection with them makes the connection the Church of the East in Baghdad and Chang'an shared and why they shared it easier to understand. Not only was it the case that speakers of Persian languages and holders of Sasanian institutions were being made part of Abbasid court culture in this period, these individuals and the cross-section of the Abbasid courtiers to which they were connected became both the targets and the bearers of Abbasid imperial ideology at the same time. This had parallels within the Tang and Abbasid Church of the East, as the church was beginning to give the Tang the ability to project imperial power back into Central Asia through the aid of the church and other non-Han.[43] Ascertaining how the church was pulled into the Abbasid court's orbit through the use of Persian traditions allows better understanding of parallel processes taking place with regards to the Abbasid court's projection into Central Asia.

Before discussing the role of speakers of Persian and Iranian languages outside the Church of the East and their participation in the Abbasid revolution and ideology, it is expedient to draw attention first to the way in which the Church of the East began connections to the Abbasid court through Timothy I, as represented by Timothy I's dialogues with caliph Al-Mahdi (r.775–85). As has been pointed out by Dimitri Gutas and others, the origins of the famous Bayt al-Hakim, or House of Wisdom, through which the East Syrian Christians and leaders such as Timothy I emerge as representatives of the scientific cosmopolitan culture of Hellenism, was a Sasanian institution.[44] While the Sasanian background of this institution and how it was actually first founded is controversial, what is beyond dispute is that the name of the institution itself is of Sasanian origin, and that Church of the East and its leaders negotiated relationships between the church and the new imperial power that ruled Baghdad after 762, just as the church had done for centuries in the Sasanian period.[45]

The famous Contract of Omar, as mentioned and reproduced in the East Syrian *Chronicle of Se'ert*, while it may not have been as old as the *Chronicle* asserts, emerged within the Bayt al-Hakim and within the negotiations between church and empire that developed in the early Abbasid setting.[46] The first translations completed at the institution were books on Sasanian courtly etiquette and on kingship.[47] Thus it is possible to say that the Bayt al-Hakim is linked with the translation, literally, of the Sasanian royal heritage; ways in which the Church of the East was both pulled into the Abbasid ideological fold and in some cases represented it as well can also be studied in relation to the translation movement. The Bayt al-Hakim was a *majlis*, a 'court', of sorts, where the institutionalising of the translation culture would come later, and where the Church of the East would play such a large role. The Xi'an monument's reference to astrology and scientific work within the Church of the East can be seen in connection to the role of the Church of the East in the translation movement. The monument refers to Yisi and says 'his science, *shu*, surpassed that of the three dynasties and his 'arts were extensive' *yi bo*') and in all respects complete' [*shi quan* 十全].[48]

There is now a large, diverse, and growing body of research literature on the Abbasid translation movement, and part of this literature charts the quintessential role of the Church of the East in this multifaceted development.[49] Much of the research on the Abbasid translation movement that focuses on the growing closeness between the Abbasid court and the Church of the East, which developed through and in conjunction with the movement, gravitates towards the role of Patriarch Timothy I.[50]

The dialogue that was to transpire between Timothy and Caliph Mahdi over two days in the 760s adds to what can be understood of this.[51] The content of the dialogues, which do not overtly treat politics and secular philosophy, belies the backdrop of the Church of the East's roles in translating Greek scientific texts into Arabic for the Abbasid court and the camaraderie that developed between church and court in this period.[52] While much of what takes place in the dialogue concerns standard Muslim objections to Christian theology that had developed by the early Abbasid setting, there are several striking things about the debates.

One is the air of collegiality found here and the respect proffered from both sides. Time and time again Patriarch Timothy I refers to the caliph as 'king of kings', an appellation that would have been used to refer to Sasanian kings. Other titles, that again signal camaraderie among co-religionists, are the appellations 'our God-loving King' and 'our virtuous king'.[53] The Patriarch signals his closeness not only to the king but to the culture of the king in several ways, for example by suggesting the culture of the Patriarch's church is closer to the Arab culture and Islamic religion of the Caliph than that of the Jews.[54] There are scathing comments made about the Roman Empire as well, suggesting the overall thrust of loyalty found in the pragmatics of the text. And the theological slight that is made against the Syrian Orthodox church that occurs along with these statements is intended to make the East Syrian theological position palatable to Muslims.[55] Whether or not the Caliph's agreement to Timothy I's slights against the theology of the theopaschites – 'those who make God suffer' – really occurred, is beside the point.[56] A common thread running through the dialogue is the Church of the East's orthodoxy both from a Christian theological point of view and within an Abbasid ideological point of view.[57]

Differing scholarly views exist on the role played within the Abbasid revolution of Persian speakers and those maintaining various Sasanian traditions at the time of the revolution.[58] Muhammad Shaban, for example, refutes the previously widely held thesis of Vloten and Wellhausen that the revolution stemmed from, as Shaban summarises their thesis, that 'the inveterate hatred of the subject population against its oppressor, of a foreign race (i.e. Arabs), Shia'ism, and the expectation of a liberator messiah caused the Khurasanis to embrace the cause of the house of the prophet'.[59] Shaban argues this and against positing a strong Iranian dimension to the revolt. He maintains instead that Arabs led the revolution. These were Arabs who had lost their privileges of the Arab ruling class and who had become subject to the rule of non-Muslims in the region of Khurasan, more specifically the city of Merv, and where Arabs had melded into the Iranian population.[60] While the revolutionaries were joined by some of the Mawali, i.e. functionary converts to Islam, these participants were not numerous.[61]

Wilferd Madelung also downplays the Persian factor and focuses instead upon a combination of economic and social dimensions, suggesting that ethnicity is difficult to single out as a deciding factor.[62] There was indeed anti-Arab sentiment within the revolution, however, and there were Zoroastrians who had converted to Islam in the mid eighth century only to have their Arab governors suspicious of them and resentful of the tax loss incurred at their conversion.[63]

Daniel, however, writes that though the 'Abbasid revolt has been characterised as a revolt of Iranians against Arabs, of the non-Arab Muslims, of an Arab faction in Merv; it was (actually) all of these, and none of them'.[64] Rather, he says that it 'was just what historians have been most reluctant to call it: a true mass uprising'.[65] This having been said, the social and political upheavals occurring in Khurasan in the decades after 750, which occurred in conjunction with the An Lushan Rebellion, did contain an element of pride in local rule, and there were also inherent Persian dimensions. Since these local Persian-speaking areas were in the process of losing their autonomy to the Abbasids, pride in their Persian cultural heritage would only be co-opted and made part of Abbasid hegemony for a short time. Daniel suggests that in order to understand the fragmentation of the Islamic empire and the rise of local dynasties in the ninth century, 'Khurasani history indicates a trend of the Abbasid Empire being towards a greater degree of feudalization', one that led to the eventual break-up of the Abbasid Empire itself.[66]

Hamilton Gibb places emphasis on the *Shubiya*, or non-Arab Muslims, in the revolt, but he also urges caution in the way Persian culture and sentiment related to the assertion of Persian identity in the social matrix and its developments. Gibb states that, indeed, the conflict between Perso-Aramean versus Arabic culture which was developing 'went to the heart of the struggle for the new civilization being created', but that the *Shubiya* did not have as 'their aim to destroy the Islamic empire, but [rather] to remould its political and social institutions and the inner spirit of Islamic culture on the model of the Sasanian institutions and values'.[67] This 'represented in their eyes the highest political wisdom'.[68] Gibb argues that there is no indication the original functionaries of the Abbasids were overwhelmingly *Shubiya*, and that it is 'very questionable whether the Abbasids were Persophile or even whether the Khurasani nobles of the second Islamic century were enthusiastic supporters of the Sasanian tradition'.[69] Gibb does concede, however, that an atmosphere was created at and around the Abbasid court in which the literary functionaries of the court learned Sasanian manuals of courtly etiquette, and the court's attendant world view was not only studied but in some cases learned by heart.[70] This is the context in which the pride in Persian heritage and local, semi-autonomous rule, visible in the Xi'an monument and its references to the city of Balkh, are connected to the resurgence of Persian identity seen within Abbasid Khorasan. New configurations in which imperial charisma could be transmitted within in the local context, seen in abundance in the Xi'an monument, the nativist movements of Abbasid ruled Central Asia, and the rise of Persiannate Abbasid functionaries arrayed around the court, paralleled developments seen within the Church of the East stemming from Timothy I's Patriarchate.[71]

The 'Sasanian solution', which was embraced by the Abbasid caliphs in order to bring these Persians into the Abbasid Empire, was a strategy actually taken up first by the Umayyad caliphs.[72] In the eastern regions that became part of the Abbasid territories there was a continuous state of war between Zoroastrians and Arabs until the late seventh century, creating a situation in which these regions had to be conquered and re-conquered.[73] At the same time, however, John bar Penkaye, a Christian who worked for the Umayyad dynasty during its final years, referred to the ethnic harmony that existed between the empire's ethnicities, something that carried over into the early Abbasid period.[74] The primary sources also indicate that Zoroastrians were encouraged to stay in government positions well into the early eighth century.[75] One caliph is believed to have said plainly, 'I admire these Persians, and our empire would not function without them', a statement reminiscent of the later Sasanian emperors' occasional view of that empire's Christians.[76] If through the seventh and eighth centuries the financiers of the Arab rulers were Zoroastrians, as non-Muslims were in fact desired in such positions because Islamic law said these occupations were ill-befitting a Muslim, such arrangements enabled the Persian speakers and bearers of Sasanian institutions in Central Asia to be brought easily into the Abbasid revolution and its early courts.

The paradoxical nature of the position of Persian speakers and maintainers of Sasanian institutions in the face of mid eighth-century Arab expansions can be seen in a number of other ways. There was growing pressure on non-Muslims to convert to Islam, and tax and population registers used by Arab rulers in Khurasan began to be written in Arabic rather than in Persian by the mid eighth century.[77] Figures such as Ruzbih ibn Al-Muqaffa, put to death for practising Zoroastrianism in secret, indicate a transition taking place in Abbasid ideology, one in which tolerance of Zoroastrians and Manicheans was disappearing, some of which surfaces in the letters of Timothy I.[78] He was said to have been:

> steeped in the traditional culture of the old Persian nobility, yet ever observant of the values of Arab society. In the purity of his Arabic he outshone members of the Arab ruling class, and in generosity and hospitality he seems to have tried to outdo them. He translated Middle Persian tales, some of Indian origin. His Kalīla and Demna, the Middle Persian original now lost but thought to have been entitled Karīrak ud Damanak was written by one Borzōē/Borzūya (q.v.), a Persian physician attached to the Sasanian court in the sixth century. His translation of Kalīla wa Demna was not a conscious attempt to start a new literary trend; it was clearly just one of several works of old Sasanian court literature which Ibn al-Muqaffa introduced to an exclusive readership within court circles, its function being to illustrate what should or should not be done by those aiming at political and social success. Ibn al-Muqaffa is thought to have produced an Arabic adaptation of the late Sasanian Xwadāy-nāmag, a chronicle of pre-Islamic Persian kings, princes, and warriors. A mixture of legend, myth, and fact, it served as a quasi-national history inspired by a vision of kingship as a well-ordered autocracy with a sacred duty to rule and to regulate its subjects' conduct within a rigid class system. Interspersed with maxims characteristic of andarz literature, the narrative also offered practical advice on civil and military matters. Ibn al-Muqaffa is known to have modified

certain parts of the original and excluded others, possibly to make it intelligible to his Arab Muslim readers.[79]

Extensively quoted by other writers of his time, the subjects he was most quoted on were 'on topics such as court manners and customs, military tactics, divination and physiognomy, archery, and polo – subjects typical of various works on Sasanian institutions, protocol, and entertainment'.[80] The subject of Ibn al-Muqaffa's *Kitab Mazdak*, although a piece of historical fiction, as its title implies was the leader of the revolutionary movement led by Mazdak and whose activities led to his death in the mid sixth century and contained the implied suggestion that Abbasid caliphs could learn how to manage Persian-speaking subjects by better understanding this particular episode of Sasanian history. Another work from the Sasanian Empire that Al-Muqaffa translated into Arabic was the *Nama-ye Tansar* (*The Letter of Tansar*), a political work taking its name from its likely legendary author Tansar, a Zoroastrian priestly adviser to the first Sasanian monarch, Ardašīr I (r.224–40).[81] However concessionary his translation was to Muslims, it was still Irano-centric:

> we are the best of Persians, and there is no quality or trait of excellence or nobility which we hold dearer than the fact that we have ever showed humility and lowliness ... in the service of kings, and have chosen obedience and loyalty, devotion and fidelity. Through this quality ... we came to be the head and neck of all the climes.[82]

The social capital that began to be held and wielded in the Abbasid court by those with Persian or Aramaic backgrounds must be seen as part of the patronage *habitus* and courtly milieu of the Church of the East under both Timothy I and the contemporaneous Xi'an monument community. Much recent scholarly work on the rise of the Abbasid Empire has emphasised the role of Persian speakers, Persian culture, and Persian and Aramaic/Syriac scholarly families and their ability to bind together the court and the society ruled over by the Abbasid Empire.[83] The early caliphs attempted to articulate an image that the new empire was a recapitulation of the ancient

Persian past stemming back through and even beyond the Sasanian Empire.[84]

For example, the first texts translated into Arabic during the so-called translation movement were often of Zoroastrian astrological texts, and were translated at the behest of the Caliphs themselves. Dimitri Gutas says shows that the Arabs of the Umayyad dynasty were being opposed in Khorasan based on the use of astrological texts.[85] Putting Persians in Abbasid administrative positions provided a means of doing this. Families like the Barmakids and the Nawbahts, and figures such as Ibn al-Muqaffa, involved in some of the earliest translations projects for the Abbasid caliphs, held such knowledge, as did the Church of the East in Chang'an, who were involved in similar ideological projects with regard to astrology.[86] An anonymous Muslim historian writing in Spain on the early Abbasid Caliphate paints a picture of how these currents began to converge during the period of Caliph Mansur and the interest in the translation of works of political astrology first developed.

> In the beginning of Islam, the Arabs cultivated no science other than language and a knowledge of the regulations of their religious law, with the exception of medicine ... this was the situation of the Arabs during the Umayyad dynasty. But when God almighty put an end to this dynasty by means of that of the Hashemites [the Abbasids] ... peoples' ambitions revived from their indifference and their minds awoke from their sleep. The first among the Arabs who cultivated the sciences was the second caliph, Abu Jafar al-Mansur. He was – God have mercy on him, deeply attracted to them and to their practitioners, being himself proficient in religious knowledge and playing a pioneering role in promoting philosophical knowledge and especially astrology.[87]

From Mas'udi comes the following, more detailed, glimpse into the period of Caliph Mansur and the emphasis of works of political astrology:

> He was the first caliph to favor astrologers and to act on the basis of astrological prognostications. He had in his retinue the astrologer Nawbaht the Zoroastrian, who converted to Islam upon his

instigation and who is the progenitor of his family of the Nawbahts. Also in his retinue were the astrologer Ibrahim al-Farazi, the author of an ode to the stars and other astrological and astronomical works, and the astrologer Ali ibn Isa the astrolabist.

He was the first caliph to have books translated from foreign languages in Arabic, among the Kalila wa Dhimma, and the Sindhind. There were also translated for him books by Aristotle on logic and other subjects, the Amalgamest by Ptolemy, the Arithmetic [by Nichomas of Gerasa], the books by Euclid and other ancient books from classical Greek, Byzantine Greek, Middle Persian, Neo-Persian, and Syriac. These books were published among the people, who examined them and devoted themselves to knowing them.[88]

The links between Abbasid ideology and the Abbasid court's interest in these ancient depositories of Persian and Aramaic/Babylonian learning can be gleaned when the content of some of the books translated in the Abbasid court even before the translation movement, with its near sole focus on Greek scientific and philosophical works, began. The caliph's interest in and ability to present an image of magnanimity and public charity in providing the inhabitants of his realm with the ability to read about the geographically most universal and temporally most ancient depositories of knowledge is indicated in the translation of the Zoroastrian *Denkard*, as rendered from Middle Persian to Arabic in the early Abbasid setting. Connections between royal patronage and scribal lineages were forged not only among the scribes themselves through these processes but also in the subjectivity of the new Arabic reading public and literary classes for generations to come. Book IV of the *Denkard* shows how successive generations of Persian kings are presented as forming communal bonds, i.e. a *comitatus*, transmitting imperial charisma between kings, scribes, and readers. The reproduction of such texts brought the Persian past and the non-Arab subjects of the Abbasid Empire into the imperial fold and its structures of thought. It made them not only targets of its ideological productions but co-producers of it as well. The interest in creating an image of universality, showing the inheritance of all the great empires of the past and their culmination in the Abbasid dynasty, proffered to accompany the newly devised cosmopolitan image of Islam propagated by the Abbasids, can be seen again in Abu Sahl ibn Nawbaht's *Kitab al-Nahmutan*.[89] The way in which the New Persian language was itself created partly by the translation projects connected to this and the mastery of courtly and literary class Arabic can be seen in the *Book of Nativities*, ascribed to Zoroaster.[90] The Abbasid proclivity for incorporating traditions of ancient learning into their empire, with astrology, and knowledge holders of astrological and other ancient learning, being preeminent, has parallels within the Church of the East in China, as the cosmological and astrological symbolism found in the Xi'an stele bear witness to. The cosmic symbolism in Manichean Old Turkic fragment M0919 and the role of Iranian knowledge holders transmitting and making possible the operation of imperial charisma should also be seen in conjunction.[91] One way of connecting this to the family of knowledge holding courtly ascetics of the Xi'an monument and its rhetorical assertions is by noting the way in which these knowledge holders were participating in both local and empire-wide courtly structures simultaneously.

Cosmopolitan Families on the Abbasid Silk Roads

One way of better understanding these connections is to note that, by the time the Xi'an monument stood in place in 781, China had become isolated from its Central Asian neighbours through loss of territory to these now far more powerful Tibetan and Arab empires.[92] These developments gave the Church of the East new agency as it became a cultural mediator for the Tang court. It became a shaper of an elite, trans-imperial culture, something it did within monastic units and within Christian family units having military connections. In the early 780s, and as the Xi'an monument appeared, the Tang government was in need of both new alliances within China as well as new connections abroad and into Central Asia; it was families from Central Asia, who were responsible for the Xi'an and Luoyang monuments (probably only reflecting a fraction of the whole), who were able to step in and respond to these needs. Beckwith writes that 'by the late eighth century, China was no longer a major force in Central Asian history; but central Asia and central Asians continued to be major factors in Chinese history'.[93]

The sparse nature of the documentary record unfortunately prevents any satisfactory tracing of the origins of the Persian family specifically mentioned in the Xi'an stele into the region from where they are mentioned to have come, i.e. Tocharistan and the city of Balkh. The historical record, however, is able to provide useful information about the city, the region, and the participation of wealthy families in patronage activities. These wealthy families also have links to monasticism and worldly asceticism, and thus indicate ways in which the cultivation of learning in the period, took place among subjects of imperial patronage moving across eighth century in Baghdad and Chang'an, but who also did so as families of house-holders having connections to non-house-holders/ascetics.

In charge of one the most prestigious and powerful institutions of Balkh was the Barmakid family, who we are told weathered many invasions of the region and managed to keep themselves and the wealth of the monastery intact before they served the Abbasid Caliphate for several generations after coming from the city of Balkh.[94] According to the historian Mas'udi, Barmak the Elder managed the Nawbahar in Balkh before he joined the Islamic cause.[95] Mas'udi writes:

> The extraordinary and remarkable history of the Barmakids, their great qualities, their benefactions, their noble actions, all in fact that makes the story of their lives so interesting, the poems composed in their honour, and the elegies composed after their disgrace, all these things are to be found in my historical annals and intermediate history.
>
> Here I have been merely given an outline of the facts which I have not mentioned in my pervious works. In these same books may be found the origins of the family of Barmak, before the coming of Islam, their functions in the temple of Nawbahar, that is the fire temple at Balkh, as has been said earlier; the explanation of the name Barmak, Barmak the elders' relations with the kings of the Turks, the history of his family since Islam. The small glimpses which I give here of their lives and story seem to me sufficient. God knows best the truth.[96]

There is no information about how the Barmaki family survived the initial attacks of Arab military forces to Central Asia. Perhaps moving to Baghdad to serve the Abbasid caliphs was also one of the strategies to protect the family's financial assets in the region and the worldly asceticism at the centre of the family's way of life. Mas'udi spends many pages in his narrative detailing the activities of several generations of the family who were in the service of the caliphate, however.

The Barmakid family was an early supporter of the Abbasid revolt against the Umayyads and of Al-Saffa. This gave Khalid ibn Barmak considerable influence, and his son Yahya ibn Khalid (d.806) was the vizier of the caliph Al-Mahdi (ruled 775–85) and tutor of Harun Al-Rashid (r.786–809). Yahya's two sons, Al-Fadl and Ja'far (767–803) both occupied high offices under Harun. Many Barmakids were patrons of the sciences, which greatly helped the propagation of Indian science and scholarship from the neighbouring academy of Gundishapur into the Arabic world. They patronised scholars such as Gebir and Jabril ibn Boktisho, Christian physicians.[97]

It is known that Yahya ibn Khalid al-Barmaki (d.805) was a patron of physicians and specifically of the translation of Hindu medical works into both Arabic and Persian. In all likelihood, however, his activity took place in the orbit of the caliphal court in Baghdad where, at the behest of Harun al-Rashid (786–809), such books were translated into Arabic. Khurasan and Transoxiana may have been essential in the transfer not only of this learning from India to Islam but may have shaped kingship and courtly patronage throughout the region in a way that affected the Church of the East. An analysis of the contours of the Barmakid family and its connections to the earliest phase of the Abbasid translation movement through Indian science and political astrology may provide trajectories in which to study the changing and emergent nature of royalty within the region and changes within the *habitus* of the Church of the East's elites.

One of the earliest works to be translated into Arabic was an Indian astronomical treatise called the *Siddhānta* of Brahmagupta.[98] The two astronomers associated with this are Al-Farazi and his father, both of whom seem to be called the first two Islamic astronomers.[99] During the time that these two family astronomers worked, the vizier supporting them was the Persian (i.e. Bactrian) Yahya Al-Barmaki. Numerous Indian medical works were also translated at this time. Although the notion that the theology of patronage seen within the region came from this Indian astronomy and its emphasis on the sovereign ruler as a cosmological sustainer is problematic, it occurs among the Abbasid caliphs and the Persian independence movement associated with the early Abbasid revolution that were eventually incorporated into it.[100] Kevin Van Bladel has argued that Chinese models of royal astrology, influenced by Indian models, may have passed through Central Asia, and the Persian nationalist movements of the mid eighth century, which shaped the Abbasid Revolution so decisively, passed into Abbasid understandings of kingship.[101] The way in which the Bactrian Middle Persian-speaking group from the Church of the East was linked to the Abbasid court and empire, and to Tang court and empire at the same time, and the *habitus* the group moved within, gain empirical support through such analyses. Each is also made clearer when set in relation to the corpus of Syriac writing stemming from Patriarch Timothy I.

Empire, Court and Worldly Asceticism in the Writings of Timothy I

The power of the Abbasid court and its imperial charisma radiated into Central Asia partly through the Church of the East, encapsulated in the figure of its Patriarch Timothy I. This can be examined in three ways. First, an analysis will be presented of the close relations between Timothy I and the Abbasid court during the period of Timothy's removal of political rivals, and specifically within the Persian areas of the church during the early part of his Patriarchate. Timothy's silencing of opposition to his Patriarchate, and specifically within the Persian branch of the church during the early part of his reign, can be linked to the incorporation of Persian learning and Persian modes of courtliness and kingship within the early Abbasid Empire taking place at the same time. Timothy's dialogues with Caliph al-Mahdi allow the closeness that developed between the church and the early Abbasid court to be viewed in new light.[102] Secondly, an analysis of the imperial, or royal, self-articulation appearing in some of Timothy I's extant letters, his understanding of his place in the Abbasid Empire and within the mobile structure of the church, will be presented. Thirdly, Timothy I's interest, concomitant with that of the church's interest, in missions, the imperial ideology through which these missions were articulated, and the resultant worldly asceticism will be examined.

Thomas of Marga captures the general tenor of the times and the political situation within the church during Timothy I's incumbency. This was a period not without controversy – with accusations of simony and other misdemeanours levelled at him, as Bar 'Ebroyo recounts the incident.[103] Timothy's letters also reveal more of the context, along with subsequent developments. In this jostling for Patriarchal position, it was ascendency over the Persian and academic faction within the church that Timothy needed to secure.[104] He did so successfully. The *habitus* and worldly ascetic structure Timothy was linked to and forming through these political manoeuvers that emerges in the following passage from letter XIII had Platonic associations for Timothy:

> I have read of the letters of thy holiness, in which they brought the good news of the obedience, I say, and submission to the laws of the Elamites [of the Persian faction and of Henanisho]. Joyful signs of peace and concord have been come to pass between the shepherd [Timothy], and the flock [the church]. Among the members of the spiritual community, the head of them has been erected. Now the hope and expectation of the things which have been assumed, and that which exceeds the ability of the senses, which must govern the perception of the mind, as the distributor of those he [God] has taught, has come to pass.[105]

Henanisho as the leader of the Persian faction is ridiculed in the text's following passage, where throne-related and royal language appears:

> Henanisho, of whom Your Holiness wrote, was by Sarbaziah ordained Metropolitan and given his title from us, which we coffered on him in private and between us two: 'No one is aware of you, until he approaches the throne, for which he was anointed, [and knows] you have arrived.' It was done because of the cruelty and fierceness of the Persian population. But though he tried to

make known his ordination in the royal city of the world, before it has been made [official], I found out about the secret. Never [I thought] will I lay upon him with the hand of God in the Spirit [and ordain him]. Then I went and had recourse to some friends who said: 'Do not remember such a folly. For this was done out of impatience, rather than caused by malice.'[106]

The worldly ascetic *habitus* that Timothy I is commandeering as part of his rule over the church, drawing impetus from changes within kingship and the inter-courtly character of the polities of Central Asia, surfaces in the letter in connection with the confrontation with Henanisho and the Persian faction within the church, and in connection with clothing and objects able to transmit imperial charisma:

> After long labors borne of his ordination, I commanded him, neither in the royal city, or Basra or Uballat, to remain for even an hour; but without the delay, he was sent to re-direct his way. He said: 'I must do this with expenses paid.' And I answered him: 'many of the monks of China and those who've crossed the seas to India, have only gone with a staff, and scriptures. Take heed of them and follow suit, for they have crossed the sea without a great deal of money'. He has forsaken my commandments, and been gone from the house of the royal city now for about two months and has not provided a royal visit. Later he went down to Basra and Huballat, he was convinced that he had been given his throne, and with a modesty that is not his to have. He then came with his staff and miter [Grk phakilon, i.e. cloak], as if to enter Sarbaziah.[107]

Letter XIII ends with a word about the links between Timothy and the physicians making their way into the Abbasid court at the time and giving the church inter-courtly leverage, physicians with training in Greek medicine playing a role in its late Sasanian and early Tang period (*c*.630–740):

> Our Gabriel is very keen to learn the art of medicine. Train him and his school, according to the custom of thy goodness, and

enjoin that they should take care of him. What we have done for the Lord (is seen) in our care of the poor.[108]

In Timothy's letter referring to Henanisho as representative of the church's Persian element, Henanisho is shown approaching the Patriarchal throne in an attempt to ask for money. Timothy's response is curt: 'so many have travelled the seas to India and China with nothing other than a staff and a sack. How dare you cross these long spaces with money when so many have done it with little or nothing!' This exchange may intimate that in Timothy's understanding, the ascetical regimen necessary for being part of the church's leadership needs to match that of the new, and emergent, trans-imperially appearing kingship structures of Central Asia in order that the church may continue to find a place within these courts, as it had done for centuries, but which was more urgent now that Abbasids had arisen and the church's mission field in Mesopotamia had become limited.[109] This can be interpreted as the joining of monastic ascetical regimens, as represented by the wearing of white clothing, with that of the non-white, i.e. the celibate clergy, which type existed in China and likely on the trade routes into China, the Persian Gulf, and almost certainly North India.[110] Timothy's interest in subduing the Persian element within the church may parallel the Abbasid court's interest in controlling Persian religious trends and the political aspirations of Persian speakers in Central Asia and elsewhere.

By the late eighth century those who had been given positions as heads of the centre of East Syrian monasticism, Beth Abhe, were required to prove their mettle in long and arduous missionary journeys.[111] Beth Abhe became a kind of training centre for what might be termed the vanguard of the church. Individuals sent out on missions were required to adhere to monastic disciplines and the disciple of their home monasteries, and could not adopt that of other monasteries. The physical rigour that Timothy I required of his missionaries comes through in sections of Thomas of Marga's epic work, the *Book of Governors*, reflecting an early Abbasid milieu, showing the imperial sense of the church's mission as a civilising institution seen in Timothy's letters and in the Xi'an stele at once. It was not only the case that clergy receive multilingual training to equip enterprise in foreign lands, what would today be called 'cross-cultural competence', but a sense of 'manifest destiny' is apparent as well, one in accordance with the divine providence notion found in Isho'yahb III's letters.[112] The following passage typifies the preparation of the monastic missionary candidates:

> Now in respect of this man of whom we speak, inasmuch as he is exceedingly able, very much was entrusted into his hands. When he went to Mar Timothy, who having learned of what this man was capable and having seen that he was instructed in the Syriac language and learning, and also in the Arabic and Persian tongues, he [Timothy] determined to anoint him with holy oil, and to make him hold the pastoral staff, and to send him as a shepherd and a teacher to the barbarian nations who had never received the bridle of teaching concerning God, and into whose country none of the preachers and evangelists of the kingdom of heaven had gone since the time of the apostles until the present.[113]

The cross-cultural training and competence the church's missionaries possessed links back ultimately to the imperial court and to the Catholicos' connection to the court. These themes are reiterated in the *Historia Monastica* of Thomas of Marga:

> For the countries of the barbarians who were remote from all understanding and decent manner of life, and to whose part of the world no preacher and planter of the truth had ever gone, and where the doctrine of the glad tidings of our redeemer had never been proclaimed. But why should I speak of the knowledge of Christ our lord only? For they had not even received the knowledge of God, the creator or the worlds and their governor, like the Jews and other nations, but they offered, and behold they still offer, worship to trees, graven images of wood, four footed beasts, fishes, reptiles, birds of prey and other birds and such like things and they bow down to worship fire and the stars and planets. Mar Yahb-Allaha, and Qardagh and Mar Elijah were the men who preached the doctrine of Christ in those counties of Dailomaye and Gilaye, and of the other barbarians who live beyond them, and they planted in them the light of the truth of the glad tidings of our lord, and plucked out from the simple souls

that were all the abominable thorns and tares of evil deeds which Satan had sown in their hearts. And they taught and baptised, and wrought mighty deeds, and showed forth works, and the fame of their acts was carried to all the ends of the east. And thou mayest learn clearly concerning all these things from the letter which certain merchants and king's scribes, who were going in and coming out from those countries for the purpose of trade and the business of government, wrote to Mar Timothy.[114]

In the courtly milieu in which these texts were written, Abbasid imperial ideology was developing such that its earlier tolerance for Persian religions (Manichaeism and Zoroastrianism) as practised more freely by courtly literati and intellectuals like ibn al-Muqaffa, was narrowing.[115] This changing of shape of the Abbasid court can be glimpsed in the following passage and in relation to the church's missions ideology and its worldly asceticism. Speaking of one of the church's missionaries, Thomas of Marga wrote:

and when he had entered those countries he began to teach and show them the true knowledge of his doctrine, and while he was teaching with these words, Christ our lord was confirming them by miracles which he worked, by cleansing the lepers, by healing the sick, by opening the eyes of the blind, by making the lame to walk, by raising the dead, and by making barren women fruitful, for the divine dispensation is accustomed to show forth works at the beginning of divine operations, more particularly in the case of those barbarians who from their earliest times and throughout all their generations had been led captive by evil deeds to the worship and service of their corrupt things. And by the sight of the miracles which our lord worked by the hands of the blessed man, he taught many cites and thickly peopled districts and baptised them and brought them near to the doctrine of divine life. And he built churches, and established priests and deacons in them, and he set apart some of the brethren who were with him to teach them psalms and spiritual praises, and he himself went further and further into the country until he arrived at the ends of the east in the great teaching he made among the heathen, and Marcionites and Manicheans, and against every object of worship and every impure thing: and he sowed among them the glorious light of the doctrine of the gospel, the mother of life and peace.[116]

The letters that Patriarch Timothy I wrote to the monks of the monastery of Mar Maron and to the physician Sergius (letters XLI and XLVII respectively) impart rare and precious details about the extent of the missionary enterprise which embraced all manner of 'creeds, colors and races' – including Persians, Turks, Indians, and Chinese – all of whom were now under the dominion of Patriarch Timothy I. In Letter XLI for example Timothy tells his correspondent:

> For behold, in all of the lands of Babel [Baghdad], Pars [Persia] and Athur [Assyria] and in all of the eastern lands and amongst Beth Hinduway [India] and indeed amongst Beth Sinaye [China] and amongst Beth Tuptaye [Tibet] and likewise amongst Beth Turkaye [Central Asia] and in all of the domains under his Patriarchal throne, this throne of which God commanded that we be its servants and likewise its ministers – that one is this hypostasis – who is from eternity, without increase, who was crucified on our behalf, is proclaimed, indeed in different and diverse lands and races and languages. For behold, even in our days, prior to these ten years that I have been entrusted with the service of the administration of the church, for even now I have been thirteen years more or less in this service, the king of Turkaye, with more or less all of his territory, has left the godless error from antiquity, for he has become acquainted with Christianity by the operation of the great power of the messiah, that by all are subject to him. And he has asked us in his writings [about] how he might appoint a Metropolitan for the territory of his kingdom. This alone we have done through [i.e. with the help] of God. And also the letter that we wrote to him we will send to you if it is pleasing to you.[117]

These passages show both the extent of the church's reach and Timothy I's conception of it.

The familial nature of the expanding Church of the East, so evident in the Xi'an and Luoyang monuments, was something that was needed in order for the church to survive and prosper. This can also be introduced as a reason the Chang'an and Baghdad church leaders are both seen discussing clerical clothing issues as the church's missional nature began to be shaped within Abbasid and late Tang imperialisms. The church's mission work and its far-flung nature as an ascetic social body standing in relation to the Abbasid court is an issue that has recently received attention, Berti's important contributions in this regard being among the most important.[118] Berti writes, for example, of how these developments took place not only as the church was being structured in relation to the new court and that its far-flung and expansive nature gave it prestige in court and gave the Church's leaders legitimacy as representatives of a large and taxable population, something clearly reflected in the sources.

In the early twentieth century Eduard Sachau brought to light a manuscript containing Church of the East marriage regulations, a portion of which stemmed from the pen of Patriarch Timothy. In the text Timothy explains his reasons for writing:

Therefore, let them (Muslim judges) not litigate against the saints (Christians). For they have no judgments and decrees which are not for this world and the lifestyle of mortals only. As a result, the believers (Christians) have a divine apostolic law which tells them that they should not litigate against the sinners (Muslims), but against the Saints ... Therefore I have decided, at the request of our brethren, the bishops and Metropolitans, Mar Jacob, Metropolitan of Perath-Maysan (Basra) and Mar Yallabbibhā, Metropolitan of Rhagae and many Christian lay near and far, to make a copy of the judgments and decisions and to write decisions and for two reasons. First is the desire, which I repeatedly have asked to be met, for those who transgress the divine laws, not to take any excuse to go to judges, in the absence of decisions and laws (among Christians) going to the courts and courts of non-Christians, since judgments and wisdom on this type of secular issues (among Christians) does not yet exist. Due to weakness of age – I'm now 65 years old, and as a result of serious long term illness, and anxiety and distress of soul, which surrounds the world and the church, and states of emergency, I've had to turn away from this until now…. I also lacked a solid knowledge and understanding of such matters (until now).[119]

Timothy makes it clear that these laws will apply across the wide geographical expanse of the church and be applicable to people living in different cultures and climates, writing:

There are a variety of people in the world who have very different climates and countries, and differ by gender and language, customs and law. The individual, that is to say, one's whole life, changes according to those customs, to that which they are used to, and into which they were educated. They will not at all deviate from this, nor can be moved without a thousand difficulties arising as from the changes to the original rule of their lives. For habit, as Inan has beautifully said, this is a second nature. All genera and species of created beings have an equality [in general] as well as the distinctiveness. So the nature of my presentation [of these legal statues] will be question and answer, and not in heavy difficult language, but in easily understandable language so that everyone can understand, not just those who have books to read and understand, but also those who can neither read nor write.[120]

While it is clear that most of what is found here is setting Christians apart from Muslims, a closeness to the Abbasid court is indicated in this text.

What is the punishment for those who revile and blaspheme the King? It is to be entirely exiled from the Church, the Sacraments and excluded from the Christians, both as he or anyone who operates secretly or openly with him.[121]

But there are many laws in the collection which distinguish Christians from Muslims and Persians through the use of the Church of the East's ritual regalia and charisma transmitting material culture, as seen in the appearance of the cross in the following passage:

> The Christian should not marry a non-Christian. Do not violate the children by taking the children to another religion. When a woman enters such a marriage by his own choice, at the instigation of the parents, they will all be anathematised. If it occurs not from her or his own choice, but at the behest of their parents, then their parents are alone to be given over to the Arabs. An engagement must take place through the mediation of the priest and the deacon, or bishop, or archbishop, and at least three lay people, and through the mediation of the cross. An engagement is not otherwise completed. With the gift of the cross, which our savior adorned us each engagement, which is not implemented in this way, should not be regarded as an engagement. Because in such a way our engagements differ from that of the pagans.[122]

CHAPTER 4

THE COURT OF EMPEROR TANG DEZONG AS 'IMPERIAL NET', AND THE CHURCH OF THE EAST'S PERSIAN *LONGUE DURÉE*

Introduction

The previous chapter looked out from Mesopotamia, the Church of the East's seat of power in Baghdad, and into Central Asia, as it analysed leadership within the Church of the East and its constitution as an agency-seeking social body, led by courtly ascetics, during the early Abbasid period. Connections to the city of Balkh, and its region of Tocharistan, figuring prominently in the Xi'an stele, were investigated in this regard, as this was a region beginning to export scientific learning and a culture of courtly patronage to Baghdad during the early Abbasid period.[1] Kevin Van Bladel has begun to explore ways in which this region's courtly culture, with its long-standing connections to China in addition to Central Asia, was present in the early Abbasid court at the time of Patriarch Timothy I.[2] This work builds upon a body of research coming before it exploring intersections between the courtly culture of the Abbasids, Central Asia and the Sasanians, which charts developments either in China or within inter-regionally placed institutions such as the Church of the East, but does not do both, nor does it do this in a synthetic manner with regards to the Church of the East.[3]

Recent work on mid eighth-century Central Asia also indicates that there were parallels between the Abbasid Revolution and the most important event of Middle Chinese history, the An Lushan Rebellion.[4] This scholarship points to ways that the Church of the East can be brought into the investigations begun by Van Bladel and Berti, as well as by Dickens and others on the 'emergent' nature of courtly culture and the *comitatus* within eighth-century Central Asia.[5] The reshaping of Tang society and its relations with Central Asia that occurred following the An Lushan Rebellion is particularly relevant in this regard as it provides a specific way in which to investigate the dhimmitude thesis, stemming from Saeki and others, as contoured in the introduction. The 'emperor worship' purportedly found in the Jingjiao corpus by Saeki, and which for him led to the disappearance of Christianity in early Middle China, stems from sources penned after the An Lushan Rebellion period.

As posited in the introduction, Yisi is not just shown as the wealthy donor of the stele working on his own initiative, nor is he shown as begging for support for the church from the court as an outsider, but one standing within the court and its history, acting as mediating figure in the patronage of the Jingjiao community, able to extend its charisma and open it, as a *comitatus*, to the Church of the East. This is represented metaphorically in the stele by images associated with fabric and binding, and by positing Yisi as not just binding the church to the court from *within* the court itself but doing so as a new breed of monastic court functionary: 'one heretofore unseen'.[6] Gabriel too stands within this line of signification, shown as an elite from the Golden Region, part of a 'thread' of elites, of high standing though from outside China, yet able to be 'repairing/ sustaining' the 'Imperial Net', i.e. restoring the empire's fallen state. Gabriel is able to do this as a monastic.[7]

There are certain deep structures within the Chinese imperial imaginary being engaged by the Church of the East and drawn upon as it searched for agency in this context.[8] One element is the Yellow Emperor ideology.[9] The Huangdi, or Yellow Emperor, was the third of ancient China's mythological emperors, a patron saint of Daoism, and thought to have been born and ruled in the third millennium before the Common Era. His legendary reign is credited with the introduction of the basic elements of Chinese technology.[10] Huangdi himself is credited with defeating 'barbarians' in a great battle somewhere in the region of what is now Shanxi – the victory winning him the leadership of tribes throughout the Huang He (Yellow River) plain, thus giving him his name. He is also credited with the introduction of governmental institutions and the use of coined money. His wife is posited mythically as the discoverer of silk production, and he is held up in some ancient sources as an exemplar of scholarly wisdom whose reign was a golden age.[11] Upon his death he was said to have become an immortal.

Developments in Chinese Buddhism more contemporaneous to the period of Dezong than the Yellow Emperor ideology hold another cultural paradigm standing behind and informing the interactions between the Church of the East and the Tang court in this environment. Adam and a Kapishan monk Prajña [*Bore,* 般若] worked together upon the translation of a Buddhist *sūtra* and submitted it to Emperor Dezong in the year 787.[12] Though this text did not survive, as it was rejected, the text was retranslated again one year later, this time directly from Sanskrit to Chinese and without the Iranian language intermediary; although it is not the same text, it is a similar text, and one that did survive. Section seven of the newer text contains a list of prayers, or *dhāraṇi,* to be said by the sovereign in order to offer protection for his kingdom. Emperor Dezong wrote the preface to the retranslated text.[13] Here Dezong indicates his support for use of Esoteric-imperial Buddhism and those closely associated with it in and around Dezong's court to create order and stability in the Tang Empire.[14] The phrase *wang hu qi guo* [往護其國, in order to protect his country] is found repeated in this text, as well as in another Prajñapāramitā text known as the *Renwang hu guo bore boluomiduo jing* [仁王護國般若波羅蜜多經], or *Prajñapāramitā Sūtra for a Humane King to Protect His County,* translated by Prajña in following years.[15] The fabric imagery the Church of the East turned to in order to express their understanding that they were part of the imperial charisma of the court and argue for and assert agency in relation to the *comitatus* of the court must be understood in relation to this articulation of the position of the emperor within the ascetic universe of imperial Chinese Buddhism. The emperor himself used the Imperial Net language, and did so in relation to the Church of the East, within this context.[16] The church's position and agency within the empire can be better understood by attempting to set its religiosity, cultural production and asceticism in relation to the attempt, being made within the court around them, and on occasion with them, to create a compelling ideological umbrella in order to motivate the Tang empire beyond the rebellion period of the mid Tang era.

One level of concreteness and specificity emerges when directing attention towards Adam-Jingjing, one of the main authors or initiators of the stele.[17] Recalling that for Bourdieu a *habitus* is something that endures through and is shaped by time, it must be noted that there is strong likelihood that in 781 Jingjing had just reached maturity, was around 30 years of age, and was a representative of a generation whose parents and forbearers had come to the Tang Empire to help quell the An Lushan Rebellion and whose lives had not only been deeply shaped by it, but the recent ascension to the throne of Emperor Dezong had made this memory and experience within their expatriate community even more salient.[18] Adam's father, Yisi, had almost certainly been part of the fighter units welcomed into the Tang Empire to help quell rebellion.[19] The Xi'an stele shows strong awareness of the An Lushan Rebellion in its Guo Ziyi and Emperor Suzong sections, in its reminders to its readers there and in its 'Imperial Net' section of the church's role in helping restore the Tang to power after the An Lushan Rebellion, the church's continued role in this, and its 'sharing' in the empire's 'imperial charisma'. As will be shown below, the stele reflects not only a Tang Empire that had processed the rebellion, its social lessons and its memory in the past, but particular manifestations of this processing and the opening of the Tang court's imperial charisma as a *comitatus* to the church's Persian and ascetic elites in the early Dezong period.[20]

The stele's Imperial Net 'discourse' comes open to investigation in this way too in relation to the figure of Aluoben, suggested to have been a product of Yisi's own world-view and self-conception, but who may well be the inspiration for the description of Jilie as well.[21] Yisi, described as having aided the empire in the An Lushan Rebellion, can be linked to both Aluoben and Jilie as both are larger than life figures – physically robust and rugged, 'Persian monks', connected to the cultures of the Tang's border regions, and shown able to hold and extend the charisma of Central Asia and Mesopotamia-Persian seats of power, and, in the case of Jilie, a figure who linked Central Asia and the 'Imperial Net' of the Tang court and emperor to these regions, which where cosmically inferior. Jilie and Aluoben, shown in the stele as having introduced to the Tang court a church in full allegiance with the Tang Empire, are also shown as exemplars of monasticism. The 'monastic way' rhetoric of the donor portion of the stele should therefore be considered in relation to both the 'Imperial Net' and Yisi sections of the stele, and in relation to how these sections characterise the Church of the East *not only* as a mobile and newly transplanted merchant and fighting unit, loyal to the Tang – having come to the empire during the rebellion – *but also* as a monastic unit within the empire. This is apparent when reading the 'Imperial Net', the 'white-robed' Yisi section, and *mdabranoutha* sections of the stele together:

The An Lushan Rebellion of 755–63 was not the only significant event within Middle Chinese history; the deeply connected Battle of Talas in 751, and the Abbasid Revolution followed right on its heels, constitute a shared context which is crucial to take into account as agency within the Church of the East as articulated in relation to the early court of Dezong is studied and surveyed. The picture emerging within the scholarship on the issue of how each of these two events is related is one suggesting that the An Lushan Rebellion wrought a fundamental change not only in the Tang Empire and court, but in these two entities' relationships with the Tang's neighbours to the west.[22] The term An Lushan Rebellion period is most often used to refer both to the political chaos and series of revolts occurring between 755 and 765, starting but not ending with An Lushan's rebellion, *and* the factionalism, decentralisation, and period of warlordism that occurred afterwards. A full half a century was required before the rebellion's social chaos was under control. It was within the reign of Dezong (r.780–805) and through the court that he established around him that this occurred.[23] The Tang Empire of emperors Xuanzong (r.712–56), Suzong (r.756–62), Daizong (r.762–79), and Dezong (r.780–805), the four emperors of the rebellion and post-rebellion period, was weakened, far more decentralised, and with a court continually forced to rethink its relationships with the empire's local military governors, and make continual concessions to the empire's neighbours, the Uighurs and Tibetans in particular. By the mid-780s and the period of Dezong the military governors of the northeastern provinces would still refer to themselves as kings, and in 783 a military governor in the northeast named Zhu Ci [朱泚] (743–84) attempted a virtual reprisal of the An Lushan rebellion itself, attempting to create a new empire to rival the Tang court.[24] Though stability returned to the empire under Dezong, he would flee the capital twice in response to Tibetan incursions during his reign. Zhu Ci declared himself not king but 'Emperor of Daqin' at the beginning of his rebellion, and only two years after the Xi'an stele, the 'monument for the propagation of the Luminous Religion of Daqin' was set in place.[25]

Though the Tang Empire under Dezong would regain stability, in terms of the agency the Church of the East could garner in relation to the early court of Dezong and the rhetoric it used to express this and its new uplift from the rising Abbasid Empire, the political context noted above is crucial. Until the late 780s the Tang Empire was not only weak and decentralised, the court itself was cut off diplomatically from Central Asia. One polity continually rising and falling as a concern in this environment was Tibet. As Chinese troops were withdrawn to help put down the An Lushan Rebellion, this allowed Tibet to reassert its power. In 756, as the rebellion got underway and Tibet took former Tang-held areas, regions surrounding Tibet sent envoys to the Tibetan court with reciprocation from Tibet. By 763 Tibet had taken large amounts of territory from the Tang and in that year took Chang'an itself. As Beckwith writes:

> suffice it to say that, with these new conquests, Tibet cut Tang China off from direct contacts with the West. From 763 until the end of the Tang dynasty, what little news of the West that reached China had to pass through the hostile territory of the Tibetans or the not much less hostile realm of the Uighur Turks. China was no longer a major factor in Central Asian history, but central Asia and central Asians continued to be major factors in Chinese history.[26]

One individual through whom the Tang court's relationship with Tibet underwent major changes in the Dezong period was statesman Li Mi [李泌] (722–89). Though much has been made within the scholarship about the 'militarisation' of the culture of the late Tang period, this has not been sufficiently explored in relation to him and the court's eunuch generals, whom he stood next to within the court in terms of wielding authority.[27] In terms of the empire's religious history, this is relevant because, as the weakness of the Tang and its isolation from Central Asia began to reverse during the reign of Dezong and with Li Mi, a 'militarised spirituality' can be pointed at, to which the Church of the East seems to have been developing in response, and in relation to which its rhetoric can be situated.[28] The Imperial Net rhetoric of the Xi'an stele surfacing during the reign of Dezong can be set in relation to these developments, and the notion that the church was a monastic house ('Divine Economy', *mdabranoutha*), led by Persian monastics and as part of its ascetic vocation. However contrary to Saeki's Christian convictions this may have appeared, when the Western ('Persian') elements existing within the church's politics are looked into more deeply, elements that counterbalance the church's apparent interest only in preserving and sustaining the Tang emperor and Tang court, the church's rhetoric of imperial fabrics and monastic binding begin to appear as an assertions of agency rather than an acquiescence to servitude status.

The Translation Incident of 787, the 'Imperial Net' and Agency

In 1896 Japanese scholar Junjirō Takakusu [高楠順次郎] alerted the Anglophone scholarly world to the fact that Church of the East leader Jingjing [景淨]/Adam worked together with Buddhist master Prajña (*Bore*, 般若) on the translation of a Buddhist scripture and presented it to Emperor Dezong in the year 787.[29] Though the incident took place six years after the installation of the Xi'an stele, the Imperial Net language of the stele appears in the record of the 787 incident penned by Esoteric School monk Yuan Zhao [圓照] (712–94) in his work the *Zhenyuan shijiao Lü* [真元釋教錄], or *Buddhist Record of the Zhenyuan Period*, the author from whom and text from which Takakusu learned of the incident.[30] The scripture that Adam and Esoteric Buddhist School monk Prajña worked on together and presented to Emperor Dezong was the *Dacheng liqu liu boluomiduo Jing* [大乘理趣六波羅蜜多経], or *Sūtra of the Six Mahāyāna Pāramitās*, as readers are informed by Yuanzhao.

The centrepiece of the portion of text where the meeting between Adam and Prajña is described is Prajña himself, the way in which he came to China, and his meeting with the Chinese emperor, each being part of a confluence of forces existing in the environment that may be thought of as the 'Tang court'. After relating to readers that Prajña is from Kapiśa, in contemporary northern Afghanistan, and had made a long and arduous sea journey to China because he had heard that the Bodhisattva Manjuśri had appeared there, readers are told that:

> He arrived at Guangdong/Canton after half a month's travel. And in 782 [Jianzhong year 3], he sailed to the capital. He then met a relation of his in the year 786. The *Shence* Army General Luo Haoxin was the son of Prajña's uncle. After both the sorrows [of travel] and joys [of meeting] they comforted one another upon his arrival at home. By using and extending the ties of those close to him, he extended his support network. Eunuch Luo Haoxin was close to, believed in, and held dear the three treasures [Buddhism] and invited him to translate a Buddhist *sūtra*. And with the Persian monk Jingjing from the Daqin temple, and by relying on foreign [hu] books, they translated the *Mahāyāna Sūtra on the Six Pāramitās* in seven volumes. At that point Prajña did not know the Hu language, nor did he know the language of the Tang. Jingjing did not know Sanskrit and did not understand the Buddhist teaching. Although they investigated the *sūtra* they could not obtain half its pearls. Thinking of stealing empty recognition and using fakery for their benefit, they presented a memorial [to the emperor], expecting to get it propagated. The emperor deeply knows civilised culture and is trustworthy and diligent with regards to the Buddhist scriptures. He examined how they had interpreted it, its principles, meanings and sections [and found things lacking]. Moreover, the Sangha of the Buddha and the monastery of the Daqin differing much in their customs, and their religious practices being completely different, [so it was stated by the emperor that] Jingjing should propagate the teaching of the Messiah, and the

Buddhist monk should elucidate the Buddhist texts. He [the emperor] desired to make the teachings separate so that nobody would excessively relate them. Orthodoxy and heterodoxy are different things and the rivers Jing and Wei have a different course. [In this way] *it's as if the net, in terms of its chords, have threads which are untangled.* Heaven and humanity come together in the four fold Saṅgha [who] knows the [three] refuges. There is a decree by the Secretariat-Chancellery which was dispatched Wang Xiqian by imperial order: [and because] the Buddhist teaching, being profoundly detailed in its customs of piety and reverence. When matching and conforming the Sanskrit [language and its] grammar laws to that of Chinese, it is suitable to command Wang Xiqian to in turn command an array of monks [on the project]. Thus the Tajik Monastery retranslated [the work] by decree.[31]

The Imperial Net language of the Xi'an stele, as placed into the very mouth of emperor Dezong by Yuanzhao, and as used here, appears to suggest that the Church of the East's elites had little agency in relation to the Tang court. It is impossible therefore to rescue Adam and the translation incident completely from the negative light into which Yuanzhao puts it. What comes across in this portrayal is the sheer futility of the translation effort, Emperor Dezong's strict Buddhist orthodoxy, and his no-nonsense attitude towards a Christian being involved in the translation of a Buddhist text, let alone an official one and done for the good of the empire.

The preface to the newly translated Prajñapāramitā text, a text penned by Emperor Dezong himself a decade later, wherein the Imperial Net language is found again, sheds a different light onto the question, however, which can be read back onto Yuanzhao's text in order to contour differently the agency the Church of the East's ascetic elites would have held in relation to the Imperial Net language. As the beginning portion of that text reads:[32]

The original Dao has already emerged, its action has led to the creation of its fame and merit, but it is placed now oh so under attack; [the loss of] its wit and intelligence is now oh so truly mourned; the love of evil has oh so attacked its [the Dao's] temperament; and because of this we must solidify its practice which has become soiled. Within the empire the hundred schools of thought are without social cohesion, but outside the empire the six roots are being enticed to cooperation, as Heaven's principle has been depleted and there is no knowledge of it, and the original Dao wanders lost and is forgotten and opposed. Drowning in a sea of sorrow, and being robbed and depleted, we must return the beginning. Only with this will humanity arrive at an understanding of the ancestor of the ten thousand things, the expression of the overcoming of the Three Fold World, the program is independent and will be unchanging, eternal and natural, and because of this we can inspire and lead the doubting masses, [and] aid and pull people into higher government ranks and social status.

The *Sūtra on the Six Pāramitās* is a guide for public law, the highest universal for the enlightenment of monks. Formerly, on a consistent basis, the Tathāgata's radiance gave light in the form of a Bodhisattva, but the Kalpa of degeneration was far and wide, [and so] truth had become violently cold and thin. But Mañjuśrī, in the assembly at Gṛdhrakūṭa, experiencing enlightenment with the Buddha Maitreya and his affairs, become a type of wisdom, only what a Buddha can know, and only what a Buddha can speak, and thus it is hereby declared.[33]

As seen in this passage, in the very mind of the Tang emperor the Imperial Net was closely associated with the Tang court and himself, *as* the emperor, in this context, and tied to a specific constellation of political actors, actions, and institutions. This context extended back to the beginning of the rebellion and the Tang court and empire's response to it. The Church of the East's place as an institution led by ascetic elites tied to Central Asia and the West and as part of this constellation of forces is also apparent in the passages.

The first text above, for example, shows that though it was not allowed to translate the imperial Buddhist *sūtra*, the church remained part of the empire and participated within and shared the emperor and court's charisma in a manner of speaking, in so far as it remained part of the imperial bureaucracy until 845. Allowing the church to stay within the empire, just not as visibly a part of cultural and ideological production, as the text indicates, ensured the 'Imperial Net was untangled', according to Dezong. It is clear from the latter of the two texts above that Dezong saw the need for a large imperial reintegration programme in the late 780s, using language that linked Buddhists, Daoists, and Confucians to the Imperial Net language in stating his views about it. The Church of the East would have held agency within such a programme, and within such language was understood as transmitting and able to hold the charisma of the Tang court, and as part of the Tang court as *comitatus*; and, as will be argued in stages below, as reformulated specifically within the reign of Emperor Dezong as part of the court's ongoing response to the long An Lushan rebellion.

Dezong employed the language of Buddhist cosmology in his articulation of the Imperial Net, and proffered the notion that the Tang Empire was one in the same with the Buddha Dharma, and linked to himself as a sacred emperor. He appears to speak in the second of the above texts for the Bodhisattva Manjuśri and to be a Chakravartin sovereign, the latter in the manner of Wu Zetian's political ideology, thus showing continuity with earlier Tang emperors, adding to what may be said of how the Imperial Net/ Heavenly Net language might have been understood by him and by those in his court.[34] This suggests specific ways that the 'imperial charisma' of the 'Tang court' was 'extended' by the Church of the East in the late Tang Empire through the use of the language of the Imperial Net, its An Lushan rebellion context clear enough from the Xi'an stele.

Mie Nakata and her ongoing work on this period and context has furthered our understanding of the meaning and function of the Imperial Net language of the Xi'an stele and the types of ideological pull the Church of the East would have experienced in relation to the Tang court.[35] She has suggested the 787 translation incident, for example, arose out of two specific shifts taking place within the Dezong's early court that changed the Tang court's connection to the army's and the Tang court's foreign policy establishment and its connections to Central Asia. She points first to the rise of eunuchs within the late Tang Empire and the fact that eunuchs appear in relation to the 787 incident and in connection to Esoteric-Imperial

Buddhism. She points secondly to the rise of statesman Li Mi [李泌] (722–89) and his proposal to create diplomatic channels with the Uighur and Tibetan empires, and in turn reshape the Tang court to build upon its connection to the northeast corridor where Guo Ziyi and the Church of the East fought against the rebellion. In 787, the same year the translation incident occurred, and as recorded in the *Zizhi tongjian* penned by respected Tang court historian Si Maguang [司馬光] (1019–86), 4,000 non-Han [*huke*, 胡客] 'foreign guests', were given an ultimatum – either join the Tang army or leave the empire altogether.[36] Li Mi presented this proposal to the court, and argued that the money being spent by the government to support these individuals and families who had been invited to the Tang to help quell the An Lushan rebellion, who had stayed on, and whose children were now part of a second generation and enculturated, could be much better spent by incorporating them into the empire and making them a permanent part of the *Shence Army* [神策軍].[37] Nakata also argues that the 787 translation incident would have had full support of the Tang court's eunuchs; they would have seen the *esprit de corps* it would have brought to the empire following a long series of rebellions, starting with An Lushan, but continuing up to the recent Zhu Ci rebellion.[38] The eunuchs' deep ties to Esoteric-imperial Buddhism, something they shared with the Church of the East and at least some of its elites, would have exposed them favourably to the proposal as well. The fact that the Shence Army was run by eunuchs at this time signals their likely involvement in the proposal.[39]

It is extremely likely, therefore, that both of these nodes, first the eunuchs and secondly Li Mi, were part of Dezong's thinking, the mind of the late Tang court, and thus the context in which the Imperial Net language, as used both by Dezong and the Church of the East, and as seen in the two passages above, came to the surface. Li Mi's proposals, being put forth in the early court of Dezong and having a receptive ear there, both created diplomatic channels among the Tang court and the Uighur and Tibetan empires and brought to the surface agency already held by the Church of the East as a social body with deep connections to Uighurs and Tibet, a theme that will be explored in the chapter's final two sections. A Daoist like Li Mi could understand his Yellow Emperor philosophy, something that guided his conduct as an official, in this vein and understood him and his Daoist religion as 'repairing the Imperial Net' and setting the Tang court and empire back on course following the An Lushan rebellion and string of rebellions ending with the Zhu Ci rebellion of the early Dezong reign. The emergence of men of 'talent and virtue', within the court of Dezong, as represented by Li Mi, has been suggested by researchers to represent a turn away from the dominance of the Tang court by eunuchs.[40] Contouring properly and fully the agency sought, experienced, and posited within the Persian monastic house (Gr. *oikos*) of the Church of the East and the language singled out within this chapter from the Xi'an stele stemming from this as the church sought this agency in relation to the Tang court, requires an exploration of both of these nodes.

Late Tang Eunuchs, the Buddhist Cosmopolis, Dezong's Court, and Agency

The Tang's eunuchs saw themselves as upholders of the emperor and court through their connections to Buddhism; and too, recalling that the 'repairing the Imperial Net/Heavenly Net' phraseology has Buddhist connections as well as ones native to China.[41] The reshaping of the Tang court through the connections to the northeast corridor occurring in the period of Dezong, thus influencing the Imperial Net/Heavenly Net language of the Church of the East, as explored in the previous section, would have resonated deeply with the court's eunuchs given their connections to multiple branches of the Tang government, finances, weapons production, and horse trade, and their shaping of the Tang court following the An Lushan Rebellion. The late Tang's eunuchs' ability to make the Tang's non-Han actors within the Tang imperial project following the An Lushan rebellion influenced the Imperial/Heavenly Net language of the stele aid in understanding how the Divine Economy and Persian Monk designations of the stele can be read together. As eunuchs were involved intrinsically in a type of asceticism, one reflected in the Persian monastic body of the church, and extended the charisma of the Tang emperor in such a way that this extension was part of ascetic vocation of both groups, this also influenced the emergence and meaning of these discursive pieces within the stele.[42] It is in connection to eunuchs as well that the Yellow Emperor ideology and the Humane King/Realm Protector motif came to the fore, became part of the Church of the East's religiosity, struggle for agency, and the broader ascetic template upon which this struggle took place for the Tang Buddhists and Daoists as well.[43]

The Xi'an stele contains a section in which eunuchs' ability to transmit the imperial charisma of the Tang court to the Church of the East and its leaders in very concrete ways can be seen, in ways that were part of Dezong's court specific post-An Lushan history. General Gao Lishi [高力士] (d.762), who played a decisive role in quelling the An Lushan Rebellion along with Guo Ziyi, is recorded in the stele as having been dispatched by the court of Xuanzong in order to distribute patronage goods to the church's elites.[44] This segment placed immediately after the Xi'an stele's Imperial/Heavenly Net pericope, a segment that clearly shows the church's support for the empire as an ascetic vocation and in connection to Gao Lishi.[45] The bringing of patronage goods by eunuchs to the church that restored its relations with the Tang court is a concrete example of imperial charisma transmission. The way in which this is suggested in the stele as having bound the church's elites and the court together is reminiscent of actions taking place within the Church of the East in the late Sasanian setting.[46] The emperor is referred to as the sage/holy man, and the solar symbolism and evocative visual and tactile imagery adds to the representation of charisma transference seen within the stele in terms of its clothing and fabric imagery seen elsewhere.[47]

Chinese eunuchs were positioned as an extension of the person of the Chinese emperor and the charisma of the court and empire since at least the Zhou dynasty (1046–256 BC); they were a feature within imperial courtly settings throughout the ancient and medieval world, and a phenomenon seen from the Mediterranean to the Indian Ocean and the Pacific.[48] The *Zhou li* [周禮], or *The Rites of the State of Zhou*, indicates the emperor in the state of Zhou; on the eve of the unification of China that would come with the Han period (206 BC– 220 AD), he had within his court and household one queen, three madams, nine concubines, 27 consorts, and 81 ladies of duty within the inner court.[49] As there was constant competition among these women to give birth to a royal heir, eunuchs were employed to both guard and manage the affairs of the imperial household, eventually becoming important liaisons among levels of the court and government.

In Tang-period China (617–907) courtly eunuchs became an institution so integral to the structure and functioning of the court, military, and government that these structures and the Tang Empire itself cannot be understood without reference to the institution of eunuchs. The number of courtly eunuchs reached 3,000 during the period of Empress Wu Zetian.[50] While alone in having access to the imperial palace, eunuchs were also involved in running branches of the military. As they could serve as go-betweens between the emperor, the palace household, and the bureaucracy, eunuchs could shape imperial social policy because of the large range of classes with which they were in constant contact. In periods when trust between the emperor, the bureaucracy, the aristocracy, and the military broke down, and as was the case in the late 780s when *Sūtra of the Six Mahāyāna Pāramitās* was translated, the court's eunuchs could aid an emperor in developing a style of personal rule until normalcy returned and the branches of government became more communicative with one another. Another eunuch mentioned in Yuanzhao's description and visible in the text above, is the *Nei-guan* [内官, palace functionary], and eunuch Wang Xiqian [王希遷].[51] The *Zhenyuan Record*, as can be seen in the text above, shows Wang being instrumental in carrying out the work on the retranslated text and orchestrating its placement within the monasteries of the empire.

Though the question of the function of the eunuch corps in imperial Chinese history and in the Tang Empire are vast topics, with an equally vast secondary literature, the question can be taken up in such a way that keeps the focus on the way in which the eunuchs of the Tang brought non-Han into the agency-holding space of imperial activity and the court, and metaphorically speaking and sometimes not, gave them a share in the imperial charisma.[52] Connections forged between ranks of eunuchs, the military, and the Tang court during the An Lushan Rebellion were a crucial step in forming the connections seen above. Before the An Lushan Rebellion Gao Lishi secured the throne for emperor Xuanzong in 710, and as a result was the first eunuch to be awarded the rank of a third-level minister.

As was the case with several other eunuchs in the late Tang period, he held positions in the court and military simultaneously.[53] Though Gao was executed in order to curtail his ability to wield power and shape politics once his usefulness to the emperor Xuanzong was over, the next emperor, Suzong, found eunuchs staffing the court's positions.[54] The An Lushan Rebellion gave the eunuchs working in the Tang court and military a range of new inroads and opportunities. Li Fuguo [李輔国] (d.762) was part of Emperor Suzong's (756–62) entourage, and was given a position to oversee the Yuanshi district Army Cavalry early in the rebellion.[55] Once he proved his usefulness to the court, he was given several positions in the government and military at once, eventually controlled the palace guard, the Jinjun [禁軍], and led this unit against a faction plotting to assassinate the empress. It has been suggested that Li's handling of various offices and at once and staffing them with like-minded eunuchs lead to the 'institutionalisation' of the eunuchs within the late Tang court, a phenomenon that lasted until the end of the dynasty.[56]

The way in which the eunuchs would remain a force shaping the Church of the East's relations with the court, and not simply be a phenomenon of the early 780s, becomes apparent when looking more deeply into the issue of the Shence Army, Shence Jun [神策軍, or Army as Cunning as Spirits], an institution the leaders of which could only be eunuchs.[57] Though the post-An Lushan historical record shows eunuchs holding power positions easily losing their lives when emperors' views of them changed, within the Dezong period eunuchs are seen being pardoned from capital punishment altogether, one indication of the way in which eunuch power and the Shence Army's power and authority had come to support one another. This power is seen in Yuanzhao's account of Adam and Prajña's meeting, and in the *New Tang Record* where it states:[58]

When Daizong came to the throne, in order to rid novices in the army from entering the inner chamber and to clear difficulties, they all [after purging the novices] received the name Bao Ying Gong Jun [an 'Official of Merit thus Granted Reward'] and the Bao Yin Jun [the Army Granted Reward]. In the first year of the Guangde era [763], Daizong, running from Tibet, held the imperial charisma in Xia. Yu Chaoen [i.e 'The Blessing/Grace of the Court'] assembled in Xia, a cavalry, with the *Shence* Army, [which was] a Welcoming Garrison, known and designated as the Army as Cunning as Spirits (*Shence jun*). The Son of Heaven rejoiced in/was intimately part of, its glory. And it stabilised the capital. Yu Chaoen returned the *Shence* Army to the inner chamber, himself leading it, and it became a 'fang' of the army, the likes of which were never seen before.

Though the *New Tang Record* and *Old Tang Record* both go on to indicate Yu Chaoen [魚朝恩] (722–70) was put to death due to infractions against the court, later in the passage the Shence Army leading eunuchs are shown pardoned from capital punishment altogether.[59] The Shence Army was established in 754 to guard the northwestern border.[60] When its base was overrun by Tibetan forces it was sent eastward, and with the start of the An Lushan Rebellion it was enlisted for support in this effort. By 763 it was known as a strong and reliable force.[61] Emperor Daizong [代宗] (762–79) showed his gratitude by incorporating the unit into the Palace Guard, the Jinjun [禁軍]. Yu Chaoen, appearing in the text above, was put in place as the unit's commander.[62] As the Tang court regained strength after the end of the rebellion in 763, for the first time since the collapse of the Fubing [輔兵] system, as studied in the first chapter, the court could now field an army without having to rely on local military rulers around the empire for help, local military rulers who had often proven untrustworthy in recent years. Because of these developments, Yu was able to wield power on the scale that had not been seen among Tang courtly eunuchs since the days of Empress Wu. He was also involved in the Hanlin Academy [翰林院] and choosing policy makers and court advisors.[63] Yu was executed in 770 in order to curtail his power, and though there was a brief respite in eunuch control within the court, in the 780s eunuchs were again back in military positions.

It is now possible to move back to the Yuanzhao *Zhenyuan Record* and note the way in which an understanding of the connections between Eunuch power and the Shence Army enable comprehension of the presence of imperial charisma transmission to the Church of the East in the Dezong period occurring well after the Xi'an stele's 781, but which in turn informs our understanding of currents existing at this early period of Dezong's rule as well. In the following text it is the Zhu Ci rebellion of 783 which is shown to have strengthened the hand of the eunuchs within the Shence Army, thus in the early Dezong court, in turn showing something of the position and agency of the Church of the East. As Yuanzhao writes:

> It was decreed that the Right Flank's *Gongde shi*, Wang Xiqian and the *Shence* Army commander Wang Panbu, would command the cavalry together. And then [in celebration of this], the Buddhist text [of the DLCQ] would be paraded with great fanfare and music and dancing girls, and with cash in form of a thousand bundles of teach and a large amount of incense, would be given. The emperor inspected the great labor undertaken. The *Shence* Army bestowed alms. The same day that the text translation promulgation occurred, in Fengtian the difficulty [The Zhu Ci Rebellion] was settled. The third level rank, Luo Haoxing announced that Wang Xiqian would lead a group of highly skilled in the Western Monastery for the translation project. When Luo Haoxin surrounded Zhu Ci with his meritorious army ... it was a dragon for the emperor. Wisdom holding Haoxin was a leader, and translated with light. The emperor recorded this.

Returning now to the earlier portion of text examined from Yuanzhao's *Zhenyuan Record*, one notes that it shows Prajña coming to China by sea, and through the port in Guangzhou/Canton, and then making contact not just with relatives, which he did, but with one named Luo Haoxin [羅 好心] (737–93). As a eunuch Luo would have had close access to the royal family and have known the emperor since his childhood. During the early reign of Emperor Dezong Luo was also the highest-ranking general in the Shence Army.[64] Given that the eunuchs had more than once, with the aid of the Shence Army, put an emperor back on the throne after having fled incursions to the capital (as happened with Dezong just three years before the translation incident of 787), and given the discussion in the previous paragraphs, it is clear why Dezong would have had a high degree of trust for Luo.

As Yuanzhao tells readers, it was Luo Haoxin who asked Prajña to translate the *sūtra*.

The eunuchs are seen therefore extending the charisma of the Tang emperor and court to the Church of the East not only through their connections to eunuchs, but through the eunuchs' connection to Buddhism – what has been termed the cosmopolitan realm of Sanskrit, and the Yellow Emperor and Humane King ideologies simultaneously.[65] In Yuanzhao's record of the event, Adam and Prajña are shown attempting to translate the *Sūtra of the Six Mahāyāna Pāramitās* from Sanskrit first into an Iranian language (*huben* [胡本]) and then into Chinese. Given that Sogdians had been involved with translating Buddhist texts in this way for centuries, this language was likely Sogdian, and suggests both that Adam may have been far more acquainted with Buddhism than Yuanzhao says, and that it may not have been true that Prajña and Adam had no common language in which to communicate. Sogdian was a *lingua franca* in the period and region, Bactria and Kapiśa were neighbouring city states, making Bactrian or Ghandaran a possibility too, though less likely.[66] What is more important is that Prajña trusted Adam enough not only to undertake the project, but actually to complete it with him and then present the results to Emperor Dezong. This seems hardly possible without a common language, without a high degree of trust and familiarity with one another, and a common network of relatives and expatriate business associates. These connections were facilitated not just by eunuchs but by the eunuchs' connections to central and south Asian cultural networks, the cosmopolitan realm of Sanskrit, *and* eunuchs' ability to represent the Tang emperor as realm protector and the inherent assimilative drive this created for the Tang's non-Han subjects.

These themes are better understood when post-An Lushan Rebellion China's strong independent military governors are taken into account and the way in which independent warlords had become patrons of Chinese Buddhist sects.[67] While the traditions of courtly patronage that had played a role in fostering courtly relations within the Persian-led and Central Asian-based Church of the East and the other religions of the Tang before the rebellion, the mid and late Tang and post-rebellion (An Lushan and Zhu Ci) period is characterised by the development of a popularised forms of Buddhism being tied to courts. This appears to have strengthened ties between the eunuchs, Buddhism and the court. In periods when trust between the emperor, the bureaucracy, the aristocracy, and the military broke down, and as was the case in the late 780s when *The Mahāyāna Sūtra on the Six Parāmitās* was translated, the court's eunuchs could aid an emperor in developing a style of personal rule until normalcy returned and the branches of government became more communicative with one another. Such was the case with Emperor Dezong in the late 780s.

In a society governed by a loose confederation of warlords and a weakened court reeling from the social chaos and dislocation experienced following the An Lushan Rebellion, Esoteric-Imperial Buddhism, with its proclivity towards simple doctrines, social-cohesion-producing rituals, and royal-power-affirming hierarchies, came to be extremely useful to the Tang court's eunuchs and to emperors as a way of strengthening the empire and creating social cohesion within it.[68] For non-Han residing in the Tang Empire with experience in the Tang military, these new developments would predispose them towards interest in 'Repairing the Imperial Net' and having actual opportunities to do so made available to them. This would occur and build upon traditions in which Esoteric-Imperial Buddhist masters garnered a respected place at the Tang court and within Tang society within this social mixture, as occurred with Amoghavajra (Bukong [不空] (705–74), who had a three-day mourning festival declared for him by emperor Daizong following his death.[69] Amogravajra, Vajrabodhi (Jin Gangzhi [金剛智]) (671–741), and Prajña came to China in similar ways and in similar extended family networks, which often included non-Han already living in China.[70] Bukong, Vajrabodhi's disciple, was of mixed Sogdian and Indian parentage, and his connections with the court resemble those of the multicultural Church of the East, something that appears to suggest relations with the Tang court and military for these groups were of a piece a movement making protection of the Tang Empire and its emperor part of their spiritual discipline and its military expression part of their asceticism.

The prayers for rain for the empire's crops, as seen in the Xi'an monument, were performed for the royal house in Esoteric Buddhist rites after the An Lushan Rebellion period, and were also performed for the royal house by Vajrabodhi during the period he was made a

National Teacher (*Guoshi* [國師]).[71] Rituals had been performed by Buddhist sects and various religions within the empire as an aid to end the An Lushan Rebellion, a development that had the oddly paradoxical effect of allowing the Tang's Buddhist sects to become more independent from the government and that allowed them to find patronage among regional warlords.[72] This occurred as Buddhists no longer had to refer to themselves as 'your subject' during court visits, emperors were being enlisted as disciples of the Esoteric-Imperial masters, and warlords in the empire competed with the Tang court for patronage of Esoteric-Imperial masters.[73] The way in which Esoteric Buddhism is shown to have become part of Japan and China's inter-state relations can also be connected to these developments, as shown by Kukai [空海] (774–835) and Ennin [圓仁] (794–864).[74] Residing in a temple within the same foreign quarter as the Church of the East, Ennin provides evidence of the way in which Esoteric-Imperial Buddhism could integrate those of non-Han ethnicity to the largely ethnic Han Empire.[75]

Within these connections the Tang Empire's northeastern corridor should be paid particularly close attention. Emperor Daizong [代宗] (762–69), emperor during the last phase of the An Lushan Rebellion, who preceded Emperor Dezong in the period so crucial to the Church of the East and links to the court through Esoteric Buddhism, is said to have been 'profoundly' influenced by Tantric master Bukong, something that occurred as Uighurs began to be a ubiquitous element within Tang society.[76] Suzong, in receiving an Esoteric Buddhist initiation ritual in effect making him a disciple of his teacher, Bukong, who was thought to have warded off an attack on the capital by Uighur general Puku Huai en [僕固懷恩], was encouraged by devout Buddhist eunuchs in the court such as Wang Jinn [王縉] (700–82), and Yuan Tai [元載] (d.777) (close associate of eunuch Li Fuguo) and Yu Chaoen, in this regard.[77] Mie Nakata and Zenryū Tsukamoto have analysed connections between the Tang court at the start of the An Lushan Rebellion, Sogdians, Esoteric-Imperial Buddhist master Bukong, and the monastic economy. Tsukamoto asserts that during the early period of Dezong's reign, and where the Tang's economy, and monastic orders rebounded, the court's openness to non-Han rose and began once again to follow patterns more in conformity with the pre-An Lushan period, characterized by non-Han Buddhist teachers being given the opportunity to represent the Tang emperor by extending their imperial charisma.[78]

Dezong's Court and Chancellor Li Mi

The opening within the Tang court of imperial charisma and agency to the Church of the East explored thus far can be understood further through an investigation of the rise and effect of Imperial Chancellor (*Zaixiang* [宰相]) Li Mi (722–89). For as Si Maguang indicates, Li Mi shaped the lives of the Tang's non-Han in a profound way in relation to the early court of Dezong by creating an elite space within the court for them.[79] Recent scholarship emphasising Li Mi's influence on changes in Tang foreign policy under Dezong in terms of the opening of diplomatic relations with the Tibetan and Uighur empires allows Nakata's observations that the 787 Imperial Translation incident be studied not just in relation to eunuchs to be expanded upon.[80] This confluence of forces would have given agency and leverage to the Church of the East and can be argued to have been part of its Heavenly Net/Imperial Chord rhetoric.

It is because of Si Maguang's remarks about Li Mi being a superstitious obscurantist that Li Mi's role in the court of Dezong has been overlooked.[81] It is precisely this, however, that must be re-analysed in order for the way in which Li Mi aided the Tang Empire in moving beyond its crippling by the An Lushan Rebellion, and gave agency to the Church of the East as a body of Western-connected elites to be appreciated. Li Mi's religious views and his connections to imperial Daoism must first of all be understood as part and parcel of his influence on Dezong's court; Li Mi had taught Dezong Daoist studies from his youth and at the 'Isles of the Blest Academy'.[82] A lynchpin in the 50 years of experience in government service that Li Mi had accumulated by the time he became chancellor under Dezong, changing Dezong' mind on this issue, was Li Mi's empirical know-how in dealing with the empire's border issues and viewing internal political difficulties as having intrinsic relations to border issues.[83] Li Mi would have seen his service within Dezong's court as an expression of the Yellow Emperor philosophy central to his Daoism.

Setting Si Maguang's description of Li Mi's measures in 787 for dealing with the empire's non-Han next to the two other primary source sites set out below makes this clear:

> Li Mi knew that among the migrants there were some who'd had long resided in Chang'an, even more than 40 years, many had had children and had purchased land and homes, doing business to the point of usury, living comfortably with no desire to return home, command and inspect and take the Hu businessmen who have property and stop their support. We will stop the support for all 4,000 of them. The migrants all go to the government and appeal to it, [and so] Li MI said: 'all of this is due to the errors of the Chancellor, [for] how can it be that a foreign emissary resides at the imperial court for some ten years not accepting [the need, in our view] to return home! At the present time with the route suspended by Uighurs, and the sea route which they were prevented from returning to their country, there is none wanting to return, [and so] at the present time at the Honglu Temple, as they've stated, in order to receive and be installed in a job, and receiving a salary as a Tang official. [Now if] a person takes advantage [of a situation like this] and turns it to their use, would this not result in the migrant's wicked death?' [So since] among these migrants there was none who wanted to return, Li Mi attached them all to the two *Shence* Armies, [as] sons of the King, spreading them out and making them part of either the Cavalry or Government Guards, making them all serve, as this guard. The Honglu Temple was supplied some ten or more individuals, each year saving [the government] expenditures 50,000 strings of cash.[84]

In response to this proposal, at least in the presentation by Si Maguang, the emperor then asked Li Mi about the tactics of government and how they could benefit from these guard units, suggesting Li Mi wielded a high degree of power in Dezong's court at this time. The suggestion has even been made that the influence that Li Mi had on Dezong's court can be compared to that of Esoteric masters on earlier courts and, as has been seen, on Dezong. In the *Old Tang Record*, despite the Confucian-leaning compiler's distaste for

Daoism (and Buddhism), such currents can be glimpsed. It is stated for example that:

Li Mi was inclined on the one hand to giving straight advice, but on the other to the false path of talk of immortal beings, and he 'wandered about' with [figures from ancient Daoist texts such as] and lived in the clouds with Chi Songzi, Wang Qiu, An Qi, and Ji Men. Since he taught things which were without substance, and though he took comfort in superstition, it was not the case that, at the time, this was, by the court, seen as a grave matter. When Dezong first took the throne there were especially bad prognostications being made by the by the official diviners. Earlier on, Suzong had taken seriously speech about Yin and Yang coming from the Temple Prognostication Office, employing sorcerer Wang Yu (d.768) as Chancellor, and commanding a sorceress to ride [with him] in his Swift Carriage in order to create a shock and awe effect. He then completely integrated this [Swift Carriage system] by making it part of the Civil Engineering Office and moving to ban and forbid [the latter]. When Dezong was in the Eastern Palace, he tended to know about such things, and after he took the throne, he ended the gathering of monks at the palace prayer shrine, and ended the rites of prognostication. There was a decree that the Inner Palace be destroyed, and then commanded the work. But the diviner said: with the first moon in the Big Dipper Pole Star, it is not a favorable time for construction. The emperor then said: 'according to the Spring and Autumn Annals, when the cold arrives, is not the Big Dipper is here?' and then the work started. But in the last year of the Jianzhong Era (783), and with the enemy 'on our door step', Sang Daomao spoke of the city of Fengtian, and brought forth a plan to put the palace there, and then elegantly asked Li Mi to extend the palace altar because this was outside his own authority, and moreover such an important task, if he himself talked about it [to the emperor] it would not be satisfactory. So in terms of the debate, eventually he [the emperor] came around, [as] he did not have a leg to stand on from which to speak against this.[85]

This passage indicates clearly the weakness of Dezong's position at the time and the strength of Li Mi's Daoism. Li Mi's keen understanding of Uighur relations and changes taking place between the Uighur and Tibet empires, in which they not only started cooperating with one another but were bringing other adjacent regions into their orbit, has been expertly studied within the scholarship. As the text states:[86]

The emperor again asked Li Mi to respond about tactics for the government troops. Li Mi said: 'with the country dealing with famine and rebellion, and finances being inadequate, and even if there is money we cannot buy grain, let alone have the luxury to support an army'. The emperor then said: 'then what should we do? If we send our troops home and completely reduce them, then what?' Li Mi responded: His Majesty can indeed make use of dialog with his court [and so] not to reduce the troops, not violate the common people, food provisions [not] to be adequate, [and the same for] grain provisions and daily finances, and for the success of the troops'. The emperor then said: with salaries like this, how? It cannot work!' Li Mi said: this is what is necessary to [think about here]: ten more days and time will run out [on our time to act]. At this point Tibet has long been stationed on the plain, make a barrier between them, for cattle to pass to grains, [and] if the grains run out, [the Tibetans] will seize what is not used, and will encourage the emergence within the border lands west a culture which will cause the congealing of side-taking within the upper echelons of the cities. Li Mi [went on] saying: those living on border are too few, and in terms of army officers' monthly rations, [their] grain and wheat is not sold, [and so we] must extend this money, make it much more compared to this year's coffers. The emperor said 'great', and then commanded the plan to be carried out. Li Mi then said, with more officials as sentinels on border, [and by] inviting and increasing support for the entry of grain to supply it, it will be enough for the current year'. The emperor then asked: how will your words rouse the troops?' In response Li Mi said: when troops in the imperial fields have money, this will pacify this area. They will not think of returning. In the old system, the troops were stationed for three years and then changed. Its generals were many. Now we need people to stay longer, and open up fields for cultivation. Families need to go. We will give them provisions. Although the commanders of the Heshuo area are fleeing and passing this fear on to others, they will welcome this news. They won't defect to the Barbarians. And so as the troops will have land, this has logic for the soldiers. This is good for our money woes. The emperor then happily said: 'the empire won't return to having 'incidents'. Li mi said: that is over. The court can no long use China's army for Tibetan causes. The emperor said: will this strategy make peace for us? Li Mi said: the court has already dared to say it, that [by] 'threshing the wheat and grain' will be an effective democratizing measure. The emperor then continued resolvedly in disagreement. Yet Li Mi's intentions were that Uighurs, Arabs and Vietnamese, would together surround Tibet, forcing protecting from Tibet. Knowing that the emperor hated Uighurs, fearing asking him he would not understand, he did not press the issue. But the troop movements went forward.

Li Mi, the Uighur Empire and the Church of the East's Persian *Longue Durée*

Dezong's mistrust of the Uighurs had several sources. It was based partly on witnessing Uighur disregard for Tang social norms and continued marauding after aiding in defeating the An Lushan rebels in 762. It was also based on very direct personal experience. The *New Tang Record* relates that the future Emperor Dezong, then called Li Kuo [李适], the Prince of Yong (*Yong-wang*, 雍王) was asked to perform a ritual dance of submission in front of Khaghan Mouyu (r.759–79) in the year 762 following the defeat of the An Lushan rebels.[87] Though Dezong did not perform the dance, four of the Tang's emissaries were taken captive and two were later killed.[88] Emperor Suzong had thought differently of Uighurs when they became instrumental in restoring him to the throne under General Guo Ziyi and defeating the An Lushan's rebel forces between 756 and 762, but the following two decades were characterised by distrust and non-cooperation between the two empires.[89]

Li Mi had different intentions regarding the Uighur Empire, however. Part of Li Mi's interest in Dezong's court expanding the empire into the northeast in order to counter Tibet and restore the court following the Zhu Ci rebellion relied upon changing the court's position toward the Uighur Empire. The *New Tang Record*, in its two sections devoted to the Uighur Empire, records numerous conversations (creatively imagined by its compiler) between Li Mi and Emperor Dezong, on the running of the empire, conversations often involving Uighurs and Tibetans. A common thread in these discussions, a concern over ritual propriety inter-courtly protocol between the Tang court and the Uighurs, is seen here to have been the means by which Li Mi was able to convince Dezong to change policy with regards to the Uighurs. Following Li Mi's enlisting the benefits of re-establishing diplomatic contact with the Uighurs, the text indicates the following exchange took place:

The emperor said, 'What you say is true, but on the other hand, I cannot possibly disregard Shaohua and the others, so what shall I do?' Li Mi said: I, your subject, consider that it is not you who are disregarding Shaohua, but Shaohua who disregarded Your Majesty. Furthermore, I would say that it was the leader of the Northern Barbarians who came to Your Majesty's assistance. For, when you were heir-apparent and still young, you made light of crossing the Yellow River and entered their camps, which might be called a lair of wolves and tigers. If Shaohua and the others were organising the affair they should first of all have decided on the rites to be followed at the meeting. I, your subject, should even so have thought it dangerous. Why did you go in alone? I was formerly a superior administrator of an expeditionary army under the late emperor [Suzong]. Just then Yehu[90] had come and the late emperor respectfully gave him a banquet, in his own mansion. Even when we were discussing the strategy for battle, he did not give him audience. Yehu summoned me, your subject, to his tent, but the emperor would not allow me to go, and said very politely, 'A host should entertain his guest, but will the guest entertain the host in return?' We went east and retook the capital and made an agreement saying, 'The land and people will return to the Tang, but jade, silk, and children will be conferred on the Uighurs'.

Having fought and conquered, Yehu wanted to carry out a savage pillage. Daizong got off his horse and made him a courteous salute. The Uighurs thereupon went east towards the Lo River. I, your subject, disapproved of the Generalissimo's having saluted Yehu in front of his horse, and thought that it was the fault of the emperor's assistants. But the late emperor [Suzong] said, 'The king's benevolence and filial piety are enough to manage my affairs'. He sent down a proclamation to console and to encourage Yehu, who was the uncle of Mouyu.[91] When Mouyu came to China, Your Majesty, as heir-apparent, did not pay him respect in front of his tent, but the Khaghan did not dare even slightly to infringe the rites towards Your Majesty, and you have never suffered humiliation. The late emperor paid respect to Yehu and saved the capital city.[92]

Visible in the passage is a narrative about the An Lushan Rebellion and the importance of Li Mi within the court as a shaper of the Tang's inter-imperial history, and its ability to move past the An Lushan Rebellion chaos by re-establishing ritual protocol. Liu Haixia suggests that Li Mi's understanding of the situation on the Tang northeastern border and his reassertion of the role of ritual propriety in inter-imperial diplomacy were cut from the same cloth, and ties this to discussions of the Mandate of Heaven appearing in the debate over the Uighurs and the border in precisely the same period and between Li Mi and the emperor as recorded by Si Maguang.[93] Li Mi submits that Emperor Suzong's trust of Uighurs can and should now be emulated because it was Dezong's attaché, Shaohua, who had been in the wrong in the area of ritual propriety, and not the Uighurs. Li says also that his own experience and acumen in dealing with Uighurs is trustworthy, and was on once instance more of a sure guide than Dezong's own judgement. Li Mi thus shapes for Dezong an understanding that the Uighurs had been, and may once again be, part of Tang hegemony, and couches this within a cognizance of the An Lushan Rebellion and the need to move beyond its dark clouds and back to a course steered by earlier emperors and their relations with Central Asian powers.

In terms of the agency the Church of the East arguably held in relation to the court of Dezong and these developments, and as represented in the language of the Xi'an stele singled out for study in this chapter, it is crucial at this juncture to take into consideration the place of the Sogdians as Tang and Uighur intermediaries. Though there are indications that Adam and Yisi's Middle Persian-speaking leaders of the branch of the Church of the East at Chang'an saw themselves as standing above and separate from the church's Sogdian members, this should not be over-emphasised or over-interpreted.[94] The inter-courtly, inter-imperial, and monastic subjectivity of the Sogdians provides access to the agency and self-conception of the Persian Church of the East of the period and context. The *New Tang Record*, in its two sections devoted to the Uighur Empire, indicates that by 780 and Dezong's ascension to the throne, the Sogdians had experienced persecution by the Uighur leader.[95] The same text indicates also that the Tang court knew of the Sogdians' increasing importance in Uighur culture and vital role as intermediaries between the Tang and Uighur courts.

A date between 761–2 stands within the scholarship, i.e. precisely as the An Lushan Rebellion was put down with the lion's share of aid by the Uighurs, for the conversion of Bögü Khaghan's (Mou-yu-ke-ban, 牟羽可半) to Manichaeism.[96] The conversion to Manichaeism by the Uighur leader, occurring simultaneously with the end of the An Lushan Rebellion, was deeply connected to the increase in involvement in Tang politics and society by the Uighurs that occurred during the An Lushan Rebellion, and that the Uighurs wanted to continue afterwards. As Michael Drompp writes of Bögü Khaghan, 'he saw the utility of a centralizing and unifying religion in which he could act as a defender of the faith by linking it to state patronage', a state patronage system that, it should be added, was interlinked with Tang society and its economy.[97] Not only was there no retribution from the Tang Empire in response to the Shaohua incident, in the 760s the Uighurs began receiving ranks in the Tang army, though resentment against them in the court ran deep.[98] Relations between the Tang and Uighur cultures had become so close by this stage that an edict was issued against Uighurs and Sogdians wearing Chinese style clothing.[99] The acceptance of Manichaeism by Uighur leaders also occurred as Uighur began taking Chinese brides; the economy of silk, horses, brides, and patronage gifting grew to a massive scale, and the first Manichaean temples in Uighur territory were built simultaneously with those in the Tang Empire, and where, serving as financial institutions, improvements in Tang–Central Asian commercial relations began to take place following the An Lushan Rebellion.[100]

The Karabalgassun Inscription, the Orkhoun Inscription, and Old Turkic Text M0919 can each be analysed in relation to the Xi'an stele, its language and the post-An Lushan developments in Dezong's court singled out for focus here.[101] Each of these texts contains notions of imperial charisma (OT *qut*) and show Sogdians as an elite body of monks and scholars arrayed around the Uighur courts in *comitatus* fashion, supporting their imperial rulers.[102] Old Turkic M0919 fragment declares the Khaghan to be the embodiment of the sun, with an array of scholars around him sustaining and being sustained by his imperial charisma exemplifies this.[103]

The *comitatus* elements exhibited in the above text can be contextualised in relation to the current discussion in two ways. The first is in connection to the Xi'an stele's reference to Emperor Xuanzong (r.712–46) coming to power and having ordered five princes to visit the East Syrian monastery of Chang'an to establish a *tanchang* {壇場} within the Church of the East's monastic/temple complex, *and* the solar symbolism also associated with this emperor in the monument.[104] Paul Pelliot suggests a translation of 'ordination altar' (*estrade autel*) for this term.[105] Chen Huaiyu adds that the term conforms to what is known of Esoteric Buddhist mandalas: '*tanchang* was a common term in the Chinese literature of Tantric Buddhism, which refers to a mandala, a ritual space for many tantric Buddhist rituals, including meditation, visualization, as well as healing illness'.[106] As the term and item would have been of relevance to the leading seventh- and eighth-century Esoteric masters active in the Tang, figures such as Amoghavajra (Bukong), Vajrabodhi (Jin Gangzhi), and Prajña (Bore), it is possible to say that the uses to which the text associated with the 787 translation incident would have been put, and the kinds of imperial religious activities encouraged within the Tang court by Li Mi, despite Li Mi being ordinarily thought of as a Daoist, would have been part of this universe of meaning as well. The courtly and emperor-centric worldview of the Manichaean Sogdians, which Li Mi's programmes and other political developments were causing to be brought ever closer to the Tang court and courtly religious bodies such as the Church of the East standing in its shadow, is at once better understood, yet also able to shed light on the inter-courtly subjectivity and elite agency of the Church of the East, and thus how terms and phrases like *mdabranoutha*, Persian Monk, and 'sustaining the imperial chord' would have been understood by them.

The second connection requires a return to the *New Tang Record*'s presentation of events as they transpired around Dezong's attaché Shaohua, the Uighurs, and ritual propriety. Here the bringing back of the Uighurs into Tang hegemony is articulated through the garment language of the Xi'an stele and Wu Yun, and as orchestrated by Li Mi, who, informing Dezong on how to think about these matters, notes that:

But Heaven helped you, the imposing and spiritual one, and caused the wolves [the Uighurs] tamely to submit. Bögü Khaghan, like a mother, *wrapped Your Majesty in a sable robe*, cursed those around him and urged some horsemen to escort you back from his camp. This is why I say that it is Shaohua and the others who have disregarded Your Majesty. Supposing Mouyu could be considered to have committed a crime, then the present khaghan has already killed him. The one on the throne [now] is Mouyu's first cousin. This man has done you meritorious service. Can we forget that? Moreover the Uighur Khaghan has engraved a stone and set it up on the gate of his state. It runs, 'Should a Tang ambassador come, let him know that we have in all ways and at all times rendered meritorious service to the Tang'. Now he is making a petition for a marital alliance and will certainly lead his whole tribe south and look at us in expectation. Should you not respond to it, his resentment will certainly be deep Be willing to agree to the marriage. Make an agreement with them on the basis of the former affair of the Kaiyuan period (713–42), that if, like the Tujue Khaghan, he style himself a subject, that if those who come as envoys to China do not exceed 200, that if their horses for trading do not exceed 1,000, and that if they do not take Tang subjects beyond the borders, there will be nothing impossible in the request. The emperor said, 'Very well'. He granted the sending out of a princess to the Khaghan and the Uighurs also begged permission to agree to the conditions.[107]

The reference to the Karabalgassun Inscription in the above passage and Gustav Schlegel's suggestions that vocabulary from the Xi'an stele, along with important figures serving within the Tang army under Guo Ziyi, indicate ways that a post-An Lushan Rebellion narrative is present within the conceptual universe standing behind this passage as well.[108] The mention of Kaiyuan period foreign relations does too. The use of metaphors of clothing and family relations, indicating Bögü Khaghan, 'like a mother', 'robed' the Tang emperor in the clothing of healthy inter-imperial relations, suggests as well the kind of agency standing behind Jingjing's seemingly audacious suggestion that the Church of the East, as a body of non-Han individuals, a religious body that was not part of the three religious of China as commonly thought of, could do this through its asceticism. Given that such thinking would have been encouraged by the Tang's eunuchs and by Li Mi, the suggestion appears less audacious. The level of agency suggested to be held within the Church of the East by taking into consideration these elements within the Tang court and its openness to the Church of the East sharing in its charismatic constitution is certainly more than that attributed to the church by the dhimmitude thesis and by Saeki's notion of emperor worship.

Li Mi, Tibet and Dezong's Imperial Net

The Tibetan court and Tibet's having continually moved closer to the Tang court between 780 and 790 were part of these developments too. Mackerras submits that another reason why Li Mi wanted the marriage alliance with the Uighurs shown in the texts of the previous section was that he hoped it would cause the Uighurs to assist China against the Tibetans.[109] The Zhu Ci Rebellion of 783, which the Tang hoped to quell with the aid of Tibet, yet which did not go as planned, allowed Tibet to encroach further into Tang territory and to take control of Dunhuang.[110] Dezong concluded a pact with Tibet following the Zhu Ci Rebellion, but it was not effective for long, and in 786 war broke out again between the Chinese and the Tibetans.

Plans were made for anther treaty to be concluded on 8 July 787, but the Tibetans used the occasion for further war and even took the Chinese ambassadors prisoner.[111] Denis Twitchett asserts that because the Tang lost its pasture land during the period of Tibetan king Khri Sron lde btsan (r.756–97), the Uighurs became the suppliers of horses for the Tang, and trade with cities such as Merv, Bukhara, and Samarkand (and Balkh?) was eclipsed, making Arab and Persian influence in trade through China's sea ports rise along with Tibetan cultural influence through their control of trade through Gansu and Dunhuang markets.[112]

Such developments have bearing on the inter-imperial agency held by the Church of the East and the language of its Xi'an stele used to express it. Arabic primary sources of the period indicating that one 'ruler of Tibet' from Balkh became a Muslim, an event that Beckwith considers to have been not in an area actually ruled by Tibet but one that was undergoing threat from Tibet, indicating how rulers were seeking backing from the Arabs in order to gain protection from the expanding Tibetan Empire to the Tang's south and southwest.[113] Beckwith has pointed to pieces of data such as the Greco-Roman scientific figure Galen appearing in Tibetan texts as the Church of the East had begun to rise within the Abbasid court as a supplier of court physicians.[114] The letters of Patriarch Timothy I, Tibetan sources and Chinese sources each indicate that as the kingdoms around Tibet were falling into the imperial orbit of both the Arab and Tibetan empires simultaneously, and these two empires were vying, along with the Uighur Empire, for control of the lucrative Silk Road trade leading from Chang'an to Baghdad, the Church of the East was missionising within the courts of the greater region.[115]

A text penned by Southern Chan Buddhist master Wuzhu [無住] (714–74) entitled the *Lidai fabao Ji* [歷代法宝記, *Record of Historical Transmission of the Dharma Jewel*] sheds light on these developments and allows them to be studied more closely. Included in the text is a historical narrative of the transmission of the Dharma of its own school in which Christians and Manichaeans of the Hephthalite Kingdom appear.[116] After a genealogical litany of a dozen names indicating how the Dharma was passed from Shakyamuni Buddha to Shima Bikshu, the immediate heir to Wuzhu's own school, the text reads:[117]

When Sima Bhikshu had transmitted the dharma to Śanavāsa, he then went from central India to Kashmir. The king there was named Mihrakula. This king did not believe in the Buddha dharma — he destroyed stupas, demolished monasteries, slaughtered sentient beings, and honoured the two heretics *Mo-ma-ni* (Mani) and *Mi-she-he* (Messiah, Jesus). At that time Sima Bhikshu purposely came to convert this kingdom and the pathless king with his own hands took up a sharp double edge sword and swore and oath. 'If you are a holy one, the other masters must suffer punishment.' Sima Bikshu then manifested a form where his body bled white milk. Mani and the Messiah were executed, and like ordinary men their blood splatted to the ground. The king was inspired then to take refuge in the Buddha and the disciple of Shima Bikshu to enter south India to preach extensively and liberate beings. The king also made the heterodox disciples of Mar Mani and the Messiah leave.[118]

What is said here of the Hephthalite Ruler Mihrakula (r.513–53) conflicts with the picture of Persian agency within the Church of the East in the *Life of Mar Aba* and the travelogue of Cosmas the India Traveller, who show the Church of the East acting as an arm of the Sasanian state and expanding its territory at precisely the same period.[119] Rong Xinjiang also points to ways that Wuzhu's criticisms of Christians and Manichaeans can suggest agency within the developments transpiring between the Tibetan and Uighur empires and the court of Dezong.[120] Rong notes the phonetics of the terms Mar Mani and Messiah appearing in the Tibetan texts *bka' ya dag pa'i tshad ma las mdo btus pa*, or *Summary of the Proofs of the Right Revelation*, a treatise attributed to the Tibetan king Khri Sron lde btsan (r.756–97), bears similarities to those of the Chinese phonetic spelling for the term Mar Mani.[121] Rong ties this to the effect on both Chinese and Tibetan Buddhism of diplomatic contacts that were established in 765 after the establishment of the first post-An Lushan peace treaty. As Rong indicates, manuscripts found at Dunhuang show that Tibetans began to transcribe and translate Wuzhu's Zen manual into Tibetan, and the teams of official translators involved stayed in cities such as Lingzhou 靈州, and Chengdu 成都, associated with Wuzhu's Tang Protection Temple (*Baotang si* 保唐寺) and Wuzhu's Zen response was being developed in response to the Esoteric-Imperial Buddhism already present in the Tang Buddhist world.[122] According to Rong, Wuzhu's positioning of Manichaeans and Christians in a historical narrative linked to the former Hephthalite kingdom (Bactria), as well as Wuzhu's links to the Shence Army, Guo Ziyi, and Uighurs, which he shared with Yisi and Jingjing's Xi'an-based Church of the East, sheds light on the prevalence of the 'rich and distinguished' Church of the East along the trade routes linking Tibet, Bactria, and the Tang court and the need for Tang Buddhists, also attempting to be part of the national protection ideology, to compete with it and to try to stem its influence.[123]

Tibet's encroachment into Tang territory and the resultant gain in agency for the Central Asian- and Perso-Mesopotamian-connected Church of the East are illuminated further by arguments put forth by David Wilmshurst for why the Xi'an stele and its community burst onto the stage of history at this time, and in the imperialised guise that they do.[124] He suggests the monument was an imperial showcase and a 'travel book' of sorts. He points out that the Xi'an monument emphasised its imperial connections in numerous ways – visits from past emperors, a recent emperors' calligraphy – and would have been a suggestion of more of the same found inside the monastery next to which the monument stood. These pieces of information would have reminded the Chinese literati who read the monument that the Jingjiao group was loyal at a time when many non-Han, especially those with connections to Persian religions, as well as the Tibetan, Arab, and Uighur empires, were undergoing suspicion of disloyalty and Buddhist leaders were also being patronised by the empire's independent warlords.[125] Wilmshurst argues that Jingjing, as a Bhandata (*Dade*, 大德) in the Church of the East, accomplished under his tenure the creation of something of a united front, a renewed public face for the church, part of which involved a streamlining of terminology used to refer to the church, the region it came from, and the name of Christianity.[126]

Wilmshurst's thesis is based largely on Xuanzong's official decree in 745 that the name of the Christian monasteries of the Tang Empire should be called 'Syrian monasteries', Daqin si, rather than 'Persian monasteries', in order to reflect more accurately the origin of the Christian religion. Wilmshurst's argument is that under the leadership of Jingjing an attempt was made to streamline the term used for the Christian religion in order to bring this terminology in line with official Tang usage and to present a more unified and imperially consonant public face for the church. Accepting Wilmshurst's postulations involves accepting a scheme for re-dating several of the Jingjiao texts. Two Jingjiao texts, *The Hymn in Adoration of the Transfiguration of Our Lord* (*Daqin jingjiao dasheng tongzhen guifa zan*, 大秦景教大聖通真歸法贊) and the *Book of the Origin of Origins* (*Daqin jingjiao xuanyuan ben Jing*, 大秦景教宣元本 經), have ending segments including text that indicates they were written, or at least copied, in the early eighth century. Wilmshurst has suggested, however, that the appearance of the term Jingjiao for the Church of the East's religion in these texts indicates that the texts were recopied after the edict in 745 stipulating the name of the religion be changed to Daqin Jingjiao.[127] Wilmshurst also points out that among the 35 books referred to in *Zun Jing* [*The Book of Praise*, 尊經], one of the documents found, importantly, in Dunhuang in 1908 and which is a list of texts used by the church, there are four books mentioned that have versions or copies that have also been recovered in the same caves at Dunhuang. These four books are the *Zhi xuan an le Jing* [*Book of the Secret of Peace and Joy* 志玄安樂經], the *Daqin jingjiao xuanyuanben Jing* [*Book of the Origin of Origins* 大秦景 教宣元本經], the so-called *Daqin jingjiao sanwei mengdu zan* [*Hymn in Adoration of the Holy Trinity* 大秦景教三威蒙度贊], and the so-called *Daqin jingjiao dashen tong zhen gui fa zan* [*Hymn in Adoration of the Transfiguration of Our Lord*, 大秦景教大聖通真歸法讚]. The *Zun Jing* is worth looking at in full on this point, for as it states:

Regarding the list of books, there are altogether 530 religious works of our church of Syria [Daqin], and they are all on patra leaves in the Syriac language. In the 9th Zhengguan year (635) of the emperor Daizong Bishop (sic) Aluoben came to China and presented a petition to the emperor in his native language. Fang Xuanling and Wei Cheng made known the interpretation of the words of his petition. Later by imperial order Bishop Adam of this church translated the above thirty rolls of books. The majority are on patra leaves or on leather in wrappers and have not been translated.[128]

Wilmshurst points out that if these books were written by Aluoben, as the ending segment found in the *Book of Praise* says they were, Christianity would not be referred to as Daqin Jingjiao, as the titles of these four works clearly state. Notes in the manuscripts of the *Hymn in Adoration of the Transfiguration of Our Lord* and the *Book of Origin of Origins* indicate they were produced in the Daqin temple. This suggests that these ending notes were added after 745, along with the terms Daqin Jingjiao, 'the Syrian Brilliant Teaching', in Wilmshurst's phraseology, which appear in the titles, though some of these texts bear earlier internal dates.

Wilmshurst's arguments are helpful in understanding the degree of imperialisation that was taking place in the late eighth century and that the Church of the East was extending its Persian legacy in the Tang Empire, just as was taking place in the Abbasid Empire. This would not only improve the public face of the church and make it appear that it and the imperial house were on close terms, it would force all others in the Church of the East's hierarchy in China to follow suit in their use the terminology of Jingjiao, a suggestion not contrary to the thrust of the arguments put forth by Barrett and Zhang on the name change as well.

Wilmshurst's thesis also sheds light on the issue of courtly agency being held by Yisi and Adam's Middle Persian identified group of elites in connection not just to links being maintained between the Church of the East and the Tibetan empire, but also the Arab and Uighur empires and the inter-courtly asceticism the church saw itself engaging in as reflected in the language from the Xi'an stele held up for analysis here. The final portion of the *Book of Praise* clearly indicates that Jingjing had been invited by Emperor Dezong to translate Christian texts into Chinese. Based on the arguments outlined in brief above, Wilmshurst makes the assumption that these texts were sent to Dunhuang because of the likelihood that Chinese versions of these Syriac texts already existed before Jingjing translated them anew in the imperial translation bureau. As Wilmshurst writes:

> The puzzle is to explain how it was possible for the Kaiyuan[129] documents, as I shall call them for convenience, to be translated at Dunhuang in the early 8th century, when Aluoben's Syriac text of

these lay neglected in Chang'an's imperial library; and why it was necessary for Adam/Jingjing to translate these two works into Chinese in the 780s, as the *Book of Praise* implies he did, when Chinese versions already existed at Dunhuang. I can only conjecture what might have happened. Obviously some of Aluoben's Syriac scriptures existed in China in more than one manuscript, and the monks at Dunhuang in the early eighth century had their own text of these two works. Adam, working in the imperial library at Chang'an sixty years later, probably translated Aluoben's Syriac originals in Chinese without realizing that translations had already been produced in far-off Dunhuang. Later, as the *Book of Praise* implies, he sent Chinese translations of thirty five Syriac works to Dunhuang and his new translation of the Kaiyuan documents were among them. The Dunhuang monks were evidently unwilling to destroy their Chinese translations and replace them with Adam's, and it is their version which survived, but in a copy made in the 780s.[130]

Understanding Adam/Jinging, who was likely bilingual in Chinese in Persian and who possibly read or had facility in Syriac, Arabic, and Bactrian/Sogdian, and given the involvement of Adam in the 787 translation incident, this assertion of prominence within the Xi'an Church of the East group and its dominance over the other outposts of the church does not seem far-fetched, and can be further supported through an analysis of the issue of science within the church's imperial patronage.

Divine Economy and the Late Tang Empire's Non-Han, Scientific Families

The topic of foreign religions in China has long been investigated through the study of the perceived use of science within missionising efforts, and more specifically, the perceived use of science as a way to gain access and leverage at China's imperial courts.[131] Though the courtly leverage obtained by the Church of the East in the late Tang Empire and its imperial identity can be approached in a number of ways, there are four solidly empirical bases upon which such a study should begin: 1) the references in Tang literature to Daqin as a place that produced good physicians;[132] 2) Yisi's twice being identified in the Xi'an stele as a physician;[133] 3) elements within the Xi'an stele having to do with imperialised astronomy/astrology and medicine;[134] and 4) the Church of the East's known connection to the Abbasid court as a supplier of court physicians, a *longue durée* that was built upon Sasanian foundations.[135] The chapter's final treatment of its themes – i.e. the 'Divine Economy' designation appearing within the Xi'an stele and the Church of the East as a monastic-ascetic, elite-led, Persian-Mesopotamian social body, sharing in an ability to transmit the imperial charisma of the court of Dezong as a post-An Lushan Rebellion institution, can be investigated in relation to these scientific issues. There are data sources, five pieces of epigraphy (beyond the Xi'an stele), in which the theme of family appears in such a way as to offset the strongly imperialised nature of the Church of the East's monasticism (i.e. one lacking agency and independence from the court). These are the Luoyang stele,[136] the gravestone epitaphs (*muzhiming*) of Sogdian Tang functionary Mi Jifen [米繼芬] (713–805)[137] and Tang astronomers Li Su [李素] (729–817) and 'Guatauma' Zhuan (Qutan Zhuan, 瞿曇譔) (711–76),[138] the so-called 'Pahalavi Bilingual Inscription' from early ninth-century Chang'an,[139] and the Middle Persian Christian gravestone from Constantinople.[140] Though not all of these pieces of data stem directly from the Church of the East or have connections to the role of early medieval science in imperial patronage, when taken together they illustrate the way in which long durational Persian Christian family lineage functioned in conjunction with monasticism and as part of the identity-creation mechanisms associated with the 'Divine Economy', 'Persian monk', and 'Imperial/Heavenly Net' designations within the Xi'an stele and as part of a set of historical changes taking place within and in relation to the court of Tang Dezong.

Nie Zhijun [聶志軍] has perspicaciously studied the Xi'an stele's references to Yisi as a physician and the benefit to the Tang Empire during the An Lushan Rebellion alleged by the stele stemming from his imperial service as a court physician.[141] Nie has made two particularly important contributions to the scholarship on the issue. One is to emphasise that there is not one but two references to Yisi's standing within the Tang court and the court's recent history as a physician.[142] The second reference, being far less obvious than the first, is ably studied by Nie through the use of statistical analysis and corpus linguistics, resulting in an analysis showing that the modifying phrase *shi quan* [十全] within the sentence *yi bo shi quan* [藝博十全] appears with high frequency in classical Chinese medical works such as the *Huang Di Nei Jing* [黃帝內經 or *Yellow Emperor's Inner Canon*].[143] The phrase refers to Yisi's being 'effective' (*shi quan*, 十全) not just within the court in general, but as an imperial physician; and does not merely indicate the empty praise thought by some interpreters, or a vague and undirected reference to the 'complete' or 'excellent' nature of Yisi's medical arts.[144] Secondly, Nie's wrestling with the issue of whether Yisi could have been a monk, as the stele seems to indicate, and his assertion that Yisi could not possibly have been a monk and a court physician at the same time, though likely incorrect, sheds light on several important issues.[145] First is that the agency the Church of the East wished to assert for itself and its self-understanding as a new type of courtly and monastic body is better understood. This is an agency in which the priests of the church could be courtly functionaries and monastics at the same time, could marry, could uphold Esoteric-imperial Buddhist traditions associated with militant eunuchs and with Daoist chancellors and their thaumaturgy. They could offer the Tang court inter-courtly and inter-imperial connections to Central Asia as part of the 'thread' (*xu*, 緒) of 'elites' (*gui*, 貴) from the Jincheng area (i.e. as *Jinfang guixu*, 金方貴緒) and who 'came from afar, the royal city of Balkh' [*yuan zi wangshe zhi cheng*, 遠自王舍之城] (using language similar to that used of Jilie and Aluoben) in which an East Syrian householder monastic and imperial functionaries entered the Tang Empire, 'repairing/sustaining' its Imperial/Heavenly Net, before the An Lushan Rebellion.[146]

Shedding further light on this agency are texts compiled in the Tang period such as the *Yellow Emperor's Inner Canon*, showing medicine to have been an imperial affair and under the purview of the Chinese emperor and court. The fact that the Tang Code, the *Tanglu shuyi* [唐律疏議], declared a punishment of two years' imprisonment at state labour camps for any private householder owning planetary almanacs, charts and texts about the sky, and oracular or military texts, shows that medicine and astronomy were under similar strictures.[147] The astronomy seen within the Xi'an stele, simultaneously imperially Chinese and Persian, already raised as an issue in several places within the book, bears particular importance in connection to this issue as well as to Saeki's 'emperor worship' thesis and the dhimmitude thesis holding sway in some of the Syriac scholarship.[148] This discussion can be furthered in reference to the stele's reference to *Da yao sen wen* [大耀森文], the Great Sunday.[149] The use of this phrase within the stele has been argued by Pelliot to stem from the prestige of foreign astronomy (Iranian, i.e. Persian and Sogdian, as well as Indian) in the eighth century Tang Empire and the spread of the nine planetary system early in that century due to the influence of astronomers from these backgrounds.[150] Pelliot asserts that the Middle Persian heritage of Adam and Yisi led to Adam not referring to Sunday in the Sogdian manner (Christian, Manichean or other), who would have used the character *mi* 密/蜜, a transliteration of the Sogdian word *mīr* (Sunday), linked to the Iranian goddess Mihr, a usage which made its way into common Chinese parlance for the days of the week lasting into the nineteenth century.[151] However, Saeki's dhimmitude thesis can be countered as well as engaged through this theme, as can an argument be made that monastic elites within the Church of the East, as an institution in which foreign families holding skills in the Tang Empire that were held and passed on over long stretches of time, by arguing that this is something that both gave and depleted agency, i.e. made them elites, but did not make them *dhimmis* or on an inevitable path of self-eradication within the Tang Empire and in relation to the Tang' court and culture.[152]

One particularly relevant phrase in the stele in this regard is the phrase *zhanxing xianghua wangri chaozun* [瞻星向化, 望日朝尊] and its connections to imperial Chinese astronomy.[153] This statement is made in relation to Jilie, and not Yisi, and might at first appear unconnected to astronomy. Pelliot and Deeg indicate ways in which this statement is an acquiescence to the Tang Empire as a realm of culture and transformation. An equation is made in the phrase with the east as the place of the rising sun, and China as the realm of culture *par excellence*,[154] and the west as the place where the sun sets, and by extension the place where a lower, barbarian, level of culture held sway.[155] The potential difficulty, that this has nothing to do with astronomy or medicine, disappears however when it is noted that what is said of Jilie here is similar to what is said of Yisi and Aluoben, both of whom are shown bringing scientific skill to the Tang Empire. The terms *shu* and *yi* (術 and 藝) used of Yisi have to do with 'arts/skills' that could include divining, medicine, and prognostication, as well as military arts.[156] If the emperor sat as a *primus inter pares* within the court, and as the symbolic head of a group of imperial functionaries whose skills held the empire in place given the spread of the new Nine Planetary System superimposed over a long held classical Chinese tradition, elites from India, Central Asia, and the West, seen as acting as satellites/planets sustaining the sun which in turn sustained the cosmos understood metaphorically as the Tang Empire, could well be a mindset that generated the phrase 瞻星向化, 望日朝尊.

The agency this mindset may have been linked to within the elite mentality of the Church of the East's leaders and in Adam can be investigated further by looking to the way in which scientific skills were passed on within families, and on a long durational basis, in the period and context. A comparison between the Barmakid family, hailing from Bactria, and the Church of the East as a familial and ascetic body under the Abbasids and Sasanians, was made in the previous chapter. The familial character of the Xi'an stele community is after all not only quite pronounced, Yisi and his son Adam were also clearly part of a family identifying themselves as part of a Middle Persian heritage, who stood upon a heritage in which Sasanian restoration hopes had once flourished, and which may well currently have existed in relation to hopes about Church of the East leadership having a degree of independence under the Abbasids. Looking to the strong connection between family and Persian heritage within Syriac Christianity in the Middle Persian Christian inscription from post-Sasanian Constantinople, expertly studied by Francois de Blois, and where the expatriate church is referred to as part of the 'house' (*mān*) of Êranšahr, add to this, as does the proud display of Persian heritage, though not Christian, in connection to Tang military offices, seen in the so-called Pahalvi bilingual inscription from Xi'an.[157] This set of connections is bolstered further when noting that Duke Guo Ziyi held the position of a *Jie-du shi* [節度使] in the Shuofang [朔方] region, an area in which the Shence Army was highly active in the period. The Jiedu shi were given enormous power, including the ability to maintain their own armies, collect taxes, and pass their titles on hereditarily as a type of tax collector and hiring agent for the Tang military, which was stationed in the western regions. The agency and power such ability could foster is seen in that An Lushan was a Jiedu shi. The Xi'an monument indicates that Yisi, in addition to being the donor, the *Daxu zhu* [大施主], of the monument and having the capital to afford such an amenity, served as a general W*ujiang* [武将] under Guo Ziyi while Guo was in this position.

Another piece of data, one pertaining more closely to the issue of the passing on of scientific skills within non-Han families within the Tang, is the gravestone and epitaph of Persian astronomer Li Su, discovered in 1981.[158] Though it is not certain that Li Su was part of the Church of the East, contrary to Rong Xinjiang's assertions,[159] the gravestone has much to say about the Persian character of the Church of the East's interactions with the Tang court, how these were mediated by family structures, and the ascetic cultivation that existed within the church's inter-imperial culture and within its leadership (*mdabranoutha*), and the Persian leadership within the Tang church as seemingly asserted within the Xi'an stele.[160] The growth of the Church of the East during the early Abbasid Empire, and in connection to the translation movement, and the long durational asceticism seen resulting from it, is spoken to in this regard as well. Li's grave marker indicates that he is a scion of Persian royalty. He became the head of the Tang astronomy bureau in 762, at the culmination of the An Lushan Rebellion. The text of the Li Su's grave marker refers repeatedly to his mastery within the Tuo-bai School of astronomy, refers to him having been a diviner, involved in the art of *wujian* [巫减], which are skills that cannot not have been employed or come into contact in some way with the An Lushan Rebellion.[161] Li Su's son was a *Shuofang* [*Jiedu shi*], further indicating connections to the circles inhabited by the Church of the East, and served within the *Kai fu yi tong san* [開府儀同三], an arm of the Tang bureaucracy associated with Persian General Aluohan. The gravestone refers repeatedly to the 'elite glory' [*ronggui*, 榮貴] bestowed upon Li by the court.

Another astronomer who worked in the Tang bureaucracy during Dezong's formative period as a prince and heir to the throne, and an observer of the court's handling of the long An Lushan Rebellion, was Indian astronomer Guatauma Zhan [Qu Tan, 瞿昙]. Qu Tan stood within the court upon a long durational family lineage in the way that Li Su and Yisi/Jingjing did, and in a way that sheds light on the subjectivity and agency they held and experienced as non-Han elites. Qu Tan was the fourth in a line of sons serving an Official Director [太史監府君] of the Astronomical Bureau [司天監], a position he clearly lost and regained in connection to his service as Prognostication Officer [*Shishi*, 筮仕], and his being a holder of a degree in the martial arts [*wuju*, 武举], and most importantly, in connection to the An Lushan Rebellion.[162] Qu Tan received the Purple-Golden Fish Pouch upon being reinstated, an award also given to Yisi at close proximity in time. The 'emperor' is said to be 'currently sitting upon the throne with the Imperial/Heavenly Net of the Empire restored' [今上登寶位，正乾綱] in this text, using language similar to the Xi'an stele, and for which said recipient was given the same prestige title as that of Yisi, the Grand Master of Imperial Entertainments with Silver Seal and Ribbon. That Qu Tan shows something of the subjectivity of the Tang's non-Han elites and the families in which they cultivated skills in the shadow of the court and their homelands simultaneously in the period of the court of Dezong, following the rise of Li Mi, is further attested in the fact that the writer of the epitaph was connected to the *tuntian* [屯田], lands held by the crown that were expanded by Li Mi in order to counteract Tibetan influence, a fear Qu Tan helped alleviate, as the gravestone refers to Tibet as well and Qu Tan's roles in counteracting it.[163] Qu Tan's observations of the wind and stars setting the Chinese Empire aright, as stated in the gravestone, is reminiscent of what is said of Aluoben in the Xi'an stele.

Family *longue dureé* constituted an arena of asceticism within the Church of the East and the elite non-Han cultural matrix in which it was embedded, one that in turn mediated the church's relations with the Tang court. Two pieces of epigraphy related to the Sogdian branch of the late Tang Church of the East, the Mi Jifen gravestone and the Luoyang stele, bear witness to this phenomenon and chart its contours. The former shows poignantly, for example, the way in which Mi's family relied upon the Church of the East's monastic institutions and institutions connected to the Tang court and military in order to instil leverage and agency within the family *habitus*. The Mi epitaph, for example, reads:

> The duke had two sons, the eldest was called Advance the Country, and was placed within the Spiritual Army on the Right of the Court and served the General Ningyuan, and protected the capital. The other son was called monk Siyuan and lived at a Church of the East monastery.[164]

Between these two boys existed the subjectivity associated with the late Tang's eunuch's and the world view of Jazbōzēdh and Adam, one where the Chinese imperial monastic unit, as a courtly appendage, was part of the larger *comitatus* of the Tang court itself, an entity undergoing continuous change in the period of Dezong as this court led the empire out of a 30-year period of rebellion and in which the Church of the East's connections to Central Asia had to be reconstituted and its asceticism reflected these connections.

The Luoyang stele, discovered in 2006, extends what can be said of this phenomenon.[165] Though the scholarship on the Loyang stele has termed its commentary on the nature of family within non-Han residing in the Tang to have been 'Sinicised', in its importation of Confucian notions of filial piety, that East Syrian monasticism, extended family notions, and merchant power can be seen working in tandem in the stele allows the stele's long durational components to be seen as well.[166] The abbot of the local monastery and head monks holding the Bhadanta rank have attended the burial ceremony, as seen in line 41 of the Luoyang stele; the extended family has come from afar, and the souls of the living within the family stand together with the souls of the departed within the family, as seen in line 39; holders of rank within the Tang military have rounded out the necessary display of social capital, as seen in lines 38 and 41. The solar symbolism through which the existential hopes associated with East Syrian Christianity in the text writer's mind negates any perceived lack of agency in the Xi'an stele in association with solar symbolism in connection with the Chinese emperor. Ensuring that this piece of epigraphy stems from the same larger community as that of the Xi'an stele, and the same Tang imperial milieu, is the Xi'an stele list of dozens of names of monastics in its final portion, who certainly came from a range of backgrounds. The long durational agency given to the Church of the East through Li Mi's proposals of the late 780s and later, the continued rise of the Church of the East in relation to the rise of the Baghdad church, and the presence of Sogdians in the Uighur Empire, adds further to what can be said of the agency existing behind this piece of epigraphy and in relation to family and ascetical nature of it.

A passage from the Dunhuang document stemming from the Church of the East referred to as the *Zhixuan anle Jing* [志玄安樂經, Book on Mysterious Peace and Joy], can be interpreted in light of the foregoing discussion and the theme of ascetic agency negotiated and gleaned in relation to the Tang court and military and the practice of science within familial long durational structures. As a portion of the text reads:[167]

> The Messiah[168] spoke again: if there is again someone who is going to join the army, then armor and weaponry[169] must be provided him so that his body will be protected. Having this solid armor and weaponry, the soldier will not have no fear of the enemy and thieves. Only this Religion of Jing is the supreme law of success [in this regard]. It can protect all creatures from the worries and troubles, like the armor and weaponry which protests the soldier's body. If there is again someone who is going to sail across the sea, then a ship must be provided for him so that he can sail through the wind and waves. If the ship is broken, then he will not reach the other side of the sea. Only the religion of Jing is the supreme law of success [in this regard]. It can help all living being to sail across the sea of life and death and to reach the other side of the stream where there is peace, joy, treasures and scents. If there is someone who has caught a pestilent disease, then this disease is spread to many others who then die. However upon smelling the precious sent and the mysterious air of the returning spirit, the souls of these dead shall return to life and their diseases and suffering will be rid of. Only the religion of Jing is the supreme law of success [in this regard]. If you men and women follow my words and practice the élite monastic way industriously, meditate on the law day and night, then you shall stay away from all pollution and have the real nature of purity and peace. You shall

have clear and complete wisdom that is to know that this person shall be saved. So you know that this teach will bring you profit. When all the angels follow it, they have no limit in the real realm. When people believe in love and practice this religion of non-doing, they will have no worry about difficulties when the road is bright. They will not encounter catastrophe when the road is dark. They can have peace and joy even in a foreign land and in different places. Then do not mention about practicing this religion with all efforts. You disciples and all other listeners, go into the world and carry out my teachings. Then you can help the kings to protect their borders. If is like a fire on the high mountain which can be seen by all the fellow countrymen. The élites and the kings are like that high mountain. The profit which my teaching can bring can be compared to this big fire. If the teaching can be practiced, then it shall be like a light which shines naturally.

Though it is impossible to locate this text within a specific time frame within the post-An Lushan period Tang Empire, the use of the term Jing for the Church of the East's religion indicates a provenance of post-745.[170] The text speaks of Jingjiao's ability to offer bodily healing to self and others, the Church of the East's elites' ability to cultivate asceticism in such a way that fosters healing within the Tang Empire, and in turn acceptance with the Tang Empire and as part of Tang imperial ideology. These notions are couched within references to service at the Tang court and within the Tang army.

The references to mountains in the passage and in connection with elites and kings can be understood in connection to the phrase 少分修行 [non-exerted asceticism], suggested as bearing relation to Laozi's famous notion of *wuwei* [無為, non-doing], and which suggests the world Li Mi opened to the church's elites in the late 780s and after. The Daoist mountain tradition became a central part of Tang political and religious life and during the period of Xuanzong, when Daoist influence reached its greatest influence in all of Chinese history. Rituals in which emperors visited China's sacred mountains with their Daoist monasteries, retracing the Yellow Emperor's imagined parallel voyage, reached new heights then. However, the inter-imperial, inter-courtly, and long durational Persian agency that was given to the Church of the East during the reign of Dezong was added to by the eunuchs and Li Mi. The rise of a zone of cultural mediation between Chang'an and Dunhuang in this period, as seen in the previous chapter, aided and abetted by Tibet and the Uighurs, shows how Li Mi's directives have existed within a larger context of increasing agency for the church, and as seen in Wushu's narrative of the perils of Christianity and Manichaeism being part of late Tang imperial social space, is likely present in this text as well. That a vision of science exists in which the Church of the East as a social body able to commandeer its practice with agency, one that counters the perceived lack of agency in the Xi'an stele's scientific elements, and appearing more like the vision of scientific and familial agency seen in the Li Su and Qu Tan gravestones and in conformity with the ascetically and elite-led church under Timothy I, is beyond doubt.

CONCLUSION

This book has argued that the closeness existing between the Church of the East and the late Sasanian imperial court, a subject of intense scrutiny in recent secondary literature and amply evident in Syriac sources, was carried into the Tang imperial setting. Though it changed over time, this closeness informed and shaped the Church of the East's relation with the Tang court and emperors, repositioning this within our analyses of the Christian texts stemming from the Tang Empire, among which the Xi'an stele is and will always be of paramount importance, and where Persian and courtly elements have long lain underinvestigated and whose Sasanian trajectories have not been appreciated.

In order to make this argument the study has analysed and sought to hold together three elements within the Xi'an stele (and related sources):

(1) the stele's 'together repair(ing) the Imperial Net' (*gong zhen xuangang*) reference;

(2) the designations 'Persian Religion' (*Bosi jiao*) and 'Persian monk' (*Bosi seng*) seen in Tang sources; and

(3) the Xi'an stele's reference to Divine Economy (Syr. *mdabranoutha*). The study has also been an extended justification for the interpretation 'Imperial Net' offered for phrase *xuangang*, of the Xi'an stele, and a simultaneous engagement with Saeki's 'emperor worship' thesis and an argument that the political theology standing behind the Xi'an stele can be best ascertained through

the use of Cultural History as an interpretive tool and as an aid in tracing this theology back to Sasanian Persia and the church's political disposition in Central Asian Bactria/Balkh. Each of these interests has served the other and they have ultimately been part of the argument that the Church of the East stood with agency in the Tang court and that this agency could be connected to its Persian past, and past and continuing ascetic character, even if not at every turn – i.e. at times one winds up analysing simply agency within the church and the Tang court's relations rather than 'Persian agency' or 'ascetic agency'.

Classical Chinese sources, telling us *xuangang* is identical to the word *tiangang* [天網], are a first step into this fertile ground in which the local context of the Chang'an Church of the East can be read against the primary source record in Syriac and Greek (and to a lesser degree) Arabic, Iranian, and Turkic materials, in order to address Saeki's assertions about 'emperor worship' and its ultimate effects on the church's standing in China. Recent developments in the cross-cultural study of early medieval, Central Asian courts, such as Beckwith's employment of the *comitatus* paradigm and the historical data analysed accordingly, provide another avenue for countering Saeki, and resonate well with Cultural History's interest in seeing markers of identity and structures of power as centred within the realm of culture. Bourdieu's notion of *habitus*, a part of the Cultural History framework and resonant with Late Antiquity's interest in the 'holy men' and with recent historiography's theorisations of courts and elites, aids in this argument against Saeki as well. The reading of primary sources offered in response draw from the Church of the East's connections to the Sasanian court and are shown to have facilitated the court's move into Central Asia after the Sasanians' fall, as continued and mediated by the church's known and observable connections to the Chinese court.

The study of Christianity in the Tang period is now gifted with two monograph-length commentaries on the Xi'an stele. A number of important articles coming out of the Salzburg conferences extending our understanding of the Xi'an stele's context stand alongside these two studies. The research literature on the place of Syriac Christianity within and as an extension of the Sasanian state is now well developed. It is now time to begin looking more widely and synthetically in order to understand the Christian political consciousness and identity matrix existing in the fifth- to ninth-century Church of the East – clearly one of its golden ages. Researchers need to look not just at the immediate context of the Xi'an stele to understand this, but to the long durational and paradoxically imperial identity of the church, and at how this changed through the period and held sway in an emergent fashion, i.e. held sway in more than one court at once. There was a stable early Tang period, one in which Tang hegemony was expanding and Persian culture was being absorbed into China. There was a later, far less stable period too, following the Abbasid revolution and An Lushan Rebellion, in which this earlier continuity and social formation was being transformed. The Church of the East's ascetic tradition as read at once through the church's connections to the fallen Sasanian house after 651 and the lens of Cultural History offers an avenue for exploration of the continuity and transition existing within the church within this context. Though contemporary scholarship in Religious Studies can be overly concerned with questions of agency and identity, thus losing sight of the need for empirical rigour, questions of agency and identity are inescapable when discussing Christians living under non-Christian rule. Using the *comitatus*, *habitus*, and charisma paradigms to analyse the three elements from the Xi'an stele in order to probe the primary source data with an eye to the way in which the courts of the period and region were open to their charisma being shared by elites allows for an exploration of Christian identity and agency that avoids overly modernising ways of reading the historical record as the repository of the thoughts and feelings individual actors who look and feel 'just like us'. At the same time, the danger of being overly concerned with religion, which, after all, as seen in Saeki's misconstruals, can pit individual identity against royal and courtly identities and dispositions, can be avoided too. The concern with Christian identity under early Arab rule is, of course, not simply the purview of the secular academy, but is of more existential concern to scholars connected to Christian communities. The Cultural History-derived focus on agency carried through the book suggests to both camps that agency and identity among Tang Syriac Christians can be discussed as a function of courtly elites and their Persian *longue durée*, and not the sole purview of individual actors, as a facile importation of the modern, Lockean self, would dictate.

Not every stone has been left unturned above, and the choice to focus upon certain subthemes and individual elements in support of the larger and rather sweeping narrative offered here excludes others. Starting from the late Tang context and working backwards, Li Su and Jazbōzēdh, two key figures in the conceptualisation of the subjectivity at the centre of the study, may have connections to Indic and Buddhist traditions in Dunhuang worth exploring. Sasanian traditions may be shown to be secondary to understandings of kingship stemming from Indic-influenced Central Asia, though that their courtly asceticism shows similarities and is connectable to the *zhen xuangang* phrase is a notion that will stand. Li Su's links to Esoteric Buddhism and the Tang military and the astrology that appears in the Xi'an monument might yield results through this connection. Links to similar patterns occurring within kingship in Tibet, Uighur Manicheans, China, and Abbasid-influenced polities at the same time, a research agenda already underway in the scholarship, though a vast undertaking, might be further connected to the culture of the fighting units of China's northeastern provinces and post-Abbasid Revolution Central Asia beyond what has been drawn out here. The way in which the Tang's Buddhist groups responded to the post-An Lushan context and how this is reflected in the period of Emperor Dezong may be researched more extensively to provide new insight on the stele's imperial Christian theology, the church's participation in the Tang *comitatus* and the elite subjectivity and Persian-ascetic *longue durée* standing behind it. The *Jingjiao* documents, besides the *Jesus Messiah Sūtra* and the *Discourse on Monotheism*,[1] have not been made part of the scope of inquiry either, a rather large lacuna by some standards, but is part of an agenda simply too large for one study, where the aim has been to establish that a royal Persian, ascetic, and agency-holding trajectory existed within the Tang Church of the East, standing alongside the goal to instrumentalise a research programme for contextualising this and building upon the hard evidence found in the Xi'an stele and other sources before moving to these other *Jingjiao* texts. Examining further the meaning of the name Tajik/Daqin in relation to changes within Persian culture on the edges of the Abbasid Empire is sure to open important new avenues of meaning and exploration in the post-An Lushan setting as well.

The reason imperial patronage was withdrawn from all Persian religions at once by the Tang court in 845 and its effects can also be studied in relation to the stele's 'we have repaired the Imperial Net' phrase and Saeki's mischaracterisation of the church's political nature. If it is the case that the Uighur Empire's fall at the same time caused the Tang court to see all three Persian religions as no longer useful, as the primary sources seem to suggest, this strengthens the argument that the Church of the East, along with the Sogdian Manichaeans, were inter-courtly elites. The question then arises of where this skill-set went after the expulsion, what other reasons might be found for why the expulsion took place, and how deeper understanding of this might augment the thesis that the Church of the East's elites were a courtly and Persian Christian social body commandeered by ascetic elites.

Chapter 3 attempted to examine Timothy I's extant literary corpus in relation to integration occurring between the Abbasid court and its territories in Central Asia in order to find connections to the Xi'an stele, its rhetorical assertions, and the political consciousness found there in connection to these rhetorical assertions. The argument presented was that the church's 'Imperial Net,' i.e. its inter-courtly nature, or its participation in both the small and large C *comitatus*,[2] is found in these materials and in connection to the stele's and Timothy I's shared concern over clerical clothing hierarchies. The chapter focused on the corpus of Timothy I, but only lightly treats other materials. Economic integration between the Abbasid court, the church's elites, merchants, and courts of Central Asia and China and its cultural manifestations also require further investigation. The world view of the Barmakid family, how it stems from the family's placement between the Abbasid court, Balkh, and the learned traditions of early Abbasid Sind, should be studied further in relation to the church under Timothy I and the church in Chang'an. The role of political astrology as contained in the texts the family first translated for the Abbasids and its possible connections to Li Su and the astrology of the Xi'an monument is likely to bear results if examined more deeply. An examination of the formation of Islamic orthodoxy and re-articulations of Persian political culture in relation to this and the Abbasid court could be brought in as well. But the way in which the chapter connected the stele to the early Abbasid setting and supported the book's thesis – that the Xi'an stele is better understood with reference to its Persian *longue durée* and the ascetic and royal dispositions the church carried both within and between the courts of the period, and in connection to the agency standing behind the term *mdabranoutha* as appearing in the stele – is a contribution to the field.

The early Tang chapter posited that the Church of the East stood together with Sasanian royals within the orbit of the Tang court from the early seventh to the mid-eighth century and the name 'The Persian Religion' reflects this. This brings together the thesis put forward by Italian scholars about the continuation of the Sasanian house with Christian support in Central Asia, and the eastward and Sasanian trajectory of scholars working in the Late Antiquity paradigm showing Christianity's inter-imperial positioning in this context. The Tang's colonial ideology, its changes in the period to include non-Han peoples, and the incremental effect of Arab rule in the region can be examined in greater depth in this regard. The Buddhist, Taoist, and Confucian traditions were each part of the imperial expansions and increased 'cosmopolitanism' of the early Tang period. More extensive work within the Tang annals and Buddhist and Taoist sources and in relation to the Turkic sub-hegemony that took place at the same time could expand further our understanding of the Church of the East's elite, ascetic, and post-Sasanian identity in this context, as related to their stronghold in Balkh and Tocharistan and their roles as holders of Greco-Roman and Persian scientific traditions between Turkic and Chinese courts. An examination of the historical record relating to Dabuyid dynasty, lasting roughly between the time of Aluoben's arrival in Chang'an and the name change of 745, is likely to produce important results.

The late Sasanian chapter ignores Middle Persian sources and the important, but specialised, field of Sasanian law. Relations between the Church of the East and the Sasanian court and aristocracy and the issue of open imperial charisma within the court could be better understood specifically with reference to the numismatic and sigillographic evidence, as the emperor's charisma, his *xwarrah*, is so widely represented there and in inscriptions. Armenian materials – in which the trans-imperial range of late Sasanian culture, in both Christian and Zoroastrian forms, exists – could be explored in this regard. The important question of to what extent the Hephthalites were Turkic or Iranian, whether or not the Church of the East's elites' connections to them caused Sasanian royals to flee to Central Asia rather than Rome (as Rome had aided Sasanian royals before), and what bearing this has on the issue the shape the Church of the East's elite culture took in the early Tang empire can be studied further. A wider examination of Greek and Syriac economic and cultural interactions, their connections to Syriac monasticism and worldly asceticism, with regard to the re-opening of the Silk Roads and its economics, could be undertaken beyond the shallow treatment given them here.

Seeking to do justice to the Church of the East's two-century-long relationship to the Tang Empire and the church's Middle Eastern (Persian and Abbasid) history in one study and with any sense of completeness would be an ambitious goal. This has not been the goal here. However, the Xi'an stele's writers clearly saw themselves as an extension of the Tang emperor and court and part of the Tang court's empire-supporting religious bodies and core of elites. They saw themselves as part of Persian cultural power continuing to exist under the Abbasids too, and as part of the Church of the East's long-standing tradition of ascetic and charisma-wielding holy fathers, and in the 780s were only one generation removed from the church thinking of itself as 'The Persian Religion' in China and as an extension of the Sasanian royal house into Central Asia and China as seen in the early Tang period materials. The goal in the book has thus been to explore a theme present in the sources, to contour its continuities, and to explore them in relation to the phrase 'we repaired the Imperial Net', the Xi'an stele's *mdabranoutha* reference, and the Tang sources' reference to the Church of the East as 'Persian monks'. The pride clearly exhibited in the church's ascetic traditions in the Xi'an stele as the footing from which it preached the gospel to the 'kings of the Chinese', along with the apparent audacity displayed in its *gong zhen xuangang* language, is thus made accessible to contemporary readers. The utility of emphasising and exploring the church's place as elites in the Sasanian court before and after its fall, and as refashioned in the early Abbasid context, is thus demonstrated as well. The courtly asceticism of the church and its parallels in the imperial body and imperial garment language in Wu Yun's imperial Daoist asceticism of the same post-An Lushan era, Wu Yun using precisely the same *xuangang* vocabulary, thus appears more natural, while points of divergence emerge too. The consequences of reading the Middle Chinese materials connected to the Church of the East in Tang China through a modernist (Protestant 'invisible church'), lens, as Saeki did, are thus also shown.

Reading the Xi'an stele and related materials through the lens of a culturally disembodied ecclesiology excludes the role of asceticism and the church's Persian and royalist past excludes both an important immediate context in the Tang and a more long-durational context in Iran, Central Asia, and Abbasid Baghdad. Though Saeki's characterisation of the Church of the East and the dhimmitude thesis may be somewhat accurate for the church of the late ninth century and after, though to what degree precisely is debatable, it was not accurate for the church between the early fifth century and early ninth century. A political consciousness existed there, stemming from the mutuality and agency the church had with and within courts and via its ascetics, and the Sasanian history, which is better understand when read in relation to the Xi'an stele and the vestiges of this Sasanian history that appear there and in related sources. In a world in which connections between church and state in the Western context are diminishing, where Christianity is increasingly becoming a non-Western religion, and where Eastern and Western Christians continue to debate the extent to which the original charisma of Christ inheres or should inhere in a single church leader, a range of church leaders, or within individuals and their interpretation of Scripture, along with to what extent connections with state power constitute an authentic Christian politics, such analyses have bearing on a range of contemporary debates.

APPENDIX A

PERSIAN, ARAB, CHINESE AND CHURCH OF THE EAST LEADERS, *c.*400–*c.*850

Persian Shahs		Chinese Emperors (Tang)	
Yazdegird I 399–420	Azarmidokht 630–1	Gaozu 618–26	Suzong 756–62
Bahram V 420–38	Empress Borandokht 631–2	Daizong 626–49	Daizong 762–79
Yazdegird II 438–57	Khosrow IV 631	Gaozong 650–83	Dezong 779–805
Hormizd III 457–9	Farrukh Ormizd 630–1	Zhongzong 684 (also 705–710)	Shunzong 806
Peroz I 459–84	Hormizd VI 630–1	**Interregnum of Zhou Dynasty (690–705)**	Xianzong 806–20
Balash 484–8	Yazdegird II 632–52	Shangdi 710	Muzong 821–4
Kavadh I 488–531	**Dabuyid Dynasty**	Ruizong 684–90 (also 710–2)	Jingzong 824–6
Djamasp 496–8	Gil Gavbara 642–60	Xuanzong 712–56	Wenzong 826–40
Khosrow I 531–79	Dabuya 660–712		Wuzong 840–6
Hormizd IV 579–90	Farrukhan the Great 712–28		
Khosrow II 590–628	Dadhburzmihr 728–41		
Vistahm 590–600	Farrukhan the Little 741–8		
Kavadh II 628	Khurshid of Tabaristan 740–60		
Ardashir III 628–9			
Shahrbaraz 629			
Khosrow III 629			
Shapur-i Shahrvaraz 630			
Peroz II 630			

East Syrian Patriarchs		Arab Caliphs	
Isaac 375–86/399–410	Ezekiel 567–81	Abu Bakr ibn Quhafah 632–4	Hisham 724–43
Ahha 386–93/410–14	Ishoʿyahb I 582–95	Umar ibn al-Hattab (634–4)	al-Walid II 743–4
Yahballaha I 393–8/415–20	Sabrishoʿ I 596–604	Uthman ibn Affan 644–56	Yazid III 744
Maʿna 398–420	Gregory 605–9	Ali ibn Abu Talib 656–61	Ibrahim 744
Farbokht 401–21	Ishoʿyahb II 628–45	Hasan ibn Ali 661	Marwan II 744–50
Dadishoʿ I 421–56	Maremmeh 646–9	**Umayyad Dynasty**	**Abbasid Dynasty**
Babowi 457–84	Ishoʿyahb III 649–59	Muawiyah I 661–80	al-Saffah 750–4
Barsauma 484–5	Giwargis I 661–80	Yazid I 680–3	al-Mansur 754–75
(opposed by Aqaq-Acace 485–96)	Yohannan I 680–3	Muawiyah II 683–4	al-Mahdi 775–85
Babai 497–503	vacant 683–5	Marwan I 684–5	al-Hadi 785–6
Shila 503–23	Hnanishoʿ I 686–98	Abd al-Malik 685–705	Harun al-Rashid 786–809
Elishaʿ 524–37	Timothy I 780–823	Al-Walid I 705–15	al-Amin 809–13
Paul 539	Ishoʿ Bar Nun 823–8	Sulayman 715–17	al-Maʾmun 813–33
Aba I 540–52	Giwargis II 828–31	Umar II 717–20	al-Muʿtasim 833–42
28th Joseph (552–67)	Sabrishoʿ II 831–5	Yazid II 720–4	al-Wathiq 842–7
	Abraham II 837–50		Al-Mutawakkil 847–61
	vacant 850–3		

APPENDIX B

THE XI'AN STELE IN CHINESE CHARACTERS

Line 1 ‖ 大秦景教流行中國碑頌(并序)
Line 2 ‖ ܟܬܒܐ ܕܩܕܝܫܘܬܐ ܡܫܝܚܝܬܐ
Line 3 ‖ 大秦寺僧景淨述
Line 4 ‖ 粵若. 常然真寂. 先先而無元. 窅然靈虛.
Line 5 ‖ 後後而妙有. 總玄摳而造化. 妙眾聖以元尊者.
Line 6 ‖ 其唯我三一妙身無元真主阿羅訶歟判.
Line 7 ‖ 十字以定四方. 鼓元風而生二氣.
Line 8 ‖ 暗空易而天地開. 日月運而晝夜作. 匠成萬物然立初人
Line 9 ‖ 別賜良和令鎮化海. 渾元之性虛而不盈.
Line 10 ‖ 素蕩之心本無希嗜. 洎乎娑殫施妄. 鈿飾純精.
Line 11 ‖ 間平大於此是之中. 隙冥同於彼非之內.
Line 12 ‖ 是以三百六十五種. 肩隨結轍. 競織法羅.
Line 13 ‖ 或指物以託宗. 或空有以淪二. 或禱祀以邀福.
Line 14 ‖ 或伐善以矯人. 智慮營營. 恩情役役.
Line 15 ‖ 茫然無得. 煎迫轉燒. 積昧亡途久迷休復. 於是
Line 16 ‖ 我三一分身景尊彌施訶. 戢隱真威. 同人出代.
Line 17 ‖ 神天宣慶. 室女誕聖. 於大秦景宿告祥.
Line 18 ‖ 波斯睹耀以來貢. 圓二十四聖有說之舊法.
Line 19 ‖ 理家國於大猷. 設三一淨風無言之新教.
Line 20 ‖ 陶良用於正信. 制八境之度. 鍊塵成真.
Line 21 ‖ 啟三常之門. 開生滅死. 懸景日以破暗府.
Line 22 ‖ 魔妄於是乎悉摧. 棹慈航以登明宮. 含靈於是乎既濟.
Line 23 ‖ 能事斯畢. 亭午昇真. 經留二十七部.
Line 24 ‖ 張元化以發靈關. 法浴水風. 滌浮華而潔虛白.
Line 25 ‖ 印持十字. 融四照以合無拘. 擊木震仁惠之音.
Line26 ‖ 東禮趣生榮之路. 存鬚所以有外行.
Line 27 ‖ 削頂所以無內情. 不畜臧獲. 均貴賤於人.
Line 28 ‖ 不聚貨財示罄遺於我. 齋以伏識而成. 戒以靜慎為固.
Line 29 ‖ 七時禮讚. 大庇存亡. 七日一薦. 洗心反素.
Line 30 ‖ 真常之道. 妙而難名. 功用昭彰. 強稱景教.
Line 31 ‖ 惟道非聖不弘. 聖非道不大. 道聖符契. 天下文明
Line 32 ‖ 太宗文皇帝. 光華啟運. 明聖臨人.
Line 33 ‖ 大秦國有上德. 曰阿羅本. 占青雲而載真經.
Line 34 ‖ 望風律以馳艱險. 貞觀九祀至於長安
Line 35 ‖ 帝使宰臣房公玄齡總仗西郊賓迎入內. 翻經書殿.
Line 36 ‖ 問道禁闈. 深知正真. 特令傳授.
Line 37 ‖ 貞觀十有二年秋七月. 詔曰道無常名. 聖無常體.
Line 38 ‖ 隨方設教. 密濟群生. 大秦國大德阿羅本.
Line 39 ‖ 遠將經像來獻上京. 詳其教旨. 玄妙無為. 觀其元宗.
Line 40 ‖ 生成立要. 詞無繁說. 理有忘筌. 濟物利人.
Line 41 ‖ 宜行天下. 所司即於京義寧坊造大秦寺.
Line 42 ‖ 一所度僧二十一人. 宗周德喪. 青駕西昇.
Line 43 ‖ 巨唐道光. 景風東扇. 旋令有司將
Line 44 ‖ 帝寫真轉摸寺壁. 天姿汎彩. 英朗景門. 聖跡騰祥.
Line 45 ‖ 永輝法界. 案西域圖記及漢魏史策.
Line 46 ‖ 大秦國南統珊瑚之海. 北極眾寶之山. 西望仙境花林.
Line 47 ‖ 東接長風弱水. 其土出火浣布. 返魂香. 明月珠.
Line 48 ‖ 夜光璧. 俗無寇盜. 人有樂康. 法非景不行.
Line 49 ‖ 主非德不立. 土宇廣明. 文物昌明. 高宗大帝.
Line 50 ‖ 克恭纘祖. 潤色真宗. 而於諸州各置景寺.
Line 51 ‖ 仍崇阿羅本為鎮國大法主. 法流十道. 國富元休.
Line 52 ‖ 寺滿百城. 家殷景福. 聖曆年. 釋子用壯.
Line 53 ‖ 騰口於東周. 先天末. 下士大笑. 訕謗於西鎬.
Line 54 ‖ 有若僧首羅含. 大德及烈. 並金方貴緒. 物外高僧.
Line 55 ‖ 共振玄網. 俱維絕紐玄宗至道皇帝.

Line 56 _____	令寧國等五王親臨福宇建立壇場。
Line 57 _____	法棟暫橈而更崇。道石時傾而復正。天寶初。
Line 58 _____	令大將軍高力士送五聖寫真寺內安置。賜絹百匹。
Line 59 _____	奉慶睿圖。龍髯雖遠。弓劍可攀。日角舒光。
Line 60 _____	天顏咫尺。三載大秦國有僧佶和。瞻星向化。
Line 61 _____	望日朝尊。詔僧羅含僧普論等一七人。
Line 62 _____	與大德佶和。於興慶宮修功德。於是天題寺牓。
Line 63 _____	額戴龍書。寶裝璀翠。灼爍丹霞。睿扎宏空。
Line 64 _____	騰淩激日。寵賚比南山峻極。沛澤與東海齊深。
Line 65 _____	道無不可。所可可名。聖無不作。所作可述
Line 66 _____	肅宗文明皇帝。於靈武等五郡。重立景寺。
Line 67 _____	元善資而福祚開。大慶臨而皇業建。
Line 68 _____	代宗文武皇帝。恢張聖運。從事無為。每於降誕之辰。
Line 69 _____	錫天香以告成功。頒御饌以光景眾。
Line 70 _____	且乾以美利故能廣生。聖以體元故能享眾
Line 71 _____	我建中聖神文武皇帝。披八政以黜陟幽明。
Line 72 _____	闡九疇以惟新景命。化通玄理。祝無愧心。
Line 73 _____	至於方大而虛。專靜而恕。廣慈救眾苦。善貸被群生者。
Line 74 _____	我修行之大猷。汲引之階漸也。若使風雨時。
Line 75 _____	天下靜。人能理。物能清。存能昌。歿能樂。
Line 76 _____	念生響應。情發目誠者。我景力能事之功用也。
Line 77 _____	大施主金紫光祿大夫。同朔方節度副使。
Line 78 _____	試殿中監。賜紫袈裟僧伊斯。和而好惠。
Line 79 _____	聞道勤行。遠自王舍之城。聿來中夏。術高三代。
Line 80 _____	博藝十全。始效節於丹庭。乃策名於王帳。
Line 81 _____	中書令汾陽郡王郭公子儀。初總戎於朔方也。
Line 82 _____	肅宗俾之從邁。雖見親於臥內。不自異於行間。
Line 83 _____	為公爪牙。作軍耳目。能散祿賜。不積於家。
Line 84 _____	獻臨恩之頗黎。布辭憩之金罽。或仍其舊寺。
Line 85 _____	或重廣法堂。崇飾廊宇。如翬斯飛。更效景門。
Line 86 _____	依仁施利。每歲集四寺僧徒。虔事精供。
Line 87 _____	備諸五旬。餒者來而飯之。寒者來而衣之。
Line 88 _____	病者療而起之。死者葬而安之。清節達娑。未聞斯美。
Line 89 _____	白衣景士。今見其人。願刻洪碑。以揚休烈。
Line 90 _____	詞曰真主無元。湛寂常然。權輿匠化。
Line 91 _____	起地立天。分身出代。救度無邊。日昇暗滅。
Line 92 _____	咸證真玄赫赫文皇。道冠前王。乘時撥亂。
Line 93 _____	乾廓坤張。明明景教。言歸我唐。翻經建寺。
Line 94 _____	存歿舟航。百福偕作。萬邦之康高宗纂祖。
Line 95 _____	更築精宇。和宮敞朗。遍滿中土。真道宣明。
Line 96 _____	式封法主。人有樂康。物無災苦玄宗啟聖。
Line 97 _____	克修真正。御牓揚輝。天書蔚映。皇圖璀璨。
Line 98 _____	率土高敬。庶績咸熙。人賴其慶肅宗來復。
Line 99 _____	天威引駕。聖日舒晶。祥風掃夜。祚歸皇室。
Line 100 _____	祅氛永謝。止沸定塵。造我區夏代宗孝義。
Line 101 _____	德合天地。開貸生成。物資美利。香以報功。
Line 102 _____	仁以作施。暘谷來威。月窟畢萃建中統極。
Line 103 _____	聿修明德。武肅四溟。文清萬域。燭臨人隱。
Line 104 _____	鏡觀物色。六合昭蘇。百蠻取則。道惟廣兮。
Line 105 _____	應惟密強。名言兮演三一主能作兮臣能述。
Line 106 _____	建豐碑兮頌元吉。
Line 107 _____	
Line 108 _____	大唐建中二年歲在作噩太蔟月七日大耀森文曰建立
Line 109 _____	時法主僧寧恕知東方之景眾也
Line 110 _____	朝議郎前行台州司士參軍呂秀巖書

Line 111_____ ‖ 助撿挍試太常卿賜紫袈裟寺主僧業利
Line 112_____ ‖ 撿挍建立碑僧行通
Line 113_____ ‖ 僧靈寶僧內澄僧光正
Line 114_____ ‖ 僧和明僧立本僧法源
Line 115_____ ‖ 僧審慎僧寶靈僧玄覽
Line 116_____ ‖ 僧景通老宿耶俱摩僧明一
Line 117_____ ‖ 僧保國僧志堅僧義濟
Line 118_____ ‖ 僧玄德僧利用僧元□
Line 119_____ ‖ 僧奉真僧至德僧和光
Line 120_____ ‖ 僧景福僧太和僧崇德
Line 121_____ ‖ 僧德建僧去甚僧廣德
Line 122_____ ‖ 僧福壽僧□□ 僧寶達
Line 123_____ ‖ 僧□明僧和吉僧□□
Line 124_____ ‖ 僧遙□ 僧日進 □□輪
Line 125_____ ‖ 僧延和僧崇敬僧惠通
Line 126_____ ‖ 僧□□ □居信僧文貞
Line 127_____ ‖ 僧文明僧昭德僧曜原
Line 128_____ ‖ 僧仁□ 僧玄真僧明泰
Line 129_____ ‖ 僧利□ 僧敬德僧元□
Line 130_____ ‖ 僧乾□ 僧守一僧光□
Line 131_____ ‖ 僧聞順僧普濟僧凝□
Line 132_____ ‖ 僧沖和僧英德僧靈德
Line 133_____ ‖ 僧靈壽僧還淳 □敬真
Line 134_____
Line 135_____ ‖ 後一千七十九年咸豐己未武林韓泰畢來觀幸字畫完整重造碑亭Line 136_____ ‖
覆焉惜故友吳子苾方伯不及同遊也為悵然久之。

‎ܪܫܕܝܐܩܘ‎ Line 137____ ‖
‎ܪ‎ Line 138____ ‖
‎ܪ‎ Line 139____ ‖
‎ܪ‎ Line 140____ ‖

Taisho Tripitaka Vol. 54, No. 2144 大秦景教流行中國碑頌CBETA Chinese Electronic Tripitaka V1.15
(Big5) Normalized Version, Release Date: 2009/04/23
Distributed free of charge.
Distributor: Chinese Buddhist Electronic Text Association (CBETA)

APPENDIX C

THE PILLAR FOR THE PROPAGATION OF THE LUMINOUS RELIGION IN CHINA

Behold the unchangeably true and invisible, who existed through all eternity without origin; the far-seeing perfect intelligence, whose mysterious existence is everlasting; operating on primordial substance he created the universe, being more excellent than all holy intelligences, inasmuch as he is the source of all that is honourable. This is our eternal true lord God, triune and mysterious in substance. He appointed the cross as the means for determining the four cardinal points, he moved the original spirit, and produced the two principles of nature; the sombre void was changed, and heaven and earth were opened out; the sun and moon revolved, and day and night commenced; having perfected all inferior objects, he then made the first man;[1] upon him he bestowed an excellent disposition, giving him in charge the government of all created beings; man, acting out the original principles of his nature, was pure and unostentatious; his unsullied and expansive mind was free from the least inordinate desire; until Satan introduced the seeds of falsehood, to deteriorate his purity of principle; the opening thus commenced in his virtue gradually enlarged, and by this crevice in his nature was obscured and rendered vicious; hence 365 sects followed each other in continuous track, inventing every species of doctrinal complexity; while some pointed to material objects as the source of their faith, others reduced all to vacancy, even to the annihilation of the two primeval principles, some sought to call down blessings by prayers and supplications, while others by an assumption of excellence held themselves up as superior to their fellows; their intellects and thoughts continually wavering, their minds and affections incessantly on the move, they never obtained their vast desires, but being exhausted and distressed they revolved in their own heated atmosphere; till by an accumulation of obscurity they lost their path, and after long groping in darkness they were unable to return. Thereupon, our Trinity being divided in nature, the illustrious and honourable Messiah, veiling his true dignity, appeared in the world as a man; angelic powers promulgated the glad tidings, a virgin gave birth to the Holy One in Daqin; a bright star announced the felicitous event, and Persians observing the splendour came to present tribute; the ancient dispensation, as declared by the 24 holy men [the writers of the Old Testament], was then fulfilled, and he laid down great principles for the government of families and kingdoms; he established the new religion of the silent operation of the pure spirit of the Triune; he rendered virtue subservient to direct faith; he fixed the extent of the eight boundaries, thus completing the truth and freeing it from dross; he opened the gate of the three constant principles, introducing life and destroying death; he suspended the bright sun to invade the chambers of darkness, and the falsehoods of the devil were thereupon defeated; he set in motion the vessel of mercy by which to ascend to the bright mansions, whereupon rational beings were then released, having thus completed the manifestation of his power, in clear day he ascended to his true station.

Twenty-seven sacred books [the number in the New Testament] have been left, which disseminate intelligence by unfolding the original transforming principles. By the rule for admission, it is the custom to apply the water of baptism, to wash away all superficial show and to cleanse and purify the neophytes. As a seal, they hold the cross, whose influence is reflected in every direction, uniting all without distinction. As they strike the wood, the fame of their benevolence is diffused abroad; worshiping toward the east, they hasten on the way to life and glory; they preserve the beard to symbolise their outward actions, they shave the crown to indicate the absence of inward affections; they do not keep slaves, but put noble and mean all on an equality; they do not amass wealth, but cast all their property into the common stock; they fast, in order to perfect themselves by self-inspection; they submit to restraints, in order to strengthen themselves by silent watchfulness; seven times a day they have worship and praise for the benefit of the living and the dead; once in seven days they sacrifice, to cleanse the heart and return to purity.

It is difficult to find a name to express the excellence of the true and unchangeable doctrine; but as its meritorious operations are manifestly displayed, by accommodation it is named the Illustrious Religion. Now without holy men, principles cannot become expanded; without principles, holy men cannot become magnified; but with holy men and right principles, united as the two parts of a signet, the world becomes civilised and enlightened.

In the time of the accomplished Emperor Taizong, the illustrious and magnificent founder of the dynasty, among the enlightened and holy men who arrived was the most-virtuous Aluoben, from the country of Daqin. Observing the azure clouds, he bore the true sacred books; beholding the direction of the winds, he braved difficulties and dangers. In the year of our Lord 635 he arrived at Chang-an; the Emperor sent his Prime Minister, Duke Fang Xuanling; who, carrying the official staff to the west border, conducted his guest into the interior; the sacred books were translated in the imperial library, the sovereign investigated the subject in his private apartments; when becoming deeply impressed with the rectitude and truth of the religion, he gave special orders for its dissemination.

In the seventh month of the year AD 638 the following imperial proclamation was issued:

Right principles have no invariable name, holy men have no invariable station; instruction is established in accordance with the locality, with the object of benefiting the people at large. The greatly virtuous Aluoben, of the kingdom of Daqin, has brought his sacred books and images from that distant part, and has presented them at our chief capital. Having examined the principles of this religion, we find them to be purely excellent and natural; investigating its originating source, we find it has taken its rise from the establishment of important truths; its ritual is free from perplexing expressions, its principles will survive when the framework is forgot; it is beneficial to all creatures; it is advantageous to mankind. Let it be published throughout the Empire, and let the proper authority build a Daqin church in the capital in the Yining ward, which shall be governed by 21 priests. When the virtue of the Zhou Dynasty declined, the rider on the azure ox ascended to the west; the principles of the great Tang becoming resplendent, the Illustrious breezes have come to fan the East.

Orders were then issued to the authorities to have a true portrait of the Emperor taken; when it was transferred to the wall of the church, the dazzling splendour of the celestial visage irradiated the Illustrious portals. The sacred traces emitted a felicitous influence, and shed a perpetual splendour over the holy precincts. According to the Illustrated Memoir of the Western Regions, and the historical books of the Han and Wei dynasties, the kingdom of Daqin reaches south to the Coral Sea; on the north it joins the Gem Mountains; on the west it extends toward the borders of the immortals and the flowery forests; on the east it lies open to the violent winds and tideless waters. The country produces fire-proof cloth, life-restoring incense, bright moon-pearls, and night-lustre gems. Brigands and robbers are unknown, but the people enjoy happiness and peace. None but Illustrious laws prevail; none but the virtuous are raised to sovereign power. The land is broad and ample, and its literary productions are perspicuous and clear.

The Emperor Gaozong respectfully succeeded his ancestor, and was still more beneficent toward the institution of truth. In every province he caused Illustrious churches to be erected, and ratified the honour conferred upon Aluoben, making him the great conservator of doctrine for the preservation of the State. While this doctrine pervaded every channel, the State became enriched and tranquillity abounded. Every city was full of churches, and the royal family enjoyed lustre and happiness. In the year AD 699 the Buddhists, gaining power, raised their voices in the eastern metropolis; in the year AD 713, some low fellows excited ridicule and spread slanders in the western capital. At that time there was the chief priest Lohan, the greatly virtuous Jilie, and others of noble estate from the golden regions, lofty-minded priests, having abandoned all worldly interests; who unitedly maintained the grand principles and preserved them entire to the end. The high-principled Emperor Xuanzong caused the Prince of Ning and others, five princes in all, personally to visit the felicitous edifice; he established the place of worship; he restored the consecrated timbers which had been temporarily thrown down; and re-erected the sacred stones which for a time had been desecrated.

In AD 742 orders were given to the great general Gao Lishi, to send the five sacred portraits and have them placed in the church, and a gift of a hundred pieces of silk accompanied these pictures of intelligence. Although the dragon's beard was then remote, their bows and swords were still within reach; while the solar horns sent forth their rays, and celestial visages seemed close at hand. In AD 744 the priest Kih-ho, in the kingdom of Daqin, looking toward the star [of China], was attracted by its transforming influence, and observing the sun [i.e. the Emperor], came to pay court to the most honorable. The Emperor commanded the priest Lohan, the priest Pulun, and others, seven in all, together with the greatly virtuous Jihe, to perform a service of merit in the Xingqing palace. Thereupon the Emperor composed mottoes for the sides of the church, and the tablets were graced with the royal inscriptions; the accumulated gems emitted their effulgence, while their sparkling brightness vied with the ruby clouds; the transcripts of intelligence suspended in the void shot forth their rays as reflected by the sun; the bountiful gifts exceeded the height of the southern hills; the bedewing favours were deep as the eastern sea. Nothing is beyond the range of the right principle, and what is permissible may be identified; nothing is beyond the power of the holy man, and that which is practicable may be related.

The accomplished and enlightened Emperor Suzong rebuilt the Illustrious Churches in Ling-wu and four other places; great benefits were conferred, and felicity began to increase; great munificence was displayed, and the imperial State became established. The accomplished and military Emperor Taizong magnified the sacred succession, and honoured the latent principle of nature; always, on the incarnation-day, he bestowed celestial incense, and ordered the performance of a service of merit; he distributed of the imperial viands, in order to shed a glory on the Illustrious Congregation. Heaven is munificent in the dissemination of blessings, whereby the benefits of life are extended; the holy man embodies the original principle of virtue, whence he is able to counteract noxious influences.

Our sacred and sage-like, accomplished and military Emperor Jianzhong appointed the eight branches of government, according to which he advanced or degraded the intelligent and dull; he opened up the nine categories, by means of which he renovated the Illustrious decrees; his transforming influence pervaded the most abstruse principles, while openness of heart distinguished his devotions. Thus, by correct and enlarged purity of principle, and undeviating consistency in sympathy with others; by extended commiseration rescuing multitudes from misery, while disseminating blessings on all around, the cultivation of our doctrine gained a grand basis, and by gradual advances its influence was diffused. If the winds and rains are seasonable, the world will be at rest; men will be guided by principle, inferior objects will be pure; the living will be at ease, and the dead will rejoice; the thoughts will produce their appropriate response, the affections will be free, and the eyes will be sincere; such is the laudable condition which we of the Illustrious Religion are labouring to attain.

Our great benefactor, the Imperially conferred purple-gown priest, Yisi, titular Great Statesman of the Banqueting-house, Associated Secondary Military Cornmissioner for the Northern Region, and Examination-palace Overseer, was naturally mild and graciously disposed; his mind susceptible of sound doctrine, he was diligent in the performance; from the distant city of Rajagriha, he came to visit China; his principles more lofty than those of the three dynasties, his practise was perfect in every department; at first he applied himself to duties pertaining to the palace, eventually his name was inscribed on the military roll. When the Duke Guo Ziyi, Secondary Minister of State and Prince of Fenyang, at first conducted the military in the northern region, the Emperor Suzong made him (Yisi) his attendant on his travels; although he was a private chamberlain, he assumed no distinction on the march; he was as claws and teeth to the duke, and in rousing the military he was as ears and eyes; he distributed the wealth conferred upon him, not accumulating treasure for his private use; he made offerings of the jewellery which had been given by imperial favour, he spread out a golden carpet for devotion; now he repaired the old churches, anon he increased the number of religious establishments; he honoured and decorated the various edifices, till they resembled the plumage of the pheasant in its flight; moreover, practising the discipline of the Illustrious Religion, he distributed his riches in deeds of benevolence; every year he assembled those in the sacred office from four churches, and respectfully engaged them for 50 days in purification and preparation; the naked came and were clothed; the sick were attended to and restored; the dead were buried in repose; even among the most pure and self-denying of the Buddhists, such excellence was never heard of; the white-clad members of the Illustrious Congregation, now considering these men, have desired to engrave a broad tablet, in order to set forth a eulogy of their magnanimous deeds.

ODE

The true Lord is without origin,
Profound, invisible, and unchangeable;
With power and capacity to perfect and transform,
He raised up the earth and established the heavens.

Divided in nature, he entered the world,
To save and to help without bounds;
The sun arose, and darkness was dispelled,
All bearing witness to his true original.

The glorious and resplendent, accomplished Emperor,
Whose principles embraced those of preceding monarchs,
Taking advantage of the occasion, suppressed turbulence;
Heaven was spread out and the earth was enlarged.

When the pure, bright Illustrious Religion
Was introduced to our Tang Dynasty,
The Scriptures were translated, and churches built,
And the vessel set in motion for the living and the dead;
Every kind of blessing was then obtained,
And all the kingdoms enjoyed a state of peace.

When Gaozong succeeded to his ancestral estate,
He rebuilt the edifices of purity;

Palaces of concord, large and light,
Covered the length and breadth of the land.

The true doctrine was clearly announced,
Overseers of the church were appointed in due form;
The people enjoyed happiness and peace,
While all creatures were exempt from calamity and distress.

When Xuanzong commenced his sacred career,
He applied himself to the cultivation of truth and rectitude;
His imperial tablets shot forth their effulgence,
And the celestial writings mutually reflected their splendours.

The imperial domain was rich and luxuriant,
While the whole land rendered exalted homage;
Every business was flourishing throughout,
And the people all enjoyed prosperity.

Then came Suzong, who commenced anew,
And celestial dignity marked the Imperial movements.
Sacred as the moon's unsullied expanse,
While felicity was wafted like nocturnal gales.

Happiness reverted to the Imperial household,
The autumnal influences were long removed;
Ebullitions were allayed, and risings suppressed,
And thus our dynasty was firmly built up.

Taozong the filial and just
Combined in virtue with heaven and earth;
By his liberal bequests the living were satisfied,
And property formed the channel of imparting succour.

By fragrant mementoes he rewarded the meritorious,
With benevolence he dispensed his donations;
The solar concave appeared in dignity,
And the lunar retreat was decorated to extreme.

When Jianzong succeeded to the throne,
He began the cultivation of intelligent virtue;
His military vigilance extended to the four seas,
And his accomplished purity influenced all lands.

His light penetrated the secrecies of men,
And to him the diversities of objects were seen as in a mirror;
He shed a vivifying influence through the whole realm of nature,
And all outer nations took him for example.

The true doctrine, how expansive!
Its responses are minute;
How difficult to name it!
To elucidate the three in one.

The sovereign has the power to act!
While the ministers record;
We raise this noble monument!
To the praise of great felicity.

This was erected in the second year of Jianzhong of the Tang Dynasty [AD 781], on the seventh day of the first month, being Sunday.

Written by Lü Xiuyan, Secretary to Council, formerly Military Superintendent for Taizhou; while the Bishop Ningshu had the charge of the congregations of the Illustrious in the East.

{The Following are written in Syriac, running down the right and left sides of the Chinese inscription above}.

'Adam, Deacon, Vicar-episcopal and Pope of China. In the time of the Father of Fathers, the Lord John Joshua, the Universal Patriarch.'

{The Following is in Syriac at the foot of the stone}.

'In the year of the Greeks one thousand and ninety-two, the Lord Jazbōzēdh, Priest and Vicar-episcopal of Kumdan the royal city, son of the enlightened Milis, Priest of Balkh a city of Tocharistan, set up this tablet, whereon is inscribed the Divine Economy of our Redeemer, and the preaching of the fathers of (our church) to the Kings of China.'

{After this, in Chinese characters, follows:}

'The Priest Lingpau.'

{Then follows in Syriac:}
'*Adam the Deacon, son of Jazbōzēdh, Vicar-episcopal.*
'*The Lord Sergius, Priest and Vicar-episcopal.*
Sabar Jesus, Priest.
Gabriel, Priest, Archdeacon, and Ecclesiarch of Kumdan and Sarag.'
{The following subscription is appended in Chinese:}
'*Assistant Examiner: the High Statesman of the Sacred rites, the Imperially conferred purple-gown Chief Presbyter and Priest Yeli'.*
{On the left-hand edge are the Syriac names of sixty-seven priests, and sixty-one are given in Chinese.}

APPENDIX D

THEORETICAL CONCEPTS USED IN THE STUDY AND THEIR DEFINITIONS

Agency:

Power. Freedom. The ability to have and create social mobility, but not within the Lockean and Enlightenment era view in which individual autonomy is stressed at the expense of, or without due regard for, the collective social body. This approach to agency is emphasised in the Bourdieuian *habitus* framework and relevant to the attempt to interpret ancient and medieval sources without modernising them, as attempted in the book.

Asceticism:

The delaying of gratification and bodily pleasure (here, within a Christian moral and intellectual context), the cultivation of the body, and its adornment, for the spiritual and cultural advancement of both self and community.

Charisma:

Social cohesion; the tendency for leaders' personal characteristics to be part of a collective representation (cf. Durkheim's tradition as carried on by Bourdieu) and the tendency for social bodies to transmit and reproduce these characteristics. See 'Royal dispositions'. Max Weber's work on charismatic authority, although it is usually discussed in terms of either primitive religious groups or modern evolutionary movements, Weber's concept of charisma and of political bodies, their leaders and their cultural environment, each being connected by charismatic bonds, lends itself quite readily to an analysis of the cultural production of the Church of the East as it stood between Persia, Central Asia, and China between the fifth and ninth centuries. There was a Persian conception of the divine favour, *xwarrah*, that will be brought into the discussion at a later time, but Weber's concept of charisma as well as his concept of worldly asceticism works well as we attempt to rethink the way in which the Church of the East both reflected, was connected to, and yet also stood apart from the courts that hosted them and did so on a partly localised and partly Christian basis. Weber posited, as an ideal-type, a theory of 'double charisma' — essentially the concept that a sacral bond exists between leaders and supporters in any functioning society, one in which charisma is present; this has innate religious dimensions, for he defined charisma as:

> a certain quality of an individual personality by virtue of which he is considered extraordinary and treated as endowed with supernatural, superhuman, or at least specifically exceptional powers or qualities, such as are not accessible to the ordinary person, but are regarded as of divine origin or as exemplary [within the social order].[1]

Comitatus:

Following Beckwith, a Central Asian political and social ur-form in which the sovereign leader stood at the top of society and shared semi-divine or divine status with his closest supporters, the latter sharing and transmitting the imperial charisma of the sovereign to future generations and representing it outside the court (cf. *longue durée*, and charisma). This author posits a 'Big C' *comitatus*, i.e. the definition above, but also a 'small C' *comitatus*, one which can simply mean a 'court' and the 'culture of the court'. The increasingly interlinked nature of the empires and patronage cultures of the eighth century can be pointed to as evidence for the former. The corridor between China and Arab dominated Persia, where the spread of World Religions is seen, is further evidence, in addition to the numerous pieces of evidence pointed to by Beckwith.[2]

Court:

Centralised power in an early medieval and ancient context. According to Duindam, 'a court is never an artefact or a possession, but always a process, a balance among many players'.[3] According to Elias, 'like a stock exchange, where anticipation of losses or gains lead to fluctuations in value'.[4] There exist social capital, classifying functions, and the self-discipline regimens enacted in relation to this power, which makes the court a shared and collective enterprise, and one that develops over time and an 'an underpinning of the social order'. Cf. 'asceticism', 'charisma', 'habitus', and 'longue durée.'

Elite:

Not to be defined without empirical data and context, but the theoretic usage employed here relies on the term's linguistics. The English word elite is derived from the Middle French verb *élire*, 'to choose', but cf. a Latin verb such as *texere*: 'to weave' and compare it to *textus*, 'a thing having been woven', the latter being the past passive participle. This highlights the contradictory nature of an elite's freedom and agency, and brings it into dialog with the other concepts in this list and the corporate nature of agency being argued for.

Empire:

According to Stephen Howe:

> a large political body which rules over territories outside its original borders. It has a central power or core territory − whose inhabitants usually continue to form the dominant ethnic or

national group in the entire system – and an extensive periphery of dominated areas.[5]

Habitus:

The nexus point between the social body and personhood. According to Bourdieu, 'a system of lasting, transposable dispositions which, integrating past experiences, functions at every moment as a matrix of perceptions, appreciations and actions'.[6] The instrumentalisation of this concept in the analysis of historical materials involves and presupposes a Chomskyan linguistic and Cognitive Science framework, for as Bourdieu says, it involves

> an attempt to break with Kantian dualism and to reintroduce the permanent dispositions that are constitutive of realized morality (*Sittlichkeit*), as opposed to the moralism of duty ... and an attempt to account for the systematic functioning of the social body ...[7]

and a 'react[ion] against the mechanistic tendencies seen in Saussure ... [and] close to Chomsky in whom [there is] the same concern to give practice an active, inventive intention, [and the] the generative capacities of dispositions'[8] (cf. 'agency', 'court', 'charisma', '*longue durée*').

Longue durée:

As used in this study, in contradistinction to other usages and building on the *dur* element within the French word *durée* and its connection to the English word durability, this is the tendency for imperial charisma and royal dispositions to be articulated within asceticism, within ascetic leadership, and in creating social cohesion within the house of the church (*mdabranoutha*), over long stretches of time and space.

Patronage field:

Participation in the culture of the court. Cf. 'asceticism', 'charisma, ' *comitatus*, '*habitus*', '*longue durée*', 'elite' and 'empire', etc.

Royal disposition(s):

The proclivity seen in ancient and medieval societies for the emperor's person, manner of sitting, modes of speech, facial features, etc., to be part of the moral aspirations of the society at large and of the culture of the courts that ruled them. This reflects Bourdieu's understanding of hexis, and the bodily nature of morality. Given that much of what constitutes religion concerns uses, restrictions, and freedoms placed on the body (something generalisable to ethical discourses not normally thought of as 'religious') such a concept has wide utility and application.

Subjectivity:

According to Foucault's reading of the transition from the Greco-Roman elite cultivation tradition to that of early Christianity, this is the practice of ruling over one's self in order to rule over others. In that formulation it offers a way of conceptualising society from both the top down as well as from the bottom up and analysing it from both directions. Cf. 'royal dispositions', '*habitus*', '*comitatus*' etc.

Worldly asceticism:

The working out in the world of one's spiritual discipline. Weber points to eschatological, cosmic, and social dimensions in the term with parallels to the Divine Economy notion (cf. Cosmas, Isho'yahb III, and Timothy I etc.) and where ascetics are shown driving the church forward through time and space (cf. Mar Yonan's house image) and offering agency to their social body as a whole.[9]

NOTES

Prelims

1. *Wenyuange siku quanshu dianziban* 文淵閣四庫全書電子版 (Shanghai, Renmin Chubanshe, 2002), hereafter SKQS.
2. See Chapter 3 for references.
3. See Chapter 4 for references.

Introduction

1. Ernst Kantorowicz, *The King's Two Bodies: A Study in Mediaeval Political Thought* (Princeton, NJ: Princeton University Press, 1957), p. 30, writing here of the political world view behind Shakespeare's *King Richard II*.
2. These images can be seen at http://www.sadanduseless.com/2014/02/blessed-everything (accessed 5 October 2015).
3. These images can be seen at http://www.nytimes.com/2014/08/03/world/europe/from-pilgrims-putin-seeks-political-profit.html (accessed 5 October 2015).
4. Yelizaveta Fyodorovna Romanova (1864–1918), was the granddaughter of Queen Victoria, the sibling of the last Empress of Russia and a German princess of the House of Hesse-Darmstadt; Jerrold M. Packard, *Victoria's Daughters* (New York: St Martin's Griffin, 1998), p. 176 ff.
5. On use of the term East Syrian and Syro-Persian rather than 'Nestorian', see Introduction, note 20.
6. For more discussion of Saeki's views, see the discussion further on in this chapter.
7. On the term *longue durée* see the list of theoretical terms employed in the study appearing among the appendices.
8. Domenico Agostini and Sören Stark, 'Zawulistan, Kawulistan and the Land of Bosi [波斯] – On the question of the Sasanian court-in-exile in the southern Hindukish', *Studia Iranica* 45 (2016), pp. 17–38.

9. See the appendices for an English translation of the entire stele as well as its Chinese, that translation being Alexander Wylie, in Charles F. Horne (ed.), *The Sacred Books and Early Literature of the East*, vol. 12: *Medieval China* (New York: Parke, Austin, and Lipscomb, 1917) (hereafter XS), pp. 381–92

10. Peter Yoshiro Saeki, *The Nestorian Documents and Relics in China* [1937], 2nd edn (Tokyo: Academy of Oriental Culture, 1951); Saeki also published 11 other books along with a series of articles.

11. Akira Fujieda, 'The Tunhuang manuscripts: a general description', *Zinbun IX* (1966), pp. 1–32; *Zinbun X* (1969), pp. 17–39; for a lively introduction to the early twentieth century rediscovery of the Central Asian Silk Roads, and which led to the Dunhuang cave discovery, see Peter Hopkirk, *Foreign Devils on the Silk Road* (Boston, MA: University of Massachusetts Press, 1984).

12. See Rong Xinjiang, 'The nature of the Dunhuang Library Cave and the reasons for its sealing', *Cahiers d'Extrême-Asie* 11/11 (1999), pp. 247–75.

13. Saeki was in fact awarded an honorary doctorate by Waseda University three years before his death; on these and the other main sources upon which this study stands, see the section devoted to this topic.

14. See section below and the part of this introduction which is devoted to the study's sources; note here, however, that Paul Pelliot's study of the monument, posthumously published along with several important essays by A. Forte, is the standard item in the study of the Xi'an stele, see Antonino Forte (ed.), *Paul Pelliot's L'inscription Nestorienne de Singan-fou* (Kyoto and Paris: Scuola di Studi Sull'Asia Orientale, Collège de France, Institute des Haute Études, Chinoises, 1996); Max Deeg's forthcoming *Die Strahlende Lehre*, will become a standard item along with Pelliot's commentary; both studies are closely followed below. See the appendices for the entire Chinese text of the stele and its Syriac portions, and where Arthur Waley's translation into English is also provided; James Legge, *The Nestorian Monument of Hsi-An Fu* (London: Trubner and Co., 1888; repr. Paragon, New York, 1966), offers a reliable translation in general and appears frequently below.

15. On the term agency, see the discussion below and the glossary of technical terms.

16. On the term *longue durée* and the general historiography of the courtly space undergirding the book's empirical investigations, see the discussion below, along with the glossary of technical terms included in the appendices.

17. He also capitalised the term; he too went so far as to say the East Syrian's having brought this to China (though indicating he thought it existed in Chinese history both before and after the Tang as well) influenced the Tang Chinese to have emperor worship; see Saeki, *The Nestorian Documents*, pp. 149–53.

18. Peter Yoshiro Saeki, *The Nestorian Monument in China* [1916], 2nd edn (London: SPCK, 1928), pp. 158–60.

19. See Chi-Hung Lam, 'The political activities of the Christian missionaries in the T'ang Dynasty', unpublished dissertation, University of Denver, Colorado (1975), pp. 180–95, where Saeki's influence can be seen; it is typical of

Chinese scholarship to understand the Church of the East as having been interested solely in missions work in the Tang, targeting the court and elite class only; both assumptions being unfounded; see Zhang Xiaohua (張曉華), *Jing-jiao dong-jian tan* (景教东渐探), *Zong-jiao-shi yan-jiu* (宗教史研究) 6 (1994), pp. 85–90, for a typical example; awareness in Chinese scholarship of the place of East Syrians in the Abbasid court as physicians and their similar roles in the Tang court is growing, however; see the book's final chapter on the secondary literature and arguments based on primary sources that Tang missionising towards Han and non-Han peoples outside the court could well have taken place as a by-product of the East Syrians' place as knowledge holders.

20. As most readers will be aware, this older appellation for the Church of the East identifies the church with a theological deemed heretical by the church of the Roman Empire, and is thus a term of derision — something on the order of referring to a Roman Catholic as 'Papist;' the term also obscures the Church of the East's much more significant connection to the theology of Theodore of Mopsuestia than Nestorius; see Sebastian P. Brock, 'The "Nestorian" Church: a lamentable misnomer', *Bulletin of the John Rylands Library* 78 (1996), pp. 23–35.

21. This is a questionable assertion.

22. Saeki, *The Nestorian Monument in China*, p. 158.

23. One suspects a Calvinistic 'Sovereignty of God' political theology, perhaps stemming from Saeki's Protestantism, in his interpretations, along with the anti-sacramentalism often associated with a strict aniconic Protestantism. This is ironic given that the Xi'an stele clearly contains a notion of God's sovereignty and that the church's elites were an extension of it and have carried the church's charisma, as ascetics, across the world; see Saeki, *The Nestorian Documents*, pp. 149–50.

24. Two more technical terms, elite and charisma, also part of the study's historiography of courts and courtly space participation, which are given more explicit treatment in the glossary of technical terms in the appendices.

25. See in particular the donor section of the Xi'an stele, which is in Syriac, the significance of which is discussed in this introduction.

26. A neologism in the French language and coined in 1982 by the Lebanese President Bachir Gemayel in his assertion of rights of Lebanese Christians; the term has had many uses, historical and contemporary, and is not without controversy. It is derived from the Arabic ذمي *dhimmī*, meaning 'protected person' and is a category within early Islamic law; the term was popularised by the highly polemical and not uncontroversial book by Bat Ye'or, *The Decline of Eastern Christianity under Islam: From Jihad to Dhimmitude. Seventh-Twentieth Century* (Madison/Teaneck, NJ: Fairleigh Dickinson University Press/ Associated University Presses, 1996).

27. Jérôme Labourt, *Le Christianisme Dans L'Empire Perse: Sous La Dynastie Sassanide (224–632)* (Paris: Victor Lecoffre, 1904), cited in Stephan Gero, 'Only a

change of masters? The Christians of Iran and the Muslim conquest', *Studia Iranica* 5 (1987), pp. 43–8, p. 43.

28. Ibid., p. 43.

29. Michael G. Morony, *Iraq after the Muslim Conquest* (Princeton, NJ: Princeton University Press, 1984), pp. 230–50.

30. Samuel Hugh Moffett, *A History of Christianity in Asia*, vol. 1: *Beginnings to 1500* (New York: Orbis, 1998), p. 325.

31. Lin Wushu (林悟殊), *Tangdai Jingjiao zaiyanjiu* (唐代景教再研究) (Beijing: Zhonghua Shuju, 2003), pp. 263–92; Lin has been influenced by Saeki's cultural degeneration thesis as well however; see his *Gu dai san yi jiao bian deng* (古代三異教辨登) (Beijing: Zhonghua shuju, 2005), pp. 361–6, where his view that science was only cultivated among the East Syrians in order to win converts among the Tang's elites and at court can be seen. The Huichang Rescript ended official support for Zoroastrians and Manichaeism in the empire at same time, and severely curtailed the Buddhist establishments. Often called the Huichang Rescript after its reign name (Huichang (會昌) 841–7), it can be read at JTS 18A.

32. This translation follows Tang (2004), pp. 149–50, with some emendation; see Saeki, *The Nestorian Documents*, p. 18 ff. for the original text.

33. I.e. the Christian God, or, given the recent spread of the Arab empire, the God of Abraham, though the reference may reference the Chinese emperor too.

34. Sam Lieu has put forward the very perceptive observation that since the East Syrians, during their history in Iran, were referred to by the Middle Persian name of *tarsāg* '(God) fearer' (hence Sogd. *trs'q*), this is a concept which may have surfaced in the name Jing-jiao, 'Reverent Teaching', and may also underlie the Chinese term *fu* in this passage; see Samuel N.V. Lieu, 'Epigraphica Nestoriana Serica', in Werner Sundermann, Almut Hintze and François de Blois (eds), *Exegisti monumenta: Festschrift in Honour of Nicholas Sims-Williams*, vol. 40 (Wiesbaden: Harrassowitz, 2009), pp. 227–46, p. 242; on the Syriac word *dehlatha*, 'fear', see Adam Becker, 'Martyrdom, religious difference, and 'fear' as a category of piety in the Sasanian Empire: the case of the martyrdom of Gregory and the martyrdom of Yazdpaneh', *Journal of Late Antiquity* 2/2 (2009), pp. 300–36.

35. See the extended passage in Li Tang's rendering: 'This is not due to their own effort but to that of the Heavenly Lord ... if someone disobeys the emperor and his commands, then for all human beings, this person is a rebel. If someone obeys the emperor's command, then among all men, he is the one who understands and observes the commandments ... if someone takes upon himself the commandments, but has no fear of the Heavenly Lord, then according to the law of Buddha, he does not hold a place of discipline and he is a rebel (against the empire); one should have fear of one's parents and have respect for parents as if they were the Heavenly Lord and Emperor; therefore, if someone first serves the Heavenly Lord, and the empire, then he serves his parents without failure; this person will gain blessings from God; there are no

more than three things (to keep in mind then): first, serve the Heavenly Lord; secondly serve the emperor, and thirdly serve one's parents.'

36. Saeki wrote that the 'study of Christianity in the Tang Empire begins and ends with the Xi'an stele'. Saeki, *The Nestorian Documents*, p. 125.

37. The stele's name in Chinese, as indicated on the monument itself, is revealing of its intent as viewed by its writers: *Daqin jingjiao liuxing zhongguo bei* (大秦景教流行中国碑); 'The Monument for the Propagation of *Daqin Jingjiao* in China'), in the author's rendering. See appendices for the text of the stele and a translation; the Taisho Tripiṭaka numbering scheme has not been followed here, though the online CBETA (Chinese Buddhist Electronic Text Association) of the Xi'an stele has been borrowed; this material is included in the Taisho collection at vol. 54, No. 2144, and made freely available for distribution; this portion of text of the stele is found at line 55 of the author's numbering scheme; Paul Pelliot, *L'inscription nestorienne de Si-ngan-fou, Edited with Supplements by Antonino Forte* (Kyoto: Scuola di Studi sull'Asia Orientale; Paris: Collège de France, Institut des Hautes Etudes Chinoises, 1996), discusses this line at p. 176; Deeg (forthcoming) discusses it at pp. 196−7; Legge, *The Nestorian Monument of Hsi-An Fu*, offers a reliable translation in general and appears frequently below; see Saeki's translation of the stele, not as reliable as Legge's, but in the public domain and thus usable free of charge, is reproduced in the appendices, though with some emendations.

38. See appendices for a full translation and Chinese character version of the Xi'an stele; Pelliot, *L'inscription nestorienne de Si-ngan-fou*, pp. 5−18, on the discovery of the stele and its whereabouts.

39. On the term, derived from Greek, *chorepiskopos* (actually *korepisqopa* in the Syriac of the stele: ܟܘܪܐܦܝܣܩܘܦܐ), this comes from Gr. χώρα 'country, land, district', plus *episkopos*, 'bishop', though note that Robert Payne Smith, in his, *A Compendious Syriac Dictionary: Founded Upon the Thesaurus Syriacus of R. Payne Smith* (Winona Lake, IN: Eisenbrauns, 1998), p. 210, defines this title as indicating one who 'ruled over village churches in the place of a bishop and appointed the lesser orders, but did not ordain priests or deacons, and (though?) himself belonged to the priesthood'; Adam is also called a *qasisa* (ܩܫܝܫܐ); 'elder', within this same portion, the title section, of the stele, almost certainly a translation of the Greek term γέρων, 'elder' (i.e. monastic elder); Cf. ibid., p. 522 on the Syriac term, though the term's origins in the Greek has gone unnoticed.

40. Jazbōzēdh, in the Syriac of the donor section, Middle Persian *yaz-dan buxt*; meaning 'One Saved by God'; see Philippe Gignoux, *Iranisches Personennamenbuch*, vol. 2, *Mitteliranische Personennamen*, Fasz. 3, 'Noms propres sassanides en moyen-perse; épigraphique supplément' (Vienna: Austrian Academy of Sciences, 1986), p. 192n.1061.

41. Glen L. Thompson, 'Sense Units in the Xi'an Stele', forthcoming, in Proceedings of Salzburg International Conference on Syriac Christianity in Medieval Central Asia and China, vol. 5.

42. Pelliot, *L'inscription nestorienne de Si-ngan-fou*, pp. 5–146.

43. See Michael Keevak, *The Story of a Stele: China's Nestorian Monument and Its Reception in the West, 1625–1916* (Hong Kong University Press 2008); it should be noted, however, that Keevak does not know Chinese, and to this reader does little more than process the material though the proclivities of the version of the postcolonial paradigm that characterises modern American academia; despite this Keevak does make available the relevant seventeenth- to early twentieth-century players in the Xi'an monument's reception and outline the key features of the interpretations.

44. Beate Dignas and Engelbert Winter, *Rome and Persia in Late Antiquity: Neighbours and Rivals* (Cambridge: Cambridge University Press, 2007); Michael G. Morony, 'Should Sasanian Iranian be in included in Late Antiquity?', e-Sasankia 1 (2008). Available at http://www.sasanika.org/wp-content/uploads/e-sasanika1-Morony4.pdf (accessed 3 March 2015); Richard E. Payne, *A State of Mixture: Christians, Zoroastrian, and Iranian Political Culture in Late Antiquity* (Oakland, CA: University of California Press, 2015); Joel T. Walker, 'The limits of Late Antiquity: philosophy between Rome and Iran', *The Ancient World* 33/1 (2002), pp. 45–69.

45. Max Deeg, 'A belligerent priest – Yisi and his political context', in Li Tang and Dietmar W. Winkler (eds), *From the Oxus River to the Chinese Shores: Studies on East Syriac Christianity in China and Central Asia*, Orientalia Patristica Oecumenica, vol. 5 (Zurich: Akademie Verlag, 2013), pp. 107–21, p. 117.

46. Among Dezong's fist reforming measures were his attempts to curtail the influence of the court's eunuchs and the monastic institutions of the empire to which the eunuchs were deeply connected; the church's elites' connection to eunuchs, which is explored in chapter four, is part of an on-going exploration of asceticism and the monastic heritage within the church's political connection to courts and reflection of courtly power – court eunuch's being at once courtly and ascetic.

47. See the discussion below for references.

48. This translation of *xuan-gang* follows that of Jan De Meyer, in his study of the life and work of Daoist Wu Yun (d. 778), who wrote a text called the *Xuan-gang lun* (玄綱論) at the beginning of the An Lushan rebellion and submitted it to Emperor Xuanzong about which more is said in the study's final chapter; see Jan De Meyer's *Wu Yun's Way: Life and Works of an Eighth-Century Daoist Master* (Leiden: E.J. Brill, 2006), p. 115.

49. Legge, *The Nestorian Monument of Hsi-An Fu*, p. 24.

50. Paul Pelliot in Antonino Forte (ed.), *Paul Pelliot's L'inscription Nestorienne de Singan-fou* (Kyoto: Scuola di Studi Sull'Asia Orientale, Paris: Collège de France, Institute des Hauste Études, Chinoises, 1996), p. 176; 'soulever', *Collins Robert Unabridged French–English English–French Dictionary*, ed. Christine Penman et al. (New York: HarperCollins, 2002), p. 962.

51. Deeg, *Die Strahlende Lehre*, p. 76; 'richten', *Concise Oxford German Dictionary*, ed. Michael Clark and Olaf Thyen, 3rd edn (Oxford: Oxford University Press, 2009), p. 446.

52. Richard B. Mather, 'Wang Chin's '"Dhūta Temple Inscription" as an example of Buddhist parallel prose', *Journal of the American Oriental Society* 83/3 (1963), pp. 338–59; there he notes that, 'Lu Yun [陸雲], the younger brother of Lu Qi, who was executed with him in 303] in Poem Commissioned to be Written at the Generalissimo's Banquet' (i.e. 司馬冏 Si Ma Jiong, Prince of Qi, who had just killed the usurper, 司馬倫 in 301)', translates this phrase: 'The failing cord has been restored, the numerous creatures set in order' (Wenxuan, 20.12a)'. This is one example of the origins of the phrase in Classical Chinese literature before Buddhism and its connection to Chinese imperial ideology.

53. The *Jinshu* (晉書) states that *xuan-gang* can be used interchangeably with 天網 (*tian-gang*), and is thus linked to important vocabulary in Classical and Middle Chinese stemming from 天下 (*tian-xia*) having to do with empire, the Chinese emperor and its connections to Chinese religion and cosmology (*Jinshu* 54.24); the larger context of this passage can be explored at http://zh.wikisource.org/wiki/晉書/卷54 (accessed 4 November 2014); though the Jin Dynasty, the subject of the *Jin Shu*, lasted from 265 to 420, the Jin Shu, or Book of Jin, was an early Tang period endeavour; see William Theodore de Bary and Irene Bloom (eds), *Sources of Chinese Tradition*, vol. I, 2nd edn (New York: Columbia University Press, 1999), p. 274; connections to imperial China's Yellow Emperor ideology are drawn out in the study's final chapter; the text states: '方今太清闢宇，四門啟籥，玄綱括地，天網廣羅', 'The present and greatly pure emperor, from the palace where he is locked, enlightens (and moves out) to include the empire ('the Imperial Net'), the heavenly expanse and all that it encompasses'; the 南齊書 [*Nanqi Shu*] states: '偶化兩儀，均明二耀，拯玄網於頹絕，反至道於澆淳', which may be rendered: 'When (the emperor) naturally nurtures the two instruments, reconciles and makes bright the sun and moon, and, when it's destroyed, establishes the Imperial Net, he (thus) reverses the degeneration of the Dao'; though Pelliot's caveat that *gang* (網) should be translated 'chord' rather than 'net' is well taken, Legge's choice of 'net' rather than 'chord' will be followed here; the author wishes to make it absolutely clear that his translation of *xuan-gang* as 'imperial net' rather than the much more literal rendering of 'mysterious net' is an interpretation, and one that is justifiable for what it does to bring the Persian heritage of the Church of the East's political asceticism and courtly agency back into focus.

54. For a general introduction, see Marc Abramson, *Ethnic Identity in Tang China* (Philadelphia, PA: University of Pennsylvania Press, 2008); see Chapters 3 and 5 for specific explorations with regards to the Church of the East in the Tang.

55. See discussion further in this chapter for references.

56. See appendices and the Xi'an stele's lines 137–40 for the original Syriac.

57. Payne Smith, *A Compendious Syriac Dictionary*, p. 252, where Payne Smith lists a hierarchy of meanings: (a) guidance, direction, steering, government, administration; (b) way of proceeding, course, action; (c) prudence, foresight; (d) a province, prefecture; (e) divine dispensation, the economy of God.

58. The New Testament Greek term οικονομια occurs at 1 Timothy 1:4; Ephesians 1:10; 3:2; 3:9; 1 Corinthians 9:17; Colossians 1:25. Cf. the Peshitta translation of Ephesians 1:10 with its Greek original: ܠܡܕܒܪܢܘܬܐ ܕܡܘܠܝܐ ܕܙܒܢܐ ܕܟܠ ܡܕܡ ܢܬܚܕܬ ܒܡܫܝܚܐ ܕܒܫܡܝܐ ܘܕܒܐܪܥܐ and εἰς *οἰκονομίαν* τοῦ πληρώματος τῶν καιρῶν, ἀνακεφαλαιώσα νακεφαλαιώσασθαι τὰ πάντα ἐν τῷ Χριστῷ, τὰ ἐπὶ τοῖς οὐρανοῖς καὶ τὰ ἐπὶ τῆς γῆς· ἐναὐτῷ. New American Standard Bible (NASB): 'with a view to an administration suitable to the fullness of the times, *that is*, the summing up of all things in Christ, things in the heavens and things on the earth. In Him'.

59. Geoffrey W.H. Lampe, *A Patristic Greek Lexicon* (Oxford: Oxford University Press, 1961), pp. 940–4.

60. Erica Hunter, 'The Persian contribution to Christianity in China: reflections in the Xi'an Fu Syriac inscriptions', in Li Tang and Dietmar Winkler (eds), *Hidden Treasures and Intercultural Encounters* (London: Global Marketing Publications, 2009), p. 76.

61. The original edict for the granting of official status to the church is found at Wang Pu [王溥] (922–82) (ed.), *Tang Huiyao* [唐會要, *Notabilia of Tang*] (Shanghai: Shanghai guji chubanshe, 1991) (hereafter THY), 49.1012, Du You [杜佑] (735–812) (ed.), *Tongdian* [通典, *Complete Institutes*] (compiled between 766–801) (Beijing: Zhongua shuju, 1988) (hereafter TD), 40.1103 and Wang Qinruo [王欽若] (ed.), *Cefu Yuangui* [冊府元龜, *The Great Tortoise of National Archives*, compiled between 1005–13) (Beijing: Zhonghua shuju, 1960) (hereafter CFYG), 51.20, and clearly identifies the Church as 'Persian' and its centers of activity as 'monasteries', and identifies as Sasanian liaison to the Tang Aluoben (Rabban 'leader') as a monk.

62. The gravestone and epitaph for court Astronomer Li Su is reprinted in Rong Xinjiang [荣新江], 'Yi ge rushi tangchao de Bosi jingjiao jiazu' [个入仕唐朝的波斯景教家族, A Persian Nestorian Family in Tang China], in Ye Yilang [叶奕良] (ed.), *Yilangxue zai Zhongguo lunwenji* [伊朗学在中国论文集, *A Collection of Essays on Iranian Studies in China*], II (Beijing: Beijing daxue shuban she, 1998), pp. 82–90, repr. in Rong Xinjiang, *Zhonggu Zhongguo yuwailai wenming* [中古中国与外来文明] (Beijing: Shenghuo, dushu, xinzhi sanlian shudian, 2001); the gravestone and epitaph will be briefly mentioned again below but will be discussed in depth in Chapter 4.

63. See Chapter 2.

64. *The Xi'an Stele*, trans. Waley, Arthur, in Charles F. Horne (ed.), *The Sacred Books and Early Literature of the East*, vol. 12: *Medieval China* (New York: Parke, Austin, and Lipscomb, 1917) (hereafter XS), lines 53–55.

65. For references and elaboration see the discussion further on in this chapter.

66. Timothy H. Barrett, 'Buddhism, Taoism and the eighth-century Chinese term for Christianity: a response to recent work by A. Forte and others', *Bulletin of the School of Oriental and African Studies* 65/3 (2002), pp. 555–60; Zhang Xiaogui [張小貴], 'Why did Chinese "Nestorians" change the name of their religion to Jingjiao?', 4th Salzburg International Conference on the Church of the East in China and Central Asia, 7–11 June 2013.

67. As Chinese does not have articles, this could be translated as either 'the Persian teaching', or 'Persian teaching', a grammatical point that is not without consequence: the edict is found at THY 49.1012, TD 40.1103 and CFYG 51.20.

68. Forte in *L'inscription nestorienne de Si-ngan-fou*, p. 263, gives five reasons for the name (some of which may be dispute):

    (1)   the Tang court would never have allowed the propagation of a religion based only on the visit of 'Persian monk', as is suggested by the Xi'an stele, who asked the empire avail itself to his missionising efforts;

    (2)   the welcome Aluoben was given by high-ranking official Fang Xuanling, as indicated in the Xi'an stele, would not have been offered to a wandering monk;

    (3)   when Peroz III (Yazdegird III's son) requested in 677 a 'Persian temple' be built in Chang'an, he was likely following the precedent set by his father and his court at the time of Aluoben's work as a diplomatic liaison (as seen in the Xi'an stele), suggesting this temple was probably Christian and not Zoroastrian;

    (4)   in Sasanian Persia, Christianity had received state protection such that, as Forte writes 'there is nothing strange in this being carried over into China'; and

    (5)   Church of the East leader Jilie (及烈; Syr. Gabriel) is shown sent as part of a diplomatic mission from a political body referred to as Persia in Chinese sources to the Tang court in the year 725, CFYG 975.

69. Antonino Forte, 'The edict of 638', in Forte, *L'inscription nestorienne de Si-ngan-fou*, p. 363.

70. See the discussion below for an understanding of imperial charisma transmission.

71. See Chapter 4 on the issue of internal and external disorder being connected, its recent historiography and in connection to Chancellor Li Mi.

72. De Meyer, *Wu Yun's Way*, p. 115; the entire text for which can be found in the *Quan Tang Wen* [全唐文], pp. 925–6.

73. For as Wu Yun writes: 'When the Way (the Dao) is lost, there is still Virtue. When Virtue goes in decline, there is still Humanity. When Humanity fails, there is still Righteousness; when Righteousness is deficient, there is still Propriety. When Propriety is spoiled, it is followed by anarchy/rebellion, and in that case, Knowledge will serve to cheat all under heaven. Therefore,

Propriety and Knowledge are the major precautions in curbing disorder (rebellion). The Way and its Virtue are the great mainstays for pacifying anarchy [whereas] Propriety and Knowledge are the outgrowths of the Way. He who abides by the fundamental (the mystic mainstay), acts with ease and is secure. He who acts in accord with the accessory, acts with difficulty and is in danger. Therefore a ruler of men takes the Way as his heart and Virtue as his body; he considers Humanity and Righteousness as his carriage and robes, and propriety and knowledge as his ceremonial cap. Then he lets his robe hang down, folds his hands, and the empire is transformed. If one esteems propriety and knowledge, but forgets the Way and its Virtue, what one does will be ornamented, but it will lack soul. Even though [the ruler] might preserve [all day long] and be alert at night, the empire will go to ruin', de Meyer, *Wu Yun's Way*, p. 115.

74. Use of the term 'charismatic constitution' is clarified in the introduction.

75. Ittai Gradel, *Emperor Worship and Roman Religion* (Oxford: Oxford University Press, 2002), pp. 78–98; as Deeg notes, Emperor Xuanzong had Buddha images installed in imperial temples, which artists rendered with the emperor's own facial features: Deeg, *Die Strahlende Lehre*, pp. 208–9.

76. Cf. 1 Sam. 10:1–2 for the ritual of anointing of a king, a wide variety of individuals and objects also anointed including Jewish priests (Lev. 4:3), and prophets (Is. 61:1); the Jewish Temple itself and its utensils (Ex. 40:9–11), unleavened bread (Num. 6:15), and even a non-Jewish king (Cyrus of Persia) (Is. 45:1).

77. The notion of the two bodies allowed for continuity of monarchy even when the monarch died, captured in the saying: 'The king is dead. Long live the king', and Kantorowicz's reconstruction of the Christian background of this notion led him to liturgical works, to Christian images in art, and theological polemical materials (Kantorowicz, *The King's Two Bodies*), providing, one may suggest, a Cultural History of the symbolic means by which early nation states established sovereignty and hegemony and its Early Modern demise.

78. Eusebius, *The Life of Constantine*, in Philip Schaff (ed.), *Nicene and Post-Nicene Christianity: From Constantine the Great to Gregory the Great*, AD 311–600 Edinburgh: T. & T. Clark, 1884), pp. 647–736; *Oratio de Laudibus Constantini* 1–10, *Panegyric to Constantine*, in Ivar A. Heikel (ed.), *Eusebius Werke*, vol. 1 (Leipzig: J.C. Hinrichs'sche Buchhandlung, 1902), pp. 195–223; *Triac.* 11–18: *Oratio de Laudibus Constantini* 11–18, *Treatise on the Church of the Holy Sepulchre*, ibid., pp. 223–59, where language of divine favour abounds.

79. *The Chronicle of Joshua the Stylite: Composed in Syriac AD 507*, ed. and trans. William Wright (Cambridge: Cambridge University Press, 1882).

80. Nathanael J. Andrade, 'The Syriac life of John of Tella and the frontier *politeia*', *Hugoye: Journal of Syriac Studies* 12/2 (2009), pp. 199–234.

81. Ibid., p. 203.

82. See Chapter 1 for further discussion of this specific issue and its bibliography.

83. See Chapter 3.

84. Cf. Peter Brown, *The Body and Society: Men, Women, and Sexual Renunciation in Early Christianity* (New York: Columbia University Press, 1988, p. 399), where Brown writes of the 'shift of the center of gravity on the human person' that took place in the fourth century and through the Origenist controversy, where virginity and the renunciation of the body's passions led to the ability to wield great power within society as bishops tailored the ascetic language and postures contoured over the previous century to fit the new Christian empire, and where the non-hierarchical view of the body in Origen's thought, in Brown's estimation, no longer had a place. It is important to note that in his introduction Brown makes clear his debt to Michel Foucault's volumes of the *History of Sexuality*, and the third volume in particular, *The History of Sexuality*, vol. 3: *The Care of the Self* (Cambridge: Blackwell, 1986); there, the concern is over the way in which the asceticism of the pagan Roman elite, in which one sought to rule the self in order to rule others, became a paradigm within an entire society with the coming of official Christianity.

85. The Cultural History paradigm exhibits emphasis on material culture and attempts to evoke the feel of a culture of the past by placing them into a narrative, something present in the work of Peter Brown; see Peter Burke, *What is Cultural History?* (Cambridge: Polity Press, 2005).

86. This and the previous two authors will be discussed in Chapter 1.

87. To be discussed in Chapter 1.

88. To be discussed in Chapter 3.

89. See Chapter 1 for a discussion of Mar Yonan's ocean-faring and crab-riding holy man, about which the author was made aware through Richard E. Payne's article 'Monks, dinars and date palms: hagiographical production and the expansion of monastic institutions in the early Islamic Persian Gulf, *Arabian Archaeology and Epigraphy* 22/1 (2011), pp. 97–111. See appendices of Richard Todd Godwin, 'Persian Christians at the Chinese Court: The Xi'an Stele and the Church of the East, 410–845', unpublished PhD thesis, School of Oriental and African Studies, University of London, 2016a, for the Syriac for this passage, and an English translation.

90. Elizabeth K. Fowden, *The Barbarian Plain: Saint Sergius between Rome and Iran* (Berkeley, CA: University of California Press, 1999); Scott McDonough, 'A second Constantine? The Sasanian King Yazdgard I in Christian history and historiography', *Journal of Late Antiquity* 1/1 (Spring 2008), pp. 127–40; Richard E. Payne, 'Christianity and Iranian society: saint's cults, canon law and social change in Late Sasanian and Early Islamic Iran', unpublished PhD thesis, Princeton University, 2010; Cynthia Villagomez, 'The fields, flocks, and finances of monks: economic life at Nestorian monasteries, 500–850', unpublished PhD thesis, University of California, Los Angeles, 1998; Joel T. Walker, *The Legend of Mar Qardagh: Narrative and Christian Heroism in Late Antique Iraq* (Berkeley, CA: University of California Press, 2006).

91. Sebastian P. Brock 'Christians in the Sasanian Empire. A case of divided loyalties', *Studies in Church History* 18 (1982), pp. 1–19; Arthur Christensen,

L'Iran sous les Sassanides (Copenhagen: Levin and Munksgaard, 1936); Matteo Compareti, 'The last Sasanians in China', *Eurasian Studies* 2/2 (2003), pp. 197–13; Touraj Daryaee, 'The idea of Ērāšahr: Jewish, Christian and Manichaean Views in Late Antiquity', in Florin Curta (ed.), *Borders, Barriers, and Ethnogenesis: Frontiers in Late Antiquity and Middle Ages* (Antwerp: Brepols, 2005), pp. 123–37; Antonino Forte, 'Iraniens en Chine. Bouddhisme, mazdéisme, bureaux de commerce', in Jean-Pierre Drége (ed.), *La Sérinde terre d'échanges* (Paris: La Documentation française, 2000), pp. 181–90; Antonino Forte, *The Hostage An Shigao and his Offspring: An Iranian Family in China* (Kyoto: Italian School of East Asian Studies, 1995); Janos Harmatta, 'The Middle Persian-Chinese bilingual inscription from Hsian and the Chinese-Sāsānian relations', in Enrico Cerulli et al. (eds), *La Persia nel Medioevo* (Rome: Accademia Nazionale dei Lince, 1971), pp. 363–76; Antonio Painano, 'The "Persian" identity in religious controversies: again on the case of "divided loyalty" in Sasanian Iran', in Carlo G. Certi (ed.), *Iranian Identity in the Course of History, Serie Orientale Roma, Orientalia Romana* 9, proceedings of the conference held in Rome, 21–24 September 2005, pp. 227–39; Payne, *A State of Mixture*; William G. Young, *Patriarch, Shah and Caliph* (Rawalpindi: Christian Study Centre, 1974).

92. Samuel N.C. Lieu, 'Byzantium, Persia and China: interstate relations on the eve of the Islamic conquest', *Realms of the Silk Roads: Ancient and Modern*, proceedings from the Third Conference of the Australasian Society for Inner Asian Studies, Macquarie University, 21–22 September 1998, pp. 47–65.

93. Aleksandr Nymark, 'Sogdiana, its Christians and Byzantium: a study of artistic and cultural connections in Late Antiquity and the Early Middle Ages', PhD thesis, Indiana University, 2001, pp. 168–200.

94. In the year 410 East Syrians became firmly entrenched within the political structures of the Sasanian empire. See Chapter 2 for more detail and for further remarks on the phase of East Syrian culture beginning in 410; see the chapter summaries at the end of this introduction for another statement of this central thesis and notion within the book.

95. Glen L. Thompson, 'Was Alopen a "missionary"?', in Li Tang and Dietmar Winkler (eds), *Hidden Treasures and Intercultural Encounters* (London: Global Marketing Publications, 2009), pp. 267–78. It must be noted that the conference in Salzburg Austria on the Church of the East in Medieval Central Asia and China, the 'divine leadership' of which is responsible for Thompson's article, along with articles by Deeg, Chen, Hunter and Lieu, appearing in the book's bibliography, is the vanguard of this field of study to which much appreciation is owed.

96. The Hephthalites, or 'White Huns', are so little understood that the question of whether they were Turkic or Iranian has yet to be settled; primary source evidence does exist that in the late sixth century the Hephthalites' empire came to an end, through a Sasanian and Turkic alliance. The extension of the Church of the East into Hephthalite territory at precisely the same time

occurred during the period of Patriarch Mar Aba I (r. 540–52); the existing hagiography representing the patriarch's tenure, known as the *Life of Mar Aba*, along with the move of the Church eastward into Hephthalite territory, are treated in the book's first chapter. The appearance of Chinese-style Kai-yuan coins in Sogdiana minted by Christian rulers begins at the same time; see Nymark, 'Sogdiana, its Christians and Byzantium, pp. 168–200; see Chapter 2 for further bibliography.

97. *Synodicon Orientale ou Recueil de Synods Nestoriens*, vol. 27, ed. and trans. Jean Baptiste Chabot (Paris: Imprimerie Nationale, 1902) (hereafter SO); Erica C.D. Hunter, 'The Church of the East in Central Asia', *Bulletin of John Rylands University Library of Manchester* 78/3 (1996), pp. 129–42, p. 131.

98. *Chronica Minora*, ed. and trans. Ernest W. Brookes, Ignazio Guidi and Jean Baptiste Chabot (Paris: E Typographeo Reipublicae, 1903–5) (Corpus Scriptorum Christianorum Orientalium) (hereafter CSCO) 1 (Syr. III, 4), 1903, 35 (Syr.) 28; Hunter, 'The Church of the East in Central Asia', p. 133.

99. The phrase *longue durée*, drawn, of course, from the French Annales school of historiography, is only meant loosely to denote that school's specific use of the phrase, though its interest in reconstructing 'the feel' of a period is present here as well, something also seen within the school of historiography known also as Cultural History, more of an influence here overall. Both schools of historiography express interest in themes, symbols, sentiments, rituals of power, material objects and social networks etc. in the interest of eliciting a 'feel' for life in a period of history; famous early works connecting both schools include Johan Huizinga's *The Waning of the Middle Ages* (*Herfsttij der Middeleeuwen* (Haarlem: Tjeenk Willink, 1919)) etc. See below for the way in which this term is being used in connection with the sociology of asceticism and within the Cultural History paradigm.

100. Morony, *Iraq after the Muslim Conquest*, pp. 338, 361, 375. See the further comments about Morony's thesis made in Chapter 1.

101. There is a large bibliography on this; this notion can be argued to exist widely in the literature, ranging from more general studies to more specialised studies; cf. Wilhelm Baum and Dietmar W. Winkler, *The Church of the East: A Concise Introduction*, trans. Miranda G. Henry (London: Routledge, 2003), pp. 26–31, for the notion of the Church of the East as a 'culturual intermediary' and Moffett, *A History of Christianity in Asia*, p. 134. On the presence of Greek scientific thought among the Tang East Syrians, see Samuel N.C. Lieu, 'The Romanitas of the Xi'an inscription', in Li Tang and Dietmar W. Winkler (eds), *From the Oxus River to the Chinese Shores: Studies on East Syriac Christianity in China and Central Asia*, Orientalia Patristica Oecumenica, vol. 5 (Zurich: Akademie Verlag, 2013), pp. 123–40.

102. Dimitri Gutas, *Greek Thought, Arab Culture* (London and New York: Routledge, 1998). See Chapter 4 for these arguments.

103. Adam H. Becker, *Fear of God and the Beginning of Wisdom: The School of Nisibis and the Development of Scholastic Culture in Late Antique Mesopotamia* (Philadelphia, PA: University of Pennsylvania Press, 2006).
104. As explored in Chapter 3.
105. Becker, *Fear of God*, p. 28.
106. Ibid., p. 31.
107. Ibid., pp. 31–2.
108. Ibid., pp. 34–9.
109. Ibid., pp. 128–30.
110. Ibid., pp. 175–7.
111. See Chapters 2 and 4 for further comments on ascetics and thaumaturgy.
112. The most straightforward exposition of his approach to sociology and the empirical work used in relation to it are found in the interviews with Pierre Bourdieu that appear in his *In Other Words: Essays Towards a Reflexive Sociology* (Stanford, CA: Stanford University Press, 1990). See the appendices for more on the understanding of *habitus* employed in the study.
113. See 'Worldly Asceticism' in Theoretical Concepts appendix.
114. Josef Wieshöfer, 'King, court and royal representation in the Sasanian Empire', in Anthony J. Spawforth (ed.), *The Court and Court Society in Ancient Monarchies* (Cambridge: Cambridge University Press, 2007), pp. 58–79, p. 68.
115. Ibid., p. 69. Tabari records Khosrow I's attempts to cut the lineage traditions of the great families of the empire by adopting their children into his own household and requiring them to wear certain types of clothing to signify this new relationship to him; see Ehsan Yarshater (ed.), *The History of al-Ṭabarī*, 40 vols (New York: SUNY Press, 1989–2007), Book I.897.1ff; Procopius' *The Persian Wars*, trans. H.B. Dewing (Cambridge MA: Loeb Classical Library, 1928), 1.17.26–18 records similar developments, as does Theophylact Simocatta 3.8; see *The History of Theophylact Simocatta: An English Translation with Introduction*, trans. Michael and Mary Whitby (Oxford: Oxford University Press, 1986).
116. An important term within the book: see the appendices for an explication of its use and significance.

Chapter 1   The Late Sasanian Court and Divine Economy

1. Antonino Forte, 'The edict of 638', in Antonino Forte (ed.), *Paul Pelliot's L'inscription Nestorienne de Singan-fou* (Kyoto: Scuola di Studi Sull'Asia Orientale, Paris: Collège de France, Institute des Hauste Études, Chinoises, 1996), pp. 349–73, p. 363.
2. Patricia Crone, *The Nativist Prophets of Early Islamic Iran* (Cambridge: Cambridge University Press, 2012), p. 5; cf. Donald Leslie's more informed arguments in favour of the notion, however, in his 'Persian temples in T'ang China', *Monumenta Serica* 35/1 (1981–83), pp. 275–303, p. 282; on Peroz II's

'Christian temple', see *Chang'an zhi* [長安志 10), *Wenyuange siku quanshu dianziban* [文淵閣四庫全書電子版) (Shanghai: Renmin Chubanshe, 2002) (hereafter SKQS), referred to specifically as a Persian Hu Temple, a 波斯胡寺.

3. Forte, 'The edict of 638', p. 363 ff.
4. To which may be added that Church of the East leaders were involved in interstate, Sasanian–Roman, Sasanian–Turkic relations; see the discussion of this topic below.
5. Ehsan Yarshater (ed.), *The History of al-Ṭabarī*, 40 vols (New York: SUNY Press, 1989–2007), Vol. 15, pp. 78–9.
6. Ibid., p. 89; Yazdegird III's death is also referred to in the *Histoire nestorienne inédite: Chronique de Séert*, Part 2, fasc. 2: *Patrologia Orientalis*, ed. and trans. Addaï Scher, vol. 13/4 (Paris: Librarie de Paris, 1919) (hereafter CS (1919)), pp. 437–39.
7. Ibid., pp. 79–80, and as discussed below.
8. Ibid., p. 89; see appendices of Richard Todd Godwin, 'Persian Christians at the Chinese Court: The Xi'an Stele and the Church of the East, 410–845', unpublished PhD thesis, School of Oriental and African Studies, University of London, 2016a, for the original Arabic and a linguistically-oriented English translation.
9. The Xi'an stele records Aluoben's winning of official permission for the church in 635; Forte reconstructs the original form of the 638 edict in which the Persian Religion naming designation was given ('The edict of 638', p. 354); the edict is found at Tang Huiyao 49.1012, Tong Dian 40.1103 and Cefu yuangui 51.20; Touraj Daryaee, 'Yazdgerd III's last year: coinage and history of Sistan at the end of Late Antiquity', *Iranistik: Deutschsprachige Zeitschrift fur iranistische Studien. Festschrift fur Erich Kettenhofen*, ed. Touraj Daryaee and Omid Tabibzadeh 5/1–2, 2006–7 (2009), pp. 21–30. Daryaee notes that it is necessary to ask whether 'Yazdegerd III's gravitation to Christianity may have caused erosion of Iranian loyalty to him', and why the bulk of the coinage from his last years, a period of 'wandering kingship', comes from Sistan though he was murdered in Merv (p. 22). The first of these questions is not answered by Daryaee but only suggested.
10. Though Queen Shirin (d. *c*.628) is central in these developments, it was Syrian Orthodox-linked Gabriel of Siggar, physician to the emperor and close confidant of Queen Shirin, Christian wife of Emperor Khosrow II, who seems to have caused a shift in the balance of power away from the Diophysite Church of the East and toward the Miaphysite Syrian Orthodox within the Sasanain court. Sabrisho', an East Syrian bishop well-adapted to courtly settings, also played a role. Sabrisho' and his closeness to the Sasanian court resulted in his eventually choosing to divorce his Christian wife for a Zoroastrian wife, something openly criticised by East Syrian Bishop Gregory. In response to this opposition by Bishop Gregory, Sabrisho' followed the queen's suggestion and had Gregory relocated to a monastery; it was at this time that Gabriel of Siggar switched his allegiance from the Church of the East

to the Syrian Orthodox church, and according to Samuel Moffet 'Queen Shirin followed her physician into the Miaphysite fold'; Moffett, *A History of Christianity in Asia*, vol. 1: *Beginnings to 1500* (New York: Orbis, 1998), p. 93.

11. Ibid.

12. Ibid., p. 78. He is described as fleeing on foot, carrying his belt, sword, and crown (symbol of the *comitatus*), and coming to the home of a stonecutter on the banks of the Mughad river. 'When he became careless the stone cutter killed him, and put the corpse into river.' The townspeople then killed the stone cutter, took Yazdegird III's body and material goods, and put it (together) in a wooden coffin.

13. A Marzban was a military governor of a frontier district under the Sasanians. After Khosrow I's reforms they were under the command of the Ispahbadh. But at this point a Marzban was an autonomous local ruler; Michael Morony, *Iraq after the Muslim Conquest* (Princeton, NJ: Princeton University Press, 1984), pp. 28, 131, passim; linguistically the term Marzobān or Marzbān (MP transliteration: mlcp'n', derived from *marz*, 'border, boundary' and the suffix -*bān*, 'guardian'; Modern Persian: مرزبان, Marzbān) described a class of margraves or military commanders in charge of border provinces of the Sasanian Empire. Marzbans were granted the administration of the border provinces and were responsible for maintaining the security of the trade routes. Sasanian emperors usually selected Marzbans from Bozorgan, Persian noble families who held the most powerful positions in the imperial administration, and passed down the office through a single family for generations. In connection to the *comitatus*, Marzbans of greatest seniority were permitted a silver throne, while Marzbans of the most strategic border provinces, such as the province of Armenia, were allowed a golden throne.

14. Yarshater, pp. 82–3.

15. See Wanda Wolska-Conus (ed.), *Cosmas Indicopleustès. Topographie chrétienne, Livres I–IV*, Sources chrétiennes 141 (Paris: Le Cerf, 1968); *The Christian Topography of Cosmas, an Egyptian Monk*, 1st edn, trans. John W. McCrindle (London: Hakluyt Society, 1897); Eric O. Winstedt (ed.), *The Christian Topography of Cosmas Indicopleustes* (London: Cambridge University Press, 1909).

16. *The Christian Topography of Cosmas, an Egyptian Monk*, p. 1, prologue

17. Ibid.

18. Ibid., p. 2, emphasis mine.

19. Ibid., p. 365; for the Greek text, see Windstedt, *The Christian Topography*, pp. 321–2.

20. *The Christian Topography of Cosmas, an Egyptian Monk*, pp. 338–9.

21. Knud Hannestad, 'Les relations de Byzance avec la Transcaucasie et l'Asie Centrale aux 5e et 6e siecles', *Byzantion* 25–27 (1955–57), pp. 421–56; Samuel N.C. Lieu, 'Byzantium, Persia and China: interstate relations on the eve of the Islamic conquest', *Realms of the Silk Roads: Ancient and Modern*,

proceedings from the Third Conference of the Australasian Society for Inner Asian Studies, Macquarie University, 21–22 September 1998, pp. 47–65E.

22. *The History of Menander the Guardsman*, ed. and trans. Roger C. Blockley (Liverpool: Cairns, 1985), Frag. 9.3–10.1, pp. 104–13.

23. Hannestad, 'Les relations de Byzance', p. 55.

24. Étienne de la Vaissière, *Sogdian Traders: A History* (Boston, E.J. Brill, 2005). Cosmas is discussed on p. 85; de la Vaissière asserts that the Sogdians were at this point taking silk from China to Persia, and that older routes going from Bactria ceased to operate.

25. *The Syriac Chronicle of Zachariah of Mitylene*, trans. Frederick J. Hamilton and Ernest W. Brooks (London: Methuen: 1899), p. 329 ff.; see appendices of Godwin (2016a) for the original Syriac and an English translation.

26. The important question of just how sedentary or nomadic the Hephthalites and their Turkic conquerors were in the mid to late sixth century will be dealt with below, though not to the extent it deserves.

27. *Syriac Chronicle*, p. 331.

28. *Synodicon Orientale ou Recueil de Synods Nestoriens*, vol. 27, ed. and trans. Jean Baptiste Chabot (Paris: Imprimerie Nationale, 1902) (hereafter SO), p. 37; cf. Theophylact Simocatta's statement on the 'two eyes of the world'. He writes that 'God saw to it that the whole world would be lit up from above and from the beginning by two eyes, namely by the most powerful Roman Empire and by the wisest rulers of the Persian state. For by these greatest powers the disobedient and bellicose nations are winnowed, and man's way of life is well ordered and always guided'. Letter iv.11.2–11, in the collection of primary texts from Persian and Roman relation in Late Antiquity: Beate Dignas and Engelbert Winter, *Rome and Persia in Late Antiquity: Neighbours and Rivals* (Cambridge: Cambridge University Press, 2007), p. 238.

29. Under the influence of the views of Arthur Christensen and his *L'Iran sous les Sassanides* (Copenhagen: Levin and Munksgaard, 1936); for contrary views, see Zeev Rubin, 'The reforms of Khosrow Anushirwan', in Averil Cameron and Lawrence I. Conrad (eds), *The Byzantine and Early Islamic Near East*, vol. 3: *States, Resources and Armies* (Princeton, NJ: Princeton University Press, 1995), pp. 227–97; Gheraldo Gnoli, 'The quadripartition of the Sasanian Empire', *East and West* 35 (1985), pp. 265–70.

30. Parveneh Pourshariati, *Decline and Fall of the Sasanian Empire: The Sasanian-Parthian Confederacy and the Arab Conquest of Iran* (London: I.B.Tauris, 2008), pp. 156–70.

31. *The History of Menander the Guardsman*, p. 95.

32. Eusebius, *The Life of Constantine*, in Philip Schaff (ed.), *Nicene and Post-Nicene Christianity: From Constantine the Great to Gregory the Great*, AD 311–600 Edinburgh: T. & T. Clark, 1884), pp. 647–36, I.12, IV.8; Sebastian P. Brock, 'Christians in the Sasanian Empire. A case of divided loyalties', *Studies in Church History* 18 (1982), pp. 1–19, p. 1.

33. SO, p. 225.

34. Ibid., p. 240.
35. Ibid.
36. Ibid.
37. Ibid.
38. Adam H. Becker, *Fear of God and the Beginning of Wisdom: The School of Nisibis and the Development of Scholastic Culture in Late Antique Mesopotamia* (Philadelphia, PA: University of Pennsylvania Press, 2006), p. 2.
39. Roman church historian Sozomen says nothing about Ephraim's involvement in founding the school following its move, but does refer to him as having been a teacher at earlier school. Barhadbesabba of Holwan, a much later author, records and reflects the existence of a tradition about Ephraim's disciples having founded the school. Arthur Vööbus, *History of the School of Nisibis* (Leuven: Peeters, 1985), pp. 33, 40–53.
40. In 489 a basilica dedicated to Mary as the 'Theotokos' (reflecting a theological view opposed to that of the diophysites) was set up on at the site of the former school; Vööbus, p. 32.
41. Ibid., p. 13.
42. Ibid., p. 14.
43. Ibid., p. 15.
44. Ibid., p. 20.
45. Socrates, *Ecclesiastical History*, in Philip Schaff (ed.), *Nicene and Post-Nicene Christianity: From Constantine the Great to Gregory the Great, AD 311–-600* (Edinburgh: T. & T. Clarke, 1884), 7.8.1–20, pp. 393–4.
46. Menander the Guardsman, Fragment, 13; *The History of Menander the Guardsman*, p. 90; the first was a lower level ambassadorial corps, made of younger staff, and had more specific duties and less freedom; the second rank was higher and given more freedom in negotiations. Such doctors were given guidelines and protocol to follow in interimperial negotiations but were given freedom to think on their feet because they were respected for their intelligence.
47. Evagrios, *Ecclesiastical History*, 7.8, *The Ecclesiastical History of Evagrios Scholasticus, Translated texts for Historians*, trans. Michael Whitby 33/VI 21 (Liverpool: Liverpool University Press, 2000) (hereafter EH), 7.8.1–20; SO, p. 255; Dignas and Winter, *Rome and Persia in Late Antiquity*, pp. 228–9; Moffett, *A History of Christianity in Asia*, pp. 154–5.
48. SO, p. 255.
49. Ibid.
50. See the discussion in Chapters 2 and 4 on connections between Roman medicine, East Syrian elites and Tang emperors.
51. Moffett, *A History of Christianity in Asia*, p. 154.
52. EH, 7.8.
53. Roger C. Blockley, 'Doctors and Diplomats in the sixth century AD', *Florilegium* 2 (1980), pp. 89–100, p. 94; *The History of Menander the Guardsman*, Frag. 37.

54. Procopius, *The Persian Wars*, vol. II, trans. H.B. Dewing (Cambridge MA: Loeb Classical Library, 1928), 26.31–7. Procopius says that Khosrow was of sickly disposition and needed the constant care of physicians. He says Justinian sent a Roman doctor to his aid for a year (ibid., 28.8–10); Zachariah of Mitylene claims that Khosrow's mother was a secret Christian (EH, 9.6); Evagrios claims that Khosrow converted to Christianity on his deathbed (ibid., 4.28).

55. Procopius, *The Persian Wars*, states that Stephanus had groomed Kavad for the throne.

56. *The History of Menander the Guardsman*, Frag. 37.

57. Ibid.

58. Ibid., Frag. 54, this time in Hormizid's court, but the Roman physicians are treated badly by the Persians.

59. Thomas of Marga, *The Book of Governors: The Historia Monastica of Thomas Bishop of Marga~ AD 840*, vol. II: *The Syriac Text, Introduction, etc.*, trans. Ernest A.W. Budge (London: K. Paul, Trench, Trübner, 1893), p. 76.

60. Ibid., p. 50.

61. Ibid., p. 68.

62. Ibid., p. 82. Information is contained about Yazdin in the *Khuzistan Chronicle* also. Page 81 indicates Yazdin being compared to Constantine. One of Khosrow II's sons is described as joining a monastery. Qualities of Church of the East leaders are described in this text also. This text reflects a period in which the Church of the East participated in diplomatic missions to Heraclius' court and missions to the Caspain Sea transpired as well, as described in the *Khusiztan Chronicle* (*Khuzistan Chronicle*, trans. Geoffrey Greatrex, in Geoffrey Greatrex and Samuel N.C. Lieu (eds), *The Roman Eastern Frontier and the Persian Wars*, Part II: *AD 363–630* (London: Routledge, 2002), pp. 229–37.

63. SO, p. 37; Dignas and Winter, *Rome and Persia in Late Antiquity*, p. 238.

64. Adam H. Becker, *Sources for the Study of the School of Nisibis* (Liverpool: Liverpool University Press, 2008), pp. 94–60, on the school as a lineage of monastic fathers.

65. He composed interpretations of, and commentaries on, the Bible, wrote a disputation against Jews, and a refutation of Eutyches. Three homilies were composed by him; one when Khosrow conquered Najran, because he was there at the court at that time on account of a suit/dispute for the school of Nisbis. Ibid., p. 154.

66. Rubin, 'The reforms of Khosrow Anushirwan', pp. 227–97; Gnoli, 'The quadripartition of the Sasanian Empire', pp. 265–70.

67. SO, pp. 68–80; *Syriac Chronicle*, pp. 318–32, trans. pp. 540–55. Mar Aba renewed monastic discipline, instigated liturgical and scholastic reform, and encouraged the adoption of the canons of the council of Chalcedon; Moffett, *A History of Christianity in Asia*, pp. 217–20.

68. *Life of Mar Aba*, in Paul Bedjan (ed.), *Histoire de Mar-Jabalaha, de trios autres patriarches, d'un prête, et deux laïques, nestoriens* (Leipzig and Paris:

O. Harrassowitz, 1895), pp. 206–74, pp. 217–23; *Ausgewählte Akten persicher Märtyrer*, trans. Oskar Braun (Kempten and Münich: Kösel, 1915), pp. 188–22, pp. 192–4; Paul Peeters, 'Observations sur la vie syriaque de Mar Aba', *Miscellanea Giovanni Mercati*, vol. 5 (Studi e Testi 125) (Rome: Città del Vatticano, 1948), pp. 69–12, pp. 76–84.

69. The text was edited and published by Addaï Scher in three parts early last century: *Histoire Nestorienne, Chronique de Séert*, Part 1, fasc. 1: *Patrologia Orientalis*, vol. 4 (Paris: Librarie de Paris, 1908), pp. 215–13 (hereafter CS (1908)); Part 2, fasc. 1: *Patrologia Orientalis*, vol. 7 (Paris: Librarie de Paris, 1908), pp. 99–203 (hereafter CS (1911)); and (CS (1919) – see n.6). The Life of Mar Aba is found at CS (1911), pp. 154–78.

70. CS (1911), p. 155; James Howard-Johnston, *Witnesses to a World Crisis: Historians and Histories of the Middle East in the Seventh Century* (Oxford: Oxford University Press, 2010), pp. 324–31, on the issue of dating the Chronicle of Se'ert and the sources it draws upon; Pierre Nautin, 'L'auteur de la "Chronique de Séert": Isho'denad de Basra', *Revue de l'histoire des religions* 186/2 (1974), pp. 113–26; Louis R. Sako, 'Les sources de la Chronique de Séert', *Parole de l'Orient* 14 (1987), pp. 155–65.

71. *Ausgewählte Akten persicher Märtyrer*, section 7–9, pp. 192–4.

72. Ibid., section 39, pp. 218–9; Mar Aba's relics rest in this city unto this very day.

73. Ibid.

74. Ibid., section 8, pp. 193–4.

75. CS (1911), p. 159.

76. For the phrase 'royal dialectic', see the introduction and Antonio Painano, 'The "Persian" identity in religious controversies: again on the case of "divided loyalty" in Sasanian Iran', in Carlo G. Certi (ed.), *Iranian Identity in the Course of History, Serie Orientale Roma, Orientalia Romana* 9, proceedings of the conference held in Rome, 21–24 September 2005, pp. 227–39 pp. 230, 233–4.

77. CS (1911), p. 166; emphasis mine; see appendices of Godwin (2016a) for the original Arabic and a translation.

78. Ibid.

79. *Ausgewählte Akten persicher Märtyrer*, section 37, p. 217; see the appendices in Godwin (2016a) for further bibliographic details, the original Syriac and an English translation.

80. See Touraj Daryaee, 'Bazaars, merchants, and trade in Late Antique Iran', *Comparative Studies of South Asia, Africa and the Middle East* 30/3 (2010), pp. 401–9; on the notion Zoroastrian prescriptions against involvement in commerce perhaps providing economic and cultural opportunities to Christians, see p. 404. In the late Sasanian text *Khusrow and the Page Boy*, there is a clear emphasis on courtly refinement and an anti-asceticism that differs enormously from the ascetic and merchant culture the Christians were involved with. The narrative culminates in the youth being accepted as a

courtier due to his refusal to perform an act of supererogation and the emperor finding out about it. For the text see Davoud Monchi-Zadeh, 'Xusrōv I Kavātā ut Rētak: Pahlavi text, transcription and translation', *Acta Iranica* 22 (Leiden: Brill, 1982), pp. 47–91.

81. On the extent of the border extensions that took place following the fall of the Hepthalites, the division of their territory between the Sasanians and the Turks, and the primary sources that speak to this issue, see Geo Widengren, 'Xosrau Anoširvan, les Hephthalites et les peuples Turcs', *Orientalia Suecana* 1 (1952), pp. 69–94.

82. See Moffett, *A History of Christianity in Asia*, pp. 207–8; James Howard-Johnston, *Witnesses to a World Crisis*, p. xvi; Kavad I was the son of Peroz I, another friend of the church through Catholicos Barsauma; when Peroz died he bequeathed the empire not to Kavad but to Kavad's uncle. Kavad revolted and fled across the Oxus river to the Hepthalites, who eventually helped him return to the Persian throne; he fled again to the Huns following the social chaos of the Mazdak revolt, a religion to which he also adhered, in 497, and was again returned to the Persian throne with Hephthalite help. In 484 the Hephthalites crushed the Sasanian army and the Sasanians had to pay massive tribute as a result; the Sogdian traders would have benefited from this indemnity payment; see la Vaissière, *Sogdian Traders*, pp. 110–11.

83. ܪܥܝܐ ܐܠܗܝܐ ܚܘܝܬܒܘܬ; *Ausgewählte Akten persicher Märtyrer*, sections 37–9; see appendices of Godwin (2016a), for close textual work and a translation of the extended passages.

84. Procopius, *History of the Wars*, 8.17.1–8.

85. *The History of Menander the Guardsman*, frag. 10.1–5.

86. Procopius, *History of the Wars*, 8.17.108; India here likely indicates Arabia Felix (Yemen) or Axum (Ethiopia); it is common for Late Antique writers to refer to that area as 'India', partly because they had little knowledge of India proper.

87. CS (1911), pp. 160–1.

88. Morony, *Iraq after the Muslim Conquest*, p. 361.

89. CS (1911), p. 170; the slight embellishment observable within the author's translation is not understood to be unwarranted and undertaken within a justifiable interpretive schema. Note also that the author's version of the final sentence differs in sense from Scher's version: 'En l'apercevant, le roi admira la sagesse du catholicos, son discernement et sa bonte; car il l'avait déjà vu auparavant et avait compris qui il était.'

90. There is some disagreement among scholars as to how long Isho'yahb III was Catholicos; Scott-Montcrieff suggests, following the twelfth century Mar Sulayman, that he was Catholicos for seven years; see Philip Scott-Moncrieff (ed.), *The Book of Consolations or the Pastoral Epistles of Mar Ishu'yab of Kuphlanapin Adiabene*, Part 1 (London: Luzac and Co., 1904), p. xxix; William Wright, *A Short History of Syriac Literature* (London: Adam and Charles Black,

1894), pp. 171–4; Gregory Bar Hebraeus, *Chronicon Ecclesiasticum*, 3 vols, ed. Jean Baptiste Abbeloos and Thomas J. Lamy (Louvani: Peters, 1877); Henricus Gismondi, *Maris, Amri, et Salibae: De Patriarchis Nestorianorum Commentaria I: Amri et Salibae Textus* (Rome, 1896); H. Gismondi, *Maris, Amri, et Salibae: De Patriarchis Nestorianorum Commentaria II: Maris Textus Arabicus et Versio Latina* (Rome, 1899).

91. Pourshariati, *Decline and Fall of the Sasanian Empire*, p. 4.

92. Robert G. Hoyland, *Seeing Islam as Others Saw It. A Survey and Evaluation of the Christian, Jewish and Zoroastrian Writings on Early Islam* (Darwin, NJ: Princeton, 1997), p. 176; Brock, 'Christians in the Sasanian Empire' 1982, p. 3; Moffett, *A History of Christianity in Asia*, pp. 244–6. According to tradition, following Muhammad's death in 632 the Arab community and its new religion was led by the 'rightly guided' (*rashidun*) Caliphs until 651; the first Arab leader figuring in the patronage of Syriac Christians among the caliphs of the Ummayad Clan is its second Caliph, Mu'āwiyah ibn 'Abī Sufyān (r.661–680). His creation of a tribal aristocracy served by a bureaucracy, ruled with the advice of a council of Arab elders and tribal representatives, which strengthened the bureaucracy, was built upon structures put in place during Roman rule. This system involved a postal service, a bureau of registry, and a system of distribution of payment to loyal tribes, each of which contributed to the stability of the early Ummayad state under Caliph Mu'awiyah; though Christians began to find patronage in the early Ummayad court under this system, the letters of Patriarch Isho'yahb III largely predate this system and show a world before the establishment of Ummayad patronage.

93. See the discussion on the letters of Isho'yahb III.

94. Victoria L. Erhart, 'The Church of the East during the period of the four rightly-guided caliphs', *Bulletin of the John Rylands University Library* 78/3 (1996), pp. 55–71, 62.

95. Ibid.

96. Ibid.

97. Isho'yahb II sat as Catholicos from 628 to 644, and was bishop of Balad at the time of his elevation to the Patriarchate; see Josephus S. Assemani, *Bibliotheca Orientalis Clementino-Vaticana* (Rome: Sacrae Congregationis de Propaganda Fide, 1719–28), II, pp. 416–8; III.i, pp. 105, 475; Bar Hebraeus, *Chronicon Ecclesiasticum*, II.113n.i. Isho'yahb II died in 643 and was buried at Kirkuk; see ibid., n.127, n.3; and Wright, *A Short History of Syriac Literature*, p. 842. Isho'yahb II is included in the list of Syriac authors compiled by the fourteenth-century Nestorian writer Abdisho of Nisibis; according to Abdisho, his principal writings were a commentary on the Psalms and a number of letters, histories, and homilies. A hymn of his has survived in a Nestorian psalter (MS BM Add. 14675); CS (1911) has a biography of him at pp. 554–61.

98. Ibid., p. 560.

99. Ibid., p. 620, relates Isho'yahb II's dealings with Arab Caliph Omar; on p. 618 he is recorded as having dealt with Muhammad himself, something which seems doubtful and like a creation of later times.
100. Ibid.
101. Seleucia-Ctesiphon fell to Sa'ad ibn Abi Waqqas in the spring of 637. Sa'ad carried off its gates, symbolising the rulership of central Iraq, to Kufa, and for the rest of his reign Isho'yahb II resided at Karka de Beth Slokh (modern Kirkuk) in Beth Garmai; on the 637 incident, see Robert G Hoyland (1998), 'A Chronicler of Khuzistan', in Hoyland, *Seeing Islam as Others Saw It*, p. 186; CS (1911), pp. 623–6; Thomas of Marga, *Book of Governors*, p. 126, on Isho'yahb II and the dubious Covenant of Omar.
102. Howard-Johnston, *Witnesses to a World Crisis*, pp. 324–31, on the *Chronicle of Se'ert* and the issue of dating the text and which sources it draws upon.
103. Heribert Busse, 'Omar's image as the conqueror of Jerusalem', *Jerusalem Studies in Arabic and Islam* 8 (1986), pp. 149–68; Hoyland, *Seeing Islam as Others Saw It*, pp. 69–71; Yarshater, *The History of al-Ṭabarī*, vol. IX, p. 191.
104. CS (1919), p. 574.
105. Empress Boran lived from 590–631 but was only on the throne for one year. See CS (1919), pp. 557–9; Scott-Moncrieff, *The Book of Consolations*, p. ix.
106. As discussed in the chapter's final section; *Life of Mar Aba*, pp. 466–25.
107. CS (1919), p. 558.
108. Ibid; this was not a name for the mother of Jesus that was in accord with Diophysite theology, an issue which deserves further investigation.
109. Scott-Moncrieff, *The Book of Consolations*, p. ix.
110. Thomas of Marga, *Book of Governors*, Book 2, ch. 4, vol. 2, pp. 124 ff. English, vol. 1, pp. 69–70 Syriac; emphasis mine; see appendices of Godwin (2016a) for the extended passage, the Syriac and an annotated translation.
111. Thomas of Marga, *Book of Governors*, p. lxxxiv, includes a biography of Isho'yahb III; Rabban Jacob merits further investigation.
112. This is only one conglomeration of information that ties Isho'yahb III to Persian wealth, land, urban life and its power arrangements becoming part of his leadership disposition as an ascetic during the period of early Arab rule. One reads in the letters of Isho'yahb III that he fled his land holdings during Greek and Persian fighting. Scott-Moncrieff has suggested that this was because he was attempting to protect his wealth, generated from this area and its trade (*The Book of Consolations*, p. ix); Young provides information on the possible machinations involved in Isho'yahb III coming to power within the church (William G. Young, 'The Church of the East in 650 AD: Patriarch Ishu'yahb III and India', *Indian Church History Review* 2/1 (1968), pp. 55–71, p. 57), also on the political machinations involving in getting this head of the monastery elected; cf. Thomas of Marga, *Book of Governors*, p. 59 for portions from an Isho'yahb III letter indicating Sadhona tried to persuade Persian authorities to support him instead of Isho'yahb III.

113. Thomas of Marga, *Book of Governors*, p. 38, on Mar Abraham being clearly identified with the Patriarch Abraham and as a 'type' or figure at work in monastic consciousness; cf. pp. 50 and 53 on monastic renewal, p. 65 on the end of the Sasanian monastic framework and the dispersion of the East Syrian schools throughout the empire; cf. p. 69: 'they filled the country of the east'.

114. Ibid., v. 1, p. 79 (Syriac Original), v. 2 (English translation), p. 174.

115. Ibid., v.1 pp. 79–80, v. 2 pp. 178–9; see appendices of Godwin (2016a) for the original Syriac and an English translation of this passage.

116. Rubens Duval (ed.), *Ishoyabh Patriarchae III Liber Epistularum*, vols 11–12 (Paris: Typographeo Reipublicae, 1904–5), p. 73 for Duval's Latin translation and pp. 95–6 for the original Syriac; hereafter both Latin and Syriac page numbers will be given.

117. Ibid., p. 220; according to Duval, this letter was written when Isho'yahb III was still a bishop, but about to become a Metropolitan.

118. Ibid., p. 96 for Syriac; as is indicated ibid., p. 220; this letter was written when Isho'yahb III was still a bishop, but about to become a Metropolitan.

119. The biological and familial bases of Isho'yahb III's rhetoric bear resemblances to the rhetoric of institutions studied by anthropologist Mary Douglas in her influential book *Purity and Danger: An Anthropology of* the Concepts of Pollution and Taboo (London: Routledge and Kegan Paul, 1966), where it is shown that social institutions are often sustained and created by rhetorical binaries having biological bases.

120. Duval, *Ishoyabh Patriarchae III Liber Epistularum*, p. 72.

121. Douglas, *Purity and Danger*, pp. 115–28.

122. Duval, *Ishoyabh Patriarchae III Liber Epistularum*, p. 96.

123. According to the temporal classifications given by Duval, p. 220, and Scott-Moncrieff, *Book of Consolations*, p. x, the letter stems from the period Isho'yahb III was Metropolitan, i.e. from 628–48.

124. This was an issue dealt with at the Synod of George; Cf. Hoyland, *Seeing Islam as Others Saw It*, p. 64.

125. Duval, *Ishoyabh Patriarchae III Liber Epistularum*, p. 109 Latin, p. 146 Syriac.

126. Ibid., Syriac pp. 147–8, Latin trans., p. 110; see appendices of Godwin (2016a) for the entire passage in Syriac and an annotated English translation.

127. Young, 'The Church of the East in 650 AD'; John Healey, 'The Christians of Qatar in the 7th century AD', *Studies in Honour of Clifford Edmund Bosworth*, vol. 1: *Hunter of the East: Arabic and Semitic Studies*, ed. Ian R. Netton (Leiden: Brill, 2000), pp. 222–37; John Healey, 'The Patriarch Išo'yabh and the Christians of Qatar in the first Islamic century', in *The Christian Heritage of Iraq: Collected Papers from the Christianity in Iraq I–V Seminar Days*, ed. Erica C. D. Hunter (Piscataway, NJ: Gorgias Press, 2009), pp. 1–9. The letters covering the period of his life as a bishop are numbered one to 52, the second period when he was Metropolitan are numbered one to 32, and the third

period when he was Patriarch are numbered one to 22; this group of letters comes from the period when he was Patriarch and are numbered 14–21 in the final section of the Duval collection; of interest here will be letter 14, addressed to Simeon, the secessionist bishop of Qatar, letter 15 to a learned teacher in Revardashir, 16, to all the people of Fars, 17 to the bishops of Qatar, 18 and 19 to the people of Qatar, and 20 and 21 the monks of Qatar. Duval, *Ishoyahb Patriarchae III Liber Epistularum*, pp. 221–2, for dating of the letters.

128. Robert A. Carter, 'Christianity in the Gulf during the first centuries of Islam', *Arabian Archaeology and Epigraphy* 19/1 (2008), pp. 71–108.

129. Ibid.

130. Ibid., pp. 104–5.

131. Richard E. Payne (2011), 'Monks, dinars and date palms: hagiographical production and the expansion of monastic institutions in the early Islamic Persian Gulf, *Arabian Archaeology and Epigraphy* 22/1 (2011), pp. 97–11, p. 100.

132. Hoyland, *Seeing Islam as Others Saw It*, p. 181–2 quoting Ep. 14C, p. 51.

133. Letter 17, p. 189, Syriac p. 261.

134. Letter 18, p. 192.

135. Healey, 'The Christians of Qatar', p. 226.

136. Ibid.

137. Ibid.

138. Cf. the *Synodicon Orientale* and its reference to the Patriarch of 'all of Fars and India', which came into the church as it officially adopted the Nicene Creed; following the council of Isaac, the watershed event in the church; the SO indicates that the Bishop of Fars was made a Metropolitan Bishop at this time; the relationship between India and Fars as a Metropolitanate is discussed further in Young, 'The Church of the East in 650 AD', pp. 62 ff.

139. See Chapter 4.

140. Ibn al-Ṭayyib, *Fiqh al-Naṣrānīya*, W. Hoenerbach & O. Spies (eds & trans.) *Corpus Scriptorum Christianorum Orientalium* 161–2 and 167–8. Louvain: Brepols, 1956–57), p. 120 German/p. 118 Arabic.

141. Young, 'The Church of the East in 650 AD', pp. 66–7.

142. Ibid., p. 63.

143. Ibid., p. 226.

144. Ibid.

145. Ibid., p. 229.

146. Ibid.

147. Ibid.

148. Young, 'The Church of the East in 650 AD', pp. 66–7; note that the Bishops in charge of the area are called by Isho'yahb III 'smoldering stumps, so called priests'; Isho'yahb III's martyrial-ascetic understanding of his church's identity is evinced in his reference to the fact that 'none of the Christian tribe (where you are) offer the sacrifice of blood'.

149. Young, 'The Church of the East in 650 AD', p. 68; note that Simeon here 'has closed the door' of spiritual perfection flowing from the church, on all of India; and in doing so he looks at ordination from a 'worldly' point of view'. This comes about in the political atmosphere of Arab control of the church and stems from what may be termed an *ethne* and ethnarc relationship, one being reformulated between the church and its leaders precisely within this atmosphere.

150. Duval, *Ishoyabh Patriarchae III Liber Epistularum*, Letter 21, p. 202.

151. Ibid., Letter 17, p. 189, Syriac p. 261.

Chapter 2   'Repairing the Imperial Net' before the An Lushan Rebellion

1. The edict is found at Wang Pu [王溥] (922–82) (ed.), *Tang Huiyao* [唐會要, *Notabilia of Tang*] (Shanghai: Shanghai guji chubanshe, 1991) (hereafter THY), 49.1012; Du You [杜佑] (735–812) (ed.), *Tongdian* [通典, *Complete Institutes*] (compiled between 766–801) (Beijing: Zhongua shuju, 1988) (hereafter TD), 40.1103, and Wang Qinruo [王欽若] (ed.), *Cefu Yuangui* [冊府元龜, *The Great Tortoise of National Archives*, compiled between 1005–13] (Beijing: Zhonghua shuju, 1960) (hereafter CFYG), 51.20.

2. Antonino Forte (ed.), *Paul Pelliot's L'inscription Nestorienne de Singan-fou* (Kyoto: Scuola di Studi Sull'Asia Orientale, Paris: Collège de France, Institute des Hauste Études, Chinoises, 1996); Timothy H. Barrett, 'Buddhism, Taoism and the eighth-century Chinese term for Christianity: a response to recent work by A. Forte and others', *Bulletin of the School of Oriental and African Studies* 65/3 (2002), pp. 555–60; Zhang Xiaogui [張小貴], 'Why did Chinese "Nestorians" change the name of their religion to Jingjiao?', 4th Salzburg International Conference on the Church of the East in China and Central Asia, 7–11 June 2013.

3. Antonino Forte, 'The edict of 638', in Forte, *Paul Pelliot's L'inscription Nestorienne de Singan-fou*, p. 354.

4. Lin Wushu (林悟殊) *Tangdai Jingjiao zaiyanjiu* (唐代景教再研究) (Beijing: Zhonghua Shuju, 2003), pp. 27–45.

5. As explored later in this chapter.

6. See Domenico Agostini and Sören Stark, 'Zawulistan, Kawulistan and the Land of Bosi [波斯] – On the question of the Sasanian court-in-exile in the southern Hindukish', *Studia Iranica* 45 (2016), pp. 17–38 for bibliography and the latest assessment.

7. THY 49.1011–1012; Forte, 'The edict of 638', pp. 350–1.

8. *The Xi'an Stele*, trans. Arthur Waley, in Charles F. Horne (ed.), *The Sacred Books and Early Literature of the East*, vol. 12: *Medieval China* (New York: Parke, Austin, and Lipscomb, 1917), pp. 381–92 (hereafter XS), line 25.

9. Paul Pelliot, *L'inscription nestorienne de Si-ngan-fou, Edited with Supplements by Antonino Forte* (Kyoto: Scuola di Studi sull'Asia Orientale; Paris: Collège de

France, Institut des Hautes Etudes Chinoises, 1996); see discussion of *Da-de* at pp. 222 and 231; on *Dade* see Deeg (2013), pp. 155–6, 192, 211; the character *de* appears in the 17 times, 12 of them in connection to the emperor or the empire, and five in connection to monks, indicative of the imperial nature of the Church of the East's monastic presence in the Tang; the character appears in the list of the monks' names at the end of the stele repeatedly.

10. See the discussion on this topic in Chapter 4.

11. See Chapter 4 for discussions of this issue.

12. The translation 'Middle East' may appear anachronistic here; but consider the place of Jerusalem in the thought of Isho'yahb III explored in the previous chapter, which was the centre of the cosmos within the Syriac Christians' world view, and far bigger than anything captured by a term like 'Syria' (Wayley), or 'Roman Empire; as Samuel Lieu points out, the Tang Church of the East 'situated Jesus' home-town of Nazareth within *Daqin*, {and} they placed most of the other place names found in the Gospels within the boundaries of a state called Fulin {a country which was}, according to the *Sermon of the Lord of the Universe on Almsgiving*, ruled by a Caesar (*ji-xi*, 寄悉, Sogdian *kysr*, Middle Chinese *kie-sjit*): Samuel N.C. Lieu, 'Da Qin 大秦 and Fulin 拂林 – the Chinese names for Rome', in Gunner Mikkelsen (ed.), *From Antioch to Xi'an: Silk Road Studies*, vol. 17 (Turnhout: Brepols, 2016), pp. 123–45; cf. *Xuting mishisuo(he) Jing*, in Peter Yoshiro Saeki (ed.), *The Nestorian Documents and Relics in China* [1937], 2nd edn (Tokyo: Academy of Oriental Culture, 1951), line 163 (1951): (text) p. 25 (trans.) p. 141; see also the Xi'an stele at its very title: XS, line 1. Daqin is therefore the source of all Western learning and culture, including that of some aspects of Persian learning and the culture of the Sasanian Empire.

13. XS, pp. 383–4.

14. Ibid., line 37. This translation is partly the author's own, but informed by others'; cf. Wayley's 'Right principles have no invariable name, holy men have no invariable station', ibid. James Legge (*The Nestorian Monument of Hsi-An Fu* (New York: Paragon, 1966), pp. 9–10), prefers 'systems have not always the same name, sages have not always the same personality'; Pelliot translates this: 'la Voie n'a pas de nom eternal; le saint n'a pas de mode eternal', and notes this echoes the famous first line of the Dao de Jing (*L'inscription nestorienne de Si-ngan-fou, Edited with Supplements by Antonino Forte* (Kyoto: Scuola di Studi sull'Asia Orientale; Paris: Collège de France, Institut des Hautes Etudes Chinoises, 1996), pp. 229–30. Deeg in *Die Strahlende Lehre* translates the passage: 'Das Dao is ohne beständigen Namen, der Weise ist ohne beständigen Struktur'. A discussion of the term *sheng* and Pelliot's comments on it is in order, as it pertains not only to the translation of this text but to the interpretation of it within this chapter's argument. Pelliot tells us Dai Zong is not making an equation between *dao* and *sheng* here as he did, according to Pelliot, in XS line 31: 惟道非聖不弘。聖非道不大。道聖符契。天下文

明, 'mais la sagesse, sans un saint, ne se développe pas; un saint, sans le sagesse, ne grandit pas; quand la sagesse et le saint s'adaptent comme [les deux moieties d']une taille, l'empire est police et éclairé'; this phrase was, importantly, placed by the writer right before the Aluoben section of the text. Not only can it be argued that he is proffering a notion of a divine sovereign, but of a shared imperial charisma, and that the *comitatus* is not an imported notion. For this reason a translation of 'sage' is warranted; sages speak and thus transmit wisdom outwardly; the emperor, along with the Church's Holy Men, speak and transmit 'sagacity' between one and within the context of the empire, and thus bind political bodies together, strengthen the Tang as a political unit, and form unity with its colonial entities, thus creating a shared culture, a *habitus*.

15. Chen Chang'an (ed.), 隋唐五代墓誌匯編 [*Sui tang wudai muzhi huibian. Luoyang juan*], vol. 8 (Tianjin: Tianjin guli chubanshe, 1990), p. 144.

16. Though insufficiently informed about the Mesopotamian and Central Asian nature of the Church of the East the best scholarship on the inscription is represented by Ma Xiaohe (馬小鶴), 唐代波斯國大酋長阿羅憾墓志考, 'Tang dai bosi guo da qiuzhang aluohan muzhi kao' (中外关系史 : 新史料 与新问题) (Beijing: Kexue Shubanshe, 2004), pp. 1–31, and Antonino Forte, 'On the so-called Abraham from Persia', in Forte, *Paul Pelliot's L'inscription Nestorienne de Singan-fou*.

17. *Hanyu Da Cidian* [漢語大詞典], chief ed. Luo Zhufeng [羅竹風], CD ROM 3.0 (Hong Kong: The Commercial Press, 2007) (hereafter HDC), 3.0.

18. Forte, 'The edict of 638', pp. 379, 385; on Aluoben's name as Syriac Rabban, see Deeg, *Die Strahlende Lehre*, pp. 138–40n.89, where the suggestion is made that local Iranian pronunciation stands behind the addition of the initial vowel in the name.

19. Forte, 'The edict of 638', p. 376.

20. Ibid.

21. Ma, 唐代波斯國大酋長阿羅憾墓志考, p. 18. A search of *Wenyuange siku quanshu dianzi ban* [文淵閣四庫全書電子版] (Shanghai: Renmin Chu- banshe, 2002) (hereafter SKQS) suggests reference to 吐火羅國 (Tocharistan, former Bactria) first appears in the annals of the Sui dynasty (581–618) and at Suishu 813; also see *Jiu Tangshu* [舊唐書], *Old Tang Record*, ed. Liu Xu [劉昫] (887–946) (compiled in 945) (Beijing: Zhonghua shuju, 1975) (hereafter JTS), 40, with a reference for the year 661, JTS 194 for the year 623, and JTS 198 for the year 679. Gikyo Itō suggests that envoys arrive in Japan from Tocharistan seeking refuge in the year 655 based on Nihon Shoki passages; see his 'Zoroastrians' arrival in Japan (Pahlavica I)', *Orient* 15 (1979), pp. 55–63.

22. Ma, 唐代波斯國大酋長阿羅憾墓志考, p. 19. Frantz Grenet has surveyed the scholarship and primary sources in Tibetan and Iranian languages, and asserts that a Bactrian king who ruled between 737 and 745 used the royal nomenclature 'From Kēsar' (Fu-lin Caesar) of himself; he notes as well that in a

Tibetan text known as the *Liyül Lungtenpa* it is said that the Tibetans were 'to have vanquished the Ta-zhig', whom they understood as Persians' ('A historical figure at the origin of Phrom Gesar: the state of research on Frūm Gesar, King of Kabul (737–745)', in Matthew T. Kapstein and Charles Ramble (eds), *The Many Faces of King Gesar: Homage to Rolf A. Stein* (forthcoming 2017).

23. Ma, 唐代波斯國大酋長阿羅憾墓志考, p. 17.
24. JTS 198.26a; *Xin Tangshu* [新唐書] (*The New Tang Record*, compiled in 1060), ed. Ouyang Xiu [歐陽修] and Song Qi [宋祁] (Beijing: Zhonghua shuju, 1975) (hereafter XTS), 221B, 15b–16a; Matteo Compareti, 'The last Sasanians in China', *Eurasian Studies* 2/2 (2003), pp. 197–13.
25. Ibid; Agostini and Stark, 'Zawulistan, Kawulistan and the Land of Bosi'; see the discussion below.
26. Richard N. Frye, 'The political history of Iran under the Sasanians', in *The Cambridge History of Iran*, vol. 3: *The Seleucid, Parthian and Sasanid Periods, Part 1*, ed. Ehsan Yarshater (Cambridge: Cambridge University Press, 1983), pp. 116–80, p. 176.
27. Compareti, 'The last Sasanians in China', p. 204.
28. Ibid.
29. JTS 198, p. 5312.
30. XTS 221B, p. 15b, pp. 6258–9.
31. Reading 師 as 帥 *shuai*, HDC 3.0, 'command'.
32. *zhi-zi*質子, a 'hostage', a term seen in the Li Su gravestone. *Zhi-zi* is a term going back to the Warring States period to indicate diplomatic envoys, but with the Chinese empire's growth in the Sui and Tang period this term clearly denotes important, often royal family related, persons sent to the Chinese court for a long period in the manner of inter-imperial marriages; see Christopher Beckwith (*The Tibetan Empire in Central Asia* (Princeton, NJ: Princeton University Press, 1987)) and the final chapter for these connections; JTS 198–9 shows the term in connection with the Gaocheng and Silla (Korean) kingdoms; note that the general, Pei Xingjian (619–82), picked to put Peroz and Narseh back on the Persian throne, albeit in Central Asia, was Korean.
33. David N. MacKenzie, 'Bundahišn', *Encyclopedia Iranica 4* (Costa Mesa: Mazda, 1990), pp. 547–51.
34. *Zand-Akasih, Iranian or Greater Bundahishn*, trans. Behramgore T. Anklesaria (Bombay: Mazdayasnan Sabha, 1956), p. 137.
35. As Ma asserts (唐代波斯國大酋長阿羅憾墓志考, p. 21), the possibility exists as well that this refers to the Arumeans, an issue currently still under investigation by the author.
36. Ibid., pp. 138–9.
37. Cf. Agostini and Stark, 'Zawulistan, Kawulistan and the Land of Bosi', pp. 26–9, for fuller coverage of the relevant Zoroastrian apocalyptic literature,

which points to Sasanian royals exilic location being in the Hindukush principalities of Tocharistan, Kawulistan and Zabulistan.

38. On the way in which Syriac Christians and Manichaens speaking Persian were both employing the Tajik/Daqin nomenclature for themselves, see Werner Sundermann, 'An early attestation of the name of the Tajiks', in Wojciech Skalmowski and Alois *van Tongerloo* (eds), *Medio-Iranica, Proceedings of the International Colloquium organised by the Katholieke Universiteit Leuven from the 21st to the 23rd of May 1990* (Orientalia Lovaniensia Analecta, 48) (Leuven: The University Press, 1993), pp. 163–71.

39. Richard Todd Godwin, 'Daqin, Tajiks, and their doctors – East Syrian scientists across the courts of early medieval Persia, China, and Tibet, and the possibility that "Daqin" Christians were "Tajik" Christians', *Studies on Syriac Christianity in Medieval Central Asia and China, Salzburg International Conference Proceedings*, vol. 5 (forthcoming).

40. Ibid.

41. Howard J. Wecshler, 'T'ai-tsung (reign 626–49) the Consolidator', in Denis Twitchett (ed.), *The Cambridge History of China*, vol. 3: *Sui and T'ang China, 589–906*, Part 1 (Cambridge: Cambridge University Press, 1979), pp. 193–236), pp. 220–4; Guangda Zhang and Xinjiang Rong, 'A concise history of Turfan and its exploration', *Asia Major* 11/2 (1998), pp. 13–36.

42. Ibid., p. 222.

43. Ibid.

44. Ibid.

45. The *Jimi* system consisted of three levels, the command area (都督府) prefecture (州), and county (县), known together as the *Jimi fuzhou* or the 'loosely controlled administrative units', which should be distinguished from the *Zhengzhou* (正州) or the 'regular administrative units'. There were two short-lived loosely controlled protectorates (都護府) established in the former western Turkic Khaganate around the Tarbagatai Mountains and Lake Balkash in 658. The loose control administrative units, specifically the command area and prefecture, were established shortly after a region, state or tribe was subdued and formed as a political division within the extent of a separated regular protectorate; Weiyan Zhou, 'Jimizhou', *Encyclopedia of China* (Beijing: Central Literary Publishing House, 1993).

46. The main Tang sources, besides the vast Buddhist documentary record, consist of the *Tongdian* ('Complete Institutes'), compiled between 766–801, along with the *Cefu Yuangui Record*, the *Tang Huiyao* (唐會要, 'Tang Collection of Important Documents'), compiled in 961, the Old and new Tang records, and the 資治通鑑 [*Zizhi tongjian*, Comprehensive Mirror to Aid in Government], compiled in 1065, by 司馬光 [Si Maguang] (1019–86), considered to be one of founding fathers of the rational and scientific historical study within the Chinese tradition. Denis Twitchett's *The Writing of Official History under the T'ang* (Cambridge: Cambridge University Press, 1992) is an essential introduction to these vast sources of which we are only at the beginnings our

understanding and of their relevance to early medieval Syriac Christianity in Iran, Central Asia and the land and sea Silk Routes.

47. TD 67; this passage can be read in wider context at http://ctext.org/tongdian/zh (accessed 21 April 2014).

48. This encyclopaedia was begun in 1005 and finished in 1013 and edited by 王欽若 [Wang Qinruo] (962–1025); its title *Cefu* refers to an 'imperial storehouse of literature', and *Yuangui*, meaning 'Oracle Tortoise Shells'. See Kurz Johannes, 'The compilation and publication of the *Taiping yulan* and the *Cefu yuangui*', in Florence Bretelle-Establet and Karine Chemla (eds), *Qu'est-ce qu'écrire une encyclopédie en Chine?*, Extreme Orient-Extreme Occident Hors série 1/1 (2007), pp. 39–76.

49. On this period see Twitchett's 'Hsüan-tsung (reign 712–56)', in Denis Twitchett (ed.), *The Cambridge History of China*, vol. 3: *Sui and T'ang China, 589–906, Part I* (Cambridge: Cambridge University Press, 1979), pp. 456–61.

50. CFYG 546.13, p. 6548. Saeki offers a translation of this passage in *The Nestorian Documents and Relics in China*, pp. 460–2, which differs in some areas from the translation presented here.

51. 汨 *mi*, HDC (book version), vol. 3, p. 1564, character 2, 'sink'.

52. 孚 Fu, HDC 3.0, 'believe, trust'.

53. See Introduction.

54. See Introduction.

55. See Edward Said's perceptive comments on Kipling's creation of British imperial space through narratives centred on travel through the British Empire, in his *Culture and Imperialism* (New York: Knopf, 1993), p. 135.

56. The Sabao was a fifth level civilian rank, one of over 250 government positions within the Tang bureaucracy, and under the 祠部 (*Ci-bu*, 'Department of Rites'), where immigration and foreign affairs were overseen in the early Tang; see TD 40 on the Sabao issue.

57. The most important work done on the Sabao is by Albert E. Dien; see his 'The Sa-pao problem re-examined', *Journal of the American Oriental Society* 82/3 (July–September 1962), pp. 335–46 and the more recent 'Caravans and caravan leaders in Palmyra', in Étienne de la Vaissière and Éric Trombert (eds), *Les Sogdiens en Chine* (Paris: École française d'Extrême-Orient, 2005), pp. 195–206. See also Rong Xinjiang, '*Sabao* or *Sabo*: Sogdian caravan leaders in the wall-paintings in Buddhist caves', ibid., pp. 207–15.

58. *Wei Shu* 102.90 shows that the Sogdians and Persians and their business activities were regulated through the *cibu* (祠部). See Donald Leslie, 'Persian temples in T'ang China', *Monumenta Serica* 35/1 (1981–83), pp. 275–303, p. 46.

59. The character *xian* (祆: HDC, vol. 4, p. 2388, character 10) has a variant of (祆) (ibid., p. 2388, character 13), both of which are pronounced *xian* and in first tone in Mandarin. On the history of Persian temples of all three Persian religions in the Tang; see Leslie, 'Persian temples in T'ang China'; Penelope

Riboud, 'Réflections sur les pratiques religieuses désignées sous le nom de *xian* 祆', in de la Vaissière and Trombert, *Les Sogdiens en Chine*, no. 17, pp. 72–85.

60. JTS 198, p. 5311 relates: 西域諸胡事火祆者,皆詣波期受焉 (the Western regions are all Zoroastrians, all come to Persia for their religious law); the same information is found in the THY 100.

61. See appendices in Godwin, 'Persian Christians at the Chinese Court' (2016a) for primary source info.

62. See ibid. for primary source info.

63. Ibid.

64. Leslie, 'Persian temples in T'ang China', p. 42.

65. See Riboud, 'Réflections sur les pratiques religieuses', p. 79.

66. *Wei Shu* 102.90.

67. Lin Wushu (林悟殊), *Gu dai san yi jiao bian deng* (古代三異教辨登) (Beijing: Zhonghua shuju, 2005), p. 269; primary sources indicate that policies centred on Sogdians as *sa-bao* was a way of maintaining peace in the other foreign communities of the Tang.

68. Leslie, 'Persian temples in T'ang China', p. 45.

69. Dien, 'The Sa-pao problem re-examined'.

70. For a primary source reference and wider discussion, see Gustavo Benevides, 'Buddhism, Manichaeism, markets and empires', in Luther H. Martin and Panayotis Pachis (eds), *Hellenisation, Empire and Globalisation: Lessons from Antiquity* (Thessalonika: Vanias Edition, 2004), pp. 1–24, and reference to the Sabao in connection to Bodhisattvas at p. 5; Benevides notes also that Mani was referred to as the 'world's greatest *sabao*', p. 10.

71. Ibid., p. 341.

72. Jonathan K. Skaff, 'The Sogdian trade diaspora in East Turkestan during the seventh and eighth centuries', *Journal of the Economic and Social History of the Orient* 46/4 (2003), pp. 475–24, p. 492. Mariko N. Washington in her "Sogdians and Buddhism', *Sino-Platonic Papers* 174 (2006), pp. 1–64, shows that Sogdians had been instrumental in transmitting Buddhism into China for the previous 200 years; their language skills, intercultural skills, and business acumen were an aid in this process and were in turn aided by their links to the transmission of Buddhism. On Sogdian participation in the Chinese military and its links to Iranian Sinification see Skaff, 'The Sogdian trade diaspora in East Turkestan', pp. 490–10; on Sinification processes appearing in Sogdian and Persian funerary inscriptions see ibid., p. 504; Annette L. Juliano and Judith A. Lerner (eds), *Monks and Merchants. Silk Road Treasures from Northern China. Gansu and Ningxia 4th–7th Century* (New York: H.N. Abrams and Asia Society, 2001), pp. 296–9.

73. Cf. Aristotle's *Physics*: 'It is clear, then, that though there may be countless instances of the perishing of unmoved movers, and though many things that move themselves perish and are succeeded by others that come into being, and though one thing that is unmoved moves one thing while another moves

another, nevertheless there is something that comprehends them all, and that as something apart from each one of them, and this it is that is the cause of the fact that some things are and others are not and of the continuous process of change; and this causes the motion of the other movers, while they are the causes of the motion of other things. Motion, then, being eternal, the first mover, if there is but one, will be eternal also; if there are more than one, there will be a plurality of such eternal movers'. *Physics*, 258b, 32–259a, 8, *The Complete Works of Aristotle*, vol. 1, ed. Jonathan Barnes (Princeton, NJ: Princeton University Press, 1984), p. 432. There was a very active Syriac scientific tradition that began to increase its activity in the period of Arab rule; the Western Syriac polymath and scientist Severus Sebokht (d.666/7) is one such example; Aristotle and Greek works were certainly at the centre of this activity.

74. Saeki, *The Nestorian Documents and Relics in China*, primary texts portion of the document, p. 30.

75. Ibid., translation portion of the document, pp. 161–2; though the presentation here follows Saeki slavishly, this is done because Saeki's translation reflects the basic meaning of this portion of the Discourse on Monotheism (hereafter DM) (*Yi shen lun juan di san* [一神論卷第三]; once known as the Tomioka manuscript; now held in Osaka, Japan, by Kyōu Shooku library, Tonkō-Hikyū Collection, manuscript no. 460) well enough to make the point desired at this stage of the argument.

76. Saeki, The Nestorian Documents and Relics in Chi, pp. 31–3.

77. Ibid., p. 163.

78. Paul Pelliot, 'Un traité Manichéen retrouvé in Chine' (ed. and trans. Édouard Chavannes), *Journale Asiatique* 11 (1913), pp. 346–67; Beckwith, *The Tibetan Empire in Central Asia*, pp. 297–13.

79. JTS 975.

80. Huang Lan-lan (黄蘭蘭), 'Tangdai Qin Minghe wei jing yikao' [唐代秦鳴鶴爲景醫考], *Journal of Sun Yatsen University* (Social Science Edition) 42/5 (2002), pp. 61–7, where good coverage of the secondary literature is found.

81. These include JTS 5, XTS 76, and the 資治通鑑 *Zizhi tongjian* [資治通鑑] (Beijing: Zhonhua shuhu, 1956) (hereafter ZZTJ), p. 6215.

82. This is undoubtedly Empress Wuzetian; Twitchett, 'Hsüan-tsung (reign 712–56)', p. 255, indicates that she was in virtual control of the empire by 660, though she had become Empress in 655.

83. XTS 76, p. 3477.

84. *Taiping Huanyu ji* (太平寰宇記) 184.2 (From Morrison Collection).

85. See final chapter.

86. The Sogdian pronunciation for the Jin dynasty, *chin*, gave the Greek and Latin world, and eventually modern Europe, its and our English word for China; on Tang astronomy, see Kiyoshi Yabuuchi [中国の天文暦法], *Chūgoku no tenmon rekihō* [*A History of Chinese Astronomy*] (Tōkyō: Heibonsha, 1990), p. 8.

87. Ibid., p. 94.

88. Ibid., p. 74.
89. Forte, 'The edict of 638', p. 395.
90. Although the present author does not have space to undertake this currently, Charles P. Fitzgerald, in his *The Empress Wu* (London: Crescent Press, 1968), pp. 130–7, offers useful coverage of the Buddhist alchemist, architect and technician Xue Huaiyi [薛懷義] (d.694), who designed the *Ming-tang* for the Empress during a period in which the Tang sources, uniformly hostile to the Empress and by proxy him as well, describe Xue as romantically involved with the Empress. JTS 21, upon which Fitzgerald's description of the *Ming-tang* is based, shows many ways in which elites involved with *Ming-tang* well before, and continuing through, Wuzetian's period, shared in the creation and sustaining of the royal house's imperial charisma, ensuring that it appeared to hold the Mandate of Heaven legitimately.
91. Antonino Forte, 'On the so-called Abraham from Persia', in Forte, *Paul Pelliot's L'inscription Nestorienne de Singan-fou*, p. 395 ff.
92. Samuel Lieu, Manichaeism in the Later Roman Empire and Medieval China (Tubigen: J.C.B. Mohr, 1992), p. 230.
93. Ibid.
94. Ibid., p. 232; CFYG 971.4, p. 11406; CFYG 546.13, p. 6548; Pelliot, 'Un traité Manichéen retrouvé in Chine', pp. 346–67.
95. Ibid.
96. Twitchett, 'Hsüan-tsung (reign 712–56)', pp. 310–9.
97. Forte discusses their role in this in his Political Propaganda and Ideology in China at the End of the Seventh Century: Inquiry into the Nature, Authors and Function of the Tunhuang document S.6502, followed by an annotated translation (Napoli: Istituto universitario orientale, Seminario di studi asiatici, 1976), p. 41 ff.
98. Ibid., pp. 5–7.
99. Twitchett, 'Hsüan-tsung (reign 712–56)'.
100. Hino Kaisaburō, 'Take i ryō kisaki jidai zeisetsu himen nisedo no seikō to gensō no shukusei', *Shigaku Zasshi* 87 (10), 1978, pp. 1484–1491; Richard W.L. Guisson, "The Reigns of Empress Wu, Chung-tsung and Jui-tsung (684–712)", CHC Vol 3, pp. 290–29.
101. CFYG 971.4 a18-b1, p. 11406.
102. A reconstruction of this king's name according to the tables developed by Pulleyblank suggests a rendering of *tsi-khan-na*; this may be a rendering of the Pahlavi and pan-Iranian word for king, 'shah', in addition to the Turkic title Khan in combination, i.e 'shah-khan'. The possibility is intriguing since one had to possess royal blood in order to use the title shah, and it is known both that the final Persian monarchs resided in the area of Tocharistan and Balkh and intermarried with Turkic royalty; see Edwin G. Pulleyblank, *Lexicon of Reconstructed Pronunciation of in Early Middle Chinese, Late Middle Chinese and Early Mandarin* (Vancouver: University of British Columbia Press, 1991).

103. The title *mu-she* [慕闍], it has been argued by Paul Pelliot to correspond to the Sogdian *Mwžk'* and Pahlavi *Možak*, ('magus') in 'Les traditions manichéennes au Fou-kien', *T'oung Pao* 22/3 (1923), pp. 193–08; Leslie uses the term 'astronomer-magus', perhaps without a strong basis, and indicates that the term *mushe* was used interchangeably on some occasions with the term *mu-hu* 穆護, that term having semantic resonances with the Sabao term in *mu-he*'s literal meaning of 'calm protector'; see Leslie, 'Persian temples in T'ang China', p. 279.

104. This text only makes sense if it is read in the first person and in the voice of the one involved in sending up the memorial.

105. There are various types of *gong-feng* [供奉; imperial staff positions]; serving in the Hanlin academy, the famous Confucian academy beginning in the Tang, as well know poets such as Li Bai did, was referred to as Hanlin *gongfeng*. The term was also used with reference to serving in rituals to ancestors and the Buddha; see HDC, vol. 1, p. 1320.

106. Ibid., vol. 5, p. 1043, indicates a purely Buddhist semantic domain for the term 法堂 [*fatang*], suggesting that however the Christians and other religions saw themselves, the Tang court saw them as practising a variant of Buddhism.

107. The possibility exists that the terms *ben-jiao* [本教] can be translated as 'basic teaching' or even 'our teaching', especially when followed by 供 [*gong*], referring to 'nourishing upward' (i.e. towards the emperor) and 養 [*yang*] 'to nourish downward' (i.e. towards the people) suggesting that the imperial teaching is the hope and aim of his teaching.

108. JTS 3, p. 51.

109. JTS 7, p. 148.

110. Ibid.

111. *Tsan-po*, Tibetan, 'king'; Chinese, *San-pu* [贊普].

112. There is an extensive documentary record on this princess and the period, though this has been untouched by secondary literature in any language, including Chinese; see JTS 196, XTS 78 and 216, *Quan Tang Wen*, 40, 100 and 286, CFYG, 295 and 980.

113. XTS 215, second part.

114. Bielenstein suggests that Buddhist priests sometimes tried to pose as dignitaries within the Tang court, p. 8; he also notes that Hirth and Rockhill believed references to the 'king of Fulin' appearing in the Tang annals referred to the East Syrian Patriarch in Baghdad, p. 366. It is possibly a reference to the Roman emperor or the Arab caliph as well, as the Tang Chinese certainly knew the difference between a religious leader and a political leader, however blurred the distinction became in the period at times.

115. Saeki translates 大德僧 [*Dade seng*], literally 'a monk of great virtue', as 'Bishop', but the discussion earlier indicates this is likely wrong, and simply

the use of Buddhist categories for Church of the East elites; HDC, vol. 2, p. 1391 indicates this term was applied to Taoist monks as well.

116. Robert des Rotours, vol. 2, p. 548, indicates that term *guoyi* [果毅, courage and bravery] corresponds to two military ranks, one within the Left and Right Guard of the army, without being specified as to which; the fifth and sixth ranks they refer to were both half-way up the Mandarin scale. The term is first found in the *Shujing* and appears in the *Zuo Zhuan*.

117. According to HDC, vol. 9, p. 46, Buddhist monks were not allowed to wear yellow, white, red, blue, or black robes.

118. Fifty bolts of silk was more than twice a Mandarin's annual salary; see Denis Twitchett's *Financial Administration under the T'ang* (Cambridge: Cambridge University Press, 1963), p. 25.

119. CFYG 975.

Chapter 3   The *Habitus* of Patriarch Timothy I

1. See Chapter 2.

2. Timothy H. Barrett, 'Buddhism, Taoism and the eighth-century Chinese term for Christianity: a response to recent work by A. Forte and others', *Bulletin of the School of Oriental and African Studies* 65/3 (2002), pp. 555–60.

3. On Talas and its long term effects, see Bai Shouyi (白寿彝), *Zhong-guo hui-hui min-zu shi* (中国回回民族史) (Beijing: Zhonghua shuju, 2003); on the place of Khurasan and Merv in the Abbasid revolution, a major reassessment of the scholarship of the first half of the twentieth century, and the thesis that the courts of Central Asia became integrated into the Islamic empire partly resulting in the revolution, see Muhammad A. Shaban, *The 'Abbāsid Revolution* (Cambridge: Cambridge University Press, 1979).

4. Samuel Hugh Moffett, *A History of Christianity in Asia*, vol. 1: *Beginnings to 1500* (New York: Orbis, 1998), p. 339.

5. Peter Yoshiro Saeki, *The Nestorian Documents and Relics in China* [1937], 2nd edn (Tokyo: Academy of Oriental Culture, 1951), p. 125.

6. See notes 12 and 52 for primary and secondary sources related to Timothy I.

7. Geoffrey Khan, *Arabic Documents from Early Islamic Khurasan* (London: Nour Foundation, 2007); *Bactrian Documents from Northern Afghanistan*, ed. and trans. Nicholas Sims-Williams (Oxford: Oxford University Press, 2000); on Old Turkic Manichaean fragment M0919, which will be discussed below in relation to emergent kingship, see A. von Le Coq's translation and transcription in *Türkische Manichaica aus Chotscho, III, nebst einem christlichen Bruchstück aus Bulayïq, mit 3 Tafeln, Philosophisch-historische Klasse. nr. 2* (Berlin: Abhandlungen der Preussischen Akademie der Wissenschaften, 1922), pp. 33–5; for an image of the fragment, see http://www.bbaw.de/forschung/turfanforschung/dta/m/images/m0919_seite1.jpg (accessed 31 May 2017).

8. Anatoly M. Khazanov, 'The spread of world religions in medieval nomadic Societies of the Eurasian steppes', in Michael Gervers and Wayne Schlepp (eds), *Nomadic Diplomacy, Destruction and Religion from the Pacific to the Atlantic,* Toronto Studies in Central and Inner Asia, No. 1 (Toronto: Joint Centre for Asia Pacific Studies Toronto, 1994), pp. 11–33; Mark Dickens, 'Patriarch Timothy I and the Metropolitan of the Turks', *Journal of the Royal Asiatic Society* 20/2 (2010), pp. 117–39, for a particular focus upon the Qarluq Turk's acceptance of East Syrian Christianity. On the Tibetan Empire's adoption of a theocratic and courtly-patronage centred form of Buddhism (Esoteric, Mijiao/ Vajrayāna) at this time, see Christopher Beckwith, *The Tibetan Empire in Central Asia* (Princeton, NJ: Princeton University Press, 1987), pp. 147 ff., and the discussion below. On the Uighur's adoption of Manichaeism and this moves to patronage and diplomacy; Larry Clark, 'The conversion of Bügü Khan to Manichaeism', in Ronald E. Emerick, Werner Sundermann and Peter Zieme (eds), *Studia Manichaica: IV, Internationaler Kongress zum Manichäismus* (Berlin: Akademie Verlag, 2004), pp. 83–123. On the Khazar's adoption of Judaism at this time see Omeljan Pritsakr, 'The Khazar kingdom's conversion to Judaism', *Harvard Ukrainian Studies* 2/3 (September 1978), pp. 261–81.

9. The term 'emergent' is used to denote a system, or structure, the causes and functions of which arise from more than one area within the structure and constituent parts at once; see Jeffrey Goldstein, 'Emergence as a construct: history and issues', *Emergence, Complexity and Organization* 1/1(1999), pp. 49–71.

10. 'Timothei Patriarchae I Epistolae I [Text]', *Corpus Scriptorum Christianorum Orientalium,* 74/Syr. 30, ed. and trans. Oskar Braun (Paris: J. Garbalda, 1915) (hereafter CSCO); ibid. 31. On the Bactrian documentary record (in both Arabic and Bactrian languages), see Khan, *Arabic Documents*; Sims-Williams, *Bactrian Documents*.

11. See the discussion of each of these concepts and their inter-relations found in Chapter 1.

12. See the next section; Christoph Baumer, *The Church of the East, an Illustrated History of Assyrian Christianity* (London and New York: I.B.Tauris, 2006, p. 185; Paul Pelliot, *L'inscription nestorienne de Si-ngan-fou, Edited with Supplements by Antonino Forte* (Kyoto: Scuola di Studi sull'Asia Orientale; Paris: Collège de France, Institut des Hautes Etudes Chinoises, 1996), p. 178.

13. Thomas of Marga, *The Book of Governors: The Historia Monastica of Thomas Bishop of Margā AD 840*, vol. II: *The Syriac Text, Introduction, etc.*, trans. Ernest A.W. Budge (London: K. Paul, Trench, Trübner, 1893); Ibn al-Ṭayyib, *Fiqh al-Naṣrānīya*, CSCO, 161–2 and 167–8, ed. and trans. Wilhelm Hoenerbach and Otto Spies (Louvain: Brepols, 1956–57), German p. 120/Arabic p. 118; Gregorii Barhebraei, *Chronicon Ecclesiasticum (Annotationibusque Illustrarunt Joannes Baptista Abbeloos et Thomas Josephus Lamy)* (Lovanii: Brepoli, 1872–77); the more recent scholarly convention of referring to Gregory Abu Al-Faraj as Bar 'Ebroyo rather than as Bar Hebraeus is followed.

14. On the Abbasid postal system, the *barīd*, see Adam J. Silverstein, *Postal Systems in The Pre-Modern Islamic World* (Cambridge: Cambridge University Press, 2004) and 'Documentary evidence for the early history of the Barīid', in Petra Sijpesteijn and Lennart Sundelin (eds), *Papyrology and the History of Early Islamic Egypt* (Leiden: E.J. Brill, 2007), pp. 153–61; on the spread of caravan stations, hostels and wells in the Abbasid period, see Xavier Tremblay, 'The spread of Buddhism in Serindia – Buddhism among Iranians, Tocharians and Turks before the 13th century', in Denis Sinor and Nicola Di Cosmo (eds), *The Spread of Buddhism: Handbook of Oriental Studies*, 8: *Central Asia* (Leiden: E.J. Brill, 2007), pp. 75–129.

15. *The Xi'an Stele*, trans. Waley, Arthur, in Charles F. Horne (ed.), *The Sacred Books and Early Literature of the East*, vol. 12: *Medieval China* (New York: Parke, Austin, and Lipscomb, 1917) (hereafter XS), pp. 381–92, Appendices, lines 88–9. It bears noting as well that these are the last lines of the narrative portion of the stele, followed by a paean both to Christianity and Tang China's dynstic house; lines 88–9 are translated by Pelliot, *L'inscription nestorienne de Si-ngan-fou*, p. 178: 'chez les ta-so (tarsā) aux règles pures, on n'a pas encore enendu parler d'une semblable excellence; parmi les maîtres Radieux aux vêtements blancs à présent on voit cet homme-là; on désirégraver une grande stèle, pour célébrer ces hauts faits excellents'; and by Max Deeg, *Die Strahlende Lehre: Dokumente zur Außereuropäischen Christentumsgeschichte 3 (Asien, Afrika, Lateinamerika)*, 2 vols (Wiesbaden: Harrassowitz, 2012), pp. 78–9: 'Die vorzüglichen *daso* haben (vorher) noch nicht solche Vorzüglichkeit vernommen (und) die weißgewandeten ‚Meister der Strahlenden (Lehre) sahen nun (zum ersten Mal) so einen Mann (Er) wünschte, eine Große Steininschrift einhauen zu lassen, um (damit) die herrlichen Taten aufzuzeigen.'

16. Baumer, *The Church of the East*, p. 178.

17. Pelliot, *L'inscription nestorienne de Si-ngan-fou*, p. 178.

18. This clothing distinction appears first in the philosophical schools of the Mediterranean world. Synesius of Cyrene (*c.*370–415) was a Neo-Platonist and Christian Bishop, close friend of Theophilus, Patriarch of Alexandria, and student of the well-known Hypatia of Alexandria, sister of Origen, recognised along with Origen as a leading Neo-Platonist debater and teacher in their day. Among Synesius' works and sizeable number of letters is the *Dion*, a discussion of the interdependence of philosophy, religion, and culture, which he felt are all needed for a sure grasp of reality. In this treatise he criticised both the men in white mantles (philosophers) and the men in black (Pythagoreans/mystery religion followers, and Neo-Platonist monks); see Jay Bregman, *Synesius of Cyrene* (Berkeley, CA: University of California Press, 1982).

19. Gregory Bar Hebraeus, *Chronicon Ecclesiasticum*, 3 vols, ed. Jean Baptiste Abbeloos and Thomas J. Lamy (Louvani: Peters, 1877) p. 172.

20. al-Ṭayyib, *Fiqh al-Naṣrānīya*, German p. 120/Arabic p. 118.

21. Ibid., German p. 121/Arabic p. 119.

22. See the discussion of these concepts in the introductory chapter and the subsequent discussions in each following chapter.

23. Pierre Bourdieu, *In Other Words: Essays Towards a Reflexive Sociology* (Stanford, CA: Stanford University Press, 1990), p. 13. Though Bourdieu does nothing with the etymology of the word habitus, the present author finds the monastic origins of the word highly relevant. See Charles du Cang, *Glossarium Mediæ et Infimæ Latinitatis*, 'habitus', accessible online at: http://ducange.enc.sorbonne. fr/HABITUS (accessed 31 May 2017).

24. Paula Sanders, *Ritual, Politics and the City in Fatimid Cairo* (Albany, NY: SUNY Press, 1994), pp. 29–31; Patricia Crone and Martin Hinds, *God's Caliph: Religious Authority in the First Centuries of Islam* (Cambridge: Cambridge University Press, 1986).

25. Jean-Maurice Fiey, *Chrétiens syriaques sous les Abbassides surtout à Bagdad (749– 1258)*. CSCO 420, Subs. 59 (Louvain: Secrétariat du CSCO, 1980); Hans Putman, *L'Église et l'Islam sous Timothée I (780–823). Étude sur l'Église nestorienne au temps des premiers 'Abbasides*, Recherches: l'Institut de Lettres Orientales de Beyrouth, Nouvelle Serie B, Orient Chretién 3 (Beirut: Dar el-Machreq, 1975).

26. Marga, *Book of Governors*, pp. 448–9.

27. Silverstein, *Postal Systems in the Pre-Modern Islamic World*, pp. 153–61.

28. For the also sensible explanation that the expense and work on the stele may have already been completed, and thus the community simply was not interested in re-doing the information contained in regarding the Patriarch, see Erica C.D. Hunter, 'The Persian contribution to Christianity in China: reflections in the Xi'an Fu Syriac inscriptions', in Li Tang and Dietmar Winkler (eds), *Hidden Treasures and Intercultural Encounters* (London: Global Marketing Publications, 2009), pp. 71–85, p. 189.

29. Christopher Beckwith, *Empires of the Silk Road* (Princeton, NJ: Princeton University Press, 2009), p. 118.

30. Ibid., p. 146.

31. Ibid.

32. See the introduction for Beckwith's contention that Sasanian architectural motifs surface in Tibet and the Abbasid court simultaneously; ibid., p. 147.

33. Ibid., p.148; also note Jacob Lassner's, *The Shaping of Abbasid Rule* (Princeton, NJ: Princeton University Press, 1980), p. 130 ff., where he robustly attacks a notion found in Beckwith's thought, and stemming from Charles Wendell's study, 'Baghdad: Imago Mundi and other foundational lore', *International Journal of Middle Eastern Studies* 2 (1971), pp. 98–128, positing Indian cosmological symbolism in relation to Al-Mansur's round design for Baghdad.

34. Though this is an old phenomenon in China and Iran, its spread into Central Asia and its simultaneous connectedness to Mesopotamia and China and surfacing in each of the polities between and in conjunction with their all having chosen a world religion, is a new phenomenon.

35. See Mas'udi, *Murūj al-Dhahab* (*The Meadows of Gold*), trans. and ed. Paul Lunde and Caroline S. Stone (London: Kegan Paul International, 1989).
36. On the appropriation of Muslim/Abbasid political ideology within the coinage of the Jewish Khazar kingdom, exemplified in mints employing the formula 'Musa rasul Allah' ('Moses the Prophet of Allah'), see Pritsakr, 'The Khazar kingdom's conversion to Judaism', pp. 261–81.
37. *al-Ya'qubi, Abu al-Abbas Ahmad ibn Ishaq. Ta'rikh {Historiae}*, 2 vols, ed. Muhammad Houtsma (Leiden: E.J. Brill, 1883), vol. 2, pp. 522–3; M.E. McMillan, *The Meaning of Mecca: The Politics of Pilgrimage in Early Islam* (London: Saqi Books, 2011), p. 87.
38. On the Dāgestān region and the *sarīr*, see *Encyclopedia of Islam*, E12, vol. 2, ed. Bernanrd Lewis, Charles Pellat and Joseph Schack (Leiden: E.J. Brill, 1965), pp. 85–6; EI2, vol 4., ed. Emeri Van Bonzel, Bernard. Lewis and Charles Pellat (Leiden: E.J. Brill, 1978), pp. 341–3; had Ibn Fadlan not included the vignette in his geography it would have been lost to history, as it survives in no other manuscript.
39. Ibn Fadlān, *Ibn Fadlān and the Land of Darkness: Arab Travellers in the Far North*, ed. and trans. Paul Lunde and Caroline S. Stone (London: Penguin, 2012), p. 156.
40. Braun, 'Timothei Patriarchae I Epistolae I [Text]', Latin pp. 148–9 /Syriac pp. 100–1.
41. See Chapter 1.
42. *Les letters de patriarche nestorien Timothée I: etude critique avec en appendice la letter de Timothée I aux moines de couvent de Mar Maron*, ed. and trans. Raphaël J. Bidawid, Studi e Testi 187 (Città del Vaticano: Biblioteca Apostolica Vaticana, 1956), pp. 123–4, emphasis mine.
43. As explored and argued in the next chapter.
44. Dimitri Gutas, *Greek Thought, Arab Culture* (London and New York: Routledge, 1998), p. xv ff.
45. Ibid.
46. Considerable controversy also surrounds the authenticity of the document. But its importance for the East Syrians' having secured a position within the Ummayad and Abbasid Empires and as part of the larger appropriation of the East Syrians' Sasanian past to do so, is beyond dispute.
47. Gutas, *Greek Thought, Arab Culture*, pp. xvii ff. also see the discussion below.
48. Appendices, XS, Line 79; see Chapter 4 on phrase *shi quan* and its medical connections.
49. Gutas, *Greek Thought, Arab Culture*; Fiey, *Chrétiens syriaques sous les Abbassides surtout à Bagdad*; John W. Watt, 'Greek Philosophy and Syriac culture in 'Abbasid Iraq', in Erica C.D. Hunter (ed.), *The Christian Heritage of Iraq: Collected Papers from the Christianity in Iraq I–V Seminar Days* (Piscataway, NJ: Gorgias Press, 2009), pp. 10–37.
50. On Timothy's position in the Abbasid court, see Sidney H. Griffith, 'From Patriarch Timothy I to Ḥunayn ibn Isḥāq: philosophy and Christian apology

in Abbasid times; reason, ethics and public policy', in Martin Tamcke (ed.), *Christians and Muslims in Dialogue in the Islamic Orient of the Middle Ages*, Beiruter Texte und Studien 117 (Beirut: Orient-Institut, 2007), pp. 75–98 and 'Patriarch Timothy I and an Aristotelian at the Caliph's court', in Erica C.D. Hunter (ed.), *The Christian Heritage of Iraq: Collected Papers from the Christianity in Iraq I–V Seminar Days* (Piscataway, NJ: Gorgias Press, 2009), pp. 38–53; Wolfgang Hage, 'Kalifenthron und Patriarchenstuhl. Zum Verhältnis von Staat und Kirche im Mittelalter', in Wolfgang Breul-Kunkel and Luther Vogel (eds), *Rezeption und Reform. Festschrift für Hans Schneider zu seinem 60. Geburtstag*, Quellen und Studien zur hessischen Kirchengeschichte 5 (Darmstadt/Kassel: Verlag der Hessischen Kirchengeschichtlichen Vereinigung, 2001), pp. 3–17; Martin Heimgartner, 'Die Disputatio des ostsyrischen Patriarchen Timotheos (780–823) mit dem Kalifen al-Mahdi', in Martin Tamcke (ed.), *Christians and Muslims in Dialogue in the Islamic Orient of the Middle Ages*, Beiruter Texte und Studien 117 (Beirut: Orient-Institut, 2007), pp. 45–56; Erica C.D. Hunter, 'Interfaith dialogues: the Church of the East and the Abbasids', in Sophia G. Vashaolmidze and Lutz Greisiger, Harrassowitze (eds), *Der Christliche Orient und seine Umwelt* (Weisbaden: Harrassowitz, 2007), pp. 289–302; Putman, *L'Église et l'Islam sous Timothée I*.

51. Alphonse Mingana, 'The Apology of Timothy the Patriarch before the Caliph Mahdi', *Bulletin of the John Rylands Library* 12 (1928), pp. 137–298, p. 9.

52. Timothy was asked by Caliph Al-Mahdi to translate a work of Aristotle for him personally.

53. Mingana, 'The Apology of Timothy the Patriarch', pp. 16 and 49.

54. Ibid., p. 40. These statements, rather politically incorrect by today's reckoning, appear with great frequency in late Roman Christian texts such as the writings of John Chrysostom and in church canons.

55. Ibid., p. 57.

56. Note the other references to rationality and intellectual freedom in the text: 'you granted me the full freedom of speaking in front of you' (ibid., p.49); 'the king asked philosophically (ibid., p. 50), which is then followed by a discussion of the role of reason in the soul.

57. Hunter, 'Interfaith dialogues', p. 289 ff.

58. Shaban summarises these views (*The 'Abbāsid Revolution*, p. xv ff); as does Elton L. Daniel, *The Political and Social History of Khurasan under Abbasid Rule 747–820* (Minneapolis: Biblioteca Islamica, 1979), pp. 5–25.

59. Shaban, *The 'Abbāsid Revolution*, p. xv ff.

60. Ibid.; Aptin Khanbaghi, *The Fire, The Star and the Cross: Minority Religions in Medieval and Early Islamic Iran* (New York: I.B.Tauris, 2006), p. 22, provides information on Arab settlement patterns in Khurasan.

61. Shaban, *The 'Abbāsid Revolution*, p. xvi.

62. As noted ibid.; Richard Bulliet shows that only a small number of Iranians had become Muslim at the start of the revolution and that Zoroastrian Mobeds were fact present working in the Abbasid court along with the Catholicoi of

the Church of the East; see his *Conversion to Islam in the Medieval Period: An Essay in Quantitative History* (Cambridge, MA: Harvard University Press, 1979); Khanbaghi, *The Fire, The Star and the Cross*, p. 23.

63. Such is supported in primary materials in the case of the chronicle penned by Narsharkhi; see Narsharkhi, *The History of Bukhara*, trans. R.N. Frye (Cambridge, MA: Mediaeval Academy of America, 1954); cf. Khanbagi's comments on this: Khanbaghi, *The Fire, The Star and the Cross*. Another primary text indicating how the assertion of ancient Persian identity was part of assertions of independence from the Ummayad empire, is *The Book of Government, or Rules for Kings: The Siyar al-Muluk or Siyasat-nama of Nizam al-Mulk*, trans. Hubert Darke, rev. edn (London: Routledge, 2001).

64. Daniel, *The Political and Social History of Khurasan*, p. 190; Gutas, *Greek Thought, Arab Culture*, and Khanbaghi, *The Fire, The Star and the Cross*, among others have explored the extent to which Persian speakers, such as Abu Muslim al Khurasani, came to be the main leaders of the early part of this revolution against Arab rule; a major reassessment of their views is found in Patricia Crone's *The Nativist Prophets of Early Islamic Iran* (Cambridge: Cambridge University Press, 2012).

65. Daniel, *The Political and Social History of Khurasan*.

66. Ibid., p. 198: also cf. pp. 9, 18 and 22.

67. Hamilton A.R. Gibb, *Studies on the Civilization of Islam* (London: Shaw and Polk, 1982), p. 66.

68. Ibid.

69. Ibid., p. 69.

70. Ibid., p. 66.

71. Crone, *The Nativist Prophets*, p. 145, pp. 327–32, and passim.

72. Khanbaghi, *The Fire, The Star and the Cross*, p. 18.

73. Ibid.

74. Ibid., p. 20, for John Bar Penkaye reference.

75. Ibid., citing Baladhuri, who indicates Zoroastrians were in charge of finance positions in late the Umayyad and early Abbasid settings; these where hereditary offices and passed from fathers to sons; also see Jamsheed Choksy, *Conflict and Cooperation: Zoroastrian Subalterns and Muslim Elites in Medieval Iranian Society* (New York: Columbia University Press, 1997), p. 33 on Zoroastrians as tax collectors.

76. John Bar Penkaye quoted in Khanbaghi, *The Fire, The Star and the Cross*, p. 25. Khanbaghi also notes that Qur'anic statements regarding *dhimma* communities would have eventually contributed to the decline of Zoroastrianism within Muslim power centres such as Baghdad; while the Qur'an does however distinguish Zoroastrians from 'idolaters', in one of the two schools of Islamic thought of the time a Zoroastrian held the equivalent of one quarter of a Christian or Jew in criminal proceedings and court testimonies.

77. Ibid., p. 20.

78. Ibid.
79. Encyclopedia Iranica Online, 'Ibn al-Muqaffa'. Available at http://www.irani
    caonline.org/articles/ebn-al-moqaffa (accessed 1 June 2017); François de
    Blois,, *Burzo̅y's Voyage to India and the Origin of the Book of Kali̅lah wa Dimnah*
    (London: Royal Asiatic Society, 1990).
80. Encyclopedia Iranica Online, 'Ibn al-Muqaffa'.
81. *The Letter of Tansar*, trans. Mary Boyce (Roma: Istituto Italiano per il Medio ed
    Estremo Oriente, 1968).
82. From Encyclopedia Iranica Online, *Nama-ye Tansar*, ed. Mojtaba Mīnovī
    (Tehran, 1311 Š.)/1933;. Boyce, *The Letter of Tansar*, Rome, 1968), p. 74.
    Available at http://www.iranicaonline.org/articles/andarz-precept-instruction-
    advice (1 June 2017).
83. Gutas, *Greek Thought, Arab Culture*, p. xv ff.
84. The choice to put the new capital near the site of Ctesiphon was done in order
    to create a Sasanian ambience; ibid., p. 52.
85. Ibid., p. 28 ff.
86. See the discussion in the introductory chapter, the following chapter; Kevin
    van Bladel, 'Eighth-century Indian astronomy in the two cities of peace', in
    Behnam Sadeghi, Asad Q. Ahmed, Robert Hoyland, Adam Silverstein (eds),
    Islamic Cultures, Islamic Contexts: Essays in Honor of Professor Patricia Crone
    (Leiden: E.J. Brill, 2014), pp. 295–342.
87. Gutas, *Greek Thought, Arab Culture*, p. 31.
88. Mas'udi, *Murūj al-Dhahab*, p. 131.
89. Gutas, *Greek Thought, Arab Culture*, p. 33.
90. Ibid.
91. See appendices for the original text.
92. Beckwith, *Empires of the Silk Road*, pp. 147–9.
93. Beckwith, *The Tibetan Empire in Central Asia*. See the following chapter for
    specifics.
94. About whom much more is now known, due to the excellent recent study by
    Kevin van Bladel; see his 'The Bactrian background of the Barmakids', in
    Anna Akasoy, Charles S.F. Burnett and Ronit Yoeli-Tlalim (eds), *Islam and
    Tibet: Interactions along the Musk Routes* (London: Ashgate, 2011), pp. 43–88.
95. Harold Bailey, 'Iranica', *BSOAS* 11/1 (1943), p. 2.
96. Mas'udi, *Murūj al-Dhahab*, p. 131.
97. The family is also credited with the establishment of the first paper mill in
    Baghdad; the power of the Barmakids in the early Abbasid Empire is reflected
    in *The Book of the Thousand and One Nights*; the vizier Ja'far appears in several
    stories, as well as a tale that gave rise to the expression 'Barmecide feast'. See
    Encyclopedia Iranica Online, 'Barmakids'. Available at http://www.iranicaonli
    ne.org/articles/barmakids (accessed 1 June 2017).
98. Majid Fakhry, *A History of Islamic Philosophy*, 2nd edn (New York: Columbia
    University Press, 1983), p. 45; Fakhry also notes that in his book *Tariq al-
    Hind* the Arab historian and polymath al-Biruni (c.1050) states that the

Abbasid Caliph al-Ma'mun had an embassy in India, and from India a book was brought to Baghdad that was translated into Arabic as *Sindhind*. It is generally presumed that *Sindhind* is none other than Brahmagūpta's *Brahmasphuta-Siddhānta*.

99. Fakhry, *A History of Islamic Philosophy*, referring to the *Fihrist* of Ibn Al-Nadim (Cairo: Rahmānīyah Press, 1929), p. 395.

100. Von Bladel, 'Eighth-century Indian astronomy'.

101. Ibid.

102. See the discussion below.

103. *Book of Governors*, pp. 384–5; Bar Hebreaeus, *Chronicon Ecclesiasticum*, ii. col. 171; see appendices of Godwin (2016a), 'Persian Christians at the Chinese Court' for the full text of the passage.

104. Recalling Morony's factionalism thesis, as discussed in Chapter 2, and political difficulties appearing in Ishoyahb III's letters, as discussed in chapter three.

105. Braun, 'Timothei Patriarchae I Epistolae I [Text]', Latin p. 69/Syriac p. 106.

106. Ibid., Latin p. 70/Syriac p. 107.

107. Ibid.

108. Ibid., Latin p. 70/Syriac 108.

109. Vittorio Berti, 'Idéologie et politique missionnaire de Timothée Ier, patriarche syro-oriental (780–823)', in Christelle Jullien (ed.), *Chrétiens en terre d'Iran IV. Itinéraires missionnaires: échanges et identities*, *Cahiers de Studia Iranica 44* (Paris: Association pour l'avancement des études iraniennes, 2011), pp. 71–110, p. 87.

110. Support for which is given throughout this chapter and the next.

111. Cynthia Villagomez, 'The fields, flocks, and finances of monks: economic life at Nestorian monasteries, 500–850', unpublished PhD thesis, University of California, Los Angeles, 1998, pp. 2–22, 25–35, 121 and 123 and passim; Villagomez notes that Harun Al-Rashid donated financially to East Syrian monasteries (p. 121) and that heads of monasteries were linked together in networks of social charitable organizations (p. 157).

112. See Chapter 1.

113. Marga, *Book of Governors*, English p. 479/Syriac p. 264.

114. Ibid., English p. 467/Syriac pp. 252–3.

115. John C. Reeves, *Prolegomena to a History of Islamicate Manichaeism* (Sheffield: Equinox Publications, 2011), pp. 1–25; Choksy, *Conflict and Cooperation*, pp. 1–45.

116. Marga, *Book of Governors*, English p. 480–2/Syriac p. 261.

117. *Les letters de patriarche nestorien Timothée I*, p. 125.

118. Berti, 'Idéologie et politique missionnaire de Timothée Ier', p. 87.

119. Eduard Sachau, *Syrische Rechtsbü'cher*, vol. 2 (Berlin: G. Reimer, 1907–14), pp. 56–7 (translation by the author).

120. Ibid.

121. Ibid., p. 62.

122. Ibid.

Chapter 4   The Court of Emperor Tang Dezong as 'Imperial Net', and the Church of the East's Persian *Longue Durée*

1. A search of *Wenyuange siku quanshu dianzi ban* (文淵閣四庫全書電子版) (Shanghai: Renmin Chubanshe, 2002) (hereafter SKQS) reveals Bactrian Buddhists coming to the Chinese court from the late Sui period onwards: see Wei Zheng (580–643) (ed.), *Sui Shu* {隋書, *Book of Sui*} [639], 6 vols (Beijing: Zhonghua shuju, 1973), 813; Zheng Qiao (1104-1162) (ed.), *Tong Zhi* [通志} (Taibei: Shijie shuju, 1956), 196 (these references simply indicate Buddhists came to receive Buddhist texts from the Chinese court), which may well indicate Buddhist texts being viewed as patronage objects tying the lesser royal court of Bactria to the higher royal court of China, a phenomenon relatable to the rhetoric from the Xi'an stele singled out below for focus and study, though not an issue which can be explored in the depth it deserves at the present time. On the connections between Bactria and Kashmiri Buddhism, see Kevin Van Bladel, 'Eighth-century Indian astronomy in the two cities of peace', in Behnam Sadeghi, Asad Q. Ahmed, Robert Hoyland, Adam Silverstein (eds) *Islamic Cultures, Islamic Contexts: Essays in Honor of Professor Patricia Crone* (Leiden: E.J. Brill, 2014), pp. 295–342; Xavier Tremblay, 'The spread of Buddhism in Serindia – Buddhism among Iranians, Tocharians and Turks before the 13th century' – in Denis Sinor and Nicola Di Cosmo (eds), *The Spread of Buddhism: Handbook of Oriental Studies*, 8: *Central Asia* (Leiden: E.J. Brill, 2007), pp. 75–129; Johan Elverskog, *Buddhism and Islam on the Silk Road* (Philadelphia, PA: University of Pennsylvania Press, 2010), pp. 25–32; Xinru Liu, *Silk and Religion: An Exploration of Material Life and the Thought of People*, AD 600–1200 (New Delhi: Oxford University Press, 1998)).

2. Kevin Van Bladel, 'The Bactrian background of the Barmakids', in Anna Akasoy, Charles S.F. Burnett and Ronit Yoeli-Tlalim (eds), *Islam and Tibet: Interactions along the Musk Routes* (London: Ashgate, 2011), pp. 43–88.

3. Étienne de la Vaissière, 'Chakar Sogdiens en Chine', in Étienne de la Vaissière and Éric Trombert (eds), *Les Sodiens en Chine* (Paris: Collège de France, Institut des Hautes Études Chinoises, 2006), pp. 255–60; Étienne de la Vaissière, Châkars d'Asie centrale', *Studia Iranica* (2005), pp.139–49; Yutaka Moribe, 'Non-Han in the late Tang and five dynasties military', in de la Vaissière and Trombert, *Les Sodiens en Chine*, pp. 243–54; Christopher Beckwith, 'Aspects of the early history of the Central Asian Guard Corps in Islam', *Archivum Eurasiae Medii Aevi* 4 (1984), pp. 29–43; Christopher Beckwith, *The Tibetan Empire in Central Asia* (Princeton, NJ: Princeton University Press, 1987); Christopher Beckwith, *Empires of the Silk Road* (Princeton, NJ: Princeton University Press, 2009); Mark Dickens, 'Review: Beckwith, *Empires of the Silk Road*', *Orientalistische Literaturzeitung* 106/4–5 (2011), pp. 1–4; Anatoly M. Khazanov, 'The spread of world religions in medieval nomadic Societies of the Eurasian steppes', in Michael Gervers and Wayne Schlepp (eds), *Nomadic Diplomacy, Destruction and Religion from the Pacific to the Atlantic*, Toronto

Studies in Central and Inner Asia, No. 1, (Toronto: Joint Centre for Asia Pacific Studies Toronto, 1994), pp. 11–33.

4. Beckwith writes of how both rebellions were 'planned in advance by merchants', see Beckwith, *Empires of the Silk Road*, p. 147.

5. See introductory section of Chapter 3.

6. *The Xi'an Stele*, trans. Alexander Wylie, in Charles F. Horne (ed.), *The Sacred Books and Early Literature of the East*, vol. 12: *Medieval China* (New York: Parke, Austin, and Lipscomb, 1917) (hereafter XS), pp. 381–92, lines 83–89; on the appellation Jing-jiao seng vs Jing-jiao shi see the final section of this chapter.

7. Ibid., line 54: *jinfang guixu, wuwai gaoseng* [金方貴緒, 物外高僧].

8. Using the term imaginary here as a noun of course, in the manner of, for example, Manfred B. Steger in his *The Rise of the Global Imaginary: Political Ideologies from the French Revolution to the Global War on Terror* (Oxford: Oxford University Press, 2008).

9. The *locus classicus* for which is Si Maqian's *Shi Ji* 史記 (*c.*100 BC), and its first chapter, 'The Basic Annals of the Five Emperors', [Wudi Benji 五帝本 紀]. Also see Ni Maoshing, *The Yellow Emperor's Classic of Medicine: A New Translation of the Neijing Suwen with Commentary* (Boston: Shambhala, 1995), p. 301.

10. Ibid;. Technology included wooden houses, carts, boats, the bow and arrow, and writing.

11. Ibid. He is said to have dreamed of an ideal kingdom whose tranquil inhabitants lived in harmonious accord with the natural law and possessed virtues remarkably like those espoused by early Daoism; on waking from his dream, Huangdi sought to inculcate these virtues in his own kingdom, to ensure order and prosperity among the inhabitants.

12. The primary source is Taishō Shinshū Daizōkyō 大正 新修 大藏經, Vol. 55, No. 2157; the text can be found online at: http://tripitaka.cbeta.org/ zh-cn/T55n2157-017 (accessed 10 December 2013); Junjirō Takakusu, 'The name of "Messiah" found in a Buddhist book: the Nestorian missionary Adam, Presbyter, Papas of China, translating a Buddhist sutra', *Tong Bao* (1896); R. Todd Godwin, 'Eunuchs for the Kingdom of God': Re-thinking the Imperial Translation Incident of 787, in Li Tang and Dietmar W. Winkler (eds), *Winds of Jingjiao: Studies on East Syriac Christianity in China and Central Asia*, Orientalia Patristica Oecumenica, vol. 6 (Zurich and Vienna: Akademie Verlag, 2016b), pp. 267-82.

13. *Taisho Tripitaka* vol. 33, no. 1709. Available at http://www.cbeta.org/result/ normal/T33/1709_007.htm (accessed 4 January 2014). On the background of these texts see the important work by Charles Orzech, *Politics and Transcendent Wisdom: The Scripture for Humane Kings in the Creation of Chinese Buddhism* (University Park, PA: Pennsylvania State University Press, 1998), pp. 141–50, 191–201. There are two versions of the text. The 仁王護國般 若波羅蜜經, T 246.8.834-845) though to be based mostly on an original version (仁王般若波羅蜜經, T 245.8.825-834), attributed to Kumārajīva.

14. One group of which were the late Tang military's eunuch generals, to whom an entire section within the chapter is devoted below. The use of the term Esoteric Buddhism is problematic but is used in accordance with the definition given by Stanley Weinstein (*Buddhism under the Tang* (Cambridge: Cambridge University Press, 1987)) and provided in Chapter 3; the term is also used by Chen Huaiyu in connection with the Church of the East's involvement in spiritual support for the Tang house. See further references to his work below, and his 'Cong bijiao yuyan xuekan "sanwei mengduzan" yu "dacheng ben sheng xindi guan jing" de lianxi' [从比较语言学看《三威蒙度赞》与《大乘本生心地观经》的联系 in his 景风梵声（中古宗教之诸相）] (Beijing: Zongjiao wenhua chubanshe, 2012), pp. 34–47, in which he explores connections between the Church of the East and another Mijiao text translated by Bo-re.

15. *Taishō Shinshū Daizōkyō (Taishō Revised Tripiṭaka)* [大正新脩大藏經], ed. Junjirou Takakasu, also contains the *Zhenyuan Xinding Shijiao Mulu* 貞元新定釋教目錄 (New Record of Buddhist Translations from the Zhenguan Era – 785–805), referred to here at 33.1709; Orzech, *Politics and Transcendent Wisdom.* pp. 286–93.

16. See 'Late Tang eunuchs, the Buddhist cosmopolis, Dezong's court, and agency', later in this chapter.

17. On whether or not Adam could have known Classical Chinese well enough to compose the text of the stele, see Paul Pelliot, *L'inscription nestorienne de Si-ngan-fou, Edited with Supplements by Antonino Forte* (Kyoto: Scuola di Studi sull'Asia Orientale; Paris: Collège de France, Institut des Hautes Etudes Chinoises, 1996), p. 445; Max Deeg, *Die Strahlende Lehre: Dokumente zur Außereuropäischen Christentumsgeschichte 3 (Asien, Afrika, Lateinamerika)*, 2 vols (Wiesbaden: Harrassowitz, 2012), p. 114.

18. Pierre Bourdieu, *In Other Words: Essays Towards a Reflexive Sociology* (Stanford: Stanford University Press, 1990), p. 13.

19. Minoru Inaba, 'Arab soldiers in China at the time of the An-Shi Rebellion', *Memoirs of the Touyou Bunko* 68 (2010), pp. 36–61.

20. See Max Deeg, 'Ways to go and not to go in the contextualization of the *Jingjiao* documents of the Tang period', in Li Tang and Dietmar Winkler (eds), *Hidden Treasures and Intercultural Encounters* (London: Global Marketing Publications, 2009), pp. 135–52, on the monastic element within Adam's thinking and reasons for composing the Xi'an stele and how this relates to developments taking place within the court of Dezong when he ascended the throne. On changes within the early Dezong court, also see Charles A. Peterson, 'Court and province in mid-and late T'ang', in Denis Twitchett (ed.), *The* Cambridge History of China, vol. 3: *Sui and T'ang China, 589–906*, Part 1 (Cambridge: Cambridge University Press, 1979), pp. 589–606; Yuan Zhipeng [袁志鹏], 'Li mi yu tangdezong minzu zhengce de zhuanbian' [李泌与唐德宗民族政策的轉變], [唐山師範学院报], *Journal of Tangshan Teachers College* 36/1 (January 2014), pp. 103–6, p. 103.

21. Per personal conversation with Max Deeg.

22. Denis Twitchett, 'Tibet in Tang's grand strategy', in Hans van de Ven (ed.), *Warfare in Chinese History*, (Leiden, Brill, 2000), pp. 106–79.

23. Peterson, 'Court and province in mid-and late T'ang', CHC, pp. 464-60; Michael T. Dalby, 'Court and Politics in late T'ang times', CHC, pp. 561-81.

24. Peterson, 'Court and province in mid-and late T'ang', pp. 464–560; *Xin Tangshu* [新唐書] (*The New Tang Record*, compiled in 1060), ed. Ouyang Xiu [歐陽修] and Song Qi [宋祁] (Beijing: Zhonghua shuju, 1975) (hereafter XTS), 52: 1352–3.

25. Cf. *Jiu Tangshu* [舊唐書], *Old Tang Record*, ed. Liu Xu [劉昫] (887–946), (compiled in 945) (Beijing: Zhonghua shuju, 1975) (hereafter JTS), 200b.150, where it states that Zhu Ci 'called himself emperor of Daqin' [*zi cheng Daqin Huangdi*, 自稱大秦皇帝].

26. Beckwith, *The Tibetan Empire in Central Asia*, p. 147.

27. On this general theme, see Edwin G. Pulleyblank, *The Background of the Rebellion of An Lu-Shan* (London: Oxford University Press, 1966); Edwin G. Pulleyblank, 'The An Lu-Shan Rebellion and the origins of chronic militarism in late T'ang China', in John C. Perry and Bardwell L. Smith (eds), *Essays on T'ang Society* (Leiden: E.J. Brill, 1976), pp. 75–81; for the bibliography on Li Mi and eunuchs.

28. The character 景 [*jing*], used in modern East Asian languages, is not the same as that of the Jingjiao corpus, a new character created which used not the sun radical above the character for capital, but rather the character for mouth, likely indicating that the church saw itself as preaching the imperial way of the Tang court and radiating its charisma. See the discussion on this below, and in connection to Zhang Xiaogui, 'Why did Chinese "Nestorians" change the name of their religion to Jingjiao?' *Winds of Jingjiao: Studies on East Syriac Christianity in China and Central Asia*, vol. 6, pp. 283–310.

29. Takakusu, pp. 589–91.

30. Though the text was translated again later, and this time directly from Sanskrit to Chinese and without the Iranian language intermediary, this it is not the same text. It is a similar text, however, and one that is three sections longer than the first one. *Taishō Shinshū Daizōkyō (Taishō Revised Tripiṭaka)* [大正新脩大藏經], ed. Junjirō Takakusu, contains the *Zhenyuan Xinding Shijiao Mulu* [貞元新定釋教目錄] (New Record of Buddhist Translations from the Zhenguan Era – 785–805) (hereafter T), vol. 8, no. 0245. Available at http://tripitaka.cbeta.org/T08n0246_001 (accessed 7 July 2013).

31. *Taisho Tripitaka* See appendices of Godwin, 'Persian Christians at the Chinese Court' (2016a), for original text and an English translation; see note 12 for primary source.

32. Taisho Tripitaka 8, no. 261; 全唐文55, pp. 590–1.

33. *Zi* [茲], 'hereby' it is declared: *Hanyu Da Cidian* [漢語大詞典], chief ed. Luo Zhufeng [羅竹風], CD ROM 3.0 (Hong Kong: The Commercial Press, 2007) (hereafter HDC).

34. See Chapter 3 on these issues. Deeg (forthcoming) notes, p. 208, that Xuanzong's facial features were used within imperial images of the Buddha within imperial temples, and likely may have appeared in the imperial portaits installed in the Church of the East's monastery/church at Chang'an.

35. Mie Nakata, 'Hasseiki kōhan ni okeru chūō yūrajia no dōkō to Chōan bukkyō-kai e sō-ki 'Daijō ri omomu rokki haramitsuta kyo' hon'yaku sankasha no bunseki yori' [八世紀後半における中央ユーラシアの動向と長安仏教界―得宗期『大乗理趣六波羅蜜多経』翻訳参加者の分析より, The Buddhist circle in Chang'an the movements amongst Central Eurasia during the latter half of the eighth century – from the study on participants in translation of Dacheng Liqu Liu Boluomiduo Jing [大乗理趣六波羅蜜多経 during the Era of the Emperor 德宗]', Kansaidaigaku tōzai gakujutsu kenkyūjo [関西大学東西学術研究所] (2011–14), pp. 153–89.

36. Ibid., p. 171; their number, 4,000, matches the number (4,000) given for non-Han soldiers having joined Guo Ziyi's force in 757: see Zizhi tongjian [資治通鑑] (Beijing: Zhonhua shuhu, 1956) (hereafter ZZTJ), 220 on the latter and 232 on the Hu Ke being forced to join the Tang army if they did not have sufficient capital and property. This passage in the ZZTJ is translated and discussed in relation to the argument of the chapter.

37. ZZTJ 232; see the discussion below on the Shence Army.

38. Nakata, 'Hasseiki kōhan ni okeru chūō yūrajia ...'.

39. A point given further elaboration later.

40. Chen Shipei [沈世培], 'Li Mì yu pingding fanzhen geju' [李泌与平定藩镇割据], 铁道师院学报 15/2 (April 1998), pp. 81–4, p. 81.

41. Nakata Mie [中田 美絵] 'Bukong as a leader of the Chang'an Buddhist world and of Sogdians', Fuku no Chouan Bukkyoukai Taotoi to Sogdojin [不空の長安仏教界台頭とソグド人], Tōyō Gakuho [東洋学報] (2007), pp. 89–93 and 33–65.

42. Asceticism, as defined in appendices.

43. See Godwin 2016b, p. 267, for primary source and discussion.

44. Guo Ziyi struggled constantly with the leading eunuchs of the court, and it is likely that Dezong's decision to remove Guo Ziyi as Shuofang Jiedushi came at the request of eunuchs: Xu Min [徐敏], 'Guo ziyi yu tang dai huanguan' [郭子仪与唐代宦官], History Teacher 6 (2007), pp. 105–6.

45. XS, line 58 ff.

46. See Chapter 1.

47. See introduction on holy man/sage designation, and see the chapter's final section, dealing with imperial Chinese science, on the issue of solar symbolism.

48. Maria H. Dettenhofer, 'Eunuchs, women and imperial courts', in Walter Scheidel (ed.), Rome and China: Comparative Perspectives on Ancient World Empires (Oxford: Oxford University Press, 2009), pp. 83-99.

49. Ibid., p. 71.

50. Wang Pu [王溥] (922–82) (ed.), *Tang Huiyao* [唐會要; *Notabilia of Tang*] (Shanghai: Shanghai guji chubanshe, 1991) (hereafter THY) 65, p. 1131.

51. Dates uncertain, JTS Juan 144.

52. On the An Lusan and post-An Lushan Tang empire, see Wang Shounan [王壽南], *Tangdai huanguan quanshi zhi yánjiu* [唐代宦官權勢之研究] (Taipei: Zhengzhong Shuju, 1971), pp. 117–43; Wang Shoudang [王守棟], 'An-shi zhi luan qian hou tang-chao huan-guan quan-shi de yan-bian' [安史之亂前後唐朝宦官權勢的演變], *Journal of Dezhou University* [德州学院学报] 19/3 (June 2003), pp. 61–5; Xu Min *Guo ziyi yu tang dai huanguan*.

53. THY 419 and 517.

54. Michael T. Dalby, 'Court politics in late T'ang times', in Twitchett, *The Cambridge History of China*, vol. 3, pp. 561–81, p. 572.

55. Ibid.

56. Ibid.

57. See Liu Yat-wing, 'The Shen-ts'e Armies and the Palace Commissions in China, 755–875 AD', PhD thesis, University of London, 1970; cf. pp. 116–54 on eunuchs in the Tang generally, and p. 71 for this assertion about the court of Dezong.

58. XTS 56, p. 1332.

59. See Liu, 'The Shen-ts'e Armies', pp. 116–54, on eunuchs in the Tang generally, and p. 71 for this assertion about the court of Dezong.

60. See Robert des Rotours, *Le Traité des fonctionnaries et Traité de l'armé*, 2 vols (San Francisco: Chinese Materials Center, 1974), p. 360, on this translation of the title Shence jun. For this biographical information on Luo Haoxin, see *Song gaoseng chuan* [宋高僧傳,] T50, no. 2061, p. 0716b14, and the *Zhenyuan Record*, T 55, no. 2157, p. 0892a05 p. 0737c29; on the beginnings of the unit, see XTS 216; ZZTJ 221.

61. Dalby, 'Court politics in late T'ang times', p. 573; THY 72: 1294.

62. XTS 50.

63. Ibid.

64. Taisho 50, no. 2061, p. 0716b14 and the *Zhenyuan Record*, T 55, no. 2157, p. 0892a05, p. 0737c29.

65. The notion of the 'Sanskrit Cosmopolis' appears in many places, but cf. Sheldon Pollock, *'The Sanskrit Cosmopolis*, 300–1300: transculturation, vernacularization, and the question of ideology', in Jan E.M. Houben (ed.), *Ideology and Status of Sanskrit: Contributions to the History of the Sanskrit Language*, Brill's Indological Library, vol. 13 (Leiden: Brill, 1996), pp. 197–249.

66. This is not to say the language could not have been Bactrian, Ghandari, or another Indo-Aryan language either, but given the prevalence of Sogdian, it seems more likely. The mention of the use of Sanskrit in the later re-translation appears to rule out the possibility that the first text was in Sanskrit. On the role of Sogdians in Chinese Buddhism, see Mariko N. Washington, 'Sogdians and Buddhism', *Sino-Platonic Papers* 174 (2006), pp. 1–64.

67. Weinstein, *Buddhism under the Tang*, p. 63, offers in support of this assertion that Shandao [善導], the great systemiser of Pureland Buddhism, who lived in Chang'an for some 30 years and whose writings had a large popular following, had no effect on the leading monks of the philosophical schools of the Tang before the An Lushan Rebellion.

68. See Elverskog, *Buddhism and Islam on the Silk Road*, pp. 35–9 for some introductory material on Esoteric-imperial Buddhism, where similar ideas are expounded.

69. Chen Huaiyu, 'The encounter of Nestorian Christianity with Tantric Buddhism in medieval China', in Winkler and Tang, *Hidden Treasures and Intercultural Encounters*, pp. 195–13, p. 204; T 54.

70. An issue explored further later in the book, but not that Yoritomo argues that eunuch Luo Haoxin is a relative of Prajña's mother, and a blood relative of An Lushan, and that Prajña is from the same area originally (modern Kabul) as Bukong (Amogavajra); cf. Yoritomo Motohiro [賴富 本宏], *Chūgoku mikkyō no kenkyū: Han'nya to san'nei no mikkyō rikai o chūshin to shite* [中国密教の研究: 般若と賛寧の密教理解を中心として] (Tokyo: Daitō Shuppan-sha, 1979), p.14; for basic material on Vajrabodhi, see Marc Abramson, *Ethnic Identity in Tang China* (Philadelphia, PA: University of Pennsylvania Press, 2008), pp. viii–ix, 50, 52, 74, 77, 81, 185–6, 199n.2, and on Amoghavajra, pp. 56, 74, 81, 199nn.2 and 5; on 'Persian' connections to the sea trade in the Tang, see Wang Changwen, [王承文], 'Tangdai Lingdan de Bosiren yu Bosi Wenhua' [唐代岭南的波斯人与波斯文化], *Sun Yatsen University Historical Study Collection*, vol. 1 (Guangzhou, 1991), pp. 68–82.

71. Abramson, *Ethnic Identity in Tang China*, p. 57.

72. Ibid., p. 58.

73. Ibid.

74. Jinhua Chen, 'Esoteric Buddhism and monastic institutions', in Charles Orzech (ed.), *Esoteric Buddhism and the Tantras in East Asia* (Leiden: E.J. Brill, 2011), pp. 286–93, notes how palace chapels were working in parallel with the Esoteric Buddhist centres in the capital. In 1987 an archaeological expedition uncovered an entire subterranean prayer chapel in Xi'an, structured like a Tantric mandala; Chen notes that the rise of warlords following the An Lushan Rebellion made the need to strengthen court legitimacy greater, thus in turn leading to Esoteric Buddhists strengthening their ties to courts as they were able to aid in this search for legitimacy (imperial charisma, Mandate of Heaven). This can be connected to the large numbers of Buddhist seekers coming to China to study and to raise their political status in their home countries, such as occurred with Japanese pilgrims Ennin and Kukai, and in Korea; the emergent nature of eighth-century courtly culture in central Asia can be connected to this phenomenon as well.

75. Ennin's diary sheds light on several things at once in this regard. The diary shows that eunuchs may have been responsible for the mass execution of Manichaean monks which took place in the last days of the Uighur Empire

(p. 232); Ennin is shown being well aware that his Japanese embassy would do well to participate in state rituals stemming from the Esoteric tradition, despite being unprepared for the level of intensity at which they would encounter this exceeding expectations (p. 353). The emperor's tour of monasteries is shown to have disappeared during Ennin's stay and showing close connection to the fall of the Uighur state, something revealing the contours of the agency, subjectivity of the Church of the East and its agency-seeking rhetoric (p. 355), something added to by the appearance in the diary of Buddhist monks resorting to violence against Uighurs in an attempt to regain their positions, but still being executed by the Tang government for going against public order (p. 321); see *Ennin's Diary: The Record of a Pilgrimage to China in Search of the Law*, trans. Edwin O. Reischauer (New York: Ronald Press, 1955), and the accompanying volume, Edwin O. Reischauer, *Ennin's Travels in T'ang China* (New York: Ronald Press, 1955).

76. Dalby, 'Court politics in late T'ang times', p. 578.

77. Ibid., p. 579.

78. Tsukamoto has explored the Gongdeshi positon in great depth in this regard, noting also that following a period of illness in his early reign and his return to health after what he saw was a healing brought on by prayers for the royal house undertaken by imperial prayer guards instigated by the Shence Army, Dezong began to support monastic institutions and the Shence Army became an arm of the Gongdeshi. Citing a passage in the *Cefu yuangui* [王欽若] (ed.), *Cefu Yuangui* [册府元龜, *The Great Tortoise of National Archives*, compiled between 1005–13] (Beijing: Zhonghua shuju, 1960) (hereafter CFYG)), p. 275, medicine and imperial physicians being a connection that can be built upon in regard to the Church of the East's and its Western agency held in relation to the Tang court, an issue explored further in the chapter's final section; see Tsukamoto Zenryu [塚本善隆], 'Tōchūki irai no chōan no kōtokushi' [唐中期以来の長安の功德使], in *Tsukamoto Zenryū chosakushū* [塚本善隆著作集], vol. 3 (Tōkyō: Daitō Shuppan, 1974–6), pp. 253–84, pp. 253–80; Nakata, 'Bukong as a leader of the Chang'an Buddhist world and of Sogdians'.

79. ZZTJ 220 and ZZTJ 232, the latter on the *Hu Ke* being forced to join the Tang army if they did not have sufficient capital and property, a passage translated and discussed later.

80. An argument made below; on the role of Li Mi in Dezong's court and the his influence in diplomatic relations; see Chen, 'Li mi yu pingding fanzhen geju'; Liu Haixia [刘海霞], 'Kun fan zhi ce: Zhong tangmingchen Li Mi de bianjian zhanlüe' [困蕃之策：中唐名臣李泌的边疆战略], *Journal of Wenshan University* [文山学院学报] 24/5 (October 2011), pp. 57–61; Liu Haixia [刘海霞], 'You ming chen li mi kan zhong tang de biangjian jin lüe' [由名臣李泌看中唐的边疆经略], *Journal of Wenshan University* [文山学院学报]

25/4 (August 2012), pp. 21–6; Yuan, 'Li mi yu tangdezong minzu zhengce de zhuanbian'.

81. ZZTJ 232.

82. As stated by Peterson, 'Court and province in mid-and late T'ang', p. 592, for which a primary source reference has thus far not been located by this researcher.

83. See the discussion below and its bibliography.

84. ZZTJ 232, p. 7493.

85. JTS 130, pp. 3623–4.

86. ZZTJ 233, pp. 7494–5.

87. The Uighur courtiers questioned the future Dezong saying, in Mackerras' translation: 'the Khaghan has the status of a younger brother of the Tang Son of Heaven and of the uncle of the prince. How could he possibly *not* perform a ceremonial dance?' See Colin Mackerras, *The Uighur Empire According to the T'ang Dynastic Histories: A Study in Sino-Uighur Relations, 744–840* (Canberra: Australian National University, 1972, p. 75. *The New Tang Record* also states that in 762 the Prince of Yong (future Emperor Dezong) became Generalissimo over the infantry and cavalry of the empire at the same time that the two who died in the Mouyu incident, Wei Ju [魏琚] and Wei Shaohua [韋少華], should become the Battle Commanders of the Right and Left Wings, and the Assistant to the Generalissimo (Dezong), respectively, thus indicating a closeness between these members of the court and bureaucracy which may indicate the long lingering nature of Dezong's resentment towards the Uighurs over this incident; Cf. ibid., p. 78, XTS 217A, pp. 6122–3.

88. I.e, Wei Ju and Wei Shaohua.

89. Minoru Inaba, 'The identity of the Turkish soldiers to the south of the Hindukush from the 7th to 9th centuries AD', *Zinbun* 38 (2006), pp. 1–19.

90. As the *New Tang Record* states, in Mackerras' translation, Mackerras, *The Uighur Empire*, p. 106: 'That year (790), the khaghan was poisoned by the younger Khatun, Princess Ye. The khatun was the granddaughter of Puuku Huaien. Huaien's son was Uighur Yehu.'

91. As Mackerras notes, ibid., n. 31, Yehu was actually the elder brother of Mouyu (also known as Tengri 'Heavenly/God-like' Khaghan), becoming khaghan in 759.

92. XTS 217A, pp. 6122–3.

93. Cf. Liu, 'You ming chen li mi kan zhong tang de biangjian jin lüe', p. 25, where two sections from ZZTJ 233, (pp. 7510–2), are quoted: 德宗曰：'卿辭理不屈，又無好勝之志，直使朕中懷已盡屈服而不能從，此朕新以私喜於得卿也.' 泌曰: '陛下能用相尚多，今皆不論，何也？' Dezong said: 'your analysis contains Principle that is unyielding, and goodness that cannot be vanquished.' Li Mi (in turn) said: 'you are good dialog partner, commanding all I say without resistance, what more could one ask for?' And 天命，他人皆可以言之，惟君相不可言。蓋君相所以造命也。

若言命, 則禮樂刑政皆無所用矣 [The Mandate of Heaven, it is something about which all people speak [and know about], not only scholars: the top aristocrats don't steer this, if it only comes from their words, then ritual and ceremony amount to nothing more than punishment and regulation [for the populace at large].]

94. As Nakata notes, this occurred also at a time when Sogdians were changing their surnames to erase their Sogdian identity, though this had occurred earlier in Chinese history as well, Nakata, 'Hasseiki kōhan ni okeru chūō yūrajia no dōkō ...', pp. 301–2. The change of the name of Christianity to Daqin Jingjiao rather than Bosi Jiao, though appearing perhaps counterintuitive, has been linked to Persianisation within the Xi'an community, its seeing itself as top representative of all Christians within the Tang at the time, and the 'Abbasidisation' of the church, each a set of currents that would have made the Persian-oriented Xi'an group's leaders see themselves above the church's Sogdian members: see Timothy H. Barrett, 'Buddhism, Taoism and the eighth-century Chinese term for Christianity: a response to recent work by A. Forte and others', *Bulletin of the School of Oriental and African Studies* 65/3 (2002), pp. 555–60; Zhang 2016.

95. Mackerras, *The Uighur Empire*, pp. 90–1.

96. Clark arrives at this date through an analysis of Old Turkic text (U I I Ia), formulations by Chavannes and Pelliot in 1913, on the basis of the Chinese text of the Karabalgasun and the Tang annals; cf. Larry. Clark, 'The conversion of Bügü Khan to Manichaeism', in Ronald E. Emerick, Werner Sundermann and Peter Zieme (eds), *Studia Manichaica: IV, Internationaler Kongress zum Manicha'ismus* (Berlin: Akademie Verlag, 2004), pp. 83–123.

97. Michael H. Drompp, *Tang China and the Collapse of the Uighur Empire: A Documentary History* (Leiden: E.J. Brill, 2005), p. 26.

98. Mackerras, *The Uighur Empire*, p. 26.

99. XTS 217; Mackerras, *The Uighur Empire*, p. 153.

100. Cf. Christopher Beckwith, 'The impact of the horse and silk trade on the economies of T'ang China and the Uighur Empire: on the importance of international commerce in the early Middle Ages', *Journal of the Economic and Social History of the Orient* 34/3 (1991), pp. 183–98.

101. Gustaaf Schlegel, 'Die Chinesische Inschrift auf dem Uigürischen Denkmal in Kara Balgassun', *Mémoires De La Société Finno-Ougrienne* IX (1896); Talat Tekin, *A Grammar of Orkhon Turkic* (Bloomington, IN: University of Indiana Press, 1967), pp. 229–96, where the Orkhon inscriptions are found in Romanised Old Turkic and in English translation; *Turfan manicahen frament m0919, in Türkische Manichaiaca aus Chotscho, III, nebst einem christlichen Bruchstück aus Bulayïq, mit 3 Tafeln, Philosophisch-historische Klasse. nr. 2*, trans. and transcription Albert Von Le Coq (Berlin: Abhandlungen der Preussischen-Akademie der Wissenschaften, 1922), pp. 33–5.

102. For a complete listing of references to the term *qut* in the Orkhon inscriptions, see Tekin, *A Grammar of Orkhon Turkic*, p. 348.

103. *Turfan manicahen frament manichaean*, p. 33.

104. A line appearing immediately after the 'Imperial Net' phrase: XS, line 55: 令寧國等五王親臨福宇建立壇場.

105. Chen indicates this term has been translated as 'place of worship' by at least three translators, see 'The encounter of Nestorian Christianity with Tantric Buddhism', p. 201; Pelliot, *L'inscription nestorienne de Si-ngan-fou*, and suggests the necessity of understanding the 'ordination altar' as having been built within the *fu-yu* [福宇, bâtiments fortunes, blessed/chrismated buildings]. Deeg (forthcoming), p. 200, notes that 福宇 is a Buddhist translation for Skt gṛha, 'house', and is similar to *futing* [福庭, merit garden], *fushe* [福舍, merit house] and *fu tang* [福堂, merit Hall]; the *mdabranoutha* of the church will be signified here as well. Given that the term means house in Greek, and an 'imperially chrismated' house as well, Deeg notes also that Xuanzong, whose reign is being referred to in this passage of the stele text, had decreed against what he'd seen as abuses in Buddhist ordinations of his predecessors, and suggests therefore that Jingjing, for propaganda purposes, is referring to the situation of the Buddhist *Kaiyuan si* [開元寺] and the Daoist *Kaiyuan guan* [開元觀] and this close relationship between the Imperial House and the Tang's religious bodies transpiring through these institutions, thus suggesting the ritual care of the imperial family and the kingdom given by the church and other religious bodies through them and before Empress Wu and Xuanzong, be re-established. This would be tantamount to, one might add, 'sustaining the Imperial Net' and 'rebinding the threads which had been broken.'

106. Ibid., p. 203.

107. XTS 142A; Mackerras, *The Uighur Empire*, p. 97; emphasis mine.

108. Though a topic that deserves closer scrutiny than time permits here, or that given by Schlegel, writing nearly 120 years ago and when the field of scholarship was level far below what it is now, Schlegel notes that the characters *wei* [微] and *miao* [妙, subtle, mysterious] appear in the both Xi'an stele and the Karabalgassun Inscription, and the latter's reference to Shi Siming [史思明] (fl.750–60), a Uighur general who fought for the Tang against the An Lushan forces and with Guo Ziyi, therefore locates the Karabalgassun Inscription within a post-An Lushan narrative and an inter-courtly agency shared by the Xi'an stele; see Schlegel, 'Die Chinesische Inschrift auf dem Uigürischen Denkmal in Kara Balgassun', p. 37 and p. 57 respectively.

109. ZZTJ 233.7504.

110. Twitchett, 'Tibet in Tang's grand strategy', p. 155.

111. See Yuan, 'Li mi yu tangdezong minzu zhengce de zhuanbian', pp. 104-5, on primary source reference and how this was a complete reversal of the thawing of relations between the two empires that had taken place starting in 780, and as the Xi'an stele was put in place.

112. Twitchett, 'Tibet in Tang's grand strategy', p. 144.

113. Orzech, *Politics and Transcendent Wisdom*, p. 162; Beckwith, *The Tibetan Empire in Central Asia*, pp. 162–3. This ruler is from Balkh, interestingly.

114. Christopher Beckwith, 'The introduction of Greek medicine into Tibet in the seventh and eighth centuries', *Journal of the American Oriental Society* 99/2 (1979), pp. 297–13.

115. See Chapter 3.

116. Rong Xinjiang [荣新江], '"Lidai fabao ji" zhong de moni he mish he – jian tan tubo wenxian de mo ni jiao he jingjiao yinsu de laili, zhonggu zhongguo yu wailai wenming' [歴代法宝記＞ 中的末尼和弥師訶 – 兼谈吐蕃文献的摩尼教和景教因素的来历，中古中国与外来文明] (Beijing: Sanlian shudian, 2001), pp. 343–6, p. 355.

117. Yanagida Seizan [柳 田聖山] (ed.), *Shoki no Zen shi* [初期の禅史] (Tōkyō: Iwanami shoten, 1972), which reproduces the original text of the *Li Dai Fa Bao Ji* [歴代法宝記], pp. 59–60.

118. Wendi L. Adamek's translation, pp. 75–6; see *The Teachings of Master Wuzhu: Zen and Religion of No-religion* (New York: Columbia University Press, 2011).

119. Litvinsky, B.A., Zhang Guang-da and R. Shabani Samghabadi (eds), *A History of Civilizations of Central Asia*, vol. 3: *The Crossroads of Civilizations, A.D. 250 to 750* (Paris: UNESCO Publications, 1996), p. 142.

120. Rong '"Lidai fabao ji" zhong de moni he mish he', pp. 343–68.

121. As transmitted in the Tibetan text the *Bstan 'gur* (Tibetan *Tripitaka* 144, no. 5839, 64a4–103b6); Aurel Stein indicates that the *Hua Hu Jing* being read by the Tibetan kings' ancestors is another possible source of the phonetic spelling for Mar Mani, as reported by Geza Uray, 'Tibet's connection with Nestorianism and Manichaeism in the 8th–10th centuries', in Ernst Steinkellner and Helmut Tauscher (eds), *Contributions on Tibetan Language, History and Culture, Proceedings of the Csoma De Körös Symposium Held at Velm-Vienna, Austria, 13–19 September 1981* (Vienna: Arbeitskreis für Tibetische und Buddhistische Studien Universität Wien, 1983), pp. 399–29, pp. 408–9.

122. Rong, '"Lidai fabao ji" zhong de moni he mish he', 2001b, pp. 343–68.

123. Ibid., p. 353 on military connections, pp. 363–55 on Guo Ziyi and Uighur connections, and p. 359 on Daqin temples and the pearl and jewel trade, something that suggests agency within the church via sea ports, and not simply the land route through Central Asia.

124. David Wilmshurst, 'The "Syrian Brilliant Teaching"', *Journal of the Hong Kong Branch of the Royal Asiatic Society* 30 (1993), pp. 44–74, pp. 55–75.

125. Chen, 'Esoteric Buddhism and monastic institutions', p. 290; Weinstein, *Buddhism under the Tang*, p. 62.

126. The name change issue has received now perspicacious study also by Barrett, 'Buddhism, Taoism and the eighth-century Chinese term for Christianity, and Zhang 2016.

127. Wilmshurst, 'The "Syrian Brilliant Teaching"', p. 70.

128. As translated by Wilmshurst, ibid., p. 74. 大秦本教經都五百卅部。並是貝葉梵音。唐太宗皇帝貞觀九年。西域太德僧阿羅本屆于中夏。並奏上本音。房玄齡魏徵宣譯奏言。後召本教大德僧景淨。譯得已上卅部卷。餘大數具在貝皮夾。猶未翻譯; see Peter Yoshiro Saeki, *The Nestorian Documents and Relics in China* [1937], 2nd edn (Tokyo: Academy of Oriental Culture, 1951), pp. 75–6 for the original text.

129. I.e. the *Hymn in Adoration of the Transfiguration of Our Lord* and the *Book of the Origin of Origins*, i.e. the two works end with textual segments indicating they were written or copied in the early eighth century.

130. Wilmshurst, 'The "Syrian Brilliant Teaching"', pp. 70–1.

131. The study of Christianity in Ming- and Ching-period China is virtually synonymous with the study of Western astronomy in the imperial patronage of Jesuits. and similar statements can be made about Western medicine in nineteenth- and twentieth-century Protestant missions in China. See Mingui Hu, 'Provenance in contest: searching for the origins of Jesuit astronomy in late Imperial China', *The International History Review* 24/1 (March 2002), pp. 1–36.

132. To the two sources and references discussed in the third chapter, one can add Du Huan {杜環,} and his travelogue, the *Jingxing ji* {經行記,}, of which, though lost, a few excerpts survive in the *Tongdian* (Du You {杜佑} (735–812) (ed.), *Tongdian* {通典, *Complete Institutes* } (compiled between 766–801) (Beijing: Zhongua shuju, 1988, (hereafter TD), books 192 and 193). The Christian religion appears closely associated there with the practice of medicine, i.e. whereas extensive information is given about Islam and its customs and beliefs, Du Huan appears to identify the region of Daqin (the Eastern Roman empire or the cultural realm of Christianity as a whole), strongly, and seemingly only, with its medical traditions and with the trepanning techniques discussed in Chapter 3; as he writes: ' 其大秦善醫眼及痢，或未病先見，或開腦出蟲,'; given that this information is so similar to what appears in the Persia section of XTS, section 221B, and in JTS 95, as discussed in Chapter 3, he, or Du You, the compiler of the *Tongdian*, may merely be passing on widely circulated material, but which may never the less indicate widespread views within the Tang court about Christian physicians.

133. This identification is found not just at XS, line 88: 病者療而起之, but also at line 80: 術高三代，藝博十全, and the author's assertion supported by Pelliot and Deeg's commentary on these lines: Pelliot, *L'inscription nestorienne de Si-ngan-fou*, p. 281, Deeg (forthcoming), pp. 258–9; see the discussion on this topic below.

134. Though these references are scant, it is certainly the case that there is imperial astrology/astronomy in the Xi'an stele. These references include: XS lines 60-1: i.e. 三載大秦國有僧佶和，瞻星向化，望日朝尊, as well as the stele's reference to Aluoben as a Daqin monastic who holds meteorological knowledge that led him safely to the Tang court and into Tang imperial patronage, i.e. XS, lines 34–5: 大秦國有上德，曰阿羅本，占青雲而載真

經, 望風律以馳艱險, 貞觀九祀至於長安, and the stele's donor section, written in Syriac, where the Middle Persian term for Sunday, *yekshambe*, is found, and written in Estrangela Syriac script, which is not included in the Taisho canon as it is not written in Chinese.

135. There is a large bibliography on this topic, set next to Gutas' work referred to in the previous chapter (Dimitri Gutas, *Greek Thought, Arab Culture* (London and New York: Routledge, 1998). Works consulted and read by this researcher are Raymond Le Coz, *Les médecins nestoriens au Moyen Age: les maîtres des Arabes* (Paris: Harmattan, 2004); Viktor Ebermann, 'Медикцинская Школа в Джундишапур' (The medical school at Gundeshapur), *Записки Коллегии Востоковедов* (*Memoirs of the Oriental College*) 1 (1925), pp. 47–72; Gerrit J. Reinink, 'Theology and medicine in Jundishapur. Cultural change in the Nestorian School tradition', in Alasdair A. MacDonald, Michael W. Twomey and Gerrit J. Reinink (eds), *Learned Antiquity. Scholarship in the Near East, the Greco-Roman World and the Early Medieval World* (Leiden: E.J. Brill, 2003), pp. 163–74.

136. See Li Tang, 'A preliminary study on the Jingjiao Inscription of Luoyang: text analyses, commentary and English translation', in Winkler and Tang, *Hidden Treasures and Intercultural Encounters*, pp. 109–32, where the Chinese text and a good introduction is given.

137. Zhou Shaoli and Zhao Chao [周紹良 and 趙超] (eds), *Tangdai muzhi huiban xuji* [唐代墓誌彙編續集] (Shanghai: Guji chubanshe, 2001, pp. 88–92.

138. See Rong Xinjiang [荣新江], 'Yi ge rushi tangchao de Bosi jingjiao jiazu' [个入仕唐朝的波斯景教家族, A Persian Nestorian Family in Tang China], in Ye Yilang [叶奕良] (ed.), *Yilangxue zai Zhongguo lunwenji* [伊朗学在中国论文集, A Collection of Essays on Iranian Studies in China], II (Beijing: Beijing daxue shuban she, 1998), pp. 82–90, where the Chinese text is given; Tansen Sen, 'Gautama Zhuan: an Indian astronomer at the Tang Court', *China Report* 31/2 (1995), pp. 197–208; Chau Huashan [晁華山], 'Tang dai tian wen xue jia qu tan zhuan mu de fa xian' [唐代天文学家瞿昙譔墓的发现], 文物 10 (1978), pp. 49–53, where the Chinese text is given, On foreign astronomers in the Tang Empire see Abramson, *Ethnic Identity in Tang China*, pp. 50–81, 185–99 and passim.

139. Hassan R. Baghbidi, 'New light on the Middle-Persian-Chinese bilingual inscription from Xi'an', in Mauro Maggi and Paola Orsatti (eds), *The Persian Language in History*, Band 32: *Beiträge zur Iranistik* (Weisbaden: Dr Ludwig Rechiert Verlag, 2011), pp. 105–15.

140. François de Blois, 'The Middle Persian Inscription from Constantinople: Sasanian or Post-Sasanian?', *Studia Iranica* 19 (1990), pp. 209–18.

141. Nie Zhigun [聂志軍], 'Jingjiao zhong "Yi si" yeshi jingyi kao' [景教中'伊斯'也是景医考], 敦煌学辑刊 [*Journal of Dunhuang Studies*] 3 (2008), pp. 119–27.

142. The first reference, XS, line 88, 病者療而起之, being evident prima facie; that there are two references, not one, being noted by Pelliot, *L'inscription*

nestorienne de Si-ngan-fou, as well, p. 281; and by Deeg (forthcoming), pp. 258–9.

143. As Harold Roth, Sarah Queen, and Nathan Sivin write: 'Three books carry the title of the Inner Canon of the Yellow Emperor – namely, the Basic Questions (Huangdi neijing suwen), its companion, the Divine Pivot (Huangdi neijing ling shu), and an overlapping compilation, the Grand Basis (Huangdi neijing taisu) ... the current versions of the first two were edited in 762 CE, and revised in the 11th century, and the third was compiled between 666–683 CE'; see 'Syncretic visions of state, society, and cosmos', in William Theodore de Bary and Irene Bloom (eds), *Sources of Chinese Tradition*, vol. I, 2nd edn (New York: Columbia University Press, 1999), pp. 235–82, p. 274. The texts of each the three mentioned can be accessed online at http://www.zh. wikisource.org/zh-hant/黃帝內經 (accessed 25 August 2014); the majority of the references to the term 十全 appear in the last five sections of the work, one of which (from Book 81) may suffice: 黃帝在明堂，雷公請曰：臣授業傳之行教，以經論從容，形法、陰陽、刺灸、湯液所滋，行治有腎不肖，未必能十 全 [in the Great Hall sat Huangdi and his attendants. Lei Gong remarked, 'I have been teaching others the medical arts and found that some of my students are not quick to grasp and their clinical results are not satisfactory}; translation by Ni Maoshing, p. 301.

144. Nie, 'Jingjiao zhong "Yi si" yeshi jingyi kao', pp. 123-26; Deeg. Ways to go and not to go', pp. 113–14 on the medical, alchemical and Daoist cosmology connected to the appellation.

145. Yisi is of course referred to in the stele as a 白衣景士, not a 波斯僧, though the stele is replete with references to East Syriac monastics as seng and as Bosi seng; see Nie, Jingjiao zhong "Yi si" yeshi jingyi kao', p. 122, on this important discussion.

146. As noted by Deeg, *Die Strahlende Lehre*, p. 258, where it is said that Yisi's medical skills are employed in an 'mesokosmischen Bereich' ('mesocosmic area'), i.e. as a way of controlling the natural environment (in the order of 'magic' or between 'heaven and earth'), though a geopolitical interpretation can be given as well, in that Yisi operated between one Central Asian 'royal city', Balkh, and a superior cosmic/imperial setting, the Chinese Empire.

147. Wuji Zhangsun [長孫無忌 等撰 長孫無忌等撰], *Tang lu shu yi san shi juan* [唐律疏議三十卷] (hereafter TLSY), 9.32, and a section of the Code reproduced at JTS 124.4A–4B.

148. See introduction.

149. Reflecting یکشنبه in Modern Persian, i.e. 'one' (*yek*), plus, or on from, 'the sabbath/Saturday' (*shambe*); cf. NT Greek usage such as Acts 20:7, where the phrase *mia ton sabbaton* [μια τον σαββατον, one in the Sabbath}, is found, and where Sabbath does not indicate a 'day' but rather a 'week', Sunday meaning therefore the first day of the week.

150. At XS, line 108; see Paul Pelliot, 'Un traiteé Manichéen retrouvé in Chine' (ed. and trans. Édouard Chavannes), *Journale Asiatique* 11, XI Série, Tome I (1913),

pp. 346–67, 1913, pp. 99–199, pp. 261–392 (see also Tome II, 1911, pp. 499–517); the nine 'planets' included: the sun, moon, five planets, and five fictive planets, p. 160; the acceptance by the Tang court of a calendar, the Jiuzhi li [九執曆] using this system came in 718 and is referred to at XTS 28B.

151. Pelliot, 'Un traiteé Manichéen retrouvé in Chine', pp. 176–7.

152. See definitions of theoretical terms in Appendix D.

153. XS, lines 60–1.

154. Recalling the discussion of *jiao hua* [教化] in Chapter 2 and in connection to the Aluohan stone.

155. Cf. Deeg (forthcoming), pp. 209–11 and the way in which he builds upon Pelliot's comments, at p. 262, in this regard and in connection to a *locus classicus* from the *Hou Han Shu*.

156. Ibid., pp. 258–9.

157. Cf. de Blois. 'The Middle Persian Inscription from Constantinople', p. 18, and the inscription as translated there, which reads: 'This tomb belongs to Xurdāδ, son of Hurmuz-Ăfrīδ, on whom, oh Lord, mayest Thou have mercy, – from the country [lit. 'House]; of Êranšahr, from the district of Călakăn (?), from the village of Xišt (?), who dwelt in Rūm for one year, in hope and studious desire for the Lord Christ, the just and victorious'. Cf. Baghbidi's translation of the Xi'an Pahlavi Bilingual inscription, 'New light on the Middle-Persian-Chinese bilingual inscription from Xi'an', p. 108: 'This is the tomb of the late Māhwaš, daughter of the late (2) Farroxzād (son) of Dādweh, from the Sūrēn [clan]. In the year 242 of the late (3) Yazdegird (3rd), in the year 260 of the Arabs, in the year 15 of the ever conquering Lord [Tang reign date of . . .], the son of God Xēm-tōn, in the month of Spandarmad and on the day of Spandarmad, (5) in the second (Chinese) month, on the 28th day, she passed away. May her place with Ohrmazd (6) and the Amahrāspands, the paradise of light and the superior life. Health!.' The Chinese portion of the grave marker saying little of interest beyond the fact that Farroxzād served in the *Shence* Army, the reader is referred to Baghbidi for the Chinese text.

158. Rong (2001), pp. 86–7, for the original text of the *muzhiming*.

159. Rong's assumption that Li Su was part of the Church of the East based on the appearance of the character *jing* (景) in each of the boy's names in the family is questionable. See Rong (2001), p. 85. However, Chen Huaiyu's assertion, which Rong mentions at p. 257, that Li Su's name appears in the Xi'an stele, though in alternate characters, is intriguing and merits further investigation. As Jinhua Chen points out, contemporary individuals associated with Dunhuang and with Esoteric Buddhism and with no demonstrable connection to Christianity or Persian religions were also part of large families in which this same character appeared in each of the son's names; 'The birth of a polymath: the genealogical background of the Tang monk-scientist Yixing (673–727)', *T'ang Studies* 18–19 (2000–1), pp. 1–39, p. 26. Also questionable is Rong's assumption that Li Su's wife's given name, Bishi, is Turkic. Pulleyblank's tables for reconstructing Middle Chinese pronunciation

and a Turkic onomastic were consulted, yielding no result; cf. László Rásonyi and Imre Baski, *Onomasticon Turcicum*, Uralic and Altaic Series, V. 172 (Bloomington, IN: Denis Sinor Institute for Inner Asian Studies, 2007). It bears pointing out as well that the name Li was on occasion chosen by Sogdians, and as such this may indicate Li Su's status as a Sogdian, his identification with Middle Persian culture thus becomes more interesting vis-à-vis his status as a non-Han intellectual elite and his family's *longue durée*.

160. It would be of momentous import if it could be proven that the patrilineal side of Li Su's family line is Persian or Sogdian, and the matrilineal side in the Li Su family grave marker Turkic, or if the patrilineal side is Persian and the matrilineal Sogdian or Turkic. This would suggests that in the same way that Uighurs were undergoing diplomatic and cultural tutelage from Sogdian Manichaeans, and intermarrying with them, Uighurs, Turks or Sogdians were also undergoing technical and cultural tutelage from Middle Persian speakers who were proud of the links to the former Sasanian Empire and cultivated the Hellenistic culture and royal *habitus* that carried and was linked to this Hellenistic culture and learning, as was seen in previous chapters. It is also important to note that Li Su is referred to in the gravestone as having been a Zhizi 'hostage', something known to have been associated with the *comitatus* system; Chen Huaiyu, 'Suowei tangdai jingjiao wenxian liangzhong bianwei bushuo', notes that the system of 'the seven luminaries' has origins in the second century and is connected with 'Persian hostages in China', p. 205; on Persian hostages in China, see Antonino Forte, *The Hostage An Shigao and his Offspring: An Iranian Family in China* (Kyoto: Italian School of East Asian Studies, 1995), pp. 1–15.

161. A search of the SKQS turned up nothing in connection to this school of astronomy.

162. He made a mistake in predictions the year the rebellion ended, and was dismissed from his post, as the epitaph indicates.

163. JTS 42 and 43 on the connection between Li Mi's programmes for imperial expansion and the Tun-tian.

164. Shaoli and Chao, *Tangdai muzhi huiban xuji*, pp. 89–92.

165. See appendices.

166. Tang, (2009), p. 113.

167. See Li Tang *A Study of the History of Nestorian Christianity in China and Its Literature in Chinese* (2004), pp. 197–9 for the translation of this passage, though only followed generally, and Saeki, *The Nestorian Documents and Relics in China*, pp. 92–5 for the original text, or as Saeki reproduces it.

168. Li Tang uses 'Misheshe' here, a usage which seems unnecessary, as the Chinese clearly indicates Messiah.

169. *Jia* [甲, armour], [*zhang* [仗, weaponry], HDC 3.0.

170. Wilmshurst, 'The "Syrian Brilliant Teaching"', pp. 70–1.

Conclusion

1. Peter Yoshirō Saeki, *The Nestorian Documents and Relics in China* [1937], 2nd edn (Tokyo: Academy of Oriental Culture, 1951), primary texts portion of the document, p. 30ff.
2. See the Introduction for this distinction and see appendices for terms and concepts.

Appendix C: The Pillar for the Propagation of the Luminous Religion in China

1. A public domain document, this translation is by Alexander Wylie, in Charles F. Horne, ed., The Sacred Books and Early Literature of the East (New York: Parke, Austin, & Lipscomb, 1917), Vol. XII, Medieval China, pp. 381–92. The text is available online at http://sourcebooks.fordham.edu/halsall/eastasia/781nestorian.asp (accessed 1 June 2017). The text has been augmented by the author in certain places.

Appendix D: Theoretical Concepts Used in the Study and Their Definitions

1. Max Weber, *Economy and Society: An Outline of Interpretive Sociology*, 2 vols, ed. Guenther Roth and Claus Wittich (Berkeley, CA: University of California Press, 1978), p. 241. In this ideally typical schematisation, transmission of power between one leader and a subsequent leader (or group of leaders) takes place as the first leader gathers about them an inner circle of disciples (elites), people who themselves are charismatic or who are able to borrow or share the charisma of the leader. The charisma of the second leader borrows from the charisma of the first in that it finds expression among those whom the latter has originally brought together uphold the original transmission; as Michael Toth writes, the martyrdom of the first charismatic leader may be either literal or figurative, i.e., real, physical death, does not have to occur'; Michael A. Toth, 'Toward a theory of the routinization of charisma', *Rocky Mountain Social Science Journal* 9/2 (April 1972), pp. 93–8, p. 96. We may note here that The English word charisma has its origins in the Greek noun χαρις, an outward sign of beauty, bestowed by a god: cf. Homer, τωγε χαριν κατεχευατ' Αθηνη [over him Athena shed grace], and the deponent verb χαριζομαι – 'to show favour, kindness', Henry G. Liddell, Robert Scott, Henry S. Jones and Roderick McKenzie, *A Greek-English Lexicon*, ed. Henry G. Liddell and Robert Scott (Oxford: Clarendon, 1995), p. 882.
2. This concept has a considerable literature and empirical engagement: see Christopher Beckwith, *Empires of the Silk Road* (Princeton, NJ: Princeton

University Press, 2008) at pp. 118, 132, and 137 for Beckwith's definition of the concept; for the connection posited in relation to the Abbasid Revolution and An Lushan Rebellion, p. 146; the Latin term *comitatus* is a collective form of the noun *comes*, i.e. *comitem*, meaning 'companion'; compare the 'boon companions' of medieval European literature such as Beowulf, and made use of within J.R.R. Tolkein's fiction and its medievalisms; the interlacing of medieval brocades and manuscript illumination has been linked to the concept as well; see John Leyerle, 'The interlace structure of Beowulf', *University of Toronto Quarterly* 33 (1967), pp. 1–17, p. 10. Beckwith presents a highly empirically based account of this and focused on the *chakr* guard corps in his article 'Aspects of the early history of the Central Asian Guard Corps in Islam', *Archivum Eurasiae Medii Aevi* 4 (1984), pp. 29–43; Beckwith notes as well that the term 'Son of Heaven', appearing in Zhou dynasty period Chinese texts, is an ancient Iranian term.

3. Jereon Duindam, 'Norbert Elias and the history of the court', *Hof und Theorie: Annänherungen an ein historiches Phänomen* (Cologne: Auflage, 2004).

4. Ibid.

5. Stephen Howe, *Empire: A Very Short Introduction* (Oxford: Oxford University Press, 2002), p. 14.

6. Pierre Bourdieu, p. 13.

7. Ibid.

8. Ibid.

9. Max Weber, *The Protestant Ethic and the Spirit of Capitalism*, trans. Talcott Parsons (London and New York: Routledge, 1992), pp. 194–5, 253–4. Weber has long been employed by secularisation proponents arguing that as modernity progresses the world is not becoming less religious and that capitalism, its asceticism, and religion are merely being worked into new configurations; see for example the sophisticated Weberian analysis presented in John Micklethwait and Adrian Wooldridge, *God is Back: How the Global Revival of Faith is Changing the World* (New York: Penguin Press, 2009).

BIBLIOGRAPHY

Primary sources and source collections in Greek and Latin

Agathias, The Histories, trans. and intro. Joseph D. Frendo (Berlin and New York: Walter de Gruyter, 1975), 2.29.9–32.4.

The Christian Topography of Cosmas, an Egyptian Monk, 1st edn, trans. John W. McCrindle (London: Hakluyt Society, 1897).

Dignas, Beate and Engelbert Winter, *Rome and Persia in Late Antiquity: Neighbours and Rivals* (Cambridge: Cambridge University Press, 2007).

Eusebius, *The Life of Constantine*, in Philip Schaff (ed.), *Nicene and Post-Nicene Christianity: From Constantine the Great to Gregory the Great, AD 311–600* (Edinburgh: T. & T. Clark, 1884), pp. 647–736.

Evagrios, *Ecclesiastical History*, 7.8, *The Ecclesiastical History of Evagrios Scholasticus, Translated texts for Historians*, trans. Michael Whitby 33/VI 21 (Liverpool: Liverpool University Press, 2000).

Heikel, Ivar A. (ed.), *Eusebius Werke*, vol. 1 (Leipzig: J.C. Hinrichs'sche Buchhandlung, 1902), pp. 195–223.

The History of Menander the Guardsman, ed. and trans. R.C. Blockley (Liverpool: Cairns, 1985).

The History of Theophylact Simocatta: An English Translation with Introduction, trans. Michaeland Mary Whitby (Oxford: Oxford University Press, 1986).

Procopius, *The Persian Wars*, trans. H.B. Dewing (Cambridge MA: Loeb Classical Library, 1928).

Schaff, Philip (ed.), 'The letters of Leo the Great', in Philip Schaff (ed.), *Nicene and Post-Nicene Fathers*, Series 2, vol. 12 (Edinbugh: T. & T. Clark, 1888).

Socrates, *Ecclesiastical History*, in Philip Schaff (ed.), *Nicene and Post-Nicene Christianity: From Constantine the Great to Gregory the Great, AD 311–600* (Edinburgh: T. & T. Clarke, 1884), 7.8.1–20, pp. 393–4.

Winstedt, Eric O. (ed.), *The Christian Topography of Cosmas Indicopleustes* (London: Cambridge University Press, 1909).

Wolska-Conus, Wanda (ed.), *Cosmas Indicopleustès. Topographie chrétienne, Livres I–IV*, Sources chrétiennes 141 (Paris: Le Cerf, 1968).

al-Ya'qubi, Abu al-Abbas Ahmad ibn Ishaq. Ta'rikh {Historiae}, 2 vols, ed. Muhammad Houtsma (Leiden: E.J. Brill, 1883).

Primary sources and source collections in Syriac and Arabic

Assemani, Josephus S., *Bibliotheca Orientalis Clementino-Vaticana* (Rome: Sacrae Congregationis de Propaganda Fide, 1719–28).

Ausgewählte Akten persicher Märtyrer, trans. Oskar Braun (Kempten and Munich: Kösel, 1915).

Barhebraei, Gregorii, *Chronicon Ecclesiasticum* (*Annotationibusque Illustrarunt Joannes Baptista Abbeloos et Thomas Josephus Lamy*) (Lovanii: Peeters, 1872–77).

Bar Hebraeus, Gregory, *Chronicon Ecclesiasticum*, 3 vols, ed. Jean Baptiste Abbeloos and Thomas J. Lamy (Louvani: Peters, 1877).

Bedjan, Paul (ed.), *Isaacus Ninivita de Perfectione Religiosa* (Paris: Otto Harrassowitz, 1909). *The Book of Government, or Rules for Kings: The Siyar al-Muluk or Siyasat-nama of Nizam al-Mulk*, trans. Hubert Darke, rev. edn (London: Routledge, 2001).

Chang Hsin-cheng [張心澂], *Wei-shu t'ung-k'ao* [偽書通考] (Shanghai: Commercial Press, 1959).

Chronica Minora, ed. and trans. Ernest W. Brookes, Ignazio Guidi and Jean Baptiste Chabot (Paris: E Typographeo Reipublicae, 1903–5).

The Chronicle of Joshua the Stylite: Composed in Syriac AD 507, ed. and trans. William Wright (Cambridge: Cambridge University Press, 1882).

Cureton, William (ed.), *John of Ephesus*, Chron[icle], Book 18.42, *The Third Part of the Ecclesiastical History of John, Bishop of Ephesus* (Oxford: Oxford University Press, 1853).

Dadisho Qatraya [Dadisho of Qatar], *Commentary on the Paradise of the Fathers*, Book 2, section 135.

Duval, Rubens (ed.), *Ishoyahb Patriarchae III Liber Epistularum*, vols 11–12 (Paris: Typographeo Reipublicae, 1904–5).

Ennin's Diary: Record of a Pilgrimage to China in Search of the Law, trans. Edwin O. Reischauer (New York: Ronald Press, 1955).

Fadlān, Ibn, *Ibn Fadlān and the Land of Darkness: Arab Travellers in the Far North*, ed. and trans. Paul Lunde and Caroline S. Stone (London: Penguin, 2012).

Gismondi, Henricus, *Maris, Amri, et Salibae: De Patriarchis Nestorianorum Commentaria I: Amri et Salibae Textus* (Rome, 1896).

———, *Maris, Amri, et Salibae: De Patriarchis Nestorianorum Commentaria II: Maris Textus Arabicus et Versio Latina* (Rome, 1899). *Histoire nestorienne inédite*, 3 parts, ed. and trans. Addaï Scher (Paris: Librarie de Paris, 1908–19).

Ibn Esfandīār, Muhammad, *The History of Tabaristan: An Abridged Translation*, ed. and trans. Edward G. Browne (Leiden: E.J. Brill; London: Bernard Quaritch, 1905).

Khan, Geoffrey (ed.), *Arabic Documents from Early Islamic Khurasan* (London: Nour Foundation, 2007).

Khuzistan Chronicle, trans. Geoffrey Greatrex, in Geoffrey Greatrex and Samuel N.C. Lieu (eds), *The Roman Eastern Frontier and the Persian Wars*, Part II: *AD363–630* (London: Routledge, 2002), pp. 229–37.

Les letters de patriarche nestorien Timothée I: etude critique avec en appendice la letter de Timothée I aux moines de couvent de Mar Maron, ed. and trans. Raphaël J. Bidawid, Studi e Testi 187 (Città del Vaticano: Biblioteca Apostolica Vaticana, 1956).

Life of Mar Aba, in Paul Bedjan (ed.), *Histoire de Mar-Jabalaha, de trios autres patriarches, d'un prête, et deux laïques, nestoriens* (Leipzig and Paris: O. Harrassowitz, 1895).

Mas'udi, *Murūj al-Dhahab (The Meadows of Gold)*, ed. and trans. Paul Lunde and Caroline S. Stone (London: Kegan Paul International, 1989).

Mingana, Alphonse (ed.), *John Bar Penkaye, Books X–XV* in *Sources Syriaques*, vol. 1 (Leipzig, 1907) (Syriac text and French translation).

——, 'The Apology of Timothy the Patriarch before the Caliph Mahdi', *Bulletin of the John Rylands Library* 12 (1928), pp. 137–298.

Al-Nadim, Ibn, *Fihrist* (Cairo: Raḥmānīyah Press, 1929).

Peeters, Paul,'Observations sur la vie syriaque de Mar Aba', *Miscellanea Giovanni Mercati*, vol. 5 (Studi e Testi 125) (Rome: Città del Vatticano, 1948), pp. 69–112.

Reischauer, Edwin O., *Ennin's Travels in T'ang China* (New York: Ronald Press, 1955).

Sachau, Eduard, *Syrische Rechtsbücher*, vol. 2 (Berlin: G. Reimer, 1907–14).

Sources for the Study of the School of Nisibis, trans. with commentary Adam H. Becker (Liverpool: Liverpool University Press, 2008).

St Isaac of Nineveh, On Ascetical Life, trans. Mary Hansbury (Crestwood, NY: St Vladimir Seminary Press, 1989).

Synodicon Orientale ou Recueil de Synods Nestoriens, vol. 27, ed. and trans. Jean Baptiste Chabot (Paris: Imprimerie Nationale, 1902).

The Syriac Chronicle of Zachariah of Mitylene, trans. Frederick J. Hamilton and Ernest W. Brooks (London: Methuen: 1899).

Tabari, Ali b. Rabbān, *The Book of Religion and Empire: A Semi-Official Defense of and Exposition of Islam Written by Order at the Court and with the Assistance of the Caliph Mutawakkil (r.847–861)*, ed. and trans. Alphonse Mingana (London: Longmans, Green & Co, 1922).

al-Ṭayyib, Ibn, *Fiqh al-Naṣrānīya*, *Corpus Scriptorum Christianorum Orientalium* 161–2 and 167–8, ed. and trans. Wilhelm Hoenerbach and Otto Spies (Louvain: Brepols, 1956–57).

Thomas of Marga, *The Book of Governors: The Historia Monastica of Thomas Bishop of Margā AD 840*, vol. II: *The Syriac Text, Introduction, etc.*, trans. Ernest A.W. Budge (London: K. Paul, Trench, Trübner, 1893).

'Timothei Patriarchae I Epistolae I [Text]', *Corpus Scriptorum Christianorum Orientalium*, 74/Syr. 30, ed. and trans. Oskar Braun (Paris: J. Garbalda, 1915).

'Timothei Patriarchae I Epistolae I [Trans.]', *Corpus Scriptorum Christianorum Orientalium*, 74/Syr. 31, ed. and trans. Oskar Braun (Paris: J. Garbalda, 1915).

Yarshater, Ehsan (ed.), *The History of al-Ṭabarī*, 40 vols (New York: SUNY Press, 1989–2007).

Primary sources and source collections in Iranian and Central and Asian languages

The Armenian History Attributed to Sebeos, ed. and trans. Robert W. Thomson (Liverpool: Liverpool University Press, 1999).

Bactrian Documents from Northern Afghanistan, ed. and trans. Nicholas Sims-Williams (Oxford: Oxford University Press, 2000).

Barber, Anthony W., *The Tibetan Tripitaka* (Taipei: SMC Publishing, 1991).

Bacot, Jacques, Frederick W. Thomas and Gustave C. Toussaint, *Documents de Touen-houang relatifs a l'histoire du Tibet* (Paris: Librairie Orientaliste, 1946).

Dotson, Brandon B., *The Old Tibetan Annals: An Annotated Translation of Tibet's First History* (Vienna: Verlag der Österreichischen Akademie der Wissenschaften, 2009).

The Letter of Tansar, trans. Mary Boyce (Roma: Istituto Italiano per il Medio ed Estremo Oriente, 1968).

Monchi-Zadeh, Davoud, 'Xusrōv I Kavātā ut Rētak: Pahlavi text, transcription and translation', *Acta Iranica* 22 (Leiden: Brill, 1982), pp. 47–91.

Narsharkhi, *The History of Bukhara*, trans. Richard N. Frye (Cambridge, MA: Mediaeval Academy of America, 1954).

Turfan manicahen frament m0919, in Türkische Manichaiaca aus Chotscho, III, nebst einem christlichen Bruchstück aus Bulayïq, mit 3 Tafeln, Philosophisch-historische Klasse. nr. 2, trans. and transcription Albert Von Le Coq (Berlin: Abhandlungen der Preussischen Akademie der Wissenschaften, 1922).

Zand-Akasih, Iranian or Greater Bundahishn, trans. Behramgore T. Anklesaria (Bombay: Mazdayasnan Sabha, 1956).

Primary sources and source collections in Chinese

Chavannes, Éduoard, (trans. and comm.), *Documents sur les Tou-Kiue (Turcs) Occidentaux* (Paris: Librairie d'Amérique et d'Orient Adrien Maisonneuve, 1903).

Dong Gao [董誥] (1740–1818) (ed.), *Quan Tang Wen* [全唐文], *Complete Tang Collection* (Shanghai: Shanghai gu ji chu ban she, 1990).

Du You [杜佑] (735–812) (ed.), *Tongdian* [通典, *Complete Institutes*] (compiled between 766–801) (Beijing: Zhonghua shuju, 1988).

Hui-Li, Shaman, *The Life of Hiuen-Tsiang: Scholar, Saint and Pilgrim*, trans. Samuel Beal (London: Kegan Paul International, 2003).

Legge, James, *The Nestorian Monument of Hsi-An Fu* (New York: Paragon, 1966).

Liu Xu [劉昫] (887–946) (ed.), (compiled in 945), *Jiu Tangshu* [舊唐書], *Old Tang Record*, (Beijing: Zhonghua shuju, 1975).

Li Rongxi, *A Biography of the Tripiṭaka Master of the Great Ci'en Monastery of the Great Tang Dynasty*, trans. Śramaṇa Huili and Shi Yancong (Berkeley, CA: Numata Center for Buddhist Translation and Research, 1995).

Ni Maoshing, *The Yellow Emperor's Classic of Medicine: A New Translation of the Neijing Suwen with Commentary* (Boston: Shambhala, 1995).

Saeki, Peter Yoshiro, *The Nestorian Monument in China* [1916], 2nd edn (London: SPCK, 1928).

——, *The Nestorian Documents and Relics in China* [1937], 2nd edn (Tokyo: Academy of Oriental Culture, 1951).

Siku Quanshu (Wen yuan ge: Digital Edition) [文淵閣四庫全書電子版] (Hong Kong: Digital Heritage Publishing, 2006).

Takakusu, Junjiro [高楠順次郎] (1866–1945), (ed.), *Taishō Shinshū Daizōkyō (Taishō Revised Tripiṭaka)* [大正新脩大藏經] contains the *Zhenyuan Xinding Shijiao Mulu* [貞元新定釋教目錄] (New Record of Buddhist Translations from the Zhenguan Era – 785–805).

Wang Pu [王溥] (922–82) (ed.), *Tang Huiyao* [唐會要, *Notabilia of Tang*] (Shanghai: Shanghai guji chubanshe, 1991).

Wang Qinruo [王欽若] (ed.) *Cefu Yuangui* [册府元龜], *The Great Tortoise of National Archives*, compiled between 1005–13) (Beijing: Zhonghua shuju, 1960).

Wei Shou (506–572) (ed.), *Wei Shu* [魏書, *Book of Wei*]. Held in Zhongguo guojiatushuguan. Photoreprint in Zhonghua zaizao shanben 中華再造善本 (Beijing: Beijing tushuguan chubanshe, 2006).

Wei Zheng (580–643) (ed.), *Sui Shu* [隋書, *Book of Sui*] [639], 6 vols (Beijing: Zhonghua shuju, 1973).

Wenyuange siku quanshu dianzi ban [文淵閣四庫全書電子版] (Shanghai: Renmin Chubanshe, 2002).

Wuji Zhangsun [長孫無忌等撰長孫無忌等撰], *Tang lu shu yi san shi juan* [唐律 疏議三十卷].

Wylie, Alexander, *The Xi'an Stele*, trans., in Charles F. Horne (ed.), *The Sacred Books and Early Literature of the East*, vol. 12: *Medieval China* (New York: Parke, Austin, and Lipscomb, 1917).

Xin Tangshu [新唐書] (*The New Tang Record*, compiled in 1060), eds Ouyang Xiu [歐陽修] and Song Qi [宋祁] (Beijing: Zhonghua shuju, 1975).

Yanagida Seizan [柳田聖山] (ed.), *Shoki no Zen shi* [初期の禅史] (Tōkyō: Iwanami shoten, 1972), contains the *Lidai fabao Ji* [歷代法宝記, *Record of Historical Transmission ofthe Dharma Jewel*] by Wuzhu [無住] (714–74).

Yang Han-Sung, Jan Yün-hua, Iida Shotaro (eds), *TheHye-Ch'o Diary: Memoir of the Pilgrimage to the Five Regions of India*, trans. Laurence W. Preston (Berkeley: the Numata Center for Buddhist Translation and Research, 1984).

Yi shen lun duan di san [神論卷第三]; once known as the Tomioka manuscript; now held in Osaka, Japan, by Kyōu Shooku library, Tonkō-Hikyū Collection.

Yoritomo Motohiro [賴富本宏], *Chūgoku mikkyō no kenkyū: Han'nya to san'nei no mikkyō rikai o chūshin to shite* [中国密教の研究: 般若と賛寧の密教理解を中 心として](Tokyo: Daitō Shuppansha, 1979).

Yue Shizhuan [楽史撰] (930–1007), *Tai Ping Huan Yu Ji* [太平寰宇記, Record of the World in the Tai Ping Era], unpublished MSS from the collection of Robert Morrison (1782–1843).

Zheng Qiao (1104–62) (ed.), *Tong zhi* [通志] (Taibei: Shijie shuju, 1956).

Zhou Shaoli and Zhao Chao [周紹良and趙超] (eds), *Tangdai muzhi huiban xuji* [唐代墓誌彙編續集] (Shanghai:Guji chubanshe, 2001).

zizhi tongjian [資治通鑑] (beijing: zhonhua shuhu, 1956).

Secondary works

Abramson, Marc, *Ethnic Identity in Tang China* (Philadelphia, PA: University of Pennsylvania Press, 2008).

Adamek, Wendi L., *The Teachings of Master Wuzhu: Zen and Religion of No-religion* (New York: Columbia University Press, 2011).

Agostini, Domenico and Sören Stark, 'Zawulistan, Kawulistan and the Land of Bosi [波斯] – on the question of the Sasanian court-in-exile in the southern Hindukish', in *Studia Iranica* 45 (2016), pp. 17–38.

Anderson, Benedict, *Imagined Communities: Reflections on the Origin and Spread of Nationalism*, rev. edn (London: Verso, 2006).

Andrade, Nathanael J., 'The Syriac life of John of Tella and the frontier *politeia*', *Hugoye: Journal of Syriac Studies* 12/2 (2009), pp. 199–234.

Aristotle, *The Complete Works of Aristotle*, ed. Jonathan Barnes (Princeton, NJ: Princeton University Press, 1984).

Baalbaki, Rohi, *Al-Mawrid: A Modern Arabic-English Dictionary*, 19th edn (Beirut: Dar El-Ilm Lilmalayin, 2005).

Baghbidi, Hassan R.,'New light on the Middle-Persian-Chinese bilingual inscription from Xi'an', in Mauro Maggi and Paola Orsatti (eds), *The Persian Language in History*, Band 32: *Beiträge zur Iranistik* (Weisbaden: Dr Ludwig Rechiert Verlag, 2011), pp. 105–15.

Bai Shouyi [白寿彝], *Zhongguo huihui minzu shi* [中国回回民族史] (Beijing: Zhonghua shuju, 2003).

Bailey, Harold, 'Iranica', Bulletin of the School of Oriental and African Studies (SOAS), 11/1 (1943), pp. 1–5.

Barfield, Thomas J., 'The shadow empires: imperial state formation along the Chinese-Nomad frontier', in Susan E. Alcock, Terence N. D'Altroy, Kathleen D. Morrison and Carla M. Sinopoli (eds), *Empires* (Cambridge, 2001), pp. 11–41.

Barrett, Timothy H., 'Buddhism, Taoism and the eighth-century Chinese term for Christianity: a response to recent work by A. Forte and others', *Bulletin of the School of Oriental and African Studies* 65/3 (2002), pp. 555–60.

Barthold, Vasily V., *Turkestan Down to the Mongol Invasion*, 4th edn (London: Gibb Memorial Trust, 1977).

Baum, Wilhelm, *Shirin: Christian, Queen, Myth of Love: a Woman of Late Antiquity: Historical Reality and Literary Effect* (Piscataway, N.J.: Gorgias Press, 2004).

—— and Dietmar W. Winkler, *The Church of the East: A Concise Introduction*, trans. Miranda G. Henry (London: Routledge, 2003).

Baumer, Christoph, *The Church of the East: An Illustrated History of Assyrian Christianity* (London and New York: I.B.Tauris, 2006).

Becker, Adam H., *Fear of God and the Beginning of Wisdom: The School of Nisibis and the Development of Scholastic Culture in Late Antique Mesopotamia* (Philadelphia, PA: University of Pennsylvania Press, 2006).

——, 'Martyrdom, religious difference, and "fear" as a category of piety in the Sasanian Empire: the case of the martyrdom of Gregory and the martyrdom of Yazdpaneh', *Journal of Late Antiquity* 2/2 (2009), pp. 300–36.

Beckwith, Christopher, 'The introduction of Greek medicine into Tibet in the seventh and eighth centuries', *Journal of the American Oriental Society* 99/2 (1979), pp. 297–313.

——, 'Aspects of the early history of the Central Asian Guard Corps in Islam', *Archivum Eurasiae Medii Aevi* 4 (1984), pp. 29–43.

——, *The Tibetan Empire in Central Asia* (Princeton, NJ: Princeton University Press, 1987).

——, 'The impact of the horse and silk trade on the economies of T'ang China and the Uighur Empire: on the importance of international commerce in the early Middle Ages', *Journal of the Economic and Social History of the Orient* 34/3 (1991), pp. 183–98.

——, *Empires of the Silk Road* (Princeton, NJ: Princeton University Press, 2009).

Benevides, Gustavo, 'Buddhism, Manichaeism, markets and empires', in Luther H. Martin and Panayotis Pachis (eds), *Hellenisation, Empire and Globalisation: Lessons from Antiquity* (Thessalonika:Vanias Edition, 2004), pp. 1–24.

Berti, Vittorio, 'Idéologie et politique missionnaire de Timothée Ier, patriarche syro-oriental (780–823)', in Christelle Jullien (ed.), *Chrétiens en terre d'Iran IV.*

Itinéraires missionnaires: échanges et identities, Cahiers de Studia Iranica 44 (Paris: Association pour l'avancement des études iraniennes, 2011), pp. 71–110.

Blockley, Roger C., 'Doctors and Diplomats in the sixth century AD', *Florilegium* 2 (1980), pp. 89–100.

Bourdieu, Pierre, *In Other Words: Essays Towards a Reflexive Sociology* (Stanford, CA: Stanford University Press, 1990).

Bregman, Jay, *Synesius of Cyrene* (Berkeley, CA: University of California Press, 1982).

Brock, Sebastian P., 'Christians in the Sasanian Empire. A case of divided loyalties', *Studies in Church History* 18 (1982), pp. 1–19.

——, 'The "Nestorian" Church: a lamentable misnomer', *Bulletin of the John Rylands Library* 78 (1996), pp. 23–35.

Brown, Peter, *The Body and Society: Men, Women, and Sexual Renunciation in Early Christianity* (New York: Columbia University Press, 1988).

Brubaker, Rogers and Frederick Cooper, 'Beyond "identity"', *Theory and Society* 29 (2000), pp. 1–47.

Bulliet, Richard, *Conversion to Islam in the Medieval Period: An Essay in Quantitative History* (Cambridge, MA: Harvard University Press, 1979).

Burke, Peter, *What is Cultural History?* (Cambridge: Polity Press, 2005).

Busse, Heribert, 'Omar's image as the conqueror of Jerusalem', *Jerusalem Studies in Arabic and Islam* 8 (1986), pp. 149–68.

Carter, Robert A., 'Christianity in the Gulf during the first centuries of Islam', *Arabian Archaeology and Epigraphy* 19/1 (2008), pp. 71–108.

Chau Huashan [晁華山], *'Tang dai tian wen xue jia qu tan zhuan mu de fa xian'* [唐代天文学家瞿曇譔墓的发现], 文物 10 (1978), pp. 49–53.

Chen Chang'an (ed.), 隋唐五代墓誌匯編 [*Sui tang wu dai mu zhi hui bian. Luoyang juan*], vol. 8 (Tianjin: Tianjinguli chubanshe, 1990), p. xxx.

Chen Huaiyu, 'The encounter of Nestorian Christianity with Tantric Buddhism in medieval China', in Dietmar W. Winklerand and Li Tang (eds), *Hidden Treasures and Intercultural Encounters* (London: Global Marketing Publications, 2009), pp. 195–213.

——, 景风梵声（中古宗教之诸相）(Beijing: Zongjiao Wenhua Chubanshe, 2012).

Chen, Jinhua, 'The birth of a polymath: the genealogical background of the Tang monk-scientist Yixing (673–727)', *T'ang Studies* 18–19 (2000–1), pp. 1–39.

——, 'Esoteric Buddhism and monastic institutions', in Charles Orzech (ed.), *Esoteric Buddhism and the Tantras in East Asia* (Leiden: E.J. Brill, 2011), pp. 286–93.

Chen Shipei [沈世培], 'Li Mi yu pingding fanzhen geju' [李泌与平定藩镇割据], 铁道师院学报 15/2 (April 1998), pp. 81–4.

Choksy, Jamsheed, *Conflict and Cooperation: Zoroastrian Subalterns and Muslim Elites in Medieval Iranian Society* (New York: Columbia University Press, 1997).

Christensen, Arthur, *L'Iran sous les Sassanides* (Copenhagen: Levin and Munksgaard, 1936).

Clark, Larry, 'The conversion of Bügü Khan to Manichaeism', in Ronald E. Emerick, Werner Sundermann and Peter Zieme (eds), *Studia Manichaica: IV, Internationaler Kongress zum Manichäismus* (Berlin: Akademie Verlag, 2004), pp. 83–123.

Collins Robert Unabridged French–English English–French Dictionary, ed. Christine Penman et al. (New York: Harper Collins, 2002).

290   PERSIAN CHRISTIANS AT THE CHINESE COURT

Compareti, Matteo, 'The last Sasanians in China', *Eurasian Studies* 2/2 (2003), pp. 197–213.

Concise Oxford German Dictionary, ed. Michael Clark and Olaf Thyen, 3rd edn (Oxford: Oxford University Press, 2009).

Crone, Patricia, *The Nativist Prophets of Early Islamic Iran* (Cambridge: Cambridge University Press, 2012).

——— and Martin Hinds, *God's Caliph: Religious Authority in the First Centuries of Islam* (Cambridge: Cambridge University Press, 1986).

Dalby, Michael T., 'Court and Politics in late T'ang times', in Denis Twitchett (ed.), *The Cambridge History of China*, vol. 3: *Sui and T'ang China*, Part 1 (Cambridge: Cambridge University Press, 1979), pp. 561–681.

Daniel, Elton L., *The Political and Social History of Khurasan underAbbasid Rule 747–820* (Minneapolis: Biblioteca Islamica, 1979).

Daryaee, Touraj, 'Bazaars, merchants, and trade in Late Antique Iran', *Comparative Studies of South Asia, Africa and the Middle East* 30/3 (2010), pp. 401–9.

———, 'The idea of Ērāšahr: Jewish, Christian and Manichaean Views in Late Antiquity', in Florin Curta (ed.), *Borders, Barriers, and Ethnogenesis: Frontiers in Late Antiquity and Middle Ages* (Antwerp: Brepols, 2005), pp. 123–37.

———, 'Yazdgerd III's last year: coinage and history of Sistan at the end of Late Antiquity', *Iranistik: Deutschsprachige Zeitschrift fur iranistische Studien. Festschrift fur Erich Kettenhofen*, ed. Touraj Daryaee and Omid Tabibzadeh 5/1–2, 2006–2007 (2009), pp. 21–30.

de Bary, William Theodore and Irene Bloom (eds), *Sources of Chinese Tradition*, vol. I, 2nd edn (New York: Columbia University Press, 1999).

Deeg, Max, 'Towards a new translation of the Chinese Nestorian documents from the Tang Dynasty', in Roman Malekand Peter (eds), *Jingjiao. The Church of the East in China and Central Asia* (Nettetal: Steyler Verlag, 2006) (Collectanea Serica), pp. 115–31.

———, 'Ways to go and not to go in the contextualization of the *Jingjiao* documents of the Tang period', in Li Tang and Dietmar Winkler (eds), *Hidden Treasures and Intercultural Encounters* (London: Global Marketing Publications, 2009), pp. 135–52.

———, *Die Strahlende Lehre: Dokumente zur Außereuropäischen Christentumsgeschichte 3 (Asien, Afrika, Lateinamerika)*, 2 vols (Wiesbaden: Harrassowitz, 2012).

———, 'A belligerent priest – Yisi and his political context', in Li Tang and Dietmar W. Winkler (eds), *From the Oxus River to the Chinese Shores: Studies on East Syriac Christianity in China and Central Asia*, Orientalia Patristica Oecumenica, vol. 5 (Zurich: Akademie Verlag, 2013), pp. 107–21.

De Blois, François, *Burzōy's Voyage to India and the Origin of the Book of Kalīlah wa Dimnah* (London: Royal Asiatic Society, 1990).

———, 'The Middle Persian Inscription from Constantinople: Sasanian or Post-Sasanian?', *Studia Iranica* 19 (1990), pp. 209–18.

De Meyer, Jan, *Wu Yun's Way: Life and Works of an Eighth-Century Daoist Master* (Leiden: E.J. Brill, 2006).

Des Rotours, Robert, *Le traité des examens* (Paris: Librairie Ernest Leroux, 1932).

———, *Le Traité des fonctionnaries et Traité de l'armé*, 2 vols (San Francisco: Chinese Materials Center, 1974).

Dettenhofer, Maria H., 'Eunuchs, women and imperial courts', in Walter Scheidel (ed.), *Rome and China: Comparative Perspectives on Ancient World Empires* (Oxford: Oxford University Press, 2009), pp. 83–99.

Dickens, Mark, 'Patriarch Timothy I and the Metropolitan of the Turks', *Journal of the Royal Asiatic Society* 20/2 (2010), pp. 117–39.

———, 'Review: Beckwith, *Empires of the Silk Road*', *Orientalistische Literaturzeitung* 106/4–5 (2011), pp. 1–4.

Dien, Albert E., 'The Sa-pao problem re-examined', *Journal of the American Oriental Society* 82/3 (July–September 1962), pp. 335–46.

———, 'Caravans and caravan leaders in Palmyra', in Étienne de la Vaissière and Éric Trombert (eds), *Les Sogdiens en Chine* (Paris: École française d'Extrême-Orient, 2005), pp. 195–206.

Douglas, Mary, *Purity and Danger: An Analysis of the Concepts of Pollution and Taboo* (London: Routledge and Kegan Paul, 1966).

Drompp, Michael H., *Tang China and the Collapse of the Uighur Empire: A Documentary History* (Leiden: E.J. Brill, 2005).

Du Cange, Carles, *Glossarium mediæ et infimæ latinitatis*, Louis Henshel, Pierre Carpentier, Johann Christoph Adelung, Leopold Favre (eds) (Paris, Librairie des sciences et des arts, 1937–38).

Duindam, Jereon, 'Norbert Elias and the history of the court' in Reinhardt Butz, Jan Hirschbiegal and Dietmar Willowei (eds), *Hof und Theorie: Annänherungen an ein historiches Phänomen* (Cologne: Auflage, 2004).

Ebermann, Viktor, 'Медикцинская Школа в Джундишапур' (The medical school at Gundeshapur), *Записки Коллегии Востоковедов* (*Memoirs of the Oriental College*) 1 (1925), pp. 47–72.

Eliade, M., *The Sacred and the Profane: The Nature of Religion* (New York: Harcourt, Brace & World, 1957).

Elverskog, Johan, *Buddhism and Islam on the Silk Road* (Philadelphia, PA: University of Pennsylvania Press, 2010).

Encyclopedia of Islam, EI2, vol. 2, ed. Bernard Lewis, Charles Pellat, and Jospeh Schack (Leiden: E.J. Brill, 1965).

———, EI2, vol. 4, ed. Emeri Van Donzel, Bernard Lewis, and Charles Pellat (Leiden: E.J. Brill, 1978).

Erhart, Victoria L., 'The Church of the East during the period of the four rightly-guided caliphs', *Bulletin of the John Rylands Library* 78/3 (1996), pp. 55–71.

Fakhry, Majid, *A History of Islamic Philosophy*, 2nd edn (New York: Columbia University Press, 1983).

Fiey, Jean-Maurice, *Chrétiens syriaques sous les Abbassides surtout à Bagdad (749–1258)*, Corpus Scriptorum Christianorum Orientalium 420, Subs. 59 (Louvain: Secrétariat du CSCO 1980).

Fitzgerald, Charles P., *The Empress Wu* (London: Crescent Press, 1968).

Forte, Antonino, *Political Propaganda and Ideology in China at the End of the Seventh Century: Inquiry into the Nature, Authors and Function of the Tunhuang document S.6502*, followed by an annotated translation (Napoli: Istituto universitario orientale, Seminario di studi asiatici, 1976).

——— (ed.), *Paul Pelliot's L'inscription Nestorienne de Singan-fou* (Kyoto: Scuola di Studi Sull'Asia Orientale, Paris: Collège de France, Institute des Hauste Études, Chinoises, 1996).

————, 'Iraniens en Chine. Bouddhisme, mazdéisme, bureaux de commerce', in Jean-Pierre Drége (ed.), *La Sérinde terred'échanges* (Paris: La Documentation française, 2000), pp. 181–90.

Foucault, Michel, *The History of Sexuality*, vol. 3: *The Care of the Self* (Cambridge: Blackwell, 1986).

Fowden, Elizabeth K., *The Barbarian Plain: Saint Sergius between Rome and Iran* (Berkeley, CA: University of California Press, 1999).

Fox, C.R. 'What, if anything, is a Byzantine?' *Celator*, vol. 10, no. 3: March 1996.

Frye, Richard N., 'The political history of Iran under the Sasanians', in *The Cambridge History of Iran*, vol. 3: *The Seleucid, Parthian and Sasanid Periods, Part 1*, ed. EhsanYarshater (Cambridge: Cambridge University Press, 1983), pp. 116–80.

Fujieda, Akira, 'The Tunhuang manuscripts: a general description', *Zinbun IX* (1966), pp. 1–32.

————, 'The Tunhuang manuscripts: a general description', *Zinbun X* (1969), pp. 17–39.

Gero, Stephan, 'Only a change of masters? The Christians of Iran and the Muslim conquest', *Studia Iranica* 5 (1987), pp. 43–8.

Gibb, Hamilton A.R., *Studies on the Civilization of Islam* (London: Shaw and Polk, 1982).

————, *Iranisches Personennamenbuch*, vol. 2, *Mitteliranische Personennamen*, Fasz. 3, 'Noms propres sassanides en moyen-perse; épigraphique supplément' (Vienna: Austrian Academy of Sciences, 1986).

Gnoli, Gheraldo, 'Farra(h)', Encyclopedia Iranica Online, retrieved 24-7-2012; K. Erdmann, 'Die Entwicklung der sāsānidischen Krone', *Ars Islamica*, vol. 15/16 (1951).

————, 'The quadripartition of the Sasanian Empire', *East and West* 35 (1985), pp. 265–70.

Godwin, Richard Todd, 'Persian Christians at the Chinese Court: The Xi'an Stele and the Church of the East, 410–845', unpublished PhD thesis, School of Oriental and African Studies, University of London, 2016a.

————, 'Eunuchs for the Kingdom of God': Re-thinking the Imperial Translation Incident of 787, in Li Tang and Dietmar W. Winkler (eds), *Winds of Jingjiao: Studies on East Syriac Christianity in China and Central Asia*, Orientalia Patristica Oecumenica, vol. 6 (Zurich and Vienna: Akademie Verlag, 2016b), pp. 267–282.

————, 'Da-Qin, Tajiks, and their doctors – East Syrian scientists across the courtsof early medieval Persia, China, and Tibet, and the Possibility that "Da-Qin" Christians were "Tajik" Christians', *Studies on Syriac Christianity in Medieval Central Asia and China, Salzburg International Conference Proceedings*, vol. 5 (forthcoming).

Goldstein, Jeffrey, 'Emergence as a construct: history and issues', *Emergence, Complexity and Organization* 1/1 (1999), pp. 49–71.

Gradel, Ittai, *Emperor Worship and Roman Religion* (Oxford: Oxford University Press, 2002).

Grenet, Franz, 'A historical figure at the origin of Phrom Gesar: the state of research on Frūm Gesar, King of Kabul (737–745)', in Matthew T. Kapstein and Charles Ramble (eds), *The Many Faces of King Gesar: Homage to Rolf A. Stein* (forthcoming 2017).

Griffith, Sidney H., 'From Patriarch Timothy I to Ḥunayn ibn Isḥāq: philosophy and Christian apology in Abbasid times; reason, ethics and public policy', in MartinTamcke (ed.), *Christians and Muslims in Dialogue in the Islamic Orient of the Middle Ages*, Beiruter Texte und Studien 117 (Beirut: Orient-Institut, 2007), pp. 75–98.

——, 'Patriarch Timothy I and an Aristotelian at the Caliph's court', in Erica C.D. Hunter (ed.), *The Christian Heritage of Iraq: Collected Papers from the Christianity in Iraq I–V Seminar Days* (Piscataway, NJ: Gorgias Press, 2009), pp. 38–53.

Guisson, Richard W.L. 'The Reigns of Empress Wu, Chung-tsung and Jui-tsung (684–712)', CHC Vol 3, pp. 290–329.

Gutas, Dimitri, *Greek Thought, Arab Culture* (London and New York: Routledge, 1998).

——, 'Primary Sources and Historiography on the Sasanian Empire', *Studia Iranica*, v. 38, no. 2, 2009, pp. 163–190.

Hage, Wolfgang, 'Kalifenthron und Patriarchenstuhl. Zum Verhältnis von Staat und Kirche im Mittelalter', in Wolfgang Breul-Kunkel and Luther Vogel (eds), *Rezeption und Reform. Festschrift für Hans Schneider zu seinem 60. Geburtstag*, Quellen und Studien zur hessischen Kirchengeschichte 5 (Darmstadt/ Kassel: Verlag der Hessischen Kirchengeschichtlichen Vereinigung, 2001), pp. 3–17.

Hannestad, K., 'Les relations de Byzance avec la Transcaucasie et l'Asie Centrale aux 5e et 6e siecles', *Byzantion* 25–27 (1955–57), pp. 421–56.

Hanyu Da Cidian [漢語大詞典], chief ed. Luo Zhufeng [羅竹風], CD ROM 3.0 (Hong Kong: The Commercial Press, 2007).

Harmatta, Janos. 'The Middle Persian-Chinese bilingual inscription from Hsian and the Chinese-Sāsānian relations', in Enrico Cerulli (eds), *La Persia nel Medioevo* (Rome: Accademia Nazionale del Lince, 1971), pp. 363–76.

Healey, John,'The Christians of Qatar in the 7th century AD', *Studies in Honour of Clifford Edmund Bosworth*, vol. 1: *Hunter of the East: Arabic and Semitic Studies*, ed. Ian R. Netton (Leiden: Brill, 2000), pp. 222–37.

Heimgartner, Martin, 'Die Disputatio des ostsyrischen Patriarchen Timotheos (780– 823) mit dem Kalifen al-Mahdi', in Martin Tamcke (ed.), *Christians and Muslims in Dialogue in the Islamic Orient of the Middle Ages*, Beiruter Texte und Studien 117 (Beirut: Orient-Institut, 2007), pp. 45–56.

——, 'The Patriarch Išoʻyabh and the Christians of Qatar in the first Islamic century', in *The Christian Heritage of Iraq: Collected Papers from the Christianity in Iraq I–V Seminar Days*, ed. Erica C.D. Hunter (Piscataway, NJ: Gorgias Press, 2009), pp. 1–9.

Hino Kaisaburō, 日野開三郎, 'Take i ryō kisaki jidai zeisetsu himen nisedo no seikō to gensō no shukusei', *Shigaku Zasshi* 87 (10), 1978, pp. 1484–91.

Hopkirk, Peter, *Foreign Devils on the Silk Road* (Boston, MA: University of Massachusetts Press, 1984).

The Hostage An Shigao and his Offspring: An Iranian Family in China (Kyoto: Italian School of East Asian Studies, 1995).

Howard-Johnston, James, *Witnesses to a World Crisis: Historians and Histories of the Middle East in the Seventh Century* (Oxford: Oxford University Press, 2010).

Howe, Stephen, *Empire: A Very Short Introduction* (Oxford: Oxford University Press, 2002).

Hoyland, Robert G., *Seeing Islam as Others Saw It. A Survey and Evaluationof the Christian, Jewish and Zoroastrian Writings on Early Islam* (Darwin, NJ: Princeton, 1997).

Hu, Mingui, 'Provenance in contest: searching for the origins of Jesuit astronomy in late Imperial China' *The International History Review* 24/1 (March 2002), pp. 1–36.

Huang, Lan-lan (黄蘭蘭), 'Tangdai Qin Minghe wei jing yi kao' (唐代秦鳴鶴爲景醫考), *Journal of Sun Yatsen University* (Social Science Edition) 42/5 (2002), pp. 61–7.

Huizinga, Johan, *Herfsttij der Middeleeuwen [The Waning of the Middle Ages]* (Haarlem: Tjeenk Willink, 1919).

Hunter, Erica C.D., 'The Church of the East in Central Asia', *Bulletin of the John Rylands Library* 78/3 (1996), pp. 129–42.

——, 'Interfaith dialogues: the Church of the East and the Abbasids', in Sophia G. Vashaolmidze and Lutz Greisiger, Harrassowitze (eds), *Der Christliche Orient und seine Umwelt* (Weisbaden: Harrassowitz, 2007), pp. 289–302.

——, 'The Persian contribution to Christianity in China: reflections in the Xi'an Fu Syriac inscriptions', in Li Tang and Dietmar Winkler (eds), *Hidden Treasures and Intercultural Encounters* (London: Global Marketing Publications, 2009), pp. 71–85.

Inaba, Minoru, 'The identity of the Turkish soldiers to the south of the Hindukush from the 7th to 9th centuries AD', *Zinbun* 38 (2006), pp. 1–19.

——, 'Arab soldiers in China at the time of the An-Shi Rebellion', *Memoirs of the Touyou Bunko* 68 (2010), pp. 36–61.

Itō, Gikyo, 'Zoroastrians' arrival in Japan (Pahlavica I)', *Orient* 15 (1979), pp. 55–63.

Johannes, Kurz, 'The compilation and publication of the *Taiping yulan* and the *Cefu yuangui*', in Florence Bretelle-Establet and Karine Chemla (eds), *Qu'est-ce qu'écrire une encyclopédie en Chine?*, Extreme Orient-Extreme Occident Hors série 1/1 (2007), pp. 39–76.

Kantorowicz, Ernst, *The King's Two Bodies: A Study in Mediaeval Political Thought* (Princeton, NJ: Princeton University Press, 1957).

Keevak, Michael, *The Story of a Stele: China's Nestorian Monument and Its Reception in the West, 1625–1916* (Hong Kong University Press, 2008).

Khanbaghi, Aptin, *The Fire, The Star and the Cross: Minority Religions in Medieval and Early Islamic Iran* (New York: I.B.Tauris, 2006).

Khazanov, Anatoly M., 'The spread of world religions in medieval nomadic Societies of the Eurasian steppes', in Michael Gervers and Wayne Schlepp (eds), *Nomadic Diplomacy, Destruction and Religion from the Pacific to the Atlantic*, Toronto Studies in Central and Inner Asia, No. 1, (Toronto: Joint Centre for Asia Pacific Studies Toronto, 1994), pp. 11–33.

Labourt, Jérôme, *Le Christianisme Dans L'Empire Perse: Sous La Dynastie Sassanide (224–632)* (Paris: Victor Lecoffre, 1904).

Lam, Chi-Hung, 'The political activities of the Christian missionaries in the T'ang Dynasty', unpublished dissertation, University of Denver, Colorado (1975).

Lampe, Geoffrey W.H., *A Patristic Greek Lexicon* (Oxford: Oxford University Press, 1961).

Lassner, Jacob, *The Shaping of Abbasid Rule* (Princeton, NJ:Princeton University Press, 1980).

Leyerle, John, 'The interlace structure of Beowulf', *University of Toronto Quarterly* 33 (1967), pp. 1–17.

Le Coz, Raymond, *Les médecins nestoriens au Moyen Age: les maîtres des Arabes* (Paris: Harmattan, 2004).

Leslie, Donald, 'Persian temples in T'ang China', *Monumenta Serica* 35/1 (1981–83), pp. 275–303.

Liddell, Henry G., Robert Scott, Henry S. Jones and Roderick McKenzie, *A Greek-English Lexicon*, ed. Henry G. Liddell and Robert Scott (Oxford: Clarendon, 1995).

Lieu, Samuel N.C., *Manichaeism in the Later Roman Empire and Medieval China* (Tubigen: J.C.B. Mohr, 1992).

———, 'Byzantium, Persia and China: interstate relations on the eve of the Islamic conquest', *Realms of the Silk Roads: Ancient and Modern*, proceedings from the Third Conference of the Australasian Society for Inner Asian Studies, Macquarie University, 21–22 September 1998, pp. 47–65.

———, 'Epigraphica Nestoriana Serica', in Werner Sundermann, Almut Hintze and François de Blois (eds), Exegisti monumenta: Festschrift in Honour of Nicholas Sims-Williams, vol. 40 (Wiesbaden: Harrassowitz, 2009), pp. 227–46.

———, 'The Romanitas of the Xi'an inscription', in Li Tang and Dietmar W. Winkler (eds), *From the Oxus River to the Chinese Shores: Studies on East Syriac Christianity in China and Central Asia*, Orientalia Patristica Oecumenica, vol. 5 (Zurich: Akademie Verlag, 2013), pp. 123–40.

———, 'Da Qin 大秦 and Fulin 拂林 – the Chinese names for Rome', in Gunner Mikkelsen (ed.), *From Antioch to Xi'an: Silk Road Studies*, vol. 17 (Turnhout: Brepols, 2016), pp. 123–145.

Lin Wushu, *Tangdai Jingjiao zaiyanjiu* (唐代景教再研究) (Beijing: Zhonghua Shuju, 2003).

———, (林悟殊), *Gu dai san yi jiao bian deng* (古代三異教辨登) (Beijing: Zhonghua shuju, 2005).

Litvinsky, B.A., Zhang Guang-da and R. Shabani Samghabadi (eds), *A History of Civilizations of Central Asia*, vol. 3: *The Crossroads of Civilizations, A.D. 250 to 750* (Paris: UNESCO Publications, 1996).

Liu Haixia [刘海霞], 'Kun fan zhi ce: Zhong tangmingchen Li Mi de bianjian zhanlüe' [困蕃之策：中唐名臣李泌的边疆战略], *Journal of Wenshan University* [文山学院学报] 24/5 (October 2011), pp. 57–61.

———, 'You ming chen li mi kan zhong tang de biangjian jin lüe' [由名臣李泌看中唐的边疆经略], *Journal of Wenshan University* [文山学院学报] 25/4 (August 2012), pp. 21–6.

Liu, Xinru, *Silk and Religion: An Exploration of Material Life and the Thought of People*, AD 600–1200 (New Delhi: Oxford University Press, 1998).

Liu Yat-wing, 'The Shen-ts'e Armies and the Palace Commissions in China, 755–875 AD', PhD thesis, University of London, 1970.

Ma Xiaohe (馬小鶴), 唐代波斯國大酋長阿羅憾墓志考, 'Tang dai bosi guo da qiuzhang aluohan muzhi kao' (中外关系史：新史料与新问题) (Beijing: Kexue Shubanshe, 2004).

MacKenzie, David N., 'Bundahišn', *Encyclopedia Iranica* 4 (Costa Mesa: Mazda, 1990), pp. 547–51.

Mackerras, Colin, *The Uighur Empire According to the T'ang Dynastic Histories: A Study in Sino-Uighur Relations, 744–840* (Canberra: Australian National University, 1972).

Mather, Richard B., 'Wang Chin's '"Dhūta Temple Inscription" as an example of Buddhist parallel prose', *Journal of the American Oriental Society* 83/3 (1963), pp. 338–59.

McDonough, Scott, 'A second Constantine? The Sasanian King Yazdgard I in Christian history and historiography', *Journal of Late Antiquity* 1/1 (Spring 2008), pp. 127–40.

McMillan, M.E., *The Meaning of Mecca: The Politics of Pilgrimage in Early Islam* (London: Saqi Books, 2011).

Micklethwait, John and Adrian Wooldridge, *God is Back: How the Global Revival of Faith is Changing the World* (New York: Penguin Press, 2009).

Moffett, Samuel Hugh, *A History of Christianity in Asia*, vol. 1: *Beginnings to 1500* (New York: Orbis, 1998).

Moribe, Yutaka, 'Non-Han in the late Tang and five dynasties military', in Étienne de la VaissièreandÉric Trombert(eds), *Les Sodiens en Chine* (Paris: Collège de France, Institut des Hautes Études Chinoises, 2006), pp. 243–54.

Morony, Michael G., *Iraq after the Muslim Conquest* (Princeton, NJ: Princeton University Press, 1984).

——, 'Should Sasanian Iranian be in included in Late Antiquity?', e-Sasankia 1 (2008). Available at http://www.sasanika.org/wp-content/uploads/e-sasanika1-Morony4.pdf (accessed 3 March 2015).

Nakata Mie [中田美絵] 'Bukong as a leader of the Chang'an Buddhist world and of Sogdians', *Fuku no Chouan Bukkyoukai Taotoi to Sogdojin* [不空の長安仏教界台頭とソグド人], *Tōyō Gakuho* [東洋学報] (2007), pp. 89–93, pp. 33–65.

——, 'Hasseiki kōhan ni okeru chūō yūrajia no dōkō to Chōan bukkyō-kai e sō-ki 'Daijō ri omomu rokki haramitsuta kyo' hon'yaku sankasha no bunseki yori' [八世紀後半における中央ユーラシアの動向と長安仏教界—得宗期『大乗理趣六波羅蜜多経』翻訳参加者の分析より], The Buddhist circle in Chang'an the movements amongst Central Eurasiaduring the latter half of the eighth century – from the study on participants in translation of Dacheng Liqu Liu Boluomiduo Jing [大乗理趣六波羅蜜多経 during the Era of the Emperor 德宗]', *Kansaidaigaku tōzai gakujutsu kenkyūjo* [関西大学東西学術研究所] (2011–14), pp. 153–89.

Nautin, Pierre, 'L'auteur de la "Chronique de Séert": Isho'denad de Basra', *Revue de l'histoire des religions* 186/2 (1974), pp. 113–26.

Ni Maoshing, *The Yellow Emperor's Classic of Medicine: A New Translation of the Neijing Suwen with Commentary* (Boston: Shambhala, 1995).

Nie Zhigun [聂志军], 'Jingjiao zhong "Yi si" yeshi jingyi kao' [景教中'伊斯'也是景医考], 敦煌学辑刊 [*Journal of Dunhuang Studies*] 3 (2008), pp. 119–27.

Nymark, Aleksandr, 'Sogdiana, its Christians and Byzantium: a study of artistic and cultural connections in Late Antiquity and the Early Middle Ages', PhD thesis, Indiana University, 2001, pp. 168–200.

Orzech, Charles, *Politics and Transcendent Wisdom: The Scripture for Humane Kings in the Creation of Chinese Buddhism* (University Park, PA: Pennsylvania State University Press, 1998).

Packard, Jerrold M., *Victoria's Daughters* (New York: St Martin's Griffin, 1998).

Painano, Antonio, 'The '"Persian" identity in religious controversies: again on the case of "divided loyalty" in Sasanian Iran', in Carlo G. Certi (ed.), *Iranian Identity in the Course of History, Serie Orientale Roma, Orientalia Romana* 9, proceedings of the conference held in Rome, 21–24 September 2005, pp. 227–39.

Payne, Richard E., 'Christianity and Iranian society: saint's cults, canon law and social change in Late Sasanian and Early Islamic Iran', unpublished PhD thesis, Princeton University, 2010.

———, 'Monks, dinars and date palms: hagiographical production and the expansion of monastic institutions in the early Islamic Persian Gulf', *Arabian Archaeology and Epigraphy* 22/1 (2011), pp. 97–111.

———, *A State of Mixture: Christians, Zoroastrian, and Iranian Political Culture in Late Antiquity* (Oakland, CA: University of California Press, 2015).

Payne-Smith, Robert, *A Compendious Syriac Dictionary: Founded Upon the Thesaurus Syriacus of R.Payne Smith* (Winona Lake, IN: Eisenbrauns, 1998).

Pelliot, Paul, 'Un traiteé Manichéen retrouvéin Chine' (ed. and trans. Édouard Chavannes), *Journale Asiatique* 11 (1913), pp. 346–67.

———, 'Les traditions manichéennes au Fou-kien', *T'oung Pao* 22/3 (1923), pp. 193–208.

———, *L'inscription nestorienne de Si-ngan-fou, Edited with Supplements by Antonino Forte* (Kyoto: Scuola di Studi sull'Asia Orientale; Paris: Collège de France, Institut des Hautes Etudes Chinoises, 1996).

Peterson, Charles A., 'Court and province in mid-and late T'ang', in Denis Twitchett (ed.), *The Cambridge History of China*, vol. 3: *Sui and T'ang China, 589–906*, Part 1 (Cambridge: Cambridge University Press, 1979), pp. 464–560.

Pritsakr, Omeljan, 'The Khazar kingdom's conversion to Judaism', *Harvard Ukrainian Studies* 2/3 (September 1978), pp. 261–81.

Pollock, Sheldon, 'The Sanskrit Cosmopolis, 300–1300: transculturation, vernacularization, and the question of ideology', in Jan E.M. Houben (ed.), *Ideology and Status of Sanskrit: Contributions to the History of the Sanskrit Language*, Brill's Indological Library, vol. 13 (Leiden: Brill, 1996), pp. 197–249.

Pourshariati, Parveneh, *Decline and Fall of the Sasanian Empire: The Sasanian-Parthian Confederacy and the Arab Conquest of Iran* (London: I.B.Tauris, 2008).

Pulleyblank, Edwin G., *The Background of the Rebellion of An Lu-Shan* (London: Oxford University Press, 1966).

———, 'The An Lu-Shan Rebellion and the origins of chronic militarism in late T'ang China', in John C. Perry and Bardwell L. Smith (eds), *Essays on T'ang Society* (Leiden: E.J. Brill, 1976), pp. 75–81.

———, *Lexicon of Reconstructed Pronunciation of in Early Middle Chinese, Late Middle Chinese and Early Mandarin* (Vancouver: University of British Columbia Press, 1991).

Putman, Hans, *L'Église et l'Islam sous Timothée I (780–823). Étude sur l'Église nestorienne au temps des premiers 'Abbasides*, Recherches: l'Institut de Lettres Orientales de Beyrouth, Nouvelle Serie B, Orient Chretién 3 (Beirut: Dar el-Machreq, 1975).

Rásonyi, László and Imre Baski, *Onomasticon Turcicum*, Uralic and Altaic Series, V. 172 (Bloomington, IN: Denis Sinor Institute for Inner Asian Studies, 2007).

Reeves, John C., *Prolegomena to a History of Islamicate Manichaeism* (Sheffield: Equinox Publications, 2011).

Reinink, Gerrit J., 'Theology and medicine in Jundishapur. Cultural change in the Nestorian School tradition', in Alasdair A. MacDonald, Michael W. Twomey and Gerrit J. Reinink (eds), *Learned Antiquity. Scholarship in the Near East, the Greco-Roman World and the Early Medieval World* (Leiden: E.J. Brill, 2003), pp. 163–74.

——, 'Réflections sur les pratiques religieuses désignées sous le nom de *xian*祆', in Étienne de la Vaissière and Éric Trombert (eds), *Les Sogdiens en Chine* (Paris: École française d'Extrême-Orient, 2005), no.17, pp. 72–85.

Rong Xinjiang [荣新江], 'The nature of the Dunhuang Library Cave and the reasons for its sealing', *Cahiers d'Extrême-Asie* 11/11 (1999), pp. 247–75.

——, 'Yi ge rushi tangchao de Bosi jingjiao jiazu' [个入仕唐朝的波斯景教家族, A Persian Nestorian Family in Tang China], in Ye Yilang [叶奕良] (ed.), *Yilangxue zai Zhongguo lunwenji* [伊朗学在中国论文集, *A Collection of Essays on Iranian Studies in China*], II (Beijing:Beijing daxue shuban she, 1998), pp. 82–90, repr. in Rong Xinjiang, *Zhonggu Zhongguo yuwailai wenming* [中古中国与外来文明] (Beijing: Shenghuo, dushu, xinzhi sanlian shudian, 2001a).

——, '"Lidai fabao ji" zhong de moni he mish he – jian tan tubo wenxian de mo ni jiao he jingjiao yinsu de laili, zhonggu zhongguo yu wailai wenming' [歷代法宝記>中的末尼和弥師訶 – 兼谈吐蕃文献的摩尼教和景教因素的来历，中古中国与外来文明] (Beijing: Sanlian shudian, 2001b), pp. 343–68.

Roth, Harold, Sarah Queen, and Nathan Sivin,'Syncretic visions of state, society, and cosmos', in William Theodore de Baryand Irene Bloom (eds), *Sources of Chinese Tradition*, vol. I, 2nd edn (New York: Columbia University Press, 1999), pp. 235–82.

Rubin, Zeev, 'The reforms of Khosrow Anushirwan', in Averil Cameron and Lawrence I. Conrad (eds), *The Byzantine and Early Islamic Near East*, vol. 3: *States, Resources and Armies* (Princeton, NJ: Princeton University Press, 1995), pp. 227–97.

Said, Edward, *Culture and Imperialism* (New York: Knopf, 1993).

——, 'Les sources de la Chronique de Séert', *Parole de l'Orient* 14 (1987), pp. 155–65.

Sanders, Paula, *Ritual, Politics and the City in Fatimid Cairo* (Albany, NY: SUNY Press, 1994).

Schlegel, Gustaaf, 'Die Chinesische Inschrift auf dem Uigürischen Denkmal in Kara Balgassun', *Mémoires De La Société Finno-Ougrienne* IX (1896).

Scott-Moncrieff, Philip (ed.), *The Book of Consolations or the Pastoral Epistles of Mar Ishu'yab of Kuphlanapin Adiabene*, Part 1(London: Luzac and Co., 1904).

Sen, Tansen, 'Gautama Zhuan: an Indian astronomer at the Tang Court', *China Report* 31/2 (1995), pp. 197–208.

Shaban, Muhammad A., *The 'Abbāsid Revolution* (Cambridge: Cambridge University Press, 1979).

Silverstein, Adam J., *Postal Systems in the Pre-Modern Islamic World* (Cambridge: Cambridge University Press, 2004).

——, 'Documentary evidence for the early history of the Bariid', in Petra Sijpesteijn and Lennart Sundelin (eds), *Papyrology and the History of Early Islamic Egypt* (Leiden: E.J. Brill, 2007), pp. 153–61.

Skaff, Jonathan K., 'The Sogdian trade diaspora in East Turkestan during the seventh and eighth centuries', *Journal of the Economic and Social History of the Orient* 46/4 (2003), pp. 475–524.

Steger, Manfred B., *The Rise of the Global Imaginary: Political Ideologies from the French Revolution to the Global War on Terror* (Oxford: Oxford University Press, 2008).

Sundermann, Werner, 'An early attestation of the name of the Tajiks', in Wojciech Skalmowski and Alois van Tongerloo (eds), *Medio-Iranica, Proceedings of the International Colloquium organised by the Katholieke Universiteit Leuven from the 21st to the 23rd of May 1990* (Orientalia Lovaniensia Analecta, 48) (Leuven: The University Press, 1993), pp. 163–71.

Takakusu, Junjiro, 'The name of "Messiah" found in a Buddhist book: the Nestorian missionary Adam, Presbyter, Papas of China, translating a Buddhist sutra', *Tong Bao* (1896), pp. 589–91.

Tang, Li, *A Study of the History of Nestorian Christianity in China and Its Literature in Chinese: Together with a New English Translation of the Dunhuang Nestorian Documents*, 2nd edn (Frankfurt: Peter Lang, 2004).

———, 'A preliminary study on the Jingjiao Inscription of Luoyang: text analyses, commentary and English translation', in Li Tang and Dietmar Winkler (eds), *Hidden Treasures and Intercultural Encounters* (London: Global Marketing Publications, 2009) pp. 109–32.

Tekin, Talat, *A Grammar of Orkhon Turkic* (Bloomington, IN: University of Indiana Press, 1967).

Thompson, Glen L., 'Was Alopen a "missionary"?', in Li Tang and Dietmar Winkler (eds), *Hidden Treasures and Intercultural Encounters* (London: Global Marketing Publications, 2009), pp. 267–78.

———, 'How Jingjiao became Nestorian: Western perceptions and Eastern realities', in Li Tang and Dietmar W. Winkler (eds), *From the Oxus River to the Chinese Shores: Studies on East Syriac Christianity in China and Central Asia*, Orientalia Patristica Oecumenica, vol. 5 (Zurich: Akademie Verlag, 2013), pp. 418–40.

Toth, Michael A, 'Toward a theory of the routinization of charisma', *Rocky Mountain Social Science Journal* 9/2 (April 1972), pp. 93–8.

Tremblay, Xavier, 'The spread of Buddhism in Serindia – Buddhism among Iranians, Tocharians and Turks before the 13th century', in Denis Sinor and Nicola Di Cosmo (eds), *The Spread of Buddhism:Handbook of Oriental Studies*, 8: *Central Asia* (Leiden: E.J. Brill, 2007), pp. 75–129.

Tsukamoto Zenryu [塚本善隆], 'Tōchūki irai no chōan no kōtokushi' [唐中期以来の長安の功德使], in *Tsukamoto Zenryū chosakushū* [塚本善隆著作集], vol. 3 (Tōkyō: Daitō Shuppan, 1974--6), pp. 253–84.

Twitchett, Denis, *Financial Administration under the T'ang* (Cambridge: Cambridge University Press, 1963).

———, 'Hsüan-tsung (reign 712–56)', in Denis Twitchett (ed.), *The Cambridge History of China*, vol. 3: *Sui and T'ang China, 589–906*, Part 1 (Cambridge: Cambridge University Press, 1979), pp. 456–61.

———, *The Writing of Official History under the T'ang* (Cambridge: Cambridge University Press, 1992).

———, 'Tibet in Tang's grand strategy', in Hans van de Ven (ed.), *Warfare in Chinese History*, (Leiden, Brill, 2000), pp. 106–79.

Uray, Geza, 'Tibet's connection with Nestorianism and Manichaeism in the 8th–10th centuries', in Ernst Steinkellner and Helmut Tauscher (eds), *Contributions on Tibetan Language, History and Culture, Proceedings of the Csoma De Körös Symposium*

Held at Velm-Vienna, Austria, 13–19 September 1981 (Vienna: Arbeitskreis für Tibetische und Buddhistische Studien Universität Wien, 1983), pp. 399–429.

Van Bladel, Kevin, 'The Bactrian background of the Barmakids', in Anna Akasoy, Charles S.F. Burnett and Ronit Yoeli-Tlalim (eds), *Islam and Tibet: Interactions along the Musk Routes* (London: Ashgate, 2011), pp. 43–88.

———, 'Eighth-century Indian astronomy in the two cities of peace', in Behnam Sadeghi, Asad Q. Ahmed, Robert Hoyland, Adam Silverstein (eds), *Islamic Cultures, Islamic Contexts: Essays in Honor of Professor Patricia Crone* (Leiden: E.J. Brill, 2014), pp. 295–342.

de la Vaissière, Étienne, *Sogdian Traders: A History* (Boston: E.J. Brill, 2005).

———, 'Châkars d'Asie centrale', *Studia Iranica* (2005), pp.139–49.

——— and ÉricTrombert (eds), *Les Sodiens en Chine* (Paris: Collège de France, Institut des Hautes Études Chinoises, 2006).

Villagomez, Cynthia, 'The fields, flocks, and finances of monks: economic life at Nestorian monasteries, 500–850', unpublished PhD thesis, University of California, Los Angeles, 1998.

Vööbus, Arthur, *History of the School of Nisibis* (Leuven: Peeters, 1985).

Walker, Joel T., 'The limits of Late Antiquity: philosophy between Rome and Iran', *The Ancient World* 33/1 (2002), pp. 45–69.

———, *The Legend of Mar Qardagh: Narrative and Christian Heroism in Late Antique Iraq* (Berkeley, CA: University of California Press, 2006).

Wang Changwen, [王承文], 'Tangdai Lingdan de Bosiren yu Bosi Wenhua' [唐代岭南的波斯人与波斯文化], *Sun Yatsen University Historical Study Collection*, vol. 1, Guangzhou, 1991, pp. 68–82.

Wang Shoudang [王守棟], 'Anshi zhi luan qian hou tangchao huanguan quanshi de yanbian' [安史之亂前後唐朝宦官權勢的演變], *Journal of Dezhou University* [德州学院学报] 19/3 (June 2003), pp. 61–5.

Wang Shounan [王壽南], *Tangdai huanguan quanshi zhi yánjiu* [唐代宦官權勢之研究] (Taipei: Zhengzhong Shuju, 1971), pp. 117–43.

Washington, Mariko N., 'Sogdians and Buddhism', *Sino-Platonic Papers* 174 (2006), pp. 1–64.

Watt, John W., 'Greek Philosophy and Syriac culture in 'Abbasid Iraq', in Erica C.D. Hunter (ed.), *The Christian Heritage of Iraq: Collected Papers from the Christianity in Iraq I–V Seminar Days* (Piscataway, NJ: Gorgias Press, 2009), pp. 10–37.

Weber, Max, *Economy and Society: An Outline of Interpretive Sociology*, 2 vols, ed. Guenther Roth and Claus Wittich (Berkeley, CA: University of California Press, 1978).

———, *The Protestant Ethic and the Spirit of Capitalism*, trans. Talcott Parsons (London and New York: Routledge, 1992).

Wechsler, Howard J., 'T'ai-tsung (reign 626–49) the Consolidator', in Denis Twitchett (ed.), *The Cambridge History of China*, vol. 3: *Sui and T'ang China, 589–906*, Part 1 (Cambridge: Cambridge University Press, 1979), pp. 193–236.

Weinstein, Stanley, 'Imperial Patronage in the Formation of T'ang Buddhism', in *Perspectives on the T'ang*. Arthur Wright and Denis Twitchett (eds) (New Haven: Yale University Press, 1973), pp. 265–306.

———, *Buddhism under the Tang* (Cambridge: Cambridge University Press, 1987).

Wendell, Charles, 'Baghdad: Imago Mundi and other foundational lore', *International Journal of Middle Eastern Studies* 2 (1971), pp. 98–128.

Widengren, Geo, Xosrau Anoširvan, les Hephthalites et les peuples Turcs', *Orientalia Suecana* 1 (1952), pp. 69–94.

Wieshöfer, Josef, 'King, court and royal representation in the Sasanian Empire', in Anthony J. Spawforth (ed.), *The Court and Court Society in Ancient Monarchies* (Cambridge: Cambridge University Press, 2007), pp. 58–79.

Wilmshurst, David, 'The "Syrian Brilliant Teaching"', *Journal of the Hong Kong Branch of the Royal Asiatic Society* 30 (1993), pp. 44–74.

Wright, William, *A Short History of Syriac Literature* (London: Adam and Charles Black, 1894).

Xu Min [徐敏], 'Guo ziyi yu tang dai huanguan' [郭子仪与唐代宦官], *History Teacher* 6 (2007), pp. 105–6.

Yabuuchi, Kiyoshi [中国の天文暦法], *Chūgoku no tenmon rekihō [A History of Chinese Astronomy]* (Tōkyō: Heibonsha, 1990).

Ye'or, Bat, *The Decline of Eastern Christianity under Islam: From Jihad to Dhimmitude. Seventh-Twentieth Century* (Madison/Teaneck, NJ: Fairleigh Dickinson University Press/Associated University Presses, 1996).

Young, William G., *Patriarch, Shah and Caliph* (Rawalpindi: Christian Study Centre, 1974).

——, 'The Church of the East in 650 AD: Patriarch Ishu'yahb III and India', *Indian Church History Review* 2/1 (1968), pp. 55–71.

Yuan Zhipeng [袁志鹏], 'Li mi yu tangdezong minzu zhengce de zhuanbian' [李泌与唐德宗民族政策的轉變], [唐山師範学院报], *Journal of Tangshan Teachers College* 36/1 (January 2014), pp. 103–6.

Zhang, Guangda and Xinjiang Rong, 'A concise history of Turfan and its exploration', *Asia Major* 11/2 (1998), pp. 13–36.

Zhang Xiaogui [張小貴], 'Why did Chinese "Nestorians" change the name of their religion to Jingjiao?', in Li Tang and Dietmar W. Winkler (eds), *Winds of Jingjiao: Studies on East Syriac Christianity in China and Central Asia*, Orientalia Patristica Oecumenica, vol.6 (Zurich and Vienna: Akademie Verlag, 2016), pp. 283–310.

Zhang Xiaohua (張曉華), *Jingjiao dongjian tan* (景教东漸探), *Zongjiaoshi yanjiu* (宗教史研究) 6 (1994), pp. 85–90.

Zhou, Weiyan, 'Jimizhou', *Encyclopedia of China* (Beijing: China's Archives Press, 1993).

INDEX

CPSIA information can be obtained
at www.ICGtesting.com
Printed in the USA
LVHW050457210221
679533LV00031B/2214